Irish Liberty, British Democracy

Irish Liberty, British Democracy

The third Irish Home Rule crisis, 1909–14

JAMES DOHERTY

CORK UNIVERSITY PRESS

First published in 2019 by Cork University Press
Boole Library
University College Cork
Cork T12 ND89
Ireland

Library of Congress Control Number: 2019949423

British Library Cataloguing in Publication Data

A CIP catalogue record for this book is available from the British Library

ISBN: 978-1-78205-360-6

Typeset by Dominic Carroll, Ardfield, County Cork
Printed by Gutenberg, Malta

www.corkuniversitypress.com

For my mother, Constance Connery,
who started me out in more ways than one

Contents

Acknowledgements

I am deeply grateful to the UK Arts and Humanities Research Council and the University of Southampton for supporting the research upon which this book is based. I offer thanks, too, to the Royal Historical Society and the British Association for Irish Studies for funding research visits to Dublin.

I owe an enormous debt of thanks to my former academic supervisor, Professor Matthew Kelly, for the unfailing accuracy of his advice, and for the generous encouragement he gave me over the course of my PhD research. I am grateful to my doctoral examiners, Professors Roy Foster and Adrian Smith, for their extensive comments on my thesis, which sharpened up this work considerably. I thank Professor Paul Readman and his colleagues at the History Department of King's College London for inspiring me to pursue this project in the first place. I extend gratitude to my agent, Jonathan Williams, to Maria O'Donovan of Cork University Press, and to my copy-editor, Dominic Carroll, for their advice and help in bringing this book to publication. I wish also to acknowledge the assistance of the staffs of the Special Collections Department at the University of Bristol and the Bodleian Libraries, Oxford, whose helpfulness was surpassed only by the superlative personnel of the Department of Manuscripts at the National Library of Ireland.

I gratefully acknowledge the permission of Her Majesty Queen Elizabeth II to make use of material from the Royal Archives at Windsor. For permission to quote from the letters of H.H. Asquith to Venetia Stanley, I thank Anna Mathias, the copyright-holder, and likewise extend thanks to Christopher Osborn, the copyright-holder of the Margot Asquith diaries, and also Susie Medley, who permitted me to make use of content from the Augustine Birrell Papers. I am grateful to the trustees of the Asquith/Bonham Carter Papers for leave to quote copyright material; I also acknowledge the permission of the Bodleian Libraries, University of Oxford, the owners of these manuscripts, to publish material in their collections.

In addition, I thank the National Library of Ireland; the warden and scholars of New College, Oxford; Nuffield College, Oxford; the Parliamentary

ix

Archives; the deputy keeper of the records, Public Record Office of Northern Ireland; University of Bristol Library Special Collections; and the board of Trinity College, Dublin for permission to quote from manuscripts in their collections. I acknowledge with thanks permission to use copyright material granted by Dr Jeremy Hogg; Margaret Masterman; Viscount Addison; Hugo Headlam; Irish Newspaper Archives; Universe Media Group; *Methodist Recorder*; Associated Newspapers Ltd; *Baptist Times*; Co-Op Press Ltd; News Licensing; *New Statesman*; Churchill Archives Centre, University of Cambridge; Dublin City Library and Archive; and the National Archives of Ireland. Should I, inadvertently, have failed to consult any copyright-holder, I apologise most sincerely, and will make good the omission in any future edition.

The tasks involved in writing this were aided, in one way or another, by the support of cherished friends and family: my late father, James Doherty, Sr., Gary Adams, Erin and Tom Littlewood, Mary Anne and Ken Breed, Jen and Matt Krenz-Erni, James Erni and Kristin Taylor, Wijay Pitumpe and Philip Lightowlers, Michael Ball, Anne and John Babineau and family, Azad Khaleel and Goran Savic, Dinzey Walters and Peter Bennett, Vernal Scott, Geetha Naran and Stuart Parker, Christine and Richard Trottier, Robert Raju and Chris Patterson, Edilson Guerreiro, Jim Metcalfe, Harlinton Leudo, and Robert Taylor and Tristram Wyatt.

My deepest thanks go to Ravindran Vadivelu, whose companionship and laughter made the time spent researching and writing this book every bit as enjoyable as it was rewarding.

Abbreviations & Acronyms

AOH	Ancient Order of Hibernians
BL	British Library
BMH.WS	Bureau of Military History [Dublin] Witness Statement
Bodl.	Bodleian Libraries, Oxford
CSORP	Chief Secretary's Office Registered Papers
DATI	Department of Agriculture and Technical Instruction
DMP	Dublin Metropolitan Police
IRB	Irish Republican Brotherhood
JP	Justice of the Peace
NA	National Archives, Kew
NAI	National Archives of Ireland, Dublin
NLI	National Library of Ireland
PA	Parliamentary Archive
PRONI	Public Record Office of Northern Ireland
RA	Royal Archives
RIC	Royal Irish Constabulary
RM	Resident magistrate
TCD	Trinity College, Dublin
U.Birm.L.	University of Birmingham Library
U.Bris.L.	University of Bristol Library
UCDA	University College Dublin Archive
UIL	United Irish League
UVF	Ulster Volunteer Force
WLF	Women's Liberal Federation

Introduction:
The Liberals and Ireland reconsidered

The Liberal government of H.H. Asquith, comprised of talented and even brilliant politicians, credited with laying the foundations of the welfare state and with curbing the power of the House of Lords, got things spectacularly wrong in Ireland. The figure of Asquith, erudite and immensely able but immersed in his own pleasures to an unusual degree, presides enigmatically over the history of the third Home Rule Bill. His secretive handling of the Irish problem deepened his personal imprimatur on a disastrous policy and the intractability of the historical problem. Yet a persistent historical focus on British party-political brinkmanship, and relative inattention to the ideological and emotional significance of Home Rule for Liberalism, has obscured important influences upon Asquith's decision-making. This volume attends to the less-often heard voices of Home Rulers – Liberal, Labour and Irish nationalist – and recounts a forgotten side of the story.

The crisis precipitated by the third attempt to devolve limited powers to an Irish parliament remains an intriguing episode for historians, not least because the unexpected outbreak of the First World War left its denouement permanently in suspense. Well-worn narratives about the 1912–14 crisis dominate the historiography. Perhaps the most influential of these is the view, in conformity with Unionist rhetoric of the time, that Ireland in 1914 stood on the brink of civil war between the Protestant north and Catholic south. The refusal of the Protestants of north-east Ulster to accept the status of a permanent minority in a unitary Irish polity, so the narrative goes, left the partition of Ireland as the sole means of averting armed insurrection by Ulster Unionists and widespread sectarian bloodshed.

This entrenched belief in 'the irreconcilable Orangeman' has ample grounding in historical fact, but notions of the inevitability of partition were embedded in popular memory in the early twentieth century by the need among new regimes in both parts of the divided island to construct a legitimising past for

1

themselves.[1] Ulster Unionist mythologising of the events of 1912–14 has left its impression on minds far beyond the borders of the northern province. Alvin Jackson's work revealed the careful twentieth-century invention of many of the elaborate 'ancient' traditions of Ulster Unionism.[2] A narrative of inevitable partition (and of persisting British occupation) also served the needs of the Irish Free State, established in the south after the Anglo-Irish war of 1919–21. Ideas of preordination distracted attention from the degree of culpability of the Sinn Féin leaders for Ireland's sundered state. So effective was the promulgation of the idea that partition was inevitable that it is today popularly regarded in Ireland, and in many other places, almost as an article of faith.[3]

It is another historical commonplace that the Irish Parliamentary Party (then representing most of Ireland at Westminster) met its 'fate' when it was swept away in the general election of 1918, devastated by the events of the First World War and by the aftermath of the 1916 Easter Rising. Perceptions of an ageing, weak and out-of-touch leadership have been sustained, even by sympathetic historians. The phenomenon persists in the profusion of books commemorating the centenary of Ireland's 'decade of revolution' of 1912–22.

Two biographies have emerged that have deepened understanding of Irish Party chairman John Redmond's character and career. The second volume of Dermot Meleady's definitive biography of Parnell's successor, *John Redmond: The national leader* (2014), substantially filled the need for a high political history, and was supplemented in 2018 by Alvin Jackson's *Judging Redmond and Carson*, an ambitious and delightfully presented dual biography of the contemporaneous leaders of Irish nationalism and Unionism. Together, these works provide the most rounded view of Redmond that we have; yet while Jackson's substantial analysis offers a great deal that is new – an insightful appreciation of Redmond's imperialism and monarchist sympathies, for example – there is also much that is familiar.

Jackson's portrait adopts the conventional view of Redmond as little more than a supplicant, outmanoeuvred by opponents and slighted by allies, and reduced, in the end, to plaintively resisting ever-widening concessions.[4] Judgements such as these arguably reflect a received narrative of a man whose temperamental limitations and outdated convictions 'fated' him to failure. No less arguable is Jackson's assertion that, as the crisis deepened, Redmond was almost entirely reliant on the goodwill of the Liberal government.[5] Redmond was certainly dependent throughout on the Liberal *Party*; his ability to con-strain the choices of the Liberal government, however, is one of the central themes of this book.

If Jackson's assessment of Redmond echoes historical orthodoxy, Ronan Fanning's *Fatal Path: British government and Irish revolution, 1910–1922*, published in 2013, recalls the vituperation of early republican historians. Fanning dismissed the third Home Rule Bill as an elaborate ruse, cynically offered by the Liberal government to preserve its parliamentary majority, in collusion with a misguided and weak-willed Redmond. Partition, he argued, became unavoidable, in some form, once the principle of temporary exclusion of Ulster was conceded, but Redmond sustained a delusional belief in the possibility of unitary self-government for Ireland.[6]

This book rejects Fanning's anachronistic presumption of the inevitability of partition. It asserts that Redmond exerted greater political leverage over British politics than has hitherto been recognised, showing him to have been much more than a passive victim of British statesmen's duplicity. The assertion of Redmond's 'delusional' thinking will be countered with analysis of the nationalist leader's calculation as to how Ulster Unionist recalcitrance was to be isolated, and the exclusion of Ulster counties abbreviated or avoided altogether. The ignominy heaped upon Redmond from time to time can, perhaps, be justly relieved by a fuller understanding of his motivations and assumptions, and of the competing demands of Irish nationalism and Westminster politics that he attempted to reconcile. While not minimising the inauspicious circumstances for achieving unitary Home Rule in 1913–14, nor the obstacles that had to be negotiated, I argue that the ultimate failure of Redmond's efforts to secure self-rule for a united Ireland rested more upon the unforeseen outbreak of war than it did upon flawed strategy.

Yet this book offers no paean to Redmondism: under Redmond's leadership the Irish Party neglected many important matters in its single-minded quest for Home Rule, leading to an abandonment of progressive allies on the women's-suffrage issue, and a dereliction of leadership during the 1913 Dublin Lockout. The party chairman acquiesced to the neglect of Irish administration, which remained in a virtually static state pending the resolution of the Home Rule question. An assertive policing policy in Ulster, which might have checked loyalist paramilitary organisation early on, was politically possible, but action was eschewed, with Redmond's full support, even as provocations grew steadily more extreme. Most damagingly, Redmond failed utterly to grapple with the legitimate fears of Ulster's Protestant population.

℘

In government from 1905 to 1915 (and in coalition thereafter until the end of the First World War), the Liberals met a remorseless set of political challenges with varying degrees of success. As a parliamentary force, however, the Liberal Party was devastated in the general election of 1918, and passed nearly into oblivion after 1923. Whether it was the unprecedented trials of the Edwardian era, the cataclysmic events of the First World War, or something of an organic nature that dealt Liberalism its mortal blow has been a matter of exhaustive debate among historians.

The Irish crisis was but one of a complex of crises besetting Asquith's Cabinet. Militant suffragettes, enraged by the failure of a Liberal administration to support the enfranchisement of women, resorted to violent protests. Windows were smashed in the West End of London, the contents of post-boxes set alight, and ministers were physically assaulted. A series of industrial disputes of unprecedented severity disrupted commerce, costing British industry thirty-six million days of labour in 1912. A combination of falling real wages and rising prices led to increasing union militancy and to the rise of syndicalism.[7] Troops were deployed on numerous occasions to break strikes and quell disorder, as tens of thousands of railwaymen, miners and dockworkers struck for better wages and working conditions. The shocking scale of this 'great unrest' of 1910–14 seemed poised to paralyse the nation.

The political upheaval in Britain, as elsewhere in Europe, had broader societal effects. In the worlds of art and culture, old certainties were breaking down. Cubism and Futurism brought unintelligible and seemingly primitive images to the galleries of London. Impressionist music, with its unconventional tonality and harmonies, jarred the ears of concert-goers. To many, these modernist innovations were grotesque and meaningless. To others, they represented a deliberate break with the old: a conceptual dissection of perception, emotion and symbolism. Rising working-class militancy and spasms of civil disorder, the intrusion of strange and provocative cultural forms, and a bruising new style of politics seemed to betoken, to some middle-class observers, a general decline of civilisation. Amid these rumblings of seismic change, the imminence of universal manhood suffrage exacerbated fears of revolution against the social and economic order.

The 'nervous breakdown' of British democracy in Edwardian society was evocatively captured in the 1930s by George Dangerfield's *The Strange Death of Liberal England*. 'Dangerfield' – a book so iconic it is often referred to simply by the author's name – charted the extraordinary travails that bedevilled Asquith's government, which, in addition to industrial unrest and suffragette militancy, included the Tory Party's struggles against the Parliament Act of 1911 (which abolished the absolute veto of the House of Lords) and Irish Home Rule. Dangerfield asserted that each element of this array of violent controversies was symptomatic of the crumbling of the old order before the advance of the downtrodden classes of society. In memorable and dramatic prose, Dangerfield cast the overthrow of Liberalism as an epochal shift in political history, proof of the inadequacy of middle-class reformists to meet the demands of burgeoning working-class democracy.[8]

Historians have contested Dangerfield's deterministic thesis over the years, criticising his pronouncement of Liberalism's death as impressionistic and premature. Among the more prominent of these critics was Peter Clarke, whose *Lancashire and the New Liberalism* (1971) asserted that popular political allegiances had already shifted from community and confessional lines to those of class by 1910. Liberalism, Clarke argued, had successfully adjusted to the altered political landscape, and had joined, with the fledgling Labour Party, in a progressive alliance wedded to social reform.[9] Clarke's study influentially altered the view of a bourgeois Liberal Party destined to obsolescence due to insistent demands for proletarian political representation. Revisionist historians asserted that the Liberal Party was in rude health until it was run down by the juggernaut of war.[10]

The critiques of Clarke and others practically transformed a historical problem into a branch of historiography. The decline of Liberalism has provided a seemingly inexhaustible seam at the historical coalface for the application of different approaches, techniques and styles of argument. Electoral results have been scrutinised and regions compared, and the debates have, broadly speaking, divided historians between those who see irreversible signs of the Liberal Party's displacement before the First World War and others who ascribe the party's obliteration almost wholly to illiberal policy, strategic blunders and leadership rivalry in wartime.[11] Yet with the notable exception of Patricia Jalland, author of *The Liberals and Ireland: The Ulster question in British politics to 1914* (1980), these later historians have mostly neglected the role of Ireland in the Liberal Party's decline and fall.

The Home Rule controversy was, arguably, the most serious of the pre-war crises facing the Liberals. The spectre of civil war in Ireland was whipped up and sustained by the British Conservative and Unionist Party,* which not

---

* The Conservative and Unionist Party, as it is still formally entitled, adopted the term 'Unionist' in 1886 to emphasise its commitment to preservation of the Act of Union of 1800,

only encouraged unlawful resistance by the Ulstermen but was probably also engaged in efforts to arm them.[12] In an oblique endorsement of armed rebellion, Andrew Bonar Law, the leader of the Tories from 1911, pledged that there was 'no length of resistance' to which Ulster might go that he would not support. Against the very modest measure of self-government for Ireland that was contemplated, the words and deeds of British Unionist leaders in the 1912–14 Irish crisis seem so extreme and disproportionate as to almost defy comprehension.

Fifty years later, Maurice Bonham Carter, Asquith's former private secretary, reflected that memory of the events of 1910–14 had faded due to the First World War and to the post-war shift of focus from constitutional issues to economic problems. Yet Bonham Carter also suggested that the historiography might reflect a degree of selective memory on the part of historians of the Conservative Party, who dominated the early field:

> It is much more comfortable and convenient for the Tory party that the memory of the lunacy of their diehard predecessors should fade into the background of history. As the events … recede down the years the more fantastic does the performance of the Tory leaders appear and the more inexplicable both to their successors and even to us who witnessed it.[13]

The Liberal response to the outrageous lengths to which the Tories resorted is a phenomenon that has been little explored by historians, an omission that this volume will seek to remedy. What will be revealed, amid the vicissitudes of the crisis, is the perception of an assault upon democracy concealed within the challenge to Irish Home Rule. I argue that the significance of the concept of democracy to twentieth-century Liberalism and the desire to reap the harvest of the 1911 Parliament Act were crucial factors in the course of the crisis. The imperative of overriding the veto of the House of Lords by enacting Home Rule, and the deep disillusionment with ministers seemingly indifferent to that democratic precedent, have been overlooked by historians assessing the Liberal Party's state of health going into the First World War. The vigorous

---

which created the United Kingdom of Great Britain and Ireland. The change of name placed opposition to Irish Home Rule at the forefront of the party's advertised principles. In line with the terminology used in the early years of the twentieth century, the Conservative Party, as it is more commonly now known, will mostly hereafter be referred to as the Unionist Party.

response of Liberal supporters to what many saw as a failure to defend the party's core doctrine is absent from histories of its declining years by Clarke, Trevor Wilson and Michael Bentley.[14] Even Dangerfield said nothing of the pre-war revolt of the Liberal rank and file against their errant leaders. Yet it seems probable that the tensions between leaders and led laid bare by the third Home Rule Crisis established the fracture lines along which the party was to shatter after the war.

❦

Irish Liberty, British Democracy examines Irish Home Rule's journey from its re-emergence as a dominating issue in British politics in 1909 to its wartime passage in suspended form in 1914. The book considers the third Home Rule Crisis from three perspectives: put simply, what the propagandists said, how the public received it, and what the politicians did. This structure unfolds the book's main arguments about the leverage that Redmond exercised over the Liberal Party, and how Home Rule came to be seen as the vindicating instrument of British democracy.

Chapter 1 sets the stage for what follows by placing the third Home Rule Bill in the context of its failed predecessor measures, and by assessing the state of the Liberal Party in the early years of the twentieth century. In considering the ideological relationship of Irish Home Rule to the Liberal Party, it adopts the approach of Eugenio Biagini, whose *British Democracy and Irish Nationalism, 1876–1906* argued that Ireland remained the central issue of Liberal politics into the twentieth century, sustaining the devotion of the rank and file by an appeal to fundamental principles of humanitarianism. Biagini contended that by identifying Home Rule with liberty, the issue of Irish self-government retained lasting appeal for Liberals.[15]

Persuasive as these assertions are for the period to 1895, they are rather less plausible after Home Rule was cleaned from the slate of Liberal priorities by Lord Rosebery. Hidden from prominence for more than a decade, the Irish cause inevitably lost its emotional charge. The insufficiency of Biagini's argument in the later period of his study prompts questions about the nature of the twentieth-century ideology of Home Rule and efforts to revive moribund Liberal sentiment, both of which will be explored in Chapter 1. The chapter delineates the ways in which Liberal commentators mediated strands of twentieth-century Liberal principle, such as arguments that Irish self-government would advance the interests of British working men, and tackled thorny questions such as the security of Protestants under a prospective

Roman Catholic political regime and the most problematic question of all, the status of Protestant-majority north-east Ulster.

The second chapter is the first of three in this book that consider the high politics of the Liberal–nationalist relationship. The chapter explores the sources of the surprising hold that Irish Parliamentary Party chairman John Redmond had over the radical wing of the Liberal Party, an assertion of power that was resented by ministers but which served the nationalist leader well as the Home Rule Crisis unfolded. Redmond more or less obliged Prime Minister H.H. Asquith to restore Irish Home Rule to the Liberal pro-gramme in 1909, effectively circumscribed ministers' freedom of action in an inter-party conference with the Tories in 1910, and was instrumental in the adoption of a policy of curbing the veto powers of the House of Lords. As the chapter reveals, his efforts to influence the drafting of the Home Rule Bill in 1911/12 met with less success. Ending on the prime minister's triumphal visit to Dublin after the introduction of a new Home Rule Bill, Chapter 2 considers the Irish Party's chequered reputation in Ireland and its credibility as a truly national party as the nationalist mission for self-rule appeared to be nearing a victorious end.

Chapter 3 chronicles the response of the Liberal and allied press to the Ulster Unionists' promised rebellion. The chapter details how Liberal journal-ists struggled to reconcile the rights of the Catholic nationalist majority in Ireland with those of the intransigent Protestant Unionist minority, at one moment advocating compromise, at another calling for the government to impose its will on Ulster. Gary Peatling identified this conflict between Liberal conciliatory instincts and the prospective coercion of Ulster's Protestant com-munity as the crux of an ideological dilemma afflicting ministers and Liberal opinion formers.[16] The inability of Liberals to articulate an effective response to the injustice of depriving Ulster's Protestant population of its settled and consensual form of government, argued both Paul Bew and Richard Bourke, was the crucial weakness of the case for Home Rule.[17]

Appeals to simple majoritarian justice *were* inadequate, and Home Rule propagandists, seemingly sensing this, responded by subordinating the Ulster question to a wider one about British democracy. The benefits that Home Rule would confer on Ireland, rhetorically at least, assumed secondary importance to the role that its passage would play in advancing democratic reform in Britain. The third chapter asserts that this identification of Home Rule with Liberalism's core doctrine obscured lesser ideological contradictions, and gave focus to frustrations with ministerial hesitancy.

Chapter 4 considers the political wrangle over what to do about Ulster. Patricia Jalland's *The Liberals and Ireland*, the standard work on the third Home Rule Crisis, framed the episode as a dispute between the British parties, protracted by a deliberate policy of 'wait and see' by which Asquith hoped to disrupt, confuse or wear down the Conservative and Unionist Party's opposition while the situation in Ulster steadily deteriorated.[18] Chapter 4 overturns Jalland's influential casting of the conflict as a Liberal–Tory dispute, arguing that a practical consensus over Ulster's exclusion emerged between the Liberal and Unionist leaders early on, and that the principal struggle was, in fact, between the British parties and the Irish nationalists.

Jalland asserted that the wider Liberal Party exerted little influence over Cabinet decisions, and she largely omitted consideration of Irish nationalist leverage over the prime minister's decision-making.[19] This reflected a belief, expressed earlier by Nicholas Mansergh, that the threat of nationalist action could be disregarded.[20] Notions of Asquith's inscrutability have persisted so long, perhaps, because indications of his responsiveness to nationalist and back-bench pressures are to be found not in what he did, but in what he did not do. As Chapter 4 reveals, it was Redmond's potential for splitting the Liberal Party, even more than the possible defection of the seventy-odd Irish nationalist votes in the House of Commons, that constrained Asquith's freedom of action. That the leaders of the British governing parties were unable to impose the compromise that they jointly desired testifies to the depths of passion on both sides that were stirred by the crisis, and the power over British politics exerted by John Redmond.

A survey of the rank-and-file Liberal response to Home Rule and to Ulster agitation closes the circle of high politics, public mediation of ideas, and popular sentiment. Chapter 5 considers the lukewarm state of Liberal feeling, fears and disputes about Irish fiscal autonomy, and widespread consternation at the Irish nationalists' perverse voting record on the question of votes for women. The chapter charts a flaring of Liberal enthusiasm after the Curragh Incident, when a shift in rhetorical emphasis cast the Unionist backing for the Orangemen and their allies as a resumption of their struggle against the Parliament Act of 1911. The rush to defend the supremacy of the House of Commons, the chapter argues, electrified the Liberal movement in the summer of 1914 as no other issue had since the defence of free trade in 1906, galvanising the party against the collusive inclinations of its leaders.

Redmond's success in manipulating Liberal opinion was not matched by a cultivation of Irish nationalist consent to concessions to north-east Ulster.

Chapter 6 describes the darkening mood of nationalist Ireland as Ulster's promised defiance went unanswered and confidence in Home Rule waned. Redmond's assent to temporary exclusion in the spring of 1914 was widely regarded as a betrayal of the national ideal, and as a monstrous dismemberment of Ireland. Intense disaffection from the extreme reaches of nationalism was communicated to Irish Party supporters through the medium of the Irish Volunteer paramilitary movement, and by 1914 outraged nationalist sentiment was constraining Redmond's own choices. The chapter on the state of nationalist feeling argues that the Irish Volunteers increased the difficulties of the Irish Parliamentary Party by radicalising the rhetoric of nationalism and by popularising the possibility of an alternative revolutionary path to nationhood. It will also reveal the prescient apprehension of provincial officials that the intent of the extremists among the Volunteers' leaders was not to make war against the Ulster Volunteer Force (UVF) but to revolt against British rule.

A final chapter on the political transactions at the climax of the crisis asserts that a reckoning with its consequences occurred on all sides. Asquith faced the realisation that an attempt to impose a settlement might shatter his government, and Redmond wrestled with serious discontent and a deteriorating political situation in nationalist Ireland. The Conservative leaders recognised just how dire a position their irresponsible actions had left them in, while the Unionists of Ulster were weighing the economic consequences of their threatened secession. The result of a wavering of Tory and Ulster Unionist resolve was an initiative to temporarily exclude Ulster on a face-saving, transitional basis.

This volume presents evidence that by the summer of 1914 Ulster Unionist leader Sir Edward Carson conceived of and desired a province reconciled to the rest of Ireland after a short span of years, and took deliberate steps in this direction. In the light of this change of view and Redmond's strategy to becalm Ulster resistance, I argue that the possibilities of a Unionist capitulation, under a flag of compromise, were not exhausted when the unexpected outbreak of the First World War altered the course of Irish and world history.

To gain fresh insight, some oddly underutilised sources have been consulted.[21] The diaries of Margot Asquith contain important material not previously published, as do the diaries of J.A. Pease, a junior government minister. A wealth of fascinating detail was found in the correspondence of George V and his aides, collected in the Royal Archives at Windsor. Clues to the motivations of Unionist leaders at key points of the controversy were gleaned from the papers of Viscount Milner, British Empire patriot and vehement opponent of Home Rule, and those of the Marquess of Lansdowne, Unionist leader in the House of Lords.

The correspondence of T.P. Gill is particularly rich.[22] Gill, a former nationalist MP, was Redmond's unofficial 'fixer' and strategist. Travelling across Ireland in the course of his work for the Department of Agriculture and Technical Instruction brought Gill into contact with a wider range of people and opinions than those accessible to the Irish Party chairman. He sought to shape opinion in the public sphere through unattributed contributions to the London *Daily Chronicle*, and privately by intercessions with Eoin MacNeill, D.P. Moran and influential figures in Britain. It was through Gill that Redmond appears to have received intelligence concerning the mood of Ireland and counsel as to arguments he thought would resonate with ministers and with British public opinion.[23]

Sir Francis Hopwood, Additional Civil Lord of the Admiralty, is revealed as an unsung but energetic British intermediary during the crisis.[24] A career civil servant, Hopwood was a trusted adviser to George V and to his private secretary, Lord Stamfordham. Hopwood was a fixture of the British establishment widely respected for the breadth of his knowledge, whose air of impartiality enabled him to move with ease among politicians of both sides. But despite this intimacy with the leading men of state, Hopwood privately regarded them with a healthy dose of contempt, and he was particularly damning of Asquith's lax leadership. With Stamfordham, Hopwood served as a conduit of political intelligence to the king.

Analysis of the public discourse and the Liberal responses to the Ulster controversy relied primarily upon British and Irish newspaper and magazine sources. Examination of the twentieth-century case for Home Rule, and efforts made to mobilise popular support, drew upon a profusion of pamphlets produced by special propaganda organisations set up by the Liberal and Irish Parliamentary parties, collected at the British Library. The National Liberal Federation and National Liberal Club archives at the University of Bristol hold valuable material suggestive of Liberal Home Rule sentiment in the country in 1912–14. The journals of Liberal and Conservative salaried constituency agents at Bristol and in the Bodleian Library, Oxford offer unique insights into the public mood.

The anxiety over the apparent end of the oligarchical order that transfixed British Conservatism in the Edwardian era affected the Liberal and Irish Parliamentary parties in parallel processes. The trajectories of increasing democratic participation and Irish autonomy, as the parties' leaders were

aware, involved the possible displacement of their moderate political movements by socialist or separatist rivals. In Ireland, the ever-diminishing fruits
of Redmondite gradualism against a mythologised Parnellite promise began
to estrange the Irish Party from grassroots nationalism. In Britain, a Liberal
government, warily embracing social democracy, was lagging behind its supporters' demand for fuller political democracy. The extremity of the opposition
challenge to Irish Home Rule, and by extension to ideals of liberty and democracy, intensified the tensions between principle and pragmatism. The trials of
the Home Rule Crisis damaged the coherence of Liberalism and constitutional
nationalism, eroding the Irish Party's dominance in Ireland and hastening a
reconstitution of progressive politics in Britain.

1

The Case for Irish Self-government, 1909–12

Liberal leader W.E. Gladstone's adoption of the cause of Irish self-government in 1885 initiated a prolonged period of disarray in the Liberal Party. The first Home Rule Bill, of 1886, triggered a party split, prompted the departure of radical visionary Joseph Chamberlain, and met defeat in the House of Commons. A second Bill, in 1893, was passed by the Commons but was thrown out by an overwhelming Tory majority in the House of Lords. The eighty-three-year-old Gladstone and his colleagues accepted the peers' rejection of their flagship policy, and mounted no serious effort to reverse the verdict of the unelected Upper Chamber. Leadership of the party passed to the brief and erratic stewardship of Lord Rosebery, no friend of Home Rule, and the Liberals were soon relegated to the opposition, where they remained for a decade.

Rejected at the polls and racked by leadership squabbles (Rosebery resigned in 1896), the Liberal Party descended into factionalism and demoralisation. Rosebery emerged from an Olympian exile in 1901 to appeal to Liberals to start afresh with a 'clean slate', a call universally understood to mean repudiation of the policy of Irish Home Rule. Rosebery could scarcely be blamed for regarding the issue as political poison, but his intervention threatened to precipitate a dispute that might once again cleave Liberalism in two. Internecine conflict, exacerbated by the South African War of 1899–1902, submerged the issue of Ireland ever deeper. Roseberyite Liberal Imperialists, who counted many of the party's luminaries among their number, quietly supported the war. They viewed the British Empire as a virtuous engine of democracy in the white-settler colonies and a benevolent institution of trusteeship for 'backward' populations elsewhere. In domestic policy the Liberal Imperialists were modernists attracted to statist ideas and 'national efficiency', from which

Leabharlanna Poiblí Chathair Baile Átha Cliath
Dublin City Public Libraries

aims sprang their pragmatic, as opposed to humanitarian, approach to social reform.[1]

At the opposite end of the spectrum were progressive radicals, who attacked imperialism on moral grounds, and advocated twin doctrines of political democracy, in the form of universal manhood suffrage (and, perhaps, women's suffrage) and social democracy, to be attained through levelling social reforms.[2] Though these 'New Liberals' were small in number in the early years of the twentieth century, their social democratic philosophy was influential. New Liberalism, as adumbrated by J.A. Hobson and L.T. Hobhouse, asserted that collectivism was not the antithesis of traditional laissez-faire Liberalism but an adaptation to modern conditions necessary for social advancement. In a capitalist society, they argued, state interventions to relieve poverty and its attendant evils would foster individual enterprise and self-improvement.[3] Graduated income tax, together with taxes on unearned income and on land, could finance social reforms to raise living standards for working people and dismantle hereditary and class privileges. Social democracy, then, was cast as the means of fulfilling the old Liberal ideals of liberty and equality. The New Liberal thought of intellectual journalists such as Hobson, Hobhouse and H.W. Massingham permeated a vibrant Liberal press.

The bulk of the Liberal Party fell somewhere between these two poles. The South African War had its own divisive effects, creating new fissures between its 'pro-Boer' opponents, supporters of the war, and an uncomfortable majority at the party's centre. Moderate Liberals, who subscribed to the Gladstonian legacy of humanitarianism, self-help and free trade, viewed jingo imperialism and collectivist social policy with equal suspicion. Prior to 1910 this core of small-government, laissez-faire Liberals, committed to the ideals of peace, retrenchment and reform, probably comprised the majority of the party's parliamentary representation. Perhaps the greatest achievement of Sir Henry Campbell-Bannerman, leader of the Liberals from 1899, was to hold together his fractured party amid the buffets of pressures old and new.

The Liberal Party was fortunate that its opposition, the Conservative and Unionist Party, was rent in two by the proposed policy of protective tariffs in 1903. The defence of free trade against 'food taxes' united Liberals as never before, and Campbell-Bannerman led his party to a victory of unprecedented scale in the 1906 general election, sweeping the Unionist government from office. The return of the Liberals, however, did not signal the restoration of a policy of Irish Home Rule. Possession of a large parliamentary majority, independent of the Irish nationalists, and the influence of Liberal Imperialists in key ministerial posts, ensured that self-rule for Ireland remained no more than an oratorical aspiration. A sop to nationalist sentiment, in the form of the Irish Council Bill of 1907, was proposed to devolve administrative, as distinct from legislative, powers to Ireland, but the measure was resoundingly rejected by an Irish Convention and had to be withdrawn. It was not until 1909, when the parliamentary arithmetic increased the Irish Parliamentary Party's leverage, that the Irish question again loomed over the British political horizon.

Where liberty had been the principal emphasis of the nineteenth-century Home Rule campaigns, democracy assumed the central focus in the twentieth century. The Reform Act of 1884 had extended the franchise to around sixty per cent of adult males in the United Kingdom; universal manhood suffrage, it was widely believed, could not be far distant. This innovation was not regarded as an unalloyed blessing. Many among the ruling classes feared the economic and social consequences of the rise of 'the multitude'. The Liberal Party, however, sworn to Gladstone's dictum to 'trust in the people', could not overlook the fact that huge swathes of the population were denied representative government. Extension of the franchise, abolition of plural voting, and (for many Liberals) women's suffrage were all anticipated as virtuous expansions of democracy.[4]

In the years since the defeat of the 1893 Home Rule Bill, the concept of democracy had evolved in a manner related to the collectivist ideas of New Liberalism. Democracy, in this sense, meant the people themselves, the working people for whom Liberalism would legislate ameliorative reforms. Democracy was used not just as a term for a responsible system of government but also as a collective noun for the aspirant working-class electorate. Sustaining the Liberal Party's claim to be the political executors of 'the democracy' was believed to be critical to its future, and part of the appeal of New Liberalism was its supposed utility in tilting the class cleavage of politics to the Liberals' advantage.

As will be seen, the mantle of Home Rule was fitted to many purposes, but democracy was the theme that bound Liberalism's diverse interests to the Irish cause. The democratic struggles of Irish nationalists and the British working classes were cast by Home Rule propagandists as twin offensives in the fight against oligarchy. The battle reached its apparent climax with the 1911 Parliament Act, which, by limiting the veto powers of the House of Lords, at last made the House of Commons the supreme authority in the land. This chapter will examine the arguments and methods by which Irish self-government was identified with the core doctrine of twentieth-century

Liberalism, and cast as a continuance of the struggle for economic and social justice for British working people.

Crafting the new demand

The miasma of electoral defeat surrounding the issue of Irish Home Rule remained undissipated in 1909/10. Liberal reluctance to campaign on Home Rule in the two general elections of 1910 arose from the memories of the electoral losses of 1886 and 1895, and from the perceived unpopularity of Home Rule in Britain. The Irish question was all but absent from the Liberal campaigns of 1910, downplayed in preference to the 'peers or people' controversy over the 1909 People's Budget. The Liberals campaigned on their record of beneficial social reforms and naval expansion, and against the promised evils of protectionism and monopoly arising from the Unionist tariff policy.

By contrast, Ireland featured prominently in the Tory campaigns of 1910, with posters depicting Irish Parliamentary Party leader John Redmond as a hound scattering Liberal hares, or as a club-wielding Fenian out 'to smash the British constitution by American dollars'. The Unionists' negative campaigning against the Liberals, as the supposed lackeys of the 'Dollar dictator', however, seems to have failed to move the electorate. Voter apathy on the issue, it appears, cut both ways. A few leading Unionists realised that Home Rule could no longer strike terror among British voters as it had in 1886 and 1893, but others believed it was still a point of vulnerability for Liberals, and with their own party bitterly divided over tariff reform, the Irish issue was, perhaps, the strongest card they had to play.

Home Rule occupied comparatively few column inches in the British press in 1906 and 1909, except for a month or so of press coverage around the time of the abortive Irish Council Bill in May 1907. With the restoration of a policy of Irish self-government to the Liberal programme in 1909, and the introduction of the third Home Rule Bill three years later, the prominence of matters Irish in the British press grew substantially. Articles about Home Rule in one selection of Liberal journals doubled in number from 1907 to 1910, and more than doubled again in 1912.

Newspapers were the principal channel for the dissemination of Home Rule rhetoric. The intensely partisan character of the Edwardian press, Liberal and Unionist, was a matter of ownership and of commercial viability. Party organisations supported their respective organs of the press financially, as the Liberals did with *The Westminster Gazette* and *Reynolds's Newspaper*, either through organising consortia of wealthy backers to bail out struggling news-papers or by means of subsidies to distressed titles from party funds.[5] Editorial compliance with the party line was, doubtless, reinforced by the knowledge that party managers expected to get their money's worth.

That said, for the greater part the Liberal press was independently minded and outspoken. Its ethos reflected the party's faith in the power of reasoned argument, though its sometimes urgent tone suggested an awareness that radical Liberal politics represented a minority taste.[6] The dominant radical editorial line of Liberal newspapers arose from the early career associations of many of their editors and contributors. Robert Donald, editor of *The Daily Chronicle* from 1904, learned his trade alongside H.W. Massingham (at the helm of *The Nation* from 1907) at *The Star* in the late 1880s under the tutelage of Irish nationalist politician and London newspaperman T.P. O'Connor.[7] Massingham and J.A. Spender, latterly of *The Westminster Gazette*, were briefly on the writing staff of *The Manchester Guardian*, whose path-breaking synthesis of Liberalism and socialism did much to define the progressive agenda. C.P. Scott, editor of *The Manchester Guardian* and one of the most influential Liberals in or out of Parliament, secured A.G. Gardiner the editorial chair at the *Daily News and Leader*.[8] Many of these men had imbibed radical principles of peace and free trade at an early age, and had been swept along by Gladstone's crusades for Home Rule in 1886 and 1893. Collectively, these journalists represented an influential progressive force promoting the advance of social and political democracy while retaining an enduring distrust of ministers.[9] They remained passionate advocates for Irish Home Rule.

In addition to the principal daily and weekly newspapers, an array of specialist titles was aimed at sectional interests and Labour supporters. A brace of Nonconformist newspapers catered to the non-Anglican Free Church sects that traditionally made up the backbone of Liberal support. *The Methodist Times* faithfully supported Liberal policy on a range of issues, while the political preoccupations of *The Baptist Times* and *The Presbyterian* tended to centre on the issue of denominational education. Frank Dilnot, a social-reform campaigner, inaugurated the halfpenny *Daily Citizen* in 1912, which provided a mixture of criticism and praise from a socialist perspective. Robert Blatchford's socialist *Clarion* newspaper was supportive of the Liberal social-reform agenda, though impatient with its pace and scope. A satirical perspective on the Home Rule debates was provided by *The Lepracaun Cartoon Monthly*, published in Dublin. So apposite and well-executed were *The Lepracaun*'s cartoons that dozens of them were reprinted in the London monthly *Review of Reviews* in 1910–14.

A surprising outlet for progressive politics was *The Catholic Times and Catholic Opinion*, edited for the best part of thirty years by P.L. Beazley.[10] Reflecting a readership of British Catholics mainly of Irish descent, *The Catholic Times* was strongly pro-labour, and sought to harness working-class interests to Irish Home Rule. While the newspaper's support for the nationalist cause was to be expected, its progressive editorial positions – particularly its support for the political organisation of labour – must have spoiled more than one Roman Catholic bishop's breakfast.

In this era, as in other times, editors and newspaper owners considered their proper function to be that of an intermediary in public affairs. Prime Minister H.H. Asquith was averse to newspapermen, but his colleagues courted Liberal editors and proprietors. Chancellor of the Exchequer David Lloyd George breakfasted with C.P. Scott, lunched with Massingham, and retained close ties to Sir Henry Dalziel MP, owner of *Reynolds's Newspaper*.[11] For a time the Chancellor appears to have concealed little from his friend and golfing partner Robert Donald of *The Daily Chronicle*.[12] T.P. O'Connor took political bearings from old journalistic colleagues Massingham and Scott, and the latter was a regular correspondent of senior Irish nationalist MP John Dillon. The intervention by Liberal editors in political negotiations was sought or proffered at various times in the 1912–14 Irish crisis by Donald, Spender, Scott and James Douglas of *The Star*. Tory newspapermen were no less active among their politicians: Lords Northcliffe and Rothermere, proprietors respectively of *The Times* and the *Daily Mail*, along with Geoffrey Robinson, H.A. Gwynne and J.A. Garvin, editors of *The Times*, *The Morning Post* and *The Observer*, were all involved behind the scenes at different stages of the Home Rule controversy.[13]

The efforts of Liberal newspapers to propagate arguments for Irish self-government were reinforced by two party organisations set up to mobilise public support. The Irish Parliamentary Party's propaganda organ, the Irish Press Agency, was revived in 1908 after a decade of inactivity. Its editor, Stephen Gwynn MP, was charged with amassing a fresh body of literature for distribution in Britain to support a new Home Rule campaign.

The Home Rule Council, generously endowed from party funds in 1911 by Alexander Murray, the Liberal chief whip, shared the considerable resources of the Liberal Publications Department.[14] The new organisation complemented the *Liberal Monthly Magazine*'s normal circulation of 200,000 copies with pamphlets, books and a monthly publication entitled *Home Rule Notes*, all pressing the case for Irish self-government.[15] Prominent Irish nationalists recruited by Gwynn's Irish Press Agency provided much of the Home Rule Council's literary output. By the end of 1912, scores of leaflets were offered with the aim of educating readers about the history of the Anglo-Irish relationship, the future work of an Irish parliament, and the safety of Irish self-government in the context of the empire, religious liberty and Ulster. By the end of the campaign, the two publicity organisations claimed to have distributed four million Home Rule leaflets and a further one million books and booklets.[16]

Arguably dominating the output of Home Rule propaganda was the one-time nationalist MP and professor of economics at University College, Dublin, T.M. (Tom) Kettle. Kettle was at the heart of the group of Irish intellectuals shaping the renewed case for constitutional nationalism. For a decade he was one of the most indefatigable speakers on matters touching Irish self-government, particularly its economic aspects, addressing meetings at the Mansion House in Dublin, the National Liberal Club, and public demonstrations in Britain and Ireland. In numerous books and British newspaper and magazine articles between 1911 and 1914, Kettle artfully pressed the case for Irish autonomy. He did so with such wit and elegance that his words were widely published and reprinted in British newspapers and journals. Kettle's book *The Open Secret of Ireland* (1911) was a tour de force distillation of arguments for self-government, and its companion of the same year, *Home Rule Finance*, was a comprehensive study of the ills of, and proposed cure for, Ireland's troubled economy.

What emerged from the welter of books, pamphlets, newspapers and journals was a coherent set of arguments for Home Rule, presenting a variety of perspectives on the case for Irish self-government. These arguments arose from a cross-fertilisation of ideas from Irish nationalist intellectual to British Liberal, and from propagandist to politician, and vice versa. Liberal pamphlets drew upon nationalist speeches, Irish nationalist politicians wrote the content of leaflets and articles in Liberal newspapers, and newspapers and pamphlets supplied the stuff of platform oratory. The circular nature of this exchange of ideas meant that the discourse in the Liberal press was indistinguishable from the Irish nationalist position, and, as often as not, was authored by an Irishman. Francis Sheehy-Skeffington penned articles for *The Morning Leader* and *The New Age* in 1912; T.P. O'Connor MP wrote a weekly column for *Reynolds's Newspaper*, dealing almost exclusively with Irish Home Rule from 1913; while nationalist civil servant T.P. Gill was an anonymous 'Special Correspondent' for *The Daily Chronicle* in 1914.[17] Liberal rhetoric around the third Home Rule Bill can therefore be described as a synthesis of mostly Irish nationalist creation. Except for critical perspectives from some socialist-leaning organs, the messages for British audiences from supporters of the Irish cause – Liberal, nationalist and Labour – were emphatic and consistent, seeking to overcome the obstacles thrown up by the previous battles for Home Rule, while accommodating new and competing popular demands.

Empire and patriotism

The argument that Irish self-government would mean the beginning of the end of the British Empire was remembered as being among the most damaging objections that Home Rulers had had to face in 1886 and 1893. Liberal and Irish nationalist propagandists again relied heavily upon historical examples to assert the idea that Home Rule was not only consistent with the British Empire but was instrumental to its existence. Canada was held up as a formerly divided and discontented colony that responsible government had transformed into a harmonious and loyal dominion, while George III's obstinate misrule in the American colonies was cited as an illustration of the perils of coercion and denial of self-government.[18] The recent granting of dominion status to the Transvaal in 1908 was regarded as the crowning example of Liberal imperialism. The defeated Boers' enthusiastic membership of the empire a half-decade after a protracted war was declared little short of miraculous.[19] These contrasting examples were used to show that self-government led to reconciliation and prosperity, while its refusal resulted in worsening discontent and an eventual rupture of the imperial tie.

The twentieth-century British Empire, propagandists asserted, was 'an agglomeration of Home Rule states'.[20] How, they asked, when there were twenty-eight parliaments in the empire, could the granting of a legislature to Ireland cause imperial bonds to instantly dissolve? Every dominion prime minister at the 1911 Imperial Conference was a Home Ruler, it was argued, because no one knew better than they the benefits that self-government bestowed.[21] The subjection of Ireland to a detested form of government damaged Britain's moral standing in the empire and in the United States. The passage of Home Rule, the *Daily News and Leader* argued, would eradicate the historical stain of British misrule in Ireland and convert her to contented membership of the British Empire; Ireland, the empire's shame, could become its glory.[22] Until the Irish demand was cleared, she would remain an obstacle to closer imperial cooperation in defence and commerce, and perhaps even federation, which many

Unionists, and some Liberals, believed was the empire's future.

The *Daily News and Leader* argued that the evident prosperity and loyalty of the settlement colonies of Canada, Australia and New Zealand were a monument to the virtues of Liberalism.[23] The 'lusty manhood' of imperialism of the 1890s, it asserted, had given way to respect for nationality and public acceptance of the wisdom of self-government.[24] Tom Kettle noted that Irishmen appreciated that the strength of the British Empire lay in its accommodation of national aspirations through grants of autonomy; but the apparent blindness of Englishmen to this fact, he said, was a source of intense annoyance to his countrymen.[25]

An inconsistency that was galling to Irishmen was the grit in the oyster of the empire. Challenges to the British Empire's legitimacy were growing in intensity in Egypt and India. Irish Home Rule, its supporters asserted, was congruous with the evolution of a self-governing empire, and offered an excellent model for its future.[26] Solution of the Irish grievance by constitutional methods pointed the way to a means of accommodating nascent nationalist forces elsewhere in the empire. Tom Kettle wrote of the need to invent a twentieth-century empire, and of Ireland's role in demonstrating to the empire 'the way forward, based on the constructive principle of Home Rule.[27]

Gladstonian Liberalism asserted that participatory self-government had brought economic and social progress to the colonies, and would do the same in Ireland. In the renewed campaign these arguments were carried further. A liberal empire – decentralised, democratic and constitutional – was cast as a beneficent agency in the world, spreading English liberty and morality. The extension of Liberal principle to Ireland would see her taking her place among the dominions, her loyalty deepened by the voluntary nature of her association. In resisting the lessons of history and by ignoring the evolution of the empire, Liberals and nationalists argued, Unionism, not Home Rule, was the anti-imperial doctrine.[28]

Nationalists protested loyalty to the empire to rebut charges of separatist intent. Ulster nationalist MP Samuel Young was among the most outspoken of 'loyal nationalists'. At the age of ninety-two, in 1912, he spoke his mind with vigour:

> Talk of disintegration! Why, sir, the King shall be our King, the Army and Navy, and a general customs and excise shall be common to the three countries. We want to glory in the success of the Empire, in the building up of which we played so great a part. We want no separation;

we would fight against it to-morrow if it were proposed. We want to belong to this country, and to be a strength to this great country.[29]

In the age of the genre of invasion literature, however, Ireland's proximity and her rebellious past roused fears that a vengeful neighbour might one day strike at Britain's flank. One such novel in the genre brought the 'green peril' to life. William Palmer's *Under Home Rule* (1912) was a lurid tale of an ecclesiastical *coup d'état* in Ireland inspiring Catholics around the world to rise, at the Pope's command, in rebellion against the British Empire.[30] Erskine Childers, Anglo-Irish author of the 1903 invasion novel *The Riddle of the Sands*, tackled the question of security in *The Framework of Home Rule* (1911). Childers argued that a great navy protecting a far-flung empire was adequate to guard St George's Channel, and pointed out that Britain did not demand the removal of the Belgian parliament to Westminster to insure against possible intrigues with Germany. Childers derided the idea that the Irish, having waited so long to govern themselves, would welcome German invaders.[31] A loyal Ireland, Childers argued, her grievances salved by self-government, would be a defensive asset worth many divisions.[32] In light of his role in the importation of German arms at Howth in 1914, Childers' ridicule of the notion of an Irish dalliance with Germany is ironic, though his later actions were intended not to sow rebellion but to defend Home Rule.

The financial question

How a self-governing Ireland was to be financed was a vexed question in the Home Rule debates of 1912–14. Its solution required balancing the demands of Ireland upon the Imperial Exchequer with the fiscal burdens to be borne by Irish taxpayers, particularly those in the industrial north. It demanded consideration of matters of historical taxation and the future connection of Britain and Ireland. Recognising the thorny nature of the case, Home Rule propagandists advanced claims that justice demanded a generous financial settlement, and emphasised the thrift with which the Irish would manage their affairs.

The 1908 Old Age Pensions Act had altered the fiscal position of Ireland vis-à-vis the rest of the United Kingdom. The enormous uptake of pensions in Ireland transformed Britain's smaller neighbour from a net contributor to the Treasury into a net liability. Home Rule's advocates acknowledged this, but stressed that Ireland's drain upon imperial finances was a recent innovation. Even so, this did not stop them from arguing the sense of Britain granting Ireland self-government if only to cut its losses.

Home Rule propagandists urged British electors to remember the historical context of Irish taxation. One pamphlet reminded readers that between the years 1787 and 1798, under Grattan's Parliament, imports of tea, coffee, sugar and tobacco increased twofold, and that revenues, trade and manufacturing were buoyant.[33] The 1800 Act of Union, it was alleged, had ended Ireland's prosperity through destruction of her industry; men of talent were forced to emigrate to find freedom and fortune. Those exiled Irishmen had risen to prominence as captains of industry, statesmen, soldiers and men of science and letters in the empire. In conditions of liberty in the United States, the pamphleteer asserted, enterprising Irishmen had 'built up and dominated the American nation'.[34]

In the century-long history of the Union, it was claimed, taxes collected in Ireland far outweighed what had been spent there. In the nineteenth century, pamphleteers alleged, an excess of £300 million over what the British government had spent in Ireland had been extracted from her.[35] Aside from putting the current position of liability into perspective, Liberal and nationalist writers argued, this century-long overtaxation strengthened the case for a broad-minded financial settlement to inaugurate Irish self-government.[36]

Tom Kettle, the most prolific writer on Home Rule finance, asserted in forceful terms where he thought Irish taxpayers' millions had gone: 'It went to pay for the establishment of a Colonial Empire, and for the consolidation of conquest in India. It went to pay for the Chinese War, and the Crimean War, and the blowing of Hindus from gun-muzzles, and the occupation of Egypt, and Majuba and Colenso.'[37] He went on to catalogue the famines and sufferings of Ireland throughout the nineteenth century against the revenues extracted from her (including £2.6 million, he claimed, in the most terrible year of the Great Famine). Kettle asserted that savings that could have been used as capital for industrial expansion had been ransacked, leaving Ireland in a permanent state of penury. He asked the reader to 'consider whether the Imperial tribute was not, in the ample and literal sense of the words, blood-money, or, if he prefers, famine-money'.[38]

If, Kettle asked, Home Rule was an issue of English conscience, how could the financial aspect be left out of the equation? He suggested that Britain's present to Ireland upon a grant of self-government should be a cheque (which drew the riposte, from F.E. Smith, that wedding presents did not ordinarily accompany a divorce).[39] For Kettle, restitution was neither a matter of charity nor of English benevolence, nor was it even a bargain, though if it were it would be one of incalculable value, he asserted, particularly in improving relations with the United States.[40] Restitution was, rather, England's way of making amends for past misdeeds, which was, he insisted, half the purpose of granting Home Rule.[41]

Kettle considered that there could be no more admirable form that reparation could take than a continued subsidy of old-age pensions. He suggested that there was, in this proposal,

> ... no irrelevant revival of the past ... the stricken and defrauded Ireland of 1835 to 1870 is not dead; it is alive and hungry ... You do not acquire a pension simply by being old; you must also be destitute. In this country there has been a division of labour: Ireland provided the aged people, Great Britain and the Union provided the destitution.[42]

The most relevant fact about the Great Famine, Kettle argued, was not its deplorable memory but that its survivors were the aged poor of 1912. 'The Ireland of the eighteen-forties and eighteen-thirties', he wrote, 'is the most living fact in our public finances today.'[43] Pensions for the relics of that age, he argued, would be a fitting gesture of restitution for the agonies visited upon Ireland under the Union.

The venerable complaint of exorbitant taxation was compounded by charges of galling extravagance of British administration. Ireland's sixty-seven costly administrative boards – 'enough ... to make her coffin', as one wit put it – made up a governmental structure so labyrinthine that it had to be 'seen to be disbelieved'.[44] Dublin Castle administration had no incentive to economise, critics complained, and, in consequence, spent British and Irish taxpayers' money prodigiously. The money lavished on Ireland was wasted on fat salaries and overstaffing that ultimately left all parts of the British Isles poorer.[45] Irish administrative costs per head of population vastly exceeded those of Scotland, owing to the employment of nearly three times as many civil servants in Ireland.[46] Kettle likened British administration in Ireland to a poor man invited to live in the house of a financier. Living a champagne lifestyle destroyed the boarder's sense of frugality and self-reliance, and his lingering presence aroused the resentment of his host.[47]

The profligacy of the Royal Irish Constabulary (RIC) had long been criticised. Expenditure on policing in Ireland per head of population was double that of England and three times more than in Scotland, despite a much lower rate of criminality.[48] So many police constables, Kettle claimed, with so few criminals to chase meant that an 'army of occupation [had] become an army of no occupation'. Kettle also compared the cost to the Exchequer of the RIC to that of the British diplomatic service, observing that 'almost precisely the same amount is spent on batoning Nationalist heads in Ireland as proclaiming and pressing imperial interests throughout the whole world'.[49]

Yet despite this lavish spending, Ireland's economy remained sluggish. Statistics were cited to demolish claims that a twenty-year period of relative prosperity had muted the demand for self-government. In 1910, it was pointed out, 340,000 Irish men and women, or seven per cent of the country's population, had emigrated. Scotland, possessing a population of a similar size to that of Ireland, yielded £3.4 million more in income tax per annum, a difference attributable to higher Scottish rates of employment in trades and professions. Decades of malinvestment had left Ireland with 3,431 miles of railways, versus 7,781 miles in Scotland, and her comparative rail revenues lagged by two-thirds.[50]

The Irish, propagandists claimed, would run their own country with the thrift of the farmer or householder. The restraint of the Irish county councils in the first eight years of their existence was offered as evidence of sound financial management. County administration in Irish hands had reduced the county rate (tax) by threepence in the pound, as contrasted with an increase in rates in England and Wales by over a shilling in the same period. 'Frugality', a Liberal Party organ wrote approvingly, 'has been the distinguishing characteristic of Irish local government.'[51] The Irish, proponents argued, knew how they wished their money to be spent, and were better placed to make budgetary choices. Experience had shown the Irish to be prudent, and the fixed provisions of Home Rule finance would force them to live within their means as a self-supporting nation.

With more productive objects for expenditure in mind, Home Rule writers asserted, a self-governing Ireland would spend on land purchase what it saved on policing, and support industry and education while cutting extravagances and jobbery. Improved drainage of flood-prone rivers, forestry development, and nationalisation of the railways were projects that an Irish government might undertake to promote commerce and underpin farming and businesses. All could be accomplished, advocates insisted, by the establishment of a responsible system of government.[52] Accountable administration was not just the guarantee of prudent expenditure, it was cast as the curative for administrative corruption and bloat. The financial arguments for Home Rule in 1912 were thus a hybrid of ideas old and new: of Gladstonian retrenchment and New Liberal collectivism. Bridging the two was the subsidy of old-age pensions, for which the case for a collectivist social good was supported by a compelling humanitarian argument.

The appeal to working men

The linkage of Irish self-government to advancement of the cause of working men in Britain was a new feature of Home Rule rhetoric. Nineteenth-century campaigns had argued that Irish prosperity would benefit the British industrial classes through more work, less wage competition from Irish labour, and lower taxation.[53] In 1912, however, proponents sought to persuade working men that they had a direct interest in the Irish cause. The struggle of the Irish against a privileged ascendancy was cast as one and the same as that of the working classes for political and economic justice. A grant of self-government to Ireland would be, Home Rulers argued, a blow struck for industrial and social reforms for the British worker.

The Catholic Times asserted that the landowning class, so hard at work against Irish Home Rule in 1912, had fought Englishmen's struggles for liberty throughout history. The English worker was urged to recognise the opponents of Irish Home Rule as the same historical enemies of his own dispossessed ancestors. The bitterness and assiduity of the assault on Home Rule by men of privilege, with no personal interest in Ireland, concealed, *The Catholic Times* contended, the true target of aristocratic spite: 'they are using the No Home Rule cry as a dam against the rising of the waters of democracy here ... Whoever else may find his interest in keeping Ireland bound, it is the British working-man's interest to make her free.'[54]

Few subjects as the land, many Liberals thought, were as central to the question of a restoration of English liberties. *The Catholic Times* applauded the government's intention to 'take in hand the tangled skeins of the land problem' in Britain, an issue supposedly of great concern to the working man.[55] The connection between grievances of the English working classes and the Irish national demand was once again made:

> The eventide of Ireland's century-long struggle for justice is the daybreak of that coming English demand for restitution of the countless acres of land which were stolen from our village peasantry by the fraud of an immoral Act of Parliament. On the day Irishmen get free, we English will begin to rattle our chains.[56]

If working-class enthusiasm was not obvious, Home Rulers asserted, it was not because workers found Home Rule objectionable but because they were more concerned with social improvement at home. The socialist *Daily Citizen* commended Home Rule to its readers on its own merits, but also because its passage would accelerate social reforms that the swelling ranks of Labour representatives demanded: 'The British working men are knocking at the door of Parliament and demanding justice', it insisted, and self-government for Ireland would aid their efforts, morally, and in practical terms, by clearing the field.[57] Ireland already benefited from reforms, such as land purchase, which were unknown in Britain; under Home Rule, *The Daily Citizen* asserted, social experimentation in self-governing Ireland could quicken the pace of reforms in the rest of the country. Ireland, already showing the way of the future in the fields of agricultural cooperation and housing, was seen as a laboratory for the Liberal/Labour programme of social reform – possibly even, the newspaper claimed in 1913, by pioneering state provision of medical treatment.[58]

Redmond cast the confrontation with the House of Lords as a battle for the self-government of the United Kingdom. The discharge of the will of the people in Britain through the assertion of the supremacy of the House of Commons, he insisted in 1910, meant practically the same thing as Home Rule in Ireland.[59] The Liberal programme of democratising legislation, Alexander Murray asserted, was a comprehensive 'attack on the evils of [the] social system' in which Home Rule for Ireland played an important part.[60] Old-age pensions, National Insurance, labour exchanges and, above all, the Parliament Act of 1911 were great strides for the cause of working people. Three principles of Liberalism, however, remained to be vindicated: religious freedom, to be advanced by disestablishment of the Welsh Church; franchise reforms, most especially universal manhood suffrage and the abolition of plural voting; and nationality and self-government, of which Irish Home Rule would be the most important symbol and an exemplar for measures for Scotland and Wales.[61]

Unionists, progressive commentators charged, fomented sectarian hatred to prevent the agricultural labourers of Ireland and the urban workers of Belfast from realising their common interests as wage earners. The *Daily News and Leader* asserted that the true cleavage of Ireland was neither racial nor religious, but a struggle for ascendancy and liberty between a small oligarchy and the mass of the people.[62] The British worker, it argued, seeing landed aristocrats and captains of industry inciting the Orange 'rabble' with disloyal oaths, might ask himself whether honest and industrious men of his own background might not be better fitted to lead in public life.[63]

Robert Blatchford's socialist *Clarion* newspaper argued that Home Rule offered an illusory solution to the Irish people's suffering. The root cause of their bondage, the newspaper asserted, was the same landowning and capitalist class that oppressed English workers; the means of breaking its hold was for the toiling classes of the two countries to unite.[64] Harold Begbie's 1912 *The Lady Next Door* asserted that the reverse polarity of the two islands had produced a bizarre outcome in which English Conservatives and Ulster socialists backed the Union, while English socialists and Irish conservatives were united for Home Rule. English Tories supported the Union, he claimed, for the preservation of the ascendancy of their class and that of their Protestant allies in Ireland. Socialists of the industrial north of Ireland desired perpetuation of the Union to escape what they thought would be the suffocating conservatism of a Dublin parliament, and 'for the sake of England's purse'. Conversely, Home Rule attracted English socialists for its democratic and reforming nature, and Irish conservatives for the prospect of displacing a Protestant, industrial hegemony with a Catholic, agrarian one of their own.[65] This was of a piece with Begbie's broader point that the British and Irish nations were economically and spiritually misaligned, a disjuncture only capable of remedy by Home Rule.

The Irish-Ireland case

Amid the flowering of the Irish cultural and Literary Revival, and the surge of popular interest in the Irish language inspired by the Gaelic League, the Liberal tenet of 'governing Ireland according to Irish ideas' had never had greater currency. Home Rule writers speculated as to how a future Dublin government might remould society in organically Irish ways, purifying it of corrupting anglicisation, and making it more harmonious and prosperous. This was by no means a frequent theme of Home Rule rhetoric in newspapers and pamphlets, but its presence points to the growing awareness of the Irish-Ireland movement, and a desire to explain its significance to British audiences.

Begbie's *The Lady Next Door* was the most substantial work to advance this thread of the case for Irish self-rule. The eponymous lady was a young woman in her cottage who told the worried gentleman next door that she wished to do her own housekeeping, which she believed she could do better and more economically herself. She desired to live in peace with her neighbours, and wished to revive no old grudges; she asked only that they buy her surplus butter and eggs.[66] Begbie's feminised allegorical imagery held little that a British audience might find threatening and much that it could admire. In conformity with the romanticised agrarianism of the time, Begbie's vision of the new Ireland was self-reliant, hard-working and pacific.

The Catholic Times insisted that Home Rule promised pastoral salvation for the British and Irish peoples:

> ... getting them in possession of the soil, which they shall till with honest work, eating the fruits they shall grow. These sweet islands of God's grace and favour, under better and juster laws, shall yet blossom with luxuriance to be compared to Paradise; for they are oases of fertility.[67]

There was an important difference between Ireland and England, in that Ireland's earthly paradise was as yet unspoiled.

British rule, Sydney Brooks asserted, had been a corrupting influence in Ireland, one that had left Irishmen 'nondescripts, half-provincial English, half-renegade and emasculated'.[68] Begbie feared that the polluting way of life under the Union would lead to the replication of the industrial anarchy and commercial brutality of England in Ireland.[69] A government of Irishmen, guided by Irish ideas, these English writers argued, offered the chance of preserving the purity of the land, the air and the spirit of the people. For what was the use of Home Rule if it meant importing the squalid life of industrial England to Ireland? *The Clarion* asked:

> What would the mass of the Irish workers gain by the building of hideous factories in the sweetest spots of their beautiful country, by making an Irwell of the Shannon, a Jarrow of Skibbereen, or a Woolwich of Killarney? ... When the laughing waters of the Kenmare are filled with gloom, grime, and stench ... when Queenstown harbour is filled with hungry swarms of Polish and Russian immigrants and the grasping Limerick land agent has given place to the grinding Jewish sweater, what will be the gain to the peasantry of Ireland?[70]

This nightmarish vision of Ireland (clearly informed by prejudice) might be in prospect if she remained under British rule or evolved into a West British imitation, claimed the newspaper.[71]

Government according to Irish ideas would be dictated by the Irish nature. Harold Begbie asserted that the mass of the people of Ireland, Roman Catholic and agrarian, was naturally conservative, desiring only peace and continuity. The farmer's life on the land was one of ancient rhythms and of deep roots to the land and family, Church and community. The concern with the spiritual over the material, Begbie argued, distinguished Irish national life from that of England. It was a fundamental clash of cultures that went to the heart of the impossibility of benign English rule. England was embarked on a course of materialism, he wrote, accruing the wealth, power and social turmoil that her choice entailed. Ireland was seeking a national life without materialism, one in which a free people could till the land in harmony with nature, and enjoy a simple life in which the spiritual remained the supreme reality.[72]

Tom Kettle, writing of 'The Catholic Future in Ireland', saw the opportunity for an Irish government inspired by Irish ideas to act as a model for other nations. An Ireland turning away from modernism and industrialisation would be, he suggested, not a backwater but a beacon illuminating a different path. A return to the land, to the community, and, Kettle argued, to the teachings of the Catholic Church would result in a society built on agriculture, local industry and cooperation. The rejection of urbanism and unbridled capitalism was, he asserted, an expression of Catholicity, and in keeping with the Irish way of life; by her example of faithfulness to her nature, he judged, 'Ireland may yet stand out as the last fortress of Western Civilisation'.[73]

Not all commentators agreed that an Irish-Ireland future would take on a form that would be pleasing to the Church. Proprietorship of the land, improved education, and technical instruction were inspiring in Ireland, said *The Nation*, new ideas and increasing self-reliance.[74] Sydney Brooks claimed that the Irish-Ireland movement was instinctively hostile to clerical intrusion. The independence of thought and social reordering that innovations like agricultural cooperation and the Irish-language movement were breeding in Ireland, Brooks argued, were cultivating a generation of people possessing a strong national identity and a progressive and increasingly secular way of thinking.[75] Like Kettle's vision, the future Ireland populated by this generation would be agricultural and cooperative, but, Brooks believed, it would be the product of dynamic, freethinking minds rather than the consummation of a Roman Catholic Arcadia.

Begbie, as a Methodist minister, could embrace neither the Catholic nor the secular point of view, but he nonetheless agreed that the Irish experiment of living without materialism would be an admirable one. A self-governing Ireland that was true to her past and her natural way of life promised to propagate, for her people, a contentment that England had lost.[76] In setting the Irish people free to follow their own path, England might be repaid with the wisdom of eternal truths that she had carelessly left behind. 'England used to think', Begbie wrote, 'that the home is the unit of the nation, that religion is the supreme law of the individual, and that it is impossible to serve both God and Mammon. On these matters … Ireland has not changed her mind.'[77] Begbie commended his British readers to honour Ireland 'for her sense of nationality … revere her for the beauty and simplicity of her life … be interested in her choice of natural simplicity, and … help her with all the power they possess'.[78]

Protestantism and Home Rule

The most sensitive issue, and the one that Home Rule propagandists felt they had to deal with at greatest length, was the fear of sectarian discrimination against the Protestant minority under a Dublin parliament. Of all the cries that might be raised against Irish self-government, 'Home Rule means Rome Rule' was recognised, by both sides of the controversy, as the one that could so inflame British opinion that the project might be wrecked altogether. The danger was thought to be especially acute for Liberals, given their reliance on Nonconformist support. To fend off the bogeys of Catholic vengeance and Protestant subjugation among this key segment of the party's supporters, Home Rule campaigners relied especially upon the contributions of Protestant Home Rulers, whose testimony, it was hoped, would allay the fears of their co-religionists.

Irish history was exhaustively cited to show that patriotic feeling had time and again overcome sectarianism and revealed a reciprocal generosity and independence of thought in Ireland's confessional communities. Grattan's exclusively Protestant parliament had given Roman Catholics the franchise in 1793, and Protestants had been instrumental in winning Catholic Emancipation in 1829. The Home Rule movement, Liberals were reminded, had been born with the assistance of Protestants and Tories. Isaac Butt, son of a Protestant minister, moved the first motion for an Irish parliament in 1870. Roman Catholic nationalists, it was said, had many times shown themselves ready to defy the power of Rome, as Daniel O'Connell did in resisting a papal rescript in 1814. Public opinion had ignored the Pope's condemnation of a public subscription to aid Charles Stewart Parnell in 1883 and a papal ban on agrarian agitation in 1888. In 1890 Redmond, despite being denounced from the altar as the Antichrist, had stood by Parnell, his chief, when the latter was disgraced by an adultery scandal. The fact that Parnell was a Protestant, one propagandist argued, made Catholics' repeated defiance of the Church in his defence all the more remarkable.[79]

The revival of Home Rule required some Nonconformist writers to restrain their native anti-Catholic tendencies. Yet support was sometimes couched in unflatteringly anti-Rome terms. Where, in 1906, *The Baptist Times* had spoken of the Vatican as the immutable and 'inveterate foe of human liberty and human progress', in 1912 Dr John Clifford, retired president of the Baptist World Alliance and paragon of Nonconformist Liberalism, deftly applied a positive spin to essentially the same rhetorical ball. Writing in the *Daily News and Leader*, Clifford suggested that nothing would better advantage Protestantism in Ireland than a full measure of liberty, as, he insisted, Roman Catholicism invariably withered in an atmosphere of freedom.[80]

A segment of Protestant supporters of Irish self-government saw no inconsistency in being fiercely anti-Catholic at the same time as being pro-Home Rule. For some Protestant commentators, Roman Catholicism had infested Dublin Castle: the Church's pernicious effects on Irish society were seen by some as being advanced and enforced by British authorities.[81] Suspicions of an unholy alliance of Roman priest and Protestant functionary dated back to Robert Peel's Maynooth Grant of 1845.[82] George Bernard Shaw observed that the English effectively policed Ireland for the Pope, while Lord Randolph Churchill recorded that the soundest Tory policy was to rule Ireland through the Roman Catholic bishops.[83] Sydney Brooks pronounced Dublin Castle's foundations to be so rotten with Romish influence, from the Lord Lieutenant to the lowliest clerk, that the Church's assent was needed to get anything done.[84]

Proof of this insidious intimacy, several Liberal commentators charged, was to be found in the Church's lack of enthusiasm for Home Rule. The Roman Catholic hierarchy, Brooks believed, supported liberty for Ireland only so long as it was sure she would not get it.[85] Joseph Hocking concurred with the view that the Church did not desire to see Home Rule, benefiting so much as it did from the existing state of affairs. Fear of Rome Rule was fantastical, he insisted, because it was almost impossible for Ireland (with the exception of Ulster) to be more oppressively ruled by Rome than it already was.[86]

The Vatican, Sydney Brooks charged, cared little for Ireland but greatly about England. The Holy See's real objection to Home Rule was that a reduction in the number of Irish representatives at Westminster would deprive English Catholics of crucial parliamentary support. Indeed, some

Nonconformists believed that the Irish Party had exercised a Catholic Church injunction over English legislation by voting against the Education Bill in 1906. The Church, Brooks suspected, dreaded a loss of influence over the imperial parliament even more than the erosion of its overwhelming power in Ireland.[87] A significant benefit of Home Rule for Nonconformists was that a reduction of Irish representation at Westminster would curtail the poisonous influence of Rome in England.

As paradoxical as it may seem, a state of near-paranoiac anti-Romanism was no bar to support for Home Rule. *The Baptist Times* spied popery at work, even in fomenting the expulsion of Catholic shipyard workers in Belfast in 1912. The Roman Catholic Church, fearing the destruction of its power in the imperial parliament and the disruption of priestcraft in Ireland, it alleged, was exercising 'those subtle means of opposition which Rome has always been so clever in bringing into play ... Protestants in England must not allow themselves to be duped by these subterranean tactics'.[88]

More level-headed Free Churchmen argued that there was much for Nonconformists to gain from Irish Home Rule. Presbyterian minister J.B. Armour claimed that members of the (Anglican) Church of Ireland ascendancy that ruled the land reserved the highest offices and salaries for themselves.[89] Much of the opposition to Home Rule, he believed, stemmed from the fears among the Anglican landowning class of a loss of its privileges. Free Churchmen, Rev. Armour argued, had little to gain from a continuation of the status quo, and less to fear from a majority-Catholic Irish parliament, since they could scarcely get fewer plums of office than they already enjoyed. The forces that sought to block Home Rule, argued Armour, 'Squire and Parson, land and Church', were the same as those that thwarted equitable treatment for Nonconformists in Ireland and Britain.[90]

Rev. W. Kingscote Greenland, in *The Methodist Times*, noted a breach between nationalists and the Roman Catholic Church, which he thought would advantage Irish Nonconformists. The Redmondites, he asserted, were using the Church and its sway over the rural poor to advance their aims; but once a Dublin parliament was in being, the Church's power would be overthrown by the new secular authority. Protestants might have to suffer some things they did not like under Home Rule, he acknowledged, but the breaking of priestly power in education would benefit Nonconformists and emancipate the minds of the Roman Catholic majority.[91]

Protestantism, Rev. W. Crawford wrote, offered an example to the Irish people of the possibilities of piety, progress and intellectual freedom without succumbing to soulless materialism.[92] Joseph Hocking asserted that the gift of religious and intellectual liberty was uniquely that of the Protestants of Ireland to give to their Roman Catholic neighbours:

> Our forefathers were not afraid of liberty, liberty to all, and in their courage they became mighty, and left to us the heritage that is our joy and our crown … Let [Nonconformists] shew their priest-bound countrymen that they at least believe in a living Christianity, the essence of which is justice and liberty and love.[93]

Viewed through this Nonconformist prism, Irish Home Rule was a vehicle for intellectual and spiritual self-improvement, a virtuous synthesis of evangelical and Liberal goals. The mission of Free Church Protestantism would be the liberation of the minds of the people. The Irish journalist and Catholic critic of the Church P.D. Kenny expressed a spiritual dimension to Home Rule with which many Nonconformists could have identified: 'the real problem is to restore the use of their wits to the Irish people. *We want peasant proprietorship in mental freedom. We want self-governorship for the peasant.*'[94] Home Rule for Ireland could mean home rule of the mind and spirit for the smallholder in his cottage. Dr John Clifford asserted that most Free Churchmen, British and Irish, could see the divine ordination of Home Rule, and answer the call of a mission to liberate and redeem Catholic Ireland.[95] Clifford and Nonconformist Home Rulers were the inheritors, and most characteristic latter-day practitioners, of Gladstone's evangelical style of Home Rule politics.

The problem of Ulster

Home Rule propagandists of 1912 asserted with confidence that their cause had the force of democracy behind it. The province of Ulster had returned a majority of Home Rule representatives in three parliamentary elections in twenty-five years. A large nationalist majority in Ireland was for Home Rule. The majority of electors in the United Kingdom, as expressed by three successive Liberal general-election victories, was, it was said, behind Home Rule. On the evidence of the opinions of colonial prime ministers and sentiment in the United States, campaigners argued, the empire and, indeed, the wider world supported Irish self-government. The resistant population of Ulster was thus, in the view of Home Rule propagandists, a minority within a minority.

The consistently narrow rivalry of nationalists and Unionists in election contests in Ulster was cited as proof that the voice of the province was not united in opposition to Home Rule. Rather, critics charged, it was *Belfast* resistance to self-government that was being amplified and exaggerated by Unionists as representing the verdict of the whole of Ulster. To accept Belfast as being indicative of Ulster opinion on Home Rule, one writer argued, was no more valid than to assume that Birmingham (home of the leading proponent of tariff reform, Joseph Chamberlain) represented British opinion on protective tariffs.[96]

'Ulster' opposition, Home Rulers asserted, flew in the face of the rights of the majority and of fair play. A segment of the population seeking to subvert the considered judgement of the majority was offensive to democratic principles. It amounted to, as Tom Kettle put it, a minority claiming that it should not merely be secure but supreme.[97] To follow the distorted logic of Ulster Unionism to its conclusion was to give licence to syndicalists, or individual householders, to pick and choose those laws they wished to follow and those they would ignore. For Home Rulers the Unionist policy of defiance would ultimately prove unsupportable, because it would undermine laws upon which the property and business interests of the north-east of Ireland relied. A position of resistance so potentially self-destructive, Liberals argued, could not be sustained.

Propagandists claimed that elaborate Orange processions and public gatherings, culminating in the signing of the Solemn League and Covenant in September 1912, were cynically orchestrated. The instigators of the Orange protests, they held, were neither men of the working class nor the businessmen who were the brains and backbone of Belfast's prosperity, but outsiders and London barristers with their personal ambitions in view. Irresponsible British politicians and local Protestant clergymen, Home Rule writers charged, were whipping north-east Ulster into a frenzy with well-rehearsed passion by manipulating the prejudices of an ignorant and superstitious populace.

The Orangemen of Ulster, in Kettle's judgement, were under the spell of a sterile set of beliefs preached by a Presbyterian clergy whose hatred of Rome surpassed their love of Ireland.[98] The ravings of platform and pulpit, Kettle asserted, aroused in the Orangeman primitive passions:

> Ritual dances, King William on his white horse, the Scarlet Woman
> on her seven hills, and grand parade of dead ideas and irrelevant
> ghosts called up in wild speech by clergymen and politicians – such
> is Orangeism in its full heat of action. Can we, with this key to its

intellectual history, be really astonished that Shankhill [*sic*] Road
should move all its life in a red mist of superstition?[99]

If the Orangemen could recover their reason, Home Rule proponents
asserted, they would see the unreality of their worries and the advantages
offered them under self-government. The Protestants of Ireland numbered
one million in a nation of four million, and were 'a minority certainly not
inferior ... in grit, in enterprise, in wealth, and above all, in conviction'.[100]
Joseph Hocking questioned whether Protestants, possessing the positions of
power that they did, really had so much to fear from their Catholic brethren.
The farmers of the south were, he claimed, 'for the most part, ignorant, unen-
lightened, and subservient to the will of the priest'. As for Belfast, its fortune
had been made by the hard work and resilient character of its Protestant
forebears. Would their inheritors allow a Dublin parliament to endanger the
city's industrial pre-eminence, even if it tried?[101]

The government's willingness to extend guarantees to the Protestant
minority in Ulster was proof, claimed its supporters, of its even-handedness
and solicitousness to northern fears. There was, in consequence, bafflement at
the Ulsterman's refusal of the hand of good faith, and at the disproportional-
ity of his threatened rebellion. All the bellicose rhetoric, with its talk of arms,
oaths and provisional governments, was rendered faintly preposterous by the
spectacle of broomstick-toting Orange bandoleros drilling. The expansive
bombast of Sir Edward Carson, leader of Ulster Unionism, accompanied by
'black robes and masks ... [of] Adelphi actors', contrasted with the apparently
feeble ability of his cohorts (prior to 1914) to deliver any meaningful action.[102]
The inconsistency invited ridicule, an invitation that Liberal propagandists
were only too happy to oblige.

Ulster resistance was variously mocked as the 'Carson Circus Troupe
of knockabout artists', or sent up as a storm in a middle-class breakfast-
table teacup.[103] 'Ye Tale of Ye Pigge', in *The Daily Citizen*, lampooned
the Ulster Unionists in the manner of an earthy Chauceresque tale. Two
yeomen, Redmond and Carson, shared ownership of a pig, but Carson, the
owner of the animal's tail, disputed its direction of travel.[104] 'King Carson,
a Renaissance Masque' featured Cardinal Redmondo, Asquith as a stage-
drunk royal porter, and a haunted Carson, pretender to the throne of Ireland,
trying to wash ghostly blood from his hands.[105] In 1913 *The Daily Citizen*
caricatured arch-Tory Lord Halsbury commending Ulster to his fellows as
the 'winning card', advising them to 'stick to Ulster and civil war 'til we scare

the Coalition into a General Election', and so overturn the Parliament Act and franchise reform.[106]

The confidence of Home Rulers that the Ulster furore was overblown was not unjustifiable in 1912. The arithmetic, parliamentary and demographic, favoured Home Rule. From the Liberal perspective, a democratic mandate from the British people had been given, and affirmed. The House of Lords had apparently been neutered. An array of carefully reasoned arguments seemed, to Home Rulers at least, to be capable of overcoming all objections. In the resort of the Conservative and Unionist Party leader Andrew Bonar Law to an abusive 'new style' in the House of Commons, and his overheated public out-pourings at Belfast and Blenheim, some saw weakness, not only of argument, but of conviction. That the concerns of Ulster's Protestant population were genuine could not be in doubt, but Liberal and nationalist critics saw artifice and opportunism in their cynical manipulation by British Unionists.[107] The Ulstermen would be abandoned, critics asserted, when the Unionist leaders saw that their efforts to stir opinion in Britain would be for naught. In any event, they insisted, the intensity of the Ulster dissidents' protests was not matched by their capacity to resist. These considerations nourished optimistic assumptions that the enactment of Home Rule under the Parliament Act would be a certainty by 1914.

While ridiculing cardboard cannon and dummy rifles occupied the bulk of the Liberal press, in some quarters there was a dawning appreciation of the potential for Ulster discontent to derail Home Rule. In January 1912 *The Nation* presciently foresaw Ulster Protestant resistance as a serious obstacle to Irish self-rule, and counselled a scheme of 'Home Rule all round' and preser-vation of the customs union with Britain as the means for avoiding it.[108] As the months passed, doubts that 'Ulsteria' was pure bluff were creeping in. In October 1912 *The Baptist Times* cautioned against underrating the sincerity of Ulster passions, misguided though they might be:

> These old bearded peasants and farmers [of the north] ... are in earnest. And in their own very unpleasant way, so are the Orangemen of Belfast. The attitude of Protestant Ulster is a real danger and dif-ficulty in the way of Home Rule, which will need the most careful and patient handling.[109]

A few observers questioned whether the province could be reconciled to Home Rule at all. Rev. William J. Oliver, Methodist minister of Roscrea,

County Tipperary, acknowledged that the religious and economic safeguards for Protestants in the Home Rule Bill could scarcely be tighter, but wrote that he knew of no one in the north-east who gave them credence. In Oliver's view, sops to Protestant sentiment in the bill seemed designed purely to quieten the fears of English Nonconformists. Anticipatory concessions were worthless on the ground in Ulster, he wrote, because neither side believed that it would long restrain the nationalist majority in a Dublin parliament.[110]

However, those few Home Rulers who foresaw trouble from Ulster in 1912 faced the prospect with equanimity. Tom Kettle wrote in *The Open Secret of Ireland* that if riots in Protestant districts greeted Home Rule,

> ... we must only remember how sorry George Stephenson was for the cow ... If rifle-levers ever click in rebellion against a Home Rule government, duly established by statute under the authority of the Crown, it will be astonishing to find that every bullet in Ireland is a member of an Orange Lodge. If 'Ulster' repudiates the arbitrament of reason, and the verdict of a free ballot, she simply puts herself outside the law. And she may be quite assured that the law, driven back on its ultimate sanction of force, will very sharply and very amply vindicate itself.[111]

Kettle's faith in the 'arbitrament of reason' and the resolve of Asquith's government to enforce the law would be put to the proof. The confident complacency of Home Rulers in 1912 would be eroded by the course of events in Ulster, and by the ministerial inaction that met them.

2

The Re-emergence of Home Rule

The foundations of political legitimacy in Britain, which had been shifting from an oligarchical to a more democratic basis for nearly a century, were still unsettled in 1909. Industrialisation, urbanisation and mass communication increased the pace of social change. The organisation of trades unions and demands for working-class political representation, given expression by the Labour Party, threatened the established economic and social order. Burgeoning cooperative and friendly societies and working-men's clubs, among other formal, working-class self-agencies, were placing a measure of effective local control into the hands of working men and women. This complex of social developments was rapidly altering notions of democracy and authority. For the Liberal Party, at risk of being displaced by Labour and the Tories, a moral ideology of social democracy – New Liberalism – promised to reinvigorate the movement and sustain it against its rivals.

Yet while the Liberal Party supported the principle of representation of the labouring classes, it did not subordinate that goal to all others as the Labour Party did. It was slow, in practice, to adopt working-class candidates, owing to the practical difficulty of working-class candidates standing without some form of subvention, and the dominance of the Liberal Party, at local and national level, by moneyed, middle-class interests.[1] Nowhere was the social insularity of the party's elites more evident than at the very top of its leadership. Men like Asquith, Secretary for War R.B. Haldane, and Sir Edward Grey, the foreign secretary, were figures loftily remote from the society and experience of working men and women. Their wealth and material interests barred an overly enthusiastic embrace of New Liberal doctrine. They, like other veterans of Gladstone's era in the Cabinet, probably were not true democrats. Doubtless, like the 'Grand Old Man' himself, they believed in liberty, but not in equality.[2] At the same time, the thoughts of some younger ministers, like Lloyd George, were turning from concepts of humanitarianism and liberty to ideas of efficiency and expediency.

The loose ideological moorings of the Liberal leaders distanced them from their often highly ideological followers. The divergence was witnessed in 1910 by Cabinet divisions over curtailment of the veto powers of the House of Lords, a policy demanded by back-bench Liberals. Some ministers opposed so-called 'single-chamber rule' on principle, but many were wary of where the radical ideology of expanding democracy was leading. Political allegiances were strained by anxiety about the Liberal Party's direction and future. The Liberal leaders, at the head not only of a 'coalition' with the Irish and Labour parties but also of a spectrum of opinion within their own party, sometimes looked for ways to duck the expectations of their progressive followers.

Irish Home Rule, unique among the controversies plaguing politics in an unsettled era, motivated the leaders of the Liberal and Unionist parties to contemplate unaccustomed combinations that would have outraged swathes of their supporters. The impulse towards collaboration, on an issue so histori-cally intractable, exhibited both the increasingly pragmatic nature of politics and the party-leaders' shared anxieties about the pace of social and political change. In consequence, the controversy over Irish Home Rule tended to be characterised as much by collusion in private as it was by conflict in public.

The grudging nature of Home Rule's revival resulted in a bill arguably drafted with greater regard for Unionist sensibilities than those of Irish nationalists. Though John Redmond, holding the parliamentary balance at Westminster, effectively set key elements of the British political agenda between 1909 and 1912, his efforts to influence the framing of the 1912 Home Rule Bill met with less success. This was in part a limitation imposed by the politically possible at Westminster, in part a product of faith in the symbolism of Home Rule over its substance, and partly, as will be seen, a matter of accident. Yet from the point of view of mid-1912, there was little cause for doubt that the Irish Party's gradual approach to national autonomy was nearing a victorious conclusion.

The 1909 Home Rule pledge

'I feel', wrote a despairing T.P. O'Connor to John Dillon in September 1909, 'as if we were going through one of our darkest hours.'[3] The fortunes of the Irish Parliamentary Party had, indeed, scarcely been at a lower ebb, and that was saying a good deal. The once-formidable nationalist party of the 1880s had been devastated in 1890 by an adultery scandal that wrecked the career and life of the Irish Party's charismatic leader, Charles Stewart Parnell, and it remained bitterly split for a decade. Though reunited under John Redmond's chairmanship in 1900, the Irish Party was racked by residual rivalry and hostility, particularly between John Dillon, T.M. Healy and William O'Brien. Under the Unionist government of the early years of the century, the party exerted little political leverage, and what successes it could claim owed more to cooperative efforts with other political forces than to any dynamism of its own. The Irish Party's political dominance in Ireland arose practically in default of effective alternative movements.

In John Redmond the Irish Parliamentary Party had a capable, if aloof, chairman. Redmond sat in the House of Commons from the age of twenty-five, with only a brief interruption until his death in 1918. A stout man in middle age, whose profile, sketch writers noted, was not unlike that of a Roman emperor, Redmond was a distinctive presence in Edwardian politics, 'a spruce, sleek figure in fashionable frock coat, garnished with a bunch of violets'.[4] Widely regarded as an eloquent, if humourless, public speaker, Redmond was, in the judgement of one interviewer, 'almost mechanically systematic and practical'.[5] As Alvin Jackson observed, his manner of expression was often characterised by over-elaborate courtesy, though Redmond was not a man to be browbeaten, and was quite capable of robustly defending his position under pressure.[6] As leader, the Irish Party chairman was remote, largely restricting his counsels to his adjutants, John Dillon and T.P. O'Connor. When not at Westminster or speaking in Ireland or North America, he remained at his country home in Augavanagh, County Wicklow with his guns and dogs.

The South African War of 1899–1902 exposed the ambiguities of Redmond's nationalism. The Irish Party chairman's imperial inclinations were rooted in his class, his family ties to the British army, and his own identity, moulded by decades of life at Westminster. The nationalist MPs whom he led in the House of Commons were, with the Labour and radical Liberal members, the war's fiercest critics, bravely facing excoriation for their 'pro-Boer' stance. John Dillon led the charge against the 'barbarous methods' of the British army's scorched-earth policy and its squalid concentration camps confining women and children. Redmond deplored the war, and said so, but pride in his family's military traditions prevented him from condemning the many Irishmen who rallied to the colours.[7] Yet despite his compromised position, the Liberal journalist W.T. Stead credited the Irish Party chairman with leading opposition in the House of Commons; but for Redmond's presence, Stead asserted, dissident 'pro-Boer' Liberals would have had no leadership.[8] The nationalists' deeply unpopular resistance to an unjust war won Redmond and his colleagues the enduring respect of the radical wing of the Liberal Party.

To historians, Redmond was, in many ways, a peculiar object of admiration for radicals. The party he led was fundamentally conservative, in that it represented powerful clerical and commercial interests in Ireland, and its nationalist ambitions were of decidedly circumscribed scope. An observant Roman Catholic, Redmond was socially conservative and opposed women's suffrage. His sympathy for tariff protection for Irish industries jarred with the Liberal free-trade creed. The Irish Party chairman was uneasy about collectivist social reforms, particularly because of their burdensome financial implications for a future self-governing Ireland, and, given the opportunity, he favoured reducing their scale. Perhaps the most credulity-stretching aspect, then and now, of viewing John Redmond as an exponent of radicalism was that at home in Ireland the Irish Parliamentary Party often bore the worst characteristics of a ruthless and corrupt political machine, of which more will be said later in this chapter.

Yet the case can be made (and was at the time) that the Irish Parliamentary Party was a progressive and democratic force in British politics. Redmond's staunch and consistent advocacy of British democratic reform (which indirectly advanced Ireland's claim to self-government) won him the respect of adherents of Cobden, Bright and Gladstone.[9] Like the Labour Party, the Irish Party was antipathetic to the aristocracy, which was exercising, through the House of Lords, a Unionist veto over the legislative programme of the majority in the elected chamber of Parliament. A decisive Tory majority in the Upper Chamber obstructed progressive legislation, and represented a permanent constitutional fetter upon duly elected Liberal governments.[10]

Like Labour, the Irish nationalists could claim to draw their financial support from the subscriptions of the working classes: in the Irish Party's case, from the workers of Ireland, Britain and North America. The nationalists had successfully lobbied for reforms for which Britain still waited; progressive Liberals in the first decade of the twentieth century might well admire a party that had secured for Ireland the right and the means for farmers to purchase their smallholdings, a home-building scheme for workers in towns, and loans from public funds to acquire plots of land and build cottages for agricultural labourers.[11] On most issues before the House of Commons, radical Liberals and Irish nationalists thought and acted as one, and Redmond, speaking for a party independent of the Liberal whip, became de facto leader of the parliamentary caucus of irreconcilables.[12]

John Dillon, Redmond's unofficial deputy, was an old Irish Party warrior and radical ally, though his progressivism was tempered by rigid Catholicism on social questions. A tall, solitary figure, Dillon possessed a more or less permanently brooding demeanour. He was jealous of the Irish Party's political hegemony, and intensely hostile to initiatives that might deflect it from its central demand for self-government. From Dillon's perspective, efforts to reconcile the nationalist political movement with its Unionist Anglo-Irish hereditary enemies would inevitably diminish the force of the Home Rule demand.[13] He thus bore deep enmity for advocates of conciliation, such as William O'Brien MP and Sir Horace Plunkett, whose new Department of Agriculture and Technical Instruction (DATI) Dillon reportedly regarded as a Machiavellian device to seduce Ireland from nationalism.[14] Dillon's narrow-minded suspicions acted as a restraint upon any impetus to bold or imaginative courses of action, and, as both Philip Bull and Alvin Jackson have suggested, his antagonism may have been motivated by a desire to preserve his personal influence.[15]

The breakthrough on the land question had emerged from the Land Conference of 1902, a meeting of landlords and tenant representatives (who included Redmond and William O'Brien). The revolutionary Wyndham Land Act of 1903 at last enabled tenant farmers to purchase their agricultural plots in a scheme backed by Treasury annuities. Redmond, who had advocated conciliation of the landlord class since the 1890s, was gratified by the outcome, though he was cautious about the broader application of O'Brien's 'conference plus business' policy. The Irish Party chairman did not turn his face against its possibilities, however, and he initially welcomed Lord Dunraven's ill-fated devolution proposal of 1904.[16] Redmond desired, at this stage, to infuse new blood and new ideas into the party. He hoped to recruit men reflective of the wider spectrum of nationalism, such as the barrister and historian R. Barry O'Brien, General Sir William Butler, and the president of the Gaelic League, Douglas Hyde. These suggestions, however, alarmed O'Connor, who, like Dillon, was opposed to the adoption of independently minded candidates who might be inclined towards broadened conciliation efforts.[17]

In moves designed to erect a bulwark against the tendency towards conciliation, Dillon instigated a revival of agrarian agitation against graziers in the west of Ireland (the 'Ranch War' of 1906–09), and mounted a political vendetta against party members suspected of consorting with O'Brienites.[18]

Combating conciliation also appears to have been his motivation for supporting the activities of Joseph Devlin, the young Belfast political organiser cultivating the growth of the Ancient Order of Hibernians (AOH) in the north of Ireland.[19] Devlin's AOH, a fiercely Roman Catholic mutual-aid society, was in many ways the mirror image of the Orange Order in Ulster. The Hibernians, piously dedicated to the defence of faith and fatherland, acquired a reputation for ruffianism and intimidation.

The lines separating the AOH from the Irish Party blurred as the Hibernians' influence spread throughout Ireland. Devlin, at Dillon's instigation, displaced an ally of O'Brien's to become general secretary of the party's local-membership network, the United Irish League (UIL), in 1904. The installation of the Hibernian grandmaster at the head of the Irish Parliamentary Party's grass-roots political machine, together with the party's embrace of an unruly and aggressively sectarian organisation, undermined its claim to be a truly national party. Dillon and Devlin's command of the party's organisation, and its unofficial enforcement arm, tempered Redmond's authority. Dillon's assertion of a competing node of power within the Irish Party was one of the ways, as one wag noted, in which its chair had to be content to be sat upon.[20]

John Dillon took no part in the leadership of the AOH, but lavishly praised its piety. His biographer ascribed his attitude towards the organisation to uncharacteristic naivety.[21] If Dillon's support for the AOH was indeed intended to thwart O'Brienite conciliation, the creation of a militantly Roman Catholic mass movement achieved its short-term goal. The longer-term consequence of the tactic's success, however, was to widen the cultural and sectarian gulf in Irish society, particularly between the Protestants of north-east Ulster and the rest of the country, with damaging implications for the attainment of unitary self-rule.

The return to confrontation with the Anglo-Irish ascendancy class in Ireland also weakened the party's links with the nationalist heartlands. The resumption of an anti-grazier campaign between 1906 and 1909 proved divisive for the nationalist movement, as many of the ranchers targeted for attack were themselves nationalists. The concerns of the huge class of newly propertied smallholders were neglected, and the Irish Party leaders obstructed the work of the Irish Agricultural Organisation Society and the Department of Agriculture and Technical Instruction, which might have benefited farmers.[22] Both innovations were products of despised conciliation, and so faced the hostility of the party's machine. Dillon's retrograde influence, it seems, had many and far-reaching consequences.

Another senior party figure, T.P. O'Connor, was the nationalists' crucial go-between with Liberal ministers, and, for a time, was an intimate of the mercurial Chancellor of the Exchequer, David Lloyd George. O'Connor's long-standing journalistic pursuits in Britain made him an effective propagandist for Irish nationalism, though his decision to stand for the Irish Party in a Liverpool constituency in 1885 rendered him suspect for ever after among nationalists in Ireland and America. Though 'Tay Pay' was regarded with affection in the House of Commons, his remoteness from Irish feelings was publicly criticised in Ireland, and seen as problematic by some of his party colleagues.[23]

The Liberal landslide of 1906 at once raised and dampened nationalist hopes. The premiership of Home Ruler Sir Henry Campbell-Bannerman gave cause for cheer, but his government, bowing to residual Liberal Imperialist influence, forswore Home Rule in the new parliament. For the Irish Party this created an uncomfortable choice between supporting putative political allies pledged against offering that upon which its existence depended, and a Unionist opposition, which offered no comfort at all.

The failure of the Irish Council Bill of 1907, initially supported by Redmond but furiously thrown out by an Irish National Convention, rendered further 'step-by-step' progress impossible.[24] Following the rout, Sinn Féin, which advocated Irish self-reliance and the withdrawal of Irish representatives from Westminster, won an unsettling level of support in local elections and parliamentary by-elections in 1907/08.[25] In an effort to rehabilitate his standing, Redmond embarked on a wide-ranging speaking tour in August 1907. The content of Redmond's speeches made plain his awareness of the damage inflicted upon the party by the Council Bill rejection, and of the need to match the substance of Sinn Féin's appeal while reasserting the value of parliamentary nationalism.[26]

In the absence of a Home Rule Bill, Redmond privately pressed ministers for the ameliorative legislation outlined in his speeches. Progressive legislation for Ireland, he argued, was vital if the party was to retain support and to continue to fortify the Liberals in the division lobbies of the House of Commons.[27] He had a firm ally in Cabinet in the Irish chief secretary, Augustine Birrell, who sedulously fought the nationalist corner among his colleagues in idiosyncratically witty fashion. The efforts of Redmond, Dillon and Birrell were rewarded (as has been alluded to) by a harvest of beneficial legislation, including the Labourers (Ireland) Act, 1906; the Town Tenants Act, 1906; the Evicted Tenants Act, 1907; the Irish (Catholic) University Act, 1908; the Housing of the Working Classes (Ireland) Act, 1908; the Land

Act of 1909; and the application in Ireland of the Old Age Pensions Act in 1908, which benefited close to 200,000 Irish men and women over the age of seventy.

These achievements notwithstanding, the Irish Party remained in the doldrums. Sinn Féin's dramatic rise had stalled by 1909, but criticism of the Irish Party continued unabated. The lack of progress on Home Rule, and rumoured concessions over reduced sums for land purchase, elicited scathing commentary. The once proudly obstructionist party of Parnell appeared to many as prone to being pushed around by the Liberals. 'Verily', wrote one critic in 1909, 'the chairman of the Irish Party is now on castors.'[28] Disenchantment with parliamentarianism was felt keenly in North America. T.P. O'Connor's predictions of the imminence of Home Rule were booed by sparse and sceptical Irish-American audiences in 1909. One Irish-American predicted that Redmond's fundraising efforts there that year would yield less than £5,000; in the event, O'Connor's trip raised only £4,000.[29]

Efforts to unite all sections of parliamentary nationalism under Redmond's leadership only intermittently reconciled two influential figures. William O'Brien MP, whose successes at the Land Conference of 1902 convinced him that conciliation of Unionists offered the only path to a united Ireland, was frequently at odds with the Irish Party leadership, despite a temporary return to the fold in 1908.[30] T.M. Healy MP, a barrister of obstreperous temperament and acid tongue, was out of the party more often than he was in. The pronounced egotism of Healy and O'Brien meant that Redmond was deprived of the counsels of two of the most creative minds of Irish nationalism.[31] O'Brien and Healy, both critical of alliance with the Liberals but nominally Irish Party members in early 1909, formed a nucleus of dissent in the ranks of parliamentary nationalism.

The Young Ireland Branch of the United Irish League, founded in 1905, was dedicated to nurturing the political capacity of younger nationalists and pressing for a policy of no minor measures.[32] Francis Cruise O'Brien, Richard Hazleton and Tom Kettle all served as president in the branch's early years, while other prominent members included Francis and Hanna Sheehy-Skeffington, as well as future leaders of the 1916 Easter Rising, Joseph Plunkett and Thomas MacDonagh. The Young Ireland Branch's welcome of nationalists sympathetic to Sinn Féin, and its advocacy of parliamentary obstructionism, attracted the ire of the standing committee of the UIL, which eventually barred the group from its meeting rooms. Despite this, the branch claimed over 100 members in 1909.[33]

The Irish Party faced a confluence of discontented factions at the infamous 'Baton Convention' of that year. William O'Brien was howled down by Hibernians, and one of his supporters was attacked on the platform, in Redmond's presence. The incident precipitated O'Brien's final exit from the party and the formation of his All-for-Ireland League from his Cork stronghold. Much worse was the discredit that the disgraceful scenes attached to the Irish Party. *The Times* gleefully contrasted Redmond's opening plea for the convention to exhibit the Irish genius for conduct in public life with his tacit approval of the meeting's undignified disintegration.[34] Humiliation turned to farce when a prosecution for assault in connection with the convention was brought in the magistrates' court, and Redmond – pleading ignorance of all wrongdoing – was cross-examined by T.M. Healy.[35]

Criticism from Ireland persuaded the nationalist leaders to adopt a more insistent line with the Liberals, and irritation with the government's Land Bill was sowing doubts in their minds as to ministerial trustworthiness.[36] Redmond considered sending Irish MPs home en masse in the summer of 1909 as a pointed means of abstention on the Land Bill's remaining clauses.[37] The Irish Party chairman's dissatisfaction over the bill grew so intense that he was inclined to oppose the government on everything – including an impending by-election at Dumfries – but a last-minute meeting with Lloyd George patched up matters.[38]

Lloyd George's 1909 'People's Budget' opened up a further serious breach. The dispute arose not from the most revolutionary and contentious aspects of the budget – graduated taxation on higher incomes, a 'super tax' on the wealthiest, and land taxes – but on liquor and licence duties that would hit Irish commercial interests especially hard. The Chancellor of the Exchequer's elastic interpretation of agreements meant that a dispute over the 'whisky tax', resolved in August, erupted again in September.[39] Given that the Irish Convention had passed a resolution opposing any fresh taxation, many nationalists expected the Irish Party to vote against the new levies. It was widely anticipated that the House of Lords would reject the budget, however, and Redmond hoped to exercise leverage in the upcoming battle with the Upper Chamber. At a meeting of party MPs on the eve of the Commons vote on the budget, he persuaded the Irish Party delegation to refrain from voting, and when the division in the House of Commons came on 4 November, most nationalist members abstained.[40]

The Irish Party's role in allowing through an extremely unpopular budget provoked outrage in Ireland. Healy surrendered the party whip, and, with

O'Brien, thereafter led a front of independent opposition. The Edenderry Board of Guardians, in a unanimous resolution, called upon the Irish Party to explain why it did not vote against a budget that would (it claimed) prove ruinous to farmers. South Wexford District Council and Kilkenny Corporation and Workingmen's Club adopted similar resolutions. Addressing the Monaghan branch of the UIL, J.C. Lardner MP had to contend with truculent questioners attacking the party's cowardice and its dependence on English Liberals.[41] The Roman Catholic hierarchy, it was rumoured, was so angered by the Irish Party's role in permitting the Commons passage of a redistributive budget (and its support for what was suspected to be a secularist Liberal educational policy) that it was inclined to issue an attack on the party, coupled with an appeal to Catholics to defend Christian education and resist socialism.[42]

In a speech in Dublin on 18 November 1909, Redmond announced that if the Irish Party was to take part in the veto battle with the House of Lords, it required a declaration from the Liberal leaders that Home Rule would be an issue before the electorate at a general election.[43] The peers, who by constitutional convention did not interfere with money bills, vetoed the budget on 30 November. In breaking with precedent in this way, the Upper Chamber of Parliament plunged Britain into a constitutional crisis. In the midst of a sudden atmosphere of uncertainty, Redmond's formal demand reached H.H. Asquith, who had succeeded Campbell-Bannerman as prime minister in 1908. Redmond wrote that political conditions in Ireland were so adverse that, unless a policy of Home Rule were announced, the Irish Party would have to ask its supporters in Britain to oppose Liberal candidates. Irish opposition, he claimed, would lose the Liberals many seats in Lancashire, Yorkshire and Scotland. It was a ludicrous situation, he acknowledged, since Ireland had the greatest interest in curbing the House of Lords' power, and had no wish to indirectly aid it by withdrawing support for Liberal candidates in the prospective election. The critical passage of Redmond's letter was underlined by Asquith:

> We must … press for an official declaration which will show clearly that the Home Rule issue is involved in the issue of the House of Lords, by declaring that Government are in favour of Home Rule, and that they are determined that their hands shall be free to deal with it, not on the lines of the Council Bill, but on the lines of national self-government, subject to Imperial control, in the next Parliament.[44]

The Cabinet considered this demand as it deliberated a response to the Lords' unprecedented rejection of a budget, and Birrell reported to Redmond that ministers were in complete agreement as to the necessity of a declaration.[45] The form of the Liberal statement, however, preoccupied Redmond and Dillon, who worried that the announcement would fall short of their demands.[46] Lord Morley sought to assure Redmond that ministers were alive to the consequences of an inadequate pledge, and united, or almost so, on the necessity of Home Rule.[47]

The Cabinet resolved to call a general election to decide the question of the budget prompted by the Lords' unconstitutional action, and advised the king, Edward VII, to dissolve Parliament. Only a small part of Asquith's campaign-opening speech at the Royal Albert Hall on 10 December was devoted to Ireland, which he characterised as 'the one undeniable failure of British statesmanship'. The solution to the Irish question, he declared, lay in 'a system of full self-government in regard to purely Irish affairs', and pledged that 'in the new House of Commons the hands of the Liberal government and the Liberal majority will be in this matter entirely free'. He undertook that the Liberals would neither assume nor hold office unless unspecified safeguards to enable them to give effect to their legislative programme were secured. Such safeguards included the highly controversial measure of obtaining a guarantee from the king to create as many as 400 Liberal peers to overcome the Tory majority in the Upper Chamber.

Asquith's statement did not make explicit the contingent relationship between Home Rule and the House of Lords. Such an admission would have lent weight to Unionist allegations of a 'corrupt bargain', trading the British constitution for political advantage with Home Rule as its price.[48] The Liberals were intent on framing the issue before the electorate in the general election as one of peers versus people. As Birrell confided to Dillon, Liberals feared that an election on Home Rule would go against them and result in their political banishment for a generation.[49] T.P. O'Connor came close to validating Unionist charges when he referred, in a letter to Dillon, to 'Asquith's announcement on Home Rule, which we were compelled by opinion among our own people to extort from him'.[50]

'No veto, no budget'

The result of the January 1910 general election left the Irish Parliamentary Party's seventy MPs holding the balance of power at Westminster, and Asquith's government in a severely demoralised state. Having lost their huge majority of 1906, ministers returned to office reliant upon Irish and Labour votes in the House of Commons.[51] The Cabinet was badly split over the form and timing of action in respect of the Upper Chamber. Asquith, who was exhausted after the election campaign, retreated to Cannes for ten days at the end of January, leaving his colleagues to speculate.[52] Was the budget or the House of Lords to be dealt with first? Should the composition of the Upper House be reformed, or its veto abolished? Should the budget be altered or passed in its current form? Should a guarantee from the king to create hundreds of Liberal peers to overcome recalcitrance by the House of Lords be sought, and, if so, when?

The figure crucial to the answers to these questions was Prime Minister Herbert Henry Asquith. Born in 1852 to a middle-class Yorkshire family, Asquith secured a scholarship to Balliol College, Oxford, where he was an outstanding classics scholar. For a decade he practised as a barrister in London, which provided an entrée to Parliament, for which he stood in 1886. Asquith soon attracted the attention of the then premier, W.E. Gladstone, who appointed him as home secretary in 1892, in which post he became known as 'The Sledgehammer' for the relentless cogency of his arguments. Marriage to the flamboyant brewing heiress Margot Tennant in 1894 granted the up-and-coming politician access to a rarefied social circle, but Asquith's enthusiastic embrace of London society suggested, to some, that he possessed only superficial democratic convictions.[53]

Asquith's inadequacies as premier in the First World War overshadow his historical reputation. He was censured, in life and afterwards, for an excessive fondness for bridge and brandy, the latter indulgence earning him the epithet 'Squiffy' after a notorious appearance on the front bench, much the worse for wear, at a late-night sitting of the House of Commons.[54] His 'wait and see' riposte to hostile Commons questioners became a popular catchphrase in 1910, inspiring advertising and even a Gaumont film, but Unionist charges of indecision and indolence stuck. A few years later, on the Western Front, Tommies adopted the phrase as a sarcastic moniker for French matches, which frequently failed to light.[55] Perhaps the most searing indictment of Asquith as leader was delivered by L.S. Amery in 1914, in a judgement that prefigured what is now the preponderant historical verdict, particularly in respect of the final years of Asquith's premiership: 'For twenty years he has held a season ticket on the line of least resistance and has gone wherever the train of events has carried him, lucidly justifying his position at whatever point he happened to find himself.'[56]

The virulence of such attacks on Asquith, born of the events of the Home Rule Crisis and reinforced by the weighty judgement of George Dangerfield, blight his reputation. But to contemporary eyes prior to the war, perceptions of Asquith, particularly from a Liberal perspective, were quite different. His intellectual brilliance was undoubted, and his authority in Cabinet unquestioned. A rather stiff public bearing concealed a curiously retiring character.[57] A pronounced distaste for confrontations manifested itself in a preference for collective decisions and a tendency to procrastinate, though this trait, combined with the prime minister's private affability, may go some way to explaining his Cabinet's notable cohesion through considerable trials.[58] A.G. Gardiner of the *Daily News and Leader*, no dewy-eyed admirer of the premier, penned a profile of Asquith in 1912, in which one can discern traces both of the faults that critics condemned and the strengths that earned him the devotion of his colleagues:

> He has little imaginative vision, a cold distrust of idealism and sentiment, a dislike of anticipating the future. You cannot get him to look into the middle of next week ... It is the habit of the barrister who gets up his case overnight ... In the House of Commons it [Asquith's intellect] is almost as though it works apart from his personality. See him in a time of crisis, wedged in the front bench between his lieutenants, his movements restless, his face a little flushed, his hand passing now over his knees, now across his chin. One might imagine him flustered and beaten. He rises. It is as though a machine gun has come into action. Every word finds its mark ... there is no rhetoric, no appeal to party passion, none of the sophistry in which Mr Balfour loves to cloud his purposes, not a breath of emotion – nothing but the resistless logic of a powerful mind.

Asquith's strengths, concluded Gardiner, were those of a detached intellectual and man of business; his weaknesses lay in a lack of deep convictions or of 'roots ... in the democratic soil'.[59]

The prime minister's quick intellect, and his confessed fondness for 'hitting nails on the head', carried limitations. A memorial article on the centenary of his birth considered that Asquith's lack of imagination, absence of any moral impulse, and trained practicality of mind rendered him a reactive leader rather than a strategic one: a problem-solver, not a visionary.[60] Asquith was thus at once the 'last of the Romans', for his urbanity and eighteenth-century elegance of phrasing, and at the same time a pragmatic, managerial politician very much in the modern mould.

In the premier's absence, Grey, the foreign secretary, lobbied his Cabinet colleagues against giving the appearance of dictation by the Irish, advocating reform of the composition of the House of Lords. Lloyd George led the opposition to these 'reformists', advancing a policy of limitation of the Upper Chamber's powers. Redmond's election-campaign demands for a veto curb, the Chancellor believed, had the solid support of the bulk of Liberal backbenchers. The peers' actions, Lord Morley observed, had 'shifted the centre of gravity ... to the extreme left' on the Liberal back benches, galvanising the resolve of radicals who relished the prospect of emasculating the House of Lords.[61]

The Irish nationalists wasted no time flexing their new-found political muscle. A letter from T.P. O'Connor read to the Cabinet 'stated as a certain fact that the Irish Party led by Mr Redmond would vote against the budget unless it was assured that the passing of a bill dealing with the veto of the House of Lords was guaranteed during the present year'.[62] Redmond made the demand public in an uncompromising speech in Dublin on 10 February. Irish support in the general election had been predicated not upon Asquith's Home Rule declaration, he said, but upon his undertaking to assume office only if armed with guarantees necessary to overcome the veto of the House of Lords. To depart from that position, Redmond claimed, would be to betray the democratic demands of Britain. Further, the Irish Party chairman vowed that if guarantees sufficient to ensure the passage of a veto bill were not secured, or if the government proposed to postpone veto legislation, Ireland would oppose such half measures.[63] This was just the sort of fixity of purpose against the peers that radical backbenchers craved, and Redmond received telegrams from the *Daily News*, *The Morning Leader* and *The Nation* pledging him wholehearted Liberal support.[64]

If Redmond's 'Hibernian bombshell' worsened the ministerial malaise, Asquith's speech on the address in the House of Commons on 21 February 1910 threw the wider Liberal Party into despair. The prime minister's uncharacteristically muddled statement failed to elucidate how the Lords were to be dealt with, and confirmed, contrary to the Albert Hall pledge, that he *had* taken office without asking for guarantees to enable execution of his government's programme.[65] Redmond, in reply, protested that Liberals had put the constitutional issue, not the budget, before the electors in the late election. He indicated his willingness for Irish members to vote for the budget if a veto bill took precedence, but repeated his threat to withdraw support if a curb on the Lords was delayed.[66]

Radicals registered their annoyance with the prime-ministerial volte-face. Joseph Martin MP was among a half-dozen Liberals who criticised the confusion of policy in the House of Commons, but he commended Redmond's case to the House as the only honourable course for Liberals.[67] Forty to fifty members of the radical wing of the Liberal Party sent a deputation to the prime minister calling for limitation of the peers' veto.[68] Sir Henry Dalziel gave notice of an amendment to block any measures to reform the composition of the Upper Chamber, because, he claimed, Liberals had no mandate from the electorate for such a policy.[69] Asquith was forced to acknowledge, in a report to the king, that there was 'a good deal of anxiety, if not of mistrust as to the plans and intentions of the Government' among the Liberal rank and file.[70]

Redmond prepared a memorandum for the Cabinet, insisting that ministers introduce resolutions to the effect that the Upper Chamber's veto should be abolished without delay. Guarantees from the king to create sufficient peers to swamp the Unionist House of Lords, contingent upon their rejection of the resolution, he demanded, should be secured immediately; the budget should be set aside until the veto resolution was adopted by the House of Commons.[71] Redmond explained his tactics in a private note to T.P. Gill, his confidant and well-connected secretary to the Irish Department of Agriculture and Technical Instruction. Fearing that Liberal enthusiasm would flag if the budget passed, Redmond's plan was to prolong the crisis until a veto resolution went to the House of Lords. If the Lords rejected the resolution, he conjectured, guarantees to create hundreds of Liberal peers would be sought, and if the king refused, ministers would advise that Parliament be dissolved. 'All worth their salt in [the] Liberal Party are heartily for this', Redmond assured Gill, adding, 'Tear this up.'[72]

Protests in Ireland spread. At a meeting of Fermoy Rural Council, Irish MPs abstaining on the budget were denounced as traitors, while a Wexford councillor disputed the Irish Party's claim to be a nationalist party at all, so subservient was it to the Liberals.[73] The party's iron grip on local politics quashed dissent in many places, but the prevailing mood was ugly. Public bodies in Limerick, Kilmallock, New Ross, Tipperary, Newcastle West and Enniscorthy passed resolutions calling for the Irish Party to oppose the budget, as did the Dublin Chamber of Commerce by unanimous vote; the Hotel and Tourist Association of Ireland petitioned the lord mayor of Dublin to call an all-Ireland meeting to canvass the views of the country.[74]

The Cabinet remained shrouded in gloom. Pro-Lords reformers in the Grey camp resented Redmond's 'exorbitant demands', and favoured resignation to preserve the government's dignity.[75] Winston Churchill believed that Liberal backbenchers and supporters in the country were gravely disheartened that the government remained in office with no veto resolution in prospect, and worried that it might blunder into the morass of Lords reform.[76] The chief whip reported to the Cabinet that Redmond 'threatened the Government with immediate hostility, & an ultimate vote against the Budget unless they were prepared to assure him that the Veto Bill would this year become law'.[77] Though ministers baulked at giving such an assurance, they swiftly sanctioned the drafting of resolutions calling for limitation of the peers' veto to the lifetime of a single Parliament.[78] Asquith confirmed the policy of curbing the Lords' veto powers, and its precedence in the parliamentary timetable before debate on the budget, in the House of Commons on 28 February.[79]

On 8 March Lloyd George told Redmond that ministers had decided that the budget should be passed in the interval between the veto resolution's adoption by the Commons and its counterpart's consideration by the Lords. Redmond remained firm in his demand that a resolution to limit the Upper Chamber's veto should be passed or rejected by the House of Lords *before* consideration of the budget.[80] The Irish Party leaders trod a fine line, pressing for deferral of the budget against their allies in Cabinet who were supporting the Irish demand for contingent guarantees. They could not behave in a way that would alienate sympathetic ministers or the strong support they enjoyed on the Liberal back benches. At the same time they had to guard against Cabinet moderates trying to avoid dealing squarely with the veto of the House of Lords.[81] Redmond privately kept up the pressure, pushing for a decision over the question of guarantees and maintaining that if the Lords rejected the veto resolution, nationalist support for the government would be dependent upon an immediate election.

The final act of the budget wrangle began on 8 April, when Lloyd George airily announced to the Cabinet his intention to drop the whiskey tax, a proposition angrily disputed by most of those present.[82] The Chancellor threatened to resign and lead the radicals and nationalists in demanding guarantees. He was dissuaded from doing so by Murray, who privately suggested to him that if he left the Cabinet his party would fit under his hat.[83] When the ministers next met, on 12 April, Lloyd George reversed his position, and, in the words of a confidante, 'amid the joy and astonishment … caused by this refusal to be dictated to by the Irish, he immediately and dramatically challenged them on the question of guarantees'.[84] The Cabinet agreed that in the event of the Lords rejecting the veto resolution, it would advise the dissolution of Parliament to the king, securing in advance guarantees for the creation of hundreds of Liberal peers to overcome the Tory majority in the Upper Chamber. Asquith announced the decision, in veiled terms, after the resolution to curb the Lords' veto had its first reading in the House of Commons two days later.

As Ronan Fanning observed, this U-turn by the Chancellor bore the appearance of an artifice to manoeuvre his colleagues in the direction he wished them to go. Resistance to nationalist pressure on the whiskey tax, as Fanning asserted, was, in fact, a capitulation to Redmond on the question of guarantees.[85] Lloyd George, his confidante recorded, 'realised more and more that it was the whisky tax and the giving way to the Irish upon it, that stuck in Grey's throat', and he dissimulated to overcome the objections of his colleagues.[86] With the matter of guarantees decided, the Chancellor knew that the nationalists could hardly defeat the government over the budget, however much they objected to the whiskey tax.

The Liberals had committed themselves to introducing a Home Rule measure, the policy of curtailment of the Lords' veto had been adopted, and a Parliament Bill, embodying that policy, was being drafted. Ministers had settled on a policy of seeking guarantees for the exercise of the royal prerogative to overcome the bill's veto by the House of Lords. Veteran trade unionist and Labour MP Keir Hardie heralded Redmond as fighting 'the battle of British Radicalism as well as of Irish Nationalism'. 'Between Mr John Redmond and the Whig element in the party there was a struggle for supremacy', he claimed, and in securing the veto policy, Redmond had won.[87] In Ireland, victory was less clear-cut: opposition to the liquor and licence duties there remained vehement. The Irish Party chairman and his colleagues hoped they would be forgiven for the budget's sequel: removal of the absolute veto of the House of Lords and of the greatest barrier to Home Rule.[88]

Conference and contrivance

The death of Edward VII in May 1910, weeks after Asquith's oblique announcement that guarantees would be sought from the monarch, led to accusations of his having caused the king's untimely demise.[89] Out of sympathy for George V, the dead sovereign's inexperienced successor, a breathing space was needed. Secret contacts initiated by Lloyd George with J.L. Garvin, editor of *The Observer*, inspired the newspaper's campaign calling for resolution of the constitutional struggle as a fitting memorial to King Edward.[90] Garvin's campaign was echoed in other newspapers, and talk of a conference was in the air.

The prospect of a conference appalled the Irish Party leaders, who feared that their labours of the preceding months would be in vain. O'Connor met almost daily with ministers, seeking assurances, but he sent worrying reports to Dillon in Dublin. Dillon foresaw in the exercise 'the complete triumph of the Roseberyite section – who in the Conference would unite with [Unionist leader Arthur] Balfour &c.'. The nationalists, he said, would be driven into opposition, resulting in the destruction of the Liberal Party.[91] Despite grave Irish qualms, the proposal was adopted, and eight delegates to the Constitutional Conference – four Liberals and four Unionists – met for the first time on 14 June.[92]

The conference's objectives were to demarcate the powers of the House of Commons with respect to finance; to establish procedures for dealing with deadlock in matters of dispute between the two Houses, whether by modification of the veto, joint sitting or referendum; and to consider proposals to reform the composition of the Upper House.[93] Although the conference's terms of reference were limited to the structural workings of Parliament, its proceedings were quickly mired in matters of substance. The Unionists argued that constitutional changes – such as questions of relations between the two Houses, Irish Home Rule and the royal prerogative – should be subject to special legislative safeguards. Ireland thus came immediately to the fore. Asquith's favoured compromise formula, as yet undisclosed to the Unionists, was the Ripon Scheme, which envisaged a joint sitting of the House of Commons with a delegation of 100 peers, comprised of twenty representing the government of the day and the remainder nominated by the Lords.[94]

On 25 July, shortly before the conference suspended its deliberations for the summer recess, Lloyd George and Birrell met Redmond, who had returned to London at the insistence of an increasingly anxious Dillon. The meeting was the culmination of O'Connor's discussions with ministers since early June about possible alternatives to curtailment of the Lords' veto powers. The nationalists viewed the Ripon Scheme with great apprehension, and worried that the Liberals might accept a position of permanent inequality vis-à-vis the Unionists.

Redmond presented a memorandum, making clear the limits of nationalist sufferance of the lesser Ripon curb on the Upper House, and the consequences of any Liberal wavering. It specified that the Unionist peers selected for joint

sittings should be in a majority of no more than thirty over their Liberal counterparts, thereby enabling a Liberal majority of fifty in the House of Commons
to command an overall majority in a joint sitting. Any proposal involving
a Unionist allocation of forty peers, Redmond stated, 'would compel us to
oppose the scheme by every means in our power'. The note demanded that
the deadlock formula be the first item of business in the autumn session of
Parliament, and that the prime minister should simultaneously announce
that Home Rule would be the first great measure passed by its operation. In
the event that the scheme did not become operative immediately, he should
dissolve Parliament and place Irish Home Rule in the foreground of the Liberal
programme in a general election.[95]

On the evening of the meeting with Redmond, Birrell spoke at a meeting
of the Liberal Party's Eighty Club, where he made an unusual call for federal
Home Rule.[96] Further steps towards a federal proposition were actuated on
27 July, when Alexander Murray spoke to Harold Harmsworth, co-proprietor
of the *Daily Mail* and the *Daily Mirror*. Murray sought sympathetic coverage
for a federal arrangement of the United Kingdom, to save the conference
from break-up over Home Rule.[97] In his column in *Reynolds's Newspaper*, T.P.
O'Connor hailed the concept of federation as 'the beginning of the solution'.[98]
As Michael Wheatley observed, the timing of this sudden flowering of Home
Rule all round – most startlingly promoted by O'Connor – strongly suggests
that a policy of federal Home Rule, as a route to settlement at the conference,
was agreed by the nationalists and the Liberals at the meeting of 25 July.[99]

Lloyd George pondered the possibilities of the unaccustomed atmosphere
of compromise with the Unionists. The product of these musings, his coalition memorandum of August 1910, was, by any standard, a remarkably
imaginative document. Proposing 'a truce, for bringing the resources of the
two Parties into joint stock in order to liquidate arrears which, if much longer
neglected, may end in national impoverishment, if not insolvency', it proposed
a comprehensive programme to arrest Britain's relative decline. Sections of
the memorandum covered housing, unemployment, education, compulsory
military training and the land, prescribing interventionist reforms in each
aspect. In a retreat from Liberal principle, the door was left open to protective
tariffs, and an aspiration for imperial federation was floated. In this context,
Lloyd George suggested, settlement of the vexed relationship with Ireland
would be a natural development. A Liberal/Unionist coalition government,
he wrote, would not be 'subject to the embarrassing dictation of extreme
partisans, whether from Nationalists or Orangemen'.[100] The proposal, which

made no mention of the House of Lords, was, in effect, a programme of 'national efficiency', but one that, in its proposed establishment and methods, was fundamentally anti-democratic.

The Chancellor sat on his plan for some weeks, relating it first to Churchill, then Asquith. The document he presented to the prime minister in early October appears to have differed substantially from the August memorandum. In Margot Asquith's roughly contemporaneous account, the prime minister understood the coalition programme to be 'to resist Socialism & Tariff Reform'; he was sceptical of its chances of success.[101] He did, however, permit Lloyd George to circulate the document to Lords Crewe and Grey, who expressed guarded approval of the proposition.[102] With Asquith's blessing the Chancellor presented his plan verbally to Arthur Balfour on 11 October, thereafter meeting a number of the Unionist leaders. Lloyd George's plan underwent a chameleon-like transformation in his oral expositions of it, adopting coloration and characteristics pleasing to each hearer. The Chancellor succeeded in setting the high echelons of Unionism abuzz in the latter half of October. J.L. Garvin recorded that J.S. Sandars (Balfour's private secretary), F.E. Smith, Austen Chamberlain and Andrew Bonar Law were prepared to consider limited self-government for Ireland. For many of the leaders, a federalised United Kingdom was a price worth paying in exchange for tariff reform, steps to imperial unity, and an unfettered House of Lords.

Garvin's wooing of *Observer* proprietor Lord Northcliffe to the federal cause led to a profusion of pro-federal Home Rule articles in the Unionist press.[103] Favourable items appeared in the *Daily Mail* on 17 October, on 20 October in the *Daily Express*, and in *The Observer* on 16, 22 and 30 October.[104] Writing as 'Pacificus', F.S. Oliver, a central figure of the imperial federationist Round Table movement, wrote a series of federalist articles for *The Times*. Even *The Morning Post*, the newspaper of the Tory right wing, offered a qualified welcome to the concept of federalism, provided that special provision would be made for Ulster, and that it would be accompanied by an effort to 'imperialise' the Parliament at Westminster.[105]

Quite separately from the coalition discussions, the unwritten Home-Rule-all-round dimension of the private Liberal/nationalist compact of 25 July manifested itself while Redmond and O'Connor were fundraising in North America in the autumn. An interview with *McClure's Magazine* in New York quoted the Irish Party chairman expressing unusual warmth for federal Home Rule, stressing Irish loyalty to the British Empire and the strictly local character of the devolved legislative powers sought.[106] For Redmond, such public flirtation with the notion of federalism, at a time when nationalists had never had a stronger hand to play, was highly dangerous. Despite the risk of a repeat of the Council Bill fiasco, the Irish leaders publicly signalled (from the comparative safety of a transatlantic platform) their consent to a compromise formula agreed with the Liberals over the summer.

A firestorm of condemnation erupted in the nationalist press when news of federalist pronouncements, first from Redmond, then from O'Connor, reached Ireland.[107] Redmond's critics pounced on his apparent recantation of Gladstonian Home Rule. T.M. Healy alleged a ploy, orchestrated by Lloyd George and Murray, in a statement published in *The Times*. He noted Birrell's unexpected paean for federal Home Rule at the Eighty Club in July, and accurately conjectured that O'Connor's federalist effusions in North America were following the trend of ministerial thinking.[108]

Redmond was quite in the dark about Lloyd George's coalition scheme, but the timing of his intervention was serendipitous for the Chancellor's plan. Had the Irish Party chairman been aware of the proposal, he would, doubtless, have been mortified. Lloyd George's proposed coalition with the Unionists would have freed the Liberals from Redmond's strictures, and the nationalists would once again have been at the mercy of the English parties. In mid-October Lloyd George informed F.E. Smith that the government was too firmly wedded to some form of Irish devolution to drop the idea altogether, but that if the two dominant parties agreed on a scheme and the Irish nationalists demurred, 'the Liberals would then wash their hands of the whole affair and leave the Irish to stew in their own juice'.[109]

Rumours of a Liberal/Unionist compromise were attracting comment from all quarters. Fierce criticism from within nationalist ranks forced Redmond to repudiate his remarks favouring federal Home Rule.[110] On the Unionist side, members of the Orange Lodge of Belfast were sufficiently alarmed by the rumours to meet on 25 October and resolve their determination to be governed by the imperial parliament, to resist the disintegration of the empire, and to defend themselves if betrayed.[111] Suspicions of a surrender of Unionist principles prompted the Dublin-born barrister and newly appointed chairman of the Irish (and Ulster) Unionists, Sir Edward Carson, and the editor of *The Morning Post*, H.A. Gwynne, to write anxious letters to Balfour.[112] A storm of protest from Ulster was rapidly gathering.

Despite being intrigued by the coalition proposal, Balfour declined the offer in the first week of November, judging that the federal Home Rule aspect of Lloyd George's scheme would split the Unionist Party.[113] G.R. Searle noted Balfour's observation that, as the coalition discussions progressed, the Chancellor was increasingly reluctant to avoid an irreparable breach with the Irish. Searle speculated that by late October, Lloyd George saw hopes for a coalition fading, and was preserving a line of retreat.[114] As the possibility of a Unionist partnership receded, the importance of the nationalists to the government's parliamentary majority reasserted itself. Once the coalition talks failed, Lloyd George's scrupulous observance of the terms of Redmond's memorandum was both a political necessity and a fortuitous means of covering his tracks.

The Constitutional Conference, meanwhile, had reconvened on 1 November. Asquith and Lloyd George presented the joint-sittings proposal and a means to circumvent the obstacle of Home Rule. The Chancellor submitted that if a Home Rule Bill was presented to Parliament before a dissolution and the measure was put to the electorate at a general election, the government, if returned with a majority, would be deemed to have a mandate for Home Rule. Following such a 'referendal' general election, Home Rule would be treated as ordinary legislation in that instance, and, in the event of the bill's defeat in a joint sitting, on all subsequent occasions.

The Unionists would not accept a one-off safeguard in respect of Irish Home Rule, and sought the application of a referendal general election in any instance that Home Rule legislation was proposed. Lloyd George vehemently disagreed with Birrell and Asquith, who were inclined to concede, and he refused to assent to the proposal. A final effort to close the gap by negotiating a figure for the Unionist majority in a joint sitting of Parliament was also blocked by the Chancellor.[115]

Once Lloyd George's coalition scheme was ruled out, the Liberals had to adhere to Redmond's terms. As negotiator of the secret compact of July, Lloyd George was compelled to rebuff every attempt to put House of Lords reform on the conference table and to resist the idea of a referendum. The terms of Redmond's memorandum delimited the Liberals' final compromise formula of a single-issue general election on Home Rule. Lloyd George's insistence on the operation of the safeguard in a single instance ensured that the effect of the agreement with the nationalists was preserved. It was also the Chancellor who, mindful of Redmond's injunctions, refused to concede on the Unionist allocation of peers in a joint sitting in the abortive eleventh-hour horse-trading.

The Irish Party chairman apparently remained oblivious of the Chancellor's coalition double-dealing. In a note added for posterity in November 1910 to his copy of the Irish Party's terms from July, he registered his regret that a conference deal was narrowly missed: 'this scheme was practically agreed upon by the Conference – but Balfour &c. insisted on Home Rule being excluded from operation of scheme'.[116]

The third Home Rule Bill

Ministers resented the nationalist leader's assertion of influence. Some were stung by Unionist charges of their subordination to the 'Dollar dictator', and preferred to let him do his worst rather than suffer the ignominy of their position.[117] Grey, who, with Haldane and Asquith, had supported Lord Rosebery's recantation of Home Rule in the 1900s, found alliance with the Irish, and with Redmond in particular, distasteful.[118] Awareness that a substantial number of Liberal backbenchers looked to Redmond with admiration sharpened ministerial indignation. J.A. Pease wrote scornfully of Redmond's dictation of terms to the Cabinet in a bid to woo the radical wing of the Liberal Party.[119] Ministers repeatedly sought to circumvent the Irish Party chairman's injunctions, notably by engaging with William O'Brien and T.M. Healy, who were judged to be less inflexible than Redmond.[120] More than a little resentment of the predicament in which the Irish Party placed Liberal ministers can be seen in Lloyd George's contemplation of coalition and his desire to force a settlement upon them. Only Birrell seemed free of animus towards the nationalist leaders. The collective desire of ministers to rid themselves of Irish pressure was expressed – in sentiment, if not in diction – by Lib-Lab minister John Burns, who burst out in Cabinet in the summer of 1910, 'If you tell Redmond to go to 'ell, he'll come to 'eel.'[121]

Such was the state of the 'coalition'. Redmond's strategy had been a success in policy terms, but it was winning him few friends in the Cabinet. Asquith was at pains to dispel any perception of dictation in the December 1910 election, which was called to obtain a popular mandate for limitation of the veto of the House of Lords. At the National Liberal Federation, the premier spoke not of Home Rule but of the spirit that animated Liberal constitutional reforms, in terms that bore equal application to the government's Irish policy:

> Just as our fathers and grandfathers installed the people in power, and converted this country from an aristocratically governed to a democratically governed country, so we, in our turn, if our work is not to be made wholly unavailing, and if we are to have a reality and not a caricature of democracy, we must continue and complete what they

began, and make the people, through their representatives, truly and
effectively supreme in the legislation of this country.[122]

This noble sentiment was rewarded by the events of 1911. Having won a
second general election in twelve months (though still dependent upon the
support of seventy-four Irish nationalist and forty-two Labour MPs for its
House of Commons majority), the Liberal government proceeded with the
Parliament Bill. The intense controversy over the bill, which limited peers'
powers to a suspensory veto, consumed the attention of Westminster until its
passage by a narrow majority in the House of Lords in August. Having driven
the Cabinet to adopt the veto policy and obtain contingent royal guarantees,
Redmond appears to have played little part in the subsequent controversy
beyond dutifully delivering nationalist votes in the House of Commons. The
Irish Party leader's secondary preoccupation that year was to water down the
provisions of Lloyd George's National Insurance Bill in respect of Ireland so as
to reduce the burden of employer and employee contributions.[123] In October
Redmond claimed to have been engaged in confidential consultations on a
new Home Rule Bill, which (he suggested) was nearing completion, though
neither of these claims appears to have been true.[124] Crucially for Home Rule,
however, the Parliament Act of 1911 meant that the House of Commons
could override the Lords' rejection of a bill by passing the same legislation in
unamended form in three successive parliamentary sessions. The way was clear
for a third Irish Home Rule Bill.

Patricia Jalland has described the haphazard fashion in which the Cabinet
committee appointed to consider the Home Rule question took up its work
after January 1911. For much of the year, Birrell, Lloyd George, Churchill,
Haldane, Grey, Herbert Samuel and Lord Loreburn considered schemes for
federal Home Rule, which was still seen as likely to be more palatable to
Unionists and nonconformist Liberals.[125] A federal system of devolved subordinate parliaments was widely discussed in the British press over the summer.[126]
The Cabinet committee met infrequently, and its deliberations were neglected
by members in favour of their departmental concerns. Birrell played little part
in the committee's discussions, except to pour cold water on suggestions of
federalism.[127] Even allowing for the drama of the Parliament Bill dominating
Westminster politics, it is remarkable that the crafting of a flagship Home Rule
policy was subject to such inattention and lack of forethought by ministers.

For months the Cabinet committee made almost no progress in framing
a bill. In the absence of a firm alternative, a Gladstonian measure, based

on the 1893 bill, began to take shape in the autumn of 1911, when Birrell and Asquith took a more active interest in it.[128] A memorandum, solicited by Asquith from William O'Brien in early November 1911, submitted that since dominion Home Rule for Ireland was not a matter of practical politics, a scheme of 'experimental' Home Rule stood the best chance of passage. Finance, he insisted, would make or break the measure; he suggested that self-government be inaugurated with a large budgetary surplus in order to soothe nationalist anger concerning (what O'Brien presumed would be) the denial of control over customs and excise. Threats of civil war could be 'disregarded', he maintained, but care should be taken to avoid the north-eastern counties unduly disturbing the infant parliament.[129]

O'Brien's memorandum is revealing for its insight into the sort of measure that was considered politically practical. The 'experimental' nature of his proposal was mirrored by the 1912 bill in its transitional provisions for finance and services to be reserved to the imperial government. The bill's Liberal authors followed O'Brien's gradualist approach so as to assuage Protestant and Unionist sentiment and to ensure nationalist good behaviour.[130] No record of a similar solicitation of Irish Party views appears to have survived, although this may be because the party-leaders' public statements were deemed to have made their position sufficiently clear.

Lloyd George and Churchill shared O'Brien's inclination to accommodate the fears of north-east Ulster. In Cabinet on 6 February 1912 they proposed a temporary opt-out for Ulster by a process of county polls, an idea vigorously resisted by Lords Crewe and Loreburn.[131] Despite holding private reservations, Birrell represented the views of the nationalist leaders, and stoutly resisted special treatment for Ulster.[132] The majority in Cabinet, supported by Asquith, decided against providing for county option for Ulster in the bill, instead reserving the right to revisit the status of Ulster in the light of developments as the bill progressed.[133]

Patricia Jalland speculated that Asquith followed the trend of the discussion in Cabinet as it evolved, citing the opinion of Charles Hobhouse that the premier often tended to agree with whomever had spoken last.[134] That Asquith did not decisively favour exclusion is odd, given that he appears to have drafted a memorandum proposing Ulster exclusion at the time of the 1886 Home Rule Bill.[135] The prime minister may have doubted its necessity, given the impression that Ulster sentiment had moved on. A memorandum on the state of Ulster, received a few days later from a former undersecretary for Ireland, advised that the Ulstermen's worries about Home Rule were principally to do with finance. Provided generous proposals and substantive guarantees against confiscatory taxation of industry were offered, the memo suggested, protests from Ulster would be political rather than violent in character.[136] This view was consistent with the information that Birrell was circulating to the Cabinet around this time, based upon RIC enquiries to gauge the probable level of resistance to Home Rule.[137]

As Jalland suggested, making provision for county opt-outs for Ulster would have had strong tactical advantages: it would have been a visible symbol of sensitivity to Ulster sentiment, diminishing the force of Unionist objections, and, most importantly, it would probably have provided a means of pacifying Ulster Protestant fears under the Parliament Act without the need for Unionist consent. This failure of vision limited Asquith's later options.[138] However, in February 1912 the prime minister had justification for believing that his government held a strong hand. The signals emanating from the province were mixed, and after the experience of 1910, the attitude of British Unionists was by no means clear. In common with many of his colleagues and the Irish nationalists, Asquith anticipated that finance, not Ulster, would attract the greatest controversy.[139] The premier had little reason to believe that the coming battle, or the battle of real consequence, at any rate, would play out anywhere but in Parliament, under the control of British politicians. Few, from the perspective of February 1912, could have anticipated the magnitude of the problem that Ulster resistance would become, owing to the cynical extremity to which British Unionists were prepared to exploit the sectarian and commercial fears of Ulster for domestic political advantage.

Quite apart from the unpredictability of Ulster's reaction, however, the implications of the Parliament Act's requirement for legislation to pass repeatedly in unaltered form might have been foreseen. As a parliamentarian of two decades' standing, Asquith should have had a keener understanding of the Act's mechanics, and appreciated the prudence of retaining an option to accommodate Ulster that would not require Unionist consent. A combination of lax leadership, ministerial distraction and indifference to Ireland resulted in a clumsily drafted bill and ill-considered tactics.

Concurrent with the Cabinet committee's erratic deliberations, a committee on Irish finance had been convened under the chairmanship of Sir Henry Primrose. Among the Primrose committee's prominent members were Denis Kelly, bishop of Ross, a rare nationalist authority on Irish finance; Lord Pirrie (besides Kelly, the only Irishman); Henry Gladstone; and W.G.S. Adams, Oxford reader in politics and former Irish civil servant.[140] Redmond pledged not to interfere with the committee's work, ostensibly to preserve the Irish Party's freedom of action.[141] In a letter to party stalwart John Muldoon, published in *The Times*, Redmond said that if Home Rule were merely a matter of money, Ireland would be much better off remaining in the Union. The national question was not a matter of pounds, shillings and pence, he wrote, but a question of liberty. It was dangerous to the cause of self-government, he argued, for Irishmen to place undue emphasis on its financing.[142]

Redmond's confidence in a decision-making process from which he was excluded seemed complacent, but he drew comfort from the fact that Bishop Kelly had been installed on the Primrose committee on the recommendation of T.P. Gill.[143] Gill was in contact with Kelly and with Adams, a former civil service colleague.[144] To Adams, Gill argued that financial autonomy, including control of customs and excise, was instrumental to Home Rule's success.[145] Adams – whose conclusions, Redmond believed, would greatly influence Asquith – obligingly framed a recommendation for fiscal autonomy in a manner designed to facilitate acceptance.[146] Bishop Kelly, complimenting Gill that his 'engineering has made a good railroad', wrote that he had discussed the arguments for and against Adams' scheme with T.P. O'Connor, and expressed satisfaction that, by this route, 'my views will get into the blood of those leading Liberals'.[147]

The committee's confidential report to the Cabinet of 17 October recommended conferral on an Irish government of full powers over expenditure and revenue, save for the imposition of tariffs, and an initial subsidy of £900,000 per annum. Existing old-age pensions, it proposed, should be maintained by the Imperial Exchequer, with liability for future pensions being transferred. The report argued that self-interest and the growing equity of Irish land purchasers were guarantees enough of future payment of Treasury-backed annuities.[148] Gill's efforts had secured official recommendation of a policy of fiscal autonomy that the Irish nationalists so ardently desired.

If the Parliament Act had nullified the absolute veto of the House of Lords, the prohibitive powers of HM Treasury remained unimpaired. On 30 October Lloyd George, primed by his officials, rejected the Primrose recommendation of fiscal autonomy, citing concern for the security of land-purchase payments.[149] Asquith took soundings from colleagues, and deputed Herbert Samuel, the highly competent postmaster general, to devise an alternative scheme of finance.[150] After several iterations, Samuel's final financial arrangements began to take shape in late November. Under this proposal the Imperial Exchequer would collect all revenues, and the Irish government would have limited powers to raise taxes but full powers to reduce them as it wished. Given that indirect taxation comprised eighty-five per cent of revenues raised in Ireland, the granting of powers to the Irish parliament to reduce customs duties was recognised as the only effective method of relieving the burden of taxation upon Irish taxpayers if expenditures were curbed.[151] Birrell, preferring a grant of fiscal autonomy but citing the psychological importance attached to control of customs in Ireland, grudgingly assented to his colleague's formula.[152]

Samuel's fiendishly complex plan called for old-age pensions, National Insurance, collection of revenues, and supervision of land-purchase payments to be retained by the Imperial Exchequer, with a block grant to the Irish government for services to be transferred. The Irish parliament was to have the power to add up to ten per cent to income tax, to excise on beer and spirits, estate duties, and to any customs duties imposed by the imperial parliament. Dublin would have no power to levy customs duties on articles not on the customs tariff of Britain. It could, however, add to other excise taxes, stamps and land taxes without limit, introduce new taxes not substantially the same as an imperial tax, and reduce any tax or duty paid by the Irish. Decreases in taxation would result in a corresponding reduction of the transferred sum. Any increase in revenue owing to prosperity or to higher rates of tax was to go to the Imperial Exchequer to extinguish the initial £1.5 million-per-annum budgetary deficit.[153]

If the Irish government wished to reduce taxation, it might choose to lower customs duty on tea. The revenue collected by the imperial customs and excise would decrease, and the transferred sum would be correspondingly reduced, but Irish taxpayers would have been relieved. On the other hand, if the Irish government reduced expenditure on a transferred service, the reduction in expenditure would not affect the transferred sum, and the Irish government would be free to spend the savings as it saw fit. A memorandum prepared for Redmond suggested that expenditure might be cut by reducing the rate of old-age pensions paid in Ireland. In such an eventuality, the revenues allocated for pensions would be assumed by the Irish parliament and the transferred sum accordingly reduced; but if the sum spent on pensions were cut by a greater amount, the net gain would be for the Irish government to spend elsewhere or to use for relieving the burden of taxation.[154] Given the political difficulty of cutting bloated public services such as the RIC, and Redmond's view that expenditure of £2.5 million on old-age pensions in Ireland was an extravagance, reducing the rate of pensions payable in Ireland doubtless presented itself as an expedient means of rebalancing expenditure.[155]

The final bill provided for the establishment of a Joint Exchequer Board, which was to be composed of two delegates each from the Irish and British Treasuries, with a nominee of the Crown as chair. The Joint Exchequer Board was to determine the cost of the transferred services and the amount of 'true' Irish revenue. This latter point was important, affecting, as it did, the board's responsibility to report to Parliament when the Irish government operated a budgetary surplus. A surplus, if sustained, would trigger revision of the financial arrangements.[156] The comparative attention devoted to the bill's financial provisions, relative to the single Cabinet meeting on the issue of Ulster in February, is indicative of the direction from which ministers anticipated the principal thrust of Unionist attack.

In early December 1911, ten months after the Cabinet committee began its sporadic and irresolute enquiry into Home Rule, the second draft of the Government of Ireland [and House of Commons Devolution of Business] Bill, arising principally from the efforts of Birrell, Asquith and Samuel, was given to Dillon and Redmond. The draft bill, which, as its title suggested, provided sketchily for English, Scottish and Welsh devolution to relieve congestion of business at Westminster, was accompanied by a memorandum explaining its complex finances.[157] The Irishmen intensely disliked the financial provisions. Redmond objected to the retention by the British Treasury of collection of revenue, the limit of ten per cent on increases of tax, and powers for the imperial parliament to increase rates of tax not just in times of war but for the purpose of extinguishing the Irish deficit.[158] Consulted by Redmond, Bishop Kelly thought the scheme a terrible one, and he did not envy him the task of tapping new sources of taxation.[159]

The third Home Rule Bill asserted, above all else, the supremacy of the imperial parliament. Under the bill's provisions, Ireland would continue to send forty-two members to Westminster, while a bicameral Irish parliament, comprised of a 164-member House of Commons and a senate of forty, would legislate strictly Irish affairs. The Irish parliament was denied authority on matters concerning the Crown, the army, the navy, foreign affairs and war; honours and foreign-trade relations were also excluded. Irish ministers would be drawn from one of the two legislative chambers and so be responsible to Parliament; however, the Lord Lieutenant, who would continue to be a Crown appointment, could exercise a legislative veto. In addition to the administration of pensions and insurance and the collection of taxes, control of the post office and the RIC was to be withheld for a transitional period. In a nod to Protestant sensitivities, the bill prohibited the establishment or endowment of any religion, and outlawed religious discrimination in any form, explicitly in relation to the validity of marriages.[160]

Mischance prevented the Irish leaders from protesting against the draft bill as vigorously as they might otherwise have done. Dillon, recuperating from injuries sustained in a road accident in October, was confined to his home in Dublin, while Redmond was incapacitated for two months after an automobile collision in late December.[161] Birrell sent the Primrose committee's report to the nationalist leader and explained why its recommendations had been rejected: political rather than financial considerations, he said, had prevailed. Fiscal autonomy, Birrell claimed, would have provoked demands for the removal of Irish representation at Westminster, stoked fears of separation, and rendered more difficult imperial financial support.[162] Dillon wrote to Redmond urging him to persevere for fiscal autonomy, fearing that its humiliating refusal, after public demands, would precipitate an Irish Convention demand for amendment of the bill.[163]

Two memoranda were prepared for, or by, the convalescing Redmond in response to the draft bill. One noted, testily, that while the Irish had been assured that the financial arrangements were the result of the most detailed deliberation, they had been told that the rest of the measure 'was not the result of serious consideration, but has been thrown hurriedly together and was not to be regarded as expressing the settled view of the Cabinet'. The notes demanded that the Irish parliament should have all legislative powers except those expressly excluded, and objected to the proposed unilateral powers of the Lord Lieutenant to summon, prorogue or dissolve the Irish parliament. Not only was this unprecedented in the empire, the nationalists argued, it would also invite the interference of the imperial parliament and cause indignation in Ireland.[164] The memoranda further demanded the elimination of reference to future devolution for Scotland and Wales, on the grounds that the provision's retention would kill the bill, and strongly objected to any increase in the rate of taxes to reduce the Irish deficit.[165] Birrell circulated the substance of the Irish objections to the Cabinet on 4 March.[166]

Little business appears to have been transacted between the government and the nationalists until the end of the month because, in addition to the Irish leaders' incapacitation, Cabinet morale was low as a result of a coal strike and militant suffragette activity.[167] The nationalists succeeded in getting the second part of the November 1911 draft removed, so eliminating the last vestige of federalism from the bill. In matters of vital concern to the Irish leaders, such as control of the police, the Lord Lieutenant's powers to withhold assent from legislation, and restriction of the imperial parliament's freedom to levy taxes, their objections were overruled. Samuel blocked the transfer of powers to collect taxes on the grounds that it would impede the Imperial Exchequer's ability to draw revenue from Ireland in time of war.[168]

Given that the 1912 Home Rule Bill was so objectionable to the nationalist leaders, and in view of the influence Redmond had wielded in 1910/11, could he have done more to remould the bill into a measure more to the nationalists' liking? Accident in history certainly played a part in hindering stronger protests, for both the Irish Party's senior leaders were incapacitated at a critical time. Yet even had this not been the case, the nationalist leaders had to take care not to be seen to spurn that which they were pledged to secure. A dispute over what many Liberals might have considered the details of Irish administration risked straining the sympathy of the nationalists' radical allies. Moreover, the unsettled state of opinion in Ireland underlined the need to deliver a Home Rule Bill without delay. As a lifelong parliamentarian, Redmond doubtless calculated that securing a bill navigable through Westminster was as important as its content; this imperative influenced his acquiescence to a meagre measure in 1912, as had been his instinct in the case of the Council Bill in 1907.

Redmond was also up against what he probably knew was tepid ministerial enthusiasm for Home Rule. Samuel viewed the bill's financial provisions as a long-term arrangement, foreseeing the attainment of Irish solvency and financial revision in, perhaps, thirty years. Even then, the transfer of control of customs was not envisaged. Customs receipts were intended to remain in the Imperial Exchequer's hands as security for land-purchase annuities 'in the event of friction' between the two islands.[169] This intention, not disclosed to the nationalist leaders, constituted a heavy qualification of the degree of autonomy contemplated for decades to come. Redmond, wedded to the British Empire though he was, would likely have been appalled. The friction that Samuel sought to guard against was, in the event, partly engendered by the British limitation of the pace of advance towards self-government. This unstated boundary of Irish devolution was an indication that even moderate nationalist aspiration was outstripping what the constitutional movement could deliver; public manifestations of this gap in the next two years were to undermine the Irish Party and draw its leadership of nationalism into question.

Further tinkering with the financial arrangements by the Cabinet – once again, without consultation with the nationalists – was still underway on the eve of the bill's introduction. On 2 April Birrell informed Dillon that a surplus payment of £500,000 per annum had been agreed, despite 'some grimaces and wry faces', and that it had been decided that revision of the financial terms would be triggered when Irish revenues exceeded the transferred sum for three years. Such revision would include transference to the Irish government of the control and collection of taxes, and an Irish contribution to the Imperial Exchequer. The Irish chief secretary stressed the 'deadly' danger of any mention of transferring land-purchase-payment collections in the bill, which might arouse suspicions of tampering with huge credit obligations to the British Treasury.[170]

Redmond, who returned to London at the end of March, met Asquith the week before the bill's introduction.[171] The financial terms had not been finalised the day before the bill's debut. Reduction of the surplus payment, Birrell wrote on 10 April 1912, was to begin a 'short number of years' after Home Rule came into operation, and Asquith and the Treasury, he said, were disinclined to extend the period. The chief secretary reported that the prime minister refused to quantify the Irish contribution after revision, and though Birrell stressed the need for security for land-purchase charges in this context, he made no mention of the intention to withhold customs indefinitely.[172] This remarkably slapdash bill, so portentous for Ireland, was introduced by Asquith in the House of Commons on 11 April 1912. It was not published until 17 April.

Reactions and reflections

The revival of Home Rule sparked considerable enthusiasm in Ireland. A fortnight before the bill's introduction, thousands of people, many of them conveyed to Dublin by special trains laid on for the purpose, gathered at great demonstrations in the city centre. Patrick Pearse, future leader of the 'Army of the Irish Republic' in the 1916 Easter Rising, vigorously commended the constitutional settlement of Ireland's national claim to the crowds gathered at Middle Abbey Street. Speaking before an audience comprised mainly of students assembled at the O'Connell monument, Professor Eoin MacNeill of University College, Dublin – later to found the Irish Volunteer militia – also hailed the coming bill.[173]

Following the Home Rule Bill's introduction, an Irish Convention was convened on 23 April 1912 to register its verdict on the measure. Even *The Times* agreed it was a triumph for Redmond, though the Unionist newspaper's congratulations were restricted to the party's success in managing the delegates' votes. A crowd of over 3,000 filled the Round Room of the Mansion House to hear Redmond speak, while Dillon and O'Connor addressed an overflow meeting to loud cheers outside. To a roar of applause, Redmond moved the resolution that the convention welcomed the bill as a generous attempt to resolve the Irish question. A second resolution, moved by a Roman Catholic clergyman and seconded by a Protestant one, significantly left the question of amendments entirely to the Irish Party's discretion, thus giving it, effectively, a blank cheque.[174] The convention was, indeed, a well-staged pageant, but with a Home Rule Bill before the House of Commons, the nationalist mood was susceptible to cajolery.

Critical voices were not absent, however. Trade union agitator Jim Larkin professed that though he might be an ex-convict, he would not stoop to attending a sham convention. 'They would all say, Aye, aye', he said, 'and shout "Hurrah".'[175] The Irish Women's Franchise League vowed to defy the ban on women attending, but its members were forcibly barred by AOH doorkeepers. Patricia Hoey, of the Irish League for Women's Suffrage, had her UIL card ripped from her hand and was refused entry.[176] Hanna Sheehy-Skeffington resigned her membership of the Young Ireland Branch of the UIL in protest at the attacks upon women by the Irish Party's hired hooligans.[177]

Laurence Ginnell MP pledged to attempt to amend the bill to secure control of customs and land purchase. The General Council of Irish County Councils, a wholly nationalist body, adopted a report condemning the financial provisions and calling for fiscal autonomy as the minimum legislative demand.[178] The convention's proceedings were criticised by Francis Sheehy-Skeffington, who wrote that if the performance of Joseph Devlin's AOH at the gathering was anything to go by, freedom of opinion would be brutally suppressed if the police were in his hands. There were plenty of grumbles under the surface, he alleged, and he predicted that if the bill failed to become law, after such dragooning of public opinion, the Irish Party would face a heavy reckoning.[179]

Amendments were suggested from all quarters. Irish Protestants advanced ideas to allay their co-religionists' fears. A committee of twenty-four prominent Irishmen, chaired by Lord Dunraven, wrote to *The Times* objecting to the bill on the grounds of its flawed financial clauses and inadequate minority representation.[180] Another Protestant-chaired committee recommended more money and more powers for the Irish parliament, calling for a single transferable vote, a property requirement for senators, and additional powers of appeal to Westminster.[181] Redmond poured cold water on the Proportional Representation Society's plea that electoral reform would increase minority representation in Ireland.[182]

Pressures were also felt from the wider constituencies of nationalism. Patrick O'Donnell, bishop of Raphoe, wrote to Redmond seeking amendments to make explicit the preservation of the status quo in respect of entitlement to public grants of Catholic schools and training colleges. The Irish Party chairman politely dismissed these suggestions on the grounds that they would arouse latent anti-Catholic feeling in Britain and endanger the bill, but he assured the bishop that, in any event, such safeguards would be within the power of the Irish parliament to enact once it was in being.[183] Arthur Griffith, the founder of Sinn Féin, denounced the bill, insisting that it granted no liberty at all.[184] A meeting of Sinn Féin, early in 1913, passed a resolution repudiating 'the claim of any man to barter Ireland's right to independence for any concession', and denying that the bill before Parliament could be a final settlement.[185] The challenge went unanswered by Redmond.

The imminent prospect of Home Rule cast a spotlight on the Irish Party's fitness to govern. Jobbery, Roman Catholic sectarianism, and suppression of dissidence dogged the Irish Party's reputation, to the satisfaction of its opponents and the embarrassment of its supporters.[186] Echoes of the forcible smothering of dissent at the 'Baton Convention' of 1909 were implicit in Unionist criticism of the Irish Party's triumphal juggernaut in April 1912. The socialist *Clarion* newspaper contrasted the Irish Party's lofty support for British liberties with its infamy as the least democratic political machine in the empire, having imported from America, it claimed, the political boss. What were the prospects for democracy in Ireland, the newspaper asked, under a party that fought the Irish Agricultural Organisation Society's work to improve the lot of distressed farmers because it interfered with the profits of its masters, the *gombeen* men?[187]

There was a Jekyll-and-Hyde quality about the Irish Party leaders that saw them seemingly transformed by the fog of the Irish Sea. Redmond's and Dillon's high-minded democratic rhetoric at Westminster stood in sharp contrast to the political methods they employed in Ireland. The party leadership frequently sought to subvert the local selection of parliamentary candidates, not without controversy, lending credence to accusations of interference from on high.[188] The partiality of *The Freeman's Journal*, the newspaper controlled by the Irish Party leadership, was often risible. The *Freeman* self-righteously championed the downtrodden abroad while disregarding social ills at home, and fawned on the powerful, particularly the Roman Catholic hierarchy. Editorial attempts to quash debate in the pages of The *Freeman* by levelling charges of 'damaging factionalism' engendered resentment among the party's political rivals, and derision in other organs of the Irish press.

The Irish Party's dominance of Dublin municipal politics further tarnished its image. *The Irish Times* heralded Dublin Corporation as the world's worst municipal government, characterised by corruption, extravagance and mis-management.[189] Self-seeking Irish Party hacks chased sinecures and 'bungs' in the remunerative corridors of City Hall, critics charged, while Dublin's poor languished in some of the most appalling conditions in Europe. Reportage in *The Irish Times*, *The Lepracaun* and *The Leader* alleged that party council-lors and Poor Law guardians shielded slum landlords, halted prosecutions of slaughterhouses and dairies supplying tainted foodstuffs, and exacerbated the miseries of workhouse inmates. Complicity in Dublin's deplorable state was said to extend to the very top of the Irish Party's leadership. In the wake of the 1913 Church Street tenement collapse that killed seven occupants, *The Lepracaun* alleged that the owner of nearby numbers 59, 60 and 61 Beresford Street was none other than 'our own national reformer, Mr John Dillon'.[190]

Arguably, it was the Irish Party's association with the Ancient Order of Hibernians that did its reputation the greatest damage. The AOH mounted violent attacks on groups perceived to be opposing the party: Sinn Féiners, Larkinites and suffragettes were all targeted, and the organisation's rough-house tactics were notably deployed in the North Leitrim by-election campaign of 1908.[191] After the Hibernians' performance at the 1909 'Baton Convention', they were, naturally enough, hated by O'Brienites. The All-for-Ireland League's *Cork Free Press* argued that the Irish Party's embrace of sectarian hooliganism had driven even moderate Protestants into the arms of Carson.[192] One separa-tist pamphleteer agreed, charging that the AOH grandmaster, Joseph Devlin, bore greater responsibility than any man for alienating Ulster.[193] Advanced nationalists, whose meetings were also disrupted by AOH thuggery, despised the Hibernians for their political conservatism and pious cant.[194] Dillon, per-ceived as Devlin's patron and benefactor of 'wee Joe's' unruly hordes, was an object of their especial loathing.

The Irish Party's indulgence of the AOH was a source of despair even to some orthodox nationalists. Stephen Gwynn, a Protestant nationalist MP, con-fessed to disquiet about the future under the Hibernians. He told Dillon that if the prospect of the AOH in the ascendant worried him, it must have filled the Orangemen with rage and fear.[195] Francis Sheehy-Skeffington, who had wit-nessed AOH attacks on women at the 1912 convention, dreaded the day when the 'Hibernian Tammany' – the Irish Party and its AOH adjunct – 'settles down to bleed the country'.[196] With such a reputation even among supporters of Home Rule, the Irish Party was, at best, a compromised champion.

That British concerns about installing a triumphalist Roman Catholic regime were not a solely Unionist phenomenon was confirmed by a surprise amendment to the Home Rule Bill in June 1912, moved by a Liberal, Thomas Agar-Robartes. Agar-Robartes, who represented a strongly Nonconformist Cornish constituency, proposed the exclusion of the four Protestant-majority counties in Ulster from the operation of the bill.[197] The Unionists supported the amendment, openly admitting their motive of wrecking the bill by doing so, thus avoiding the appearance of abandoning southern Irish Unionists. The exclusion amendment was handily defeated, but the fact that it originated from the Liberal benches signalled widespread disquiet with the possibility that an attempt might be made to coerce the Protestants of Ulster into Home Rule. The abortive proposal left its impression: Churchill wrote to Redmond at the end of August 1912 urging consideration of the option of temporary exclusion of Ulster counties.[198]

The parliamentary Liberal Party strained under the burden of the Home Rule Bill's laborious progress through the House of Commons. The result of a momentary lapse of party discipline was a snap defeat on one of the financial clauses on 11 November 1912; in Cabinet the following day, Lloyd George urged that the Home Rule Bill be dropped, and that the government should proceed instead with the Franchise Bill, and dissolve Parliament.[199] To the fury of the Unionists, Asquith opted to negate the vote by extraordinary procedural means. Redmond must have been aware of Cabinet demoralisation and back-bench exhaustion, but he would have been disconcerted to learn that abandonment of the bill had even momentarily been considered.

Privately, nationalists did their best to stiffen ministerial resolve over Ulster. J.J. Clancy MP prepared a memorandum for the prime minister outlining unforeseen consequences of the threatened declaration of a provisional government. The memorandum itemised a long list of commercial dislocations that the proclamation of 'Carsonia' would set in train, such as the stoppage of post, telegraph and telephone communications, and a nullification of credit transactions. Land purchases would be halted over worries that annuities would be irrecoverable. And because a provisional government would be obliged on principle to refuse money distributed by an Irish parliament, many disbursements for public services would cease. New administrative departments and a whole new legal framework would be required, Clancy wrote, including – underlined on Asquith's copy of the document – 'a court of bankruptcy … [that] will probably be the busiest court of the lot'. Thus was the reality of Ulster secession, Clancy argued:

Its trade and commerce would be destroyed, its social system would be rent in pieces, its existing local government would disappear; bankruptcy would be universal. And as has been said, all this would happen without even [a] shot being fired at the 'grim, dour, determined' Covenanters. The 'provisional government' and its supporters would simply be committing suicide.[200]

So was laid out the basis of the nationalists' Ulster strategy: economic self-interest would restrain the excesses of Ulster Unionists and, even if it did not, steps to isolate the province economically could halt incipient rebellion without bloodshed.

The prime minister in Dublin

At no event was Home Rule more triumphantly heralded than on the occasion of Asquith's visit to Dublin, on 18–19 July 1912. The first ever visit to the Irish capital by a sitting prime minister was marked by enormous crowds at Kingstown (Dún Laoghaire) harbour and in the city, where 2,000 torch-bearers escorted Mr and Mrs Asquith and their party to the Gresham Hotel, which was decorated with electric lights in the shape of a harp and shamrocks.[201] The following evening, a crowd of 100,000 lined the streets for the Asquiths' carriage procession to the Theatre Royal in Hawkins Street.[202] To English observer Maurice Headlam, the cause for celebration was misapprehended by the rather self-consciously waving pair at its centre:

> The roars of delight meant only Dublin's appreciation of Redmond's skill and cunning, not in getting the Bill, which no one cared about, but in showing the hereditary enemy made a raree-show in the persons of two swaying, posturing figures, dishevelled and grotesque, for all Dublin to mock at the boasted majesty of England.[203]

The motivation of the audience at the Theatre Royal was less open to dispute. When the prime minister rose to speak, there were tumultuous cheers lasting more than five minutes, followed by the singing of 'For he's a jolly good fellow' for several minutes more.[204]

Asquith's speech covered much of the ground of the new Home Rule propaganda campaign. The application of the principle of a self-governing empire, government by consent of the people, and the discharge of the will of the two 'democracies' – British and Irish – all featured prominently. Upon the premier's pronouncement 'Ireland is a nation', there rose another sustained and thunderous ovation. A few suffragist hecklers (Francis Sheehy-Skeffington among them) were ejected, but the good-humoured throng even received the name of Arthur Balfour with a cheer.[205] This, one wit wrote, was the crowd's nearest approach to treason.[206] As for threats of civil war, the prime minister said he simply did not believe in the prospect. To another burst of loud cheers, he declared that a fragment of Ireland seeking to thwart the will of a vast majority would not win the sympathy of the British people.[207]

The presence of well-wishers from all sections of Ireland – Protestant and Catholic, southern farmer and Ulster factory worker – seemed to demonstrate, as Redmond had claimed on an earlier occasion, that Ireland was divided by many things but united for national liberty.[208] A few noticed that the inscription on the Parnell monument, bearing the great man's most famous words, had been obscured by electric lights spelling out Redmond's preferred formula, 'Ireland a nation'.[209] The exultant mood of the visit, however, did seem to confirm that Home Rule would be the final, and enthusiastically received, settlement of the Irish people's demand. The excitement of nationalist Dublin was indisputable, and the high spirits and gratification of the leaders and their adherents apparent, even if, as *The Times* claimed, the visit only induced a temporary forgetfulness of Ulster.[210] In the summer of 1912 it was possible to believe, as Asquith told the crowd, that the clouds really had rolled away.

3

Answering the Challenge of Ulster, 1912–14

In 1911 the inhabitants of the nine counties of Ulster were 56.3% Protestant to 43.7% Roman Catholic; excluding Belfast, the figures were 50.01% Catholic to 49.99% Protestant. Only four of the province's constituent counties, Antrim, Down, Derry and Armagh, were majority Protestant.[1] Yet despite accounting for a quarter of Ireland's population, Ulster generated a third of the country's revenues. In 1913/14 the rateable value of land in the northern province was said to stand at £5.5 million versus £10 million in the rest of the country; Ulster's bank deposits totalled £5.8 million against £7.2 million in the much more populous south. Customs and Inland Revenue collections in Ulster totalled £3.2 million, while the rest of Ireland yielded £4.9 million.[2] Ulster possessed not only a far more heterogeneous population, in sectarian terms, than its southern neighbours, its inhabitants were also wealthier (especially Protestants, who often secured better-paid work than Catholics) and more likely to live in cities or towns and to be employed in industry. The religious, socio-economic and cultural distinctiveness of the Protestant population of Ulster, celebrated by the traditions of Orangeism, was not uncommonly viewed and expressed in racial terms.

This supposed 'racial' distinction arose from the very different history of Ulster from the rest of Ireland, and its position, in the eyes, at least, of its majority population, as a besieged outpost of Protestantism. Many of the province's Protestant inhabitants traced their lineage back to the seventeenth-century plantation of Ulster, during which time lands were confiscated from the native Catholic Irish (deemed hostile to the English Crown) and given over to colonists from Britain. In 1689, when the Protestant William of Orange deposed King James II of England, the Protestants of Ulster sided with William's army against Jacobite forces in control of most of Ireland. The defeat of James II's army at the Battle of the Boyne in 1690 and subsequently at Aughrim and Limerick ensured the perpetuation of British dominion and Protestant ascendancy in Ireland. The Orange Order, formed a century later, in 1795, commemorated William's historic victory and Protestant Ulster's role in securing it.

Orangemen and other Unionists, particularly from Ulster's large and strongly Unionist Presbyterian community, organised resistance to the Home Rule bills of 1886 and 1893. Serious riots in Belfast attended the ultimately unsuccessful progress of the 1893 bill. When, in 1910, a third effort to enact Irish self-rule came into view, Ulster's Unionists once again united in opposition. The Unionist base was mobilised by Captain James Craig's highly effective propaganda campaigns and stage management of public spectacles, such as the great Unionist demonstration at Craigavon in 1911 and the signing of the Solemn League and Covenant in Belfast City Hall on 28 September 1912. The Covenant, signed amid great fanfare by Ulster Unionist leader Sir Edward Carson, pledged its signatories to refuse the authority of a Dublin parliament and to defend the right to remain loyal to the Crown and the United Kingdom. The Covenant, and an analogous declaration for the women of Ulster, was ultimately signed by over 470,000 individuals.[3]

Loyalist drilling, beginning on a small scale in Ulster in 1910, steadily grew in popularity. Sectarian tensions flared in the summer of 1912 in tit-for-tat Catholic and Protestant attacks, resulting in the expulsion of Catholic workers from Belfast's shipyards and linen mills. The Unionist political leaders, hoping to restrain their followers from rioting or outrages, consolidated the patchwork of local paramilitary corps into the Ulster Volunteer Force in late 1912. By the end of 1913, the loyalist militia claimed 100,000 recruits, and with the secret assistance of senior British Tories the force was beginning to acquire arms.[4] Ulster's Unionist leaders vowed implacable resistance to Dublin rule, and promised that a provisional government, backed by the UVF, would seize control of the northern counties if the Home Rule Bill was enacted.

Liberal journalists responded to these developments with a confused editorial line. Home Rule writers were baffled by the Ulstermen's obstinate refusal of conciliatory gestures. They were at pains to urge the government to accommodate all reasonable concerns of this culturally distinct Protestant minority while satisfying the majority's demand for self-government. Liberal journalists frequently thundered against surrendering to illegality while urging, seemingly in the same breath, that no effort be spared to placate Ulster. Despite the inconsistency and equivocation, however, the evolving mood of the Liberal press, as the Ulster challenge unfolded, was of growing impatience with inaction against lawlessness.

The extremities of illegality to which British Unionists were prepared to back Ulster's Protestant population, Liberal writers claimed, betrayed hidden motivations. Liberal propagandists presented the assault on Home Rule as a fresh eruption of the constitutional struggle between peers and people, one that sought to turn the democratic tide that had been rising for decades. The Irish Home Rule Bill thus assumed for Liberal commentators an importance in Britain quite distinct from the benefits that it would confer to Ireland. This linkage of British democracy to the attainment of Irish Home Rule transformed the discourse. The dynamic response of Home Rule polemicists to Ulster resistance, and their success in refashioning the Irish question into a defence of Liberal doctrine, was instrumental in revitalising the issue of Home Rule in the Liberal heartlands.

The persistence of confidence

A cartoon in *The Lepracaun*'s January 1914 issue depicted the bright dawn of the new year greeting the jaunty figure of Irish Home Rule striding across St George's Channel.[5] The poignancy of optimistic expectations for 1914, owing to the historical significance of that year, should not obscure the fact that, from the perspective of January 1914, Home Rule for Ireland was confidently in prospect. Liberal journals had exultantly greeted each stage of the Home Rule Bill's progress in 1912/13. The Liberal rank and file were said to be solidly behind the Irish cause, though some still suspected that the issue faintly bored the public. *The Catholic Times* and *The Daily Citizen* asserted that the British electorate had been so long convinced of the justice and necessity of Irish self-government that they were a little mystified as to what the fuss was about.[6] *The Nation* argued that weariness with Ireland fed British support for Home Rule. Many electors, the journal claimed, backed settlement of the Irish question because they wanted the way cleared for social reforms.[7]

The Liberal press uniformly cited by-election results as confirming the popular will. Such tests of popular opinion, even when lost by the Liberal candidate, could be pointed to as 'Home Rule majorities' if the combined Liberal and Labour vote (which was presumed to signal support for the bill) exceeded that for the Unionists. This served to emphasise the flagship character of Home Rule in the Liberal programme, but it also signalled sensitivity to the Unionist claim that Irish self-government lacked a popular mandate in Britain. In December 1913 *The Methodist Times* tabulated the results of the twenty-three by-elections since the Home Rule Bill's introduction, and asserted that this aggregation demonstrated a majority of 15,700 votes for Home Rule.[8]

The holding firm of the combined Liberal/Labour vote, *Reynolds's Newspaper* suggested, indicated the rejection of Tory appeals to religious and 'racial' prejudice, and the transformation of Home Rule from a source of Liberal weakness to one of strength.[9] Working-class solidarity, *The Nation* asserted, underpinned support for Home Rule. 'The British workman', the newspaper wrote, 'learned his Nationalism in 1886, and has never forgotten it, and his Radicalism or his Socialism of today accepts an equal comradeship with the Dublin wharfinger and the Belfast engineer.'[10]

A nationalist by-election victory in Derry in February 1913 was widely proclaimed as indicative of the tide of opinion in Ulster. The wrenching of an urban Ulster seat from the Unionists on the very day that the House of Lords rejected the Home Rule Bill was hailed as a comprehensive answer to the charge that Ireland did not want self-rule. It was evidence, said *Reynolds's Newspaper*, that the nationalist cause was gaining ground, even in the stronghold of enemy territory.[11]

Liberal journals assured their readers that no one desired prosperity and contentment for the whole of Ireland more than nationalists. If their sincerity were only put to the test, every Orangeman who 'repented' would be greeted as a brother by nationalists.[12] *The Methodist Times* foretold that in an Irish House of Commons the quarrels of orange and green would be supplanted by the voices of liberal and conservative, and urban and rural interests, as elsewhere in the empire.[13] *The Westminster Gazette* argued that this imminent political reconfiguration meant that Ulster's objections were baseless. The prospective fresh groupings along economic and class lines in southern Ireland would disprove the Ulstermen's worries of a Catholic bloc bent on persecution.[14]

With the advent of self-government, it was anticipated that the Irish Party, its *raison d'être* attained, would dissolve. *The Daily Citizen* speculated in July 1914 that Redmond would head a Liberal ministry, and held high hopes for Joseph Devlin, whose future role, it foretold, would be to 'slay slum-landlordism and the sweating system'. O'Brienites and socialists, it said, would be the new government's main opposition.[15] *The Nation* predicted that as Protestantism's perceived enemies regrouped around new political poles, northern Unionists would remain a culturally and economically distinct political unit. The journal foresaw that when, at last, Ulster bowed to the inevitability of Home Rule, command of Irish politics would be hers.[16]

Cynics suspected that the overriding consideration for the Ulsterman was the likely effect of Home Rule on his pocketbook, and that if self-rule promised to benefit his trade, his fears would quickly evaporate. *The Freeman's Journal* suggested that, solemn Covenant or no, if a Dublin parliament introduced an advantageous scheme to compel the sale of farmland to tenants, no Orangeman would resent the title of peasant proprietor.[17] Harold Begbie believed the working men of Ulster would give more thought to their household economy than to fantastical spectres of popery, prophesying, in his poem, 'Better Times':

> The Orange poor will toil, the rich make money ...
> Workman and clerk, dismiss your dread,
> the Pope still in his prison lingers;
> Pirrie won't burn his boats, nor Ned [Carson] his fingers ...
> But this will pass.
> The wise will own, while babies are born and trade increases,
> peace is better than being blown to pieces.[18]

Liberal propagandists argued that the businessman's hard head would overcome wild talk of sedition. *The Catholic Times* asserted that a provisional government setting itself apart from both a Dublin parliament and Westminster would involve a crippling disruption of trade and civil law. With these requisites of commerce in disarray, one could expect, at the least, mischief when 'some witty Irishman will order from a Belfast merchant or shopkeeper, and laugh while the creditor appeals to his precious Ulster Assembly to put the law in motion against the debtor in Cork or Dublin'.[19] Such considerations would surely give the merchants of Belfast pause for thought; but for the manufacturers of the linen trade and shipbuilding, the losses owing to legal disputes and the interruption of supplies were incalculable. Were the scions of industry really so rash as to risk insolvency on a speculative fear? Much of the Liberal press thought not. Factory owners ran a political risk, too, if an Ulster Unionist boycott of the Irish parliament resulted in the election, en masse, of Labour representatives. The emergence of an assertive Labour Party in Belfast and environs would be a most unwelcome development for large employers in the city.[20] *The Daily Citizen* speculated that the industrialists of Ulster would not countenance armed revolt for a moment, calling it a 'mad enterprise' that would result in 'irreparable ruin'.[21] The businessmen of Ulster might engage in bluff, but bloodshed was another matter.

So confident of triumph were Home Rulers that they persisted in ridiculing 'Ulsteria'. T.P. O'Connor told a meeting in Cardiff that the reason peers and politicians were not in prison for incitement was that 'the right way to treat a lunatic was to laugh at him'.[22] As late as December 1913, *Reynolds's Newspaper* was unperturbed by the Ulster Volunteers, calling their preparations harmless amusements that would not alter the bill's progress.[23] That Home Rule's chief opponents were the same men who had fulminated impotently against the Parliament Act added a frisson of delight for one of the newspaper's commentators. Singling out the diehard Lord Willoughby de Broke, the writer commented that if 'wild pantomime tomfoolery' won battles, then the Unionists would defeat Home Rule, 'but as we have seen all this bluster and swagger and bounce and impudence before, followed by a scuttle and a scoot worthy of frightened hares, we may well laugh at these later ravings'.[24]

Responses to Unionist agitation

Liberal propagandists attacked what they saw as the insincere motives of British Unionists in backing the Ulstermen. The inconsistency of Unionist Irish policy was recalled: how the Tories had opposed schemes for local government before they passed the 1898 Local Government (Ireland) Act, and how they had fought Gladstone's land-purchase scheme in 1886 only to adopt something similar in 1903.[25] Unionist antagonism to Home Rule had not barred an electoral understanding between Parnell and Lord Salisbury in 1885, nor had it prevented Tory Irish Chief Secretary George Wyndham's blessing of a devolution scheme in 1904.[26]

Many commentators looked only a few years back to 1910, when 'Pacificus' in *The Times* and J.L. Garvin in *The Observer* were leading the chorus of Unionists urging sympathetic consideration of federal Home Rule.[27] British Unionists had had no qualms about Catholic oppression of the Protestant minority then, yet now they claimed to be desperately concerned for the industrial prosperity of Ulster and the religious liberty of her Protestant population.[28] The pamphlet *Home Rule in a Nutshell* quoted pro-Home-Rule-all-round passages published in no fewer than thirteen Unionist newspapers from October 1910.[29] *The Freeman's Journal* recalled the many faces that Toryism had shown to Ireland, from 'Carnarvon to Pigott' and from sweet reasonableness in 1910 to the revival of old rancours months later.[30] The pretended fury of British Unionists in 1912, opined *The Baptist Times*, was mere 'stage thunder'.[31]

Yet even while the Tories affected outrage, they were selective about whose resistance of the law was to be supported. Citing the Unionists' swift denunciation of the refusal of Indians in Natal to pay a £3 poll tax, *The Baptist Times* argued that it was not principle but cynical political tactics that accounted for the inconsistency.[32] Sir Edward Carson was inciting violence in Ulster at no risk to himself or his property, *The Catholic Times* asserted. When Ulster had served its purpose in the fencing between English parties, the newspaper predicted, the Tories were sure to 'throw over all the gulled Orangemen and laugh at them as heartily as the rest of us'.[33]

The churlish 'new style' of Andrew Bonar Law (who had succeeded Arthur Balfour as leader of the opposition in 1911), and his oblique incitement to violence, rendered him the target of unflattering attention. Like Carson, Bonar Law was portrayed as an opportunistic outsider spreading poisonous anarchy but possessing little sincere attachment to Ulster. *Reynolds's Newspaper* noted his glib talk about bloodshed; but, it contended, like the rest of the 'new anarchists' of the Unionist party, the Unionist leader would not 'run the risk of a bruised head'. The eventuality was unlikely to arise, however, as the Irish would refuse to be 'dragooned into lawlessness by the wild … words of a mediocre politician'.[35] The government should not dignify the vulgar bullying of 'ill-conditioned ruffians' by negotiation, maintained *Reynolds's*. If Carson and Bonar Law persisted 'in making themselves a public nuisance they must be forced to behave themselves', the newspaper insisted; 'They will very soon come to heel.'[36]

The improbability of factory workers and boilermakers following the lead of marquesses, London barristers and Belfast industrialists did not go unnoticed by the Liberal press. *The Methodist Times* noted the absence of representation of labouring interests in the prospective Ulster provisional government, making its composition anomalous in a democratic age.[37] *The Daily Citizen* claimed that getting the workers more exercised 'about Popery and King William than … about their wages' was a useful diversion for the capitalists of Belfast.[38] Tom Kettle, writing in the *Citizen*, noted the irony that Belfast, a city whose industries had flourished with free trade, had 'swallowed tariff reform without mastication' simply because English Unionists made bigotry their platform. The simple Orangeman, Kettle continued, seemed to believe that Ulster's economic vigour somehow rested on antipathy for the

Pope, and that if the north-east corner of Ireland were to refrain for a moment from 'consigning that dignitary to Hell, the looms and the great cranes would instantly go to pieces'.[39]

The conviction that the Home Rule furore was engineered to force a general election was present almost from the start of the controversy. Ulster exclusion was cast as a wedge with which the Unionists hoped to split the Liberals and nationalists, and precipitate the fall of Asquith's government. In presenting the Liberals with a bad choice of exclusion, or a worse one of civil war, the Unionist *Spectator* argued, the Tories were rendering Home Rule an impossibility. Exclusion was, it said, an absurdity, and recognised as such on all sides. Civil war, on the other hand, was unthinkable; the only course left open to the government would be retreat and withdrawal of the bill.[40] Should this result in a general election, as was likely, *The Nation* claimed, Unionists would arrange for a 'fusillade of outrages' in Ulster as a backdrop to their campaign. Ulster was being more cynically manipulated than ever, it wrote, in the belief that sectarian unrest in the province would be a powerful weapon in British constituencies.[41]

It was widely asserted that the Unionist leaders' encouragement of rebellion would rebound on them in unexpected ways. The illogic underpinning the Tory argument, claimed *The Catholic Times*, was that whenever a party threatened armed resistance to the law, the duty of the state was to yield to the demand, or else to bear moral responsibility for violence if it broke out.[42] This notion that sufficient provocation absolved an aggrieved party of responsibility for treason and illegal force, J.A. Hobson charged, was the 'sophistry of rebellion' and the 'gospel of the anarchist'.[43] The incessant refrain of 'civil war', *The Westminster Gazette* insisted, was an attempt to legitimise the Ulster Unionists' threatened action, providing a flimsy pretext for what would plainly be unlawful actions.[44]

The avenues of political mischief to which the Unionist leaders had shown the way, wrote *The Methodist Times*, were practically unlimited. The language of Carson gave sustenance and legitimacy to the advocates of violence behind a multitude of causes.[45] Incendiary speeches, it suggested, would cause more damage to Unionist interests than they would to Ireland.[46] *The Catholic Times* wondered whether, at a time of social upheaval, the party of wealth ought not to be more careful to avoid disparagement of the law upon which its security depended.[47]

'What will the landlord party say', *The Daily Citizen* asked, 'when insurgent Labour adopts and practices their principles?'[48] The intervention of Lord

Lansdowne calling upon army officers to exercise private opinions was considered to be particularly ill-judged. What would happen, *The Catholic Times* asked, when the private soldier examined his conscience? Might he not find justification for refusing to fire on his striking brothers 'struggling for more freedom and more food'?[49] Unionist leaders were nurturing, Liberal commentators asserted, the very proletarian forces that most wished to destroy Toryism. 'Go on, do what you threaten', *Reynolds's Newspaper* urged, 'you will never cease to damn the consequences.'[50] *The Catholic Times* savoured the irony that Ireland, upon which the aristocracy of England had visited such suffering, might be the instrument of its destruction in the aftermath of Carsonism.[51]

In their single-minded desire to bring down the government, Liberal writers asserted, Unionists were setting themselves an impossible task in Ireland if they regained office. Having to suppress the Irish nationalists, applying, themselves, the methods of force learned from Carson, would make 'the desert of the Opposition benches ... seem a garden of roses'.[52] Unionists would not only find nationalist Ireland ungovernable but, barring a policy of bloody suppression, would be forced to offer some form of Home Rule. This was the crowning absurdity of the British Unionist position, *The Nation* claimed in 1914, exacerbated by the fact that the armed fanaticism that Bonar Law and his colleagues had recklessly conjured into life was now refusing to follow their lead.[53]

Conciliation and alternatives

From the outset, proposals to conciliate Ulster abounded in the Liberal discourse. *The Nation* endorsed the sentiments of C.P. Scott that no opportunity should be lost for accommodation.[54] One pamphlet proposed giving north-east Ulster disproportionately greater representation in the Home Rule parliament for a period of twenty years.[55] Frederic Harrison, a veteran radical, suggested that the Ulster members of the Irish House of Commons should have sole authority to decide matters affecting the province.[56] 'A Protestant Ulsterman' advocated alternating sittings of the Irish parliament between Dublin and Armagh, 'the ecclesiastical capital of Ireland', and devolving expanded administrative powers on the four Protestant-majority counties.[57] A time-honoured means of softening up resistance was rumoured by *The Daily Citizen*: it whispered of 'promises of honours and jobs, knighthoods and baronetcies, and fat posts in the Government service' offered to prominent

Ulstermen 'if not to "rat", at any rate to render innocuous the great threatened civil war'.[58]

The Nation regretted that the bill had not been used as an opportunity to experiment with a system of proportional representation, arguing that such a scheme would give greater security to Ulster. Fuller representation of minorities, the newspaper asserted, would have facilitated the dissolution of sectarian blocs and their re-coalescence around sectional interests.[59] Sir Alfred Mond MP proposed an amendment to introduce proportional representation to Ireland's cities, intended to give nationalists perhaps three seats in Belfast, and some six seats to Unionists in Dublin and Cork.[60]

The Nation also revived federal Home Rule as a curative for the Ulster deadlock. It commended a federal reorganisation of the United Kingdom in tandem with reform of the House of Lords.[61] *The Way of Unity and Peace*, an anonymous pamphlet appearing in 1914, called for a rapid scheme of devolution to avert civil disorder in Ulster.[62] A correspondent to *The Nation* suggested improbably that a broader plan of Home Rule all round would hasten resolution of the Ulster difficulty, because it would encounter less resistance than the effort to tackle Ireland on its own.[63] The journal rejected Ulster exclusion as being incompatible with the federal ideal, and persisted in advancing federalism as a means of reconciling nationalists and Unionists well into 1914.[64]

In the effort to adopt a firm but conciliatory line, Liberal editors tended to tie themselves in knots. Home Rule commentators urged openness to pacific overtures, while stressing their determination to see the matter through. Thus, in the space of two pages *The Methodist Times* could issue an appeal to Protestants to support efforts to make peace, in the spirit of followers of John Wesley, while condemning the 'perverse obduracy' and 'impenetrable ignorance' of the Ulster Unionists.[65] *The Nation* offered indistinct and contradictory advice to ministers to stamp out sedition, but also to try to work with Unionists along cooperative lines and carry with them all men of conscience.[66] As usual, a federal fig leaf was prescribed. *Reynolds's Newspaper*'s equivocal suggestion was that a forthright but fair administration, fully conscious of its power, should be unafraid to make concessions, which were, of course, unspecified.[67] *The Contemporary Review* expressed a desire for the government to proceed confidently and to avoid any appearance of surrender to the Ulstermen, yet at the same time counselled that peace should be preserved at almost any cost. How were these conflicting aims to be achieved? Liberals, the writer suggested, should do everything in their power to satisfy all Ulster's reasonable demands, and isolate the extremists.[68] Such hazy vapidities suggested little in the way of constructive policy.

What should be done about north-east Ulster was no easier for Liberal editors to work out than it was for Liberal ministers. *The Nation* reported Carson's demand for a 'clean cut' for Ulster in July 1914, yet, just a few pages later, sought to convince its readers that county option of exclusion 'finds favour wherever it is discussed' and that Tories who professed themselves to be eager for a general election were bluffing.[69] Even at a very late stage, with the fate of large Protestant minorities in the counties of Tyrone and Fermanagh proving the insoluble difficulty, *The Nation* could offer only empty words. Appeals for an improbable and unspecified formula that would protect Protestants while not crushing the hopes of the bulk of the Irish nation were simply expressions of wishful thinking.[70]

The Westminster Gazette advertised the confusion at the head of the Liberal Party. Its Janus-faced editorial line advocated, at one time or another, an inter-party conference, a federal settlement, coercion of Ulster as a last resort, a firm stand on county option, and an Irish conference to delimit the contracting-out counties, thus nullifying the democratic rationale of county polls.[71] Readers could be forgiven for being mystified by all this, but the *Gazette*, in the end, finally summoned up a sort of noncommittal resolve: that the government should decide on some policy or another, and press it through whatever the consequences.[72] The conflict of Liberal pacific instincts with the prospective coercion of Ulster's Protestant population posed no less of an ideological dilemma for Liberal opinion-formers than it did for ministers.

The Irish Volunteers and the Liberal press

The advent of the Irish Volunteer nationalist paramilitary force (the rise of which is chronicled in Chapter 6) was attended by a mixture of admiration and alarm in Liberal journals. For the most part ignored by the British press upon its formation in November 1913, the Irish Volunteers began to attract notice only in the spring of 1914. Tom Kettle, writing in the *Daily News and Leader*, explained to Liberal readers the Volunteers' purpose of protecting the grant of freedom to Ireland.[73] *The Catholic Times* asserted that nationalists had been left with little option but to reinforce their hitherto parliamentary course by drilling: 'The Irish Nationalist has been taught that Constitutional reform was the ticket for Home Rule. He took it. But now, when he gets off at the terminus, he is told that the ticket is invalid. What can he do in the circumstances?'[74]

The Irish Volunteers burst into prominence in the British press when questions in Parliament about the movement were asked in June 1914. At first *The Nation* claimed that the Volunteers' principal purpose was political, their large numbers having already impressed British public opinion.[75] Yet the newspaper soon worried that an independent armed force might dominate the policy of a new Irish government. Redmond, *The Nation* asserted, could not tolerate a menacing standing army looking over his shoulder.[76] A similarly ambivalent interpretation of the significance of the Irish Volunteers' appearance was offered by *The Daily Citizen*, which suggested that the existence of a large nationalist force might cow Unionists or inflame a situation already getting out of hand.[77] The government, in acquiescing to Ulster Volunteer Force drilling, the newspaper wrote, had 'placed itself between two fires'.[78]

T.P. O'Connor reassured the readers of *Reynolds's Newspaper* that the Irish Volunteers' leaders remained loyal to the constitutional faith. He explained the Volunteer movement as the uncommanded response of the Irish people to the challenge to Home Rule and 'the most striking and triumphant symbol' of national revival.[79] O'Connor expressed satisfaction that with the appearance of the 'boys' in the south of Ireland, the ballyhooed Covenanters 'have begun to squeal already, and their friends in this country [England] have lost no time in calling out for "law and order"'.[80]

The existence of the Irish Volunteers, many newspapers pointed out, rendered Unionist governance of Ireland by old methods impossible. Henry Nevinson, echoing the idealistic beliefs of some of the Volunteers' founders, speculated that if an English soldier killed a loyalist rebel, Unionists and nationalists would combine to hound the occupiers from their country.[81] *The Catholic Times* asserted that the Tories and the peers, 'on their deathbed' because of the Parliament Act, were powerless to resist Home Rule because it was demanded by an Ireland in arms.[82] *The Nation* noted, with concern, that the Irish Volunteers had no intention of disbanding at the bidding of English or Irish politicians, even after Home Rule, and speculated that a break-up of the Liberal government might well precipitate an armed nationalist insurrection.[83]

The Irish Volunteers' landing of 1,500 rifles at Howth on 29 July 1914 was a publicity coup for the corps, but British troops, ineffectually despatched to intercept the Volunteers, fired on a jeering crowd at Bachelor's Walk in Dublin. The killing of four and wounding of thirty seemed proof of an inconsistent attitude towards the nationalist and Ulster militias, as 5,000 armed Ulster Volunteers had paraded unmolested through the streets of Belfast the previous day.[84] *The Daily Chronicle*'s 'Special Correspondent' (presumably T.P.

Gill) observed that after the atrocity there was a great resentment of injustice abroad in Ireland and strong anti-English feeling.[85] O'Connor, writing in *Reynolds's Newspaper*, stressed that in the changed mood of the country the Irish Party could take concessions no further, and that if it were to countenance it, 'the people of Ireland would rise in revolt against them, and decline any longer to follow their lead'.[86] The *Chronicle* (again, likely voicing Gill's thoughts) commented that Fenian sentiment was gaining ground in a receptive countryside, at the expense of the constitutional movement. Two hundred thousand Irish Volunteers, rapidly arming themselves, and with the whole of the southern population behind them, the newspaper argued, constituted a grave threat to peace.[87] 'It looks', *The Nation* commented despairingly, as the crisis approached its climax, 'as if all our Irish errors are coming back on us at one swoop.'[88]

The sunny outlook for 1914 that had graced *The Lepracaun's* pages in January darkened considerably by mid-year. Where hope and harmony had dominated its content, there was now reflected disillusionment and grim self-reliance. In June it depicted Carson's Ulster Volunteers' torch igniting a runaway Irish Volunteer brush fire.[89] 'The most popular phrase in the Irish Volunteers vocabulary at the moment', it noted the following month, 'is "Present arms!" Philanthropy in a presenting mood, please note.'[90] *The Lepracaun's* final depiction of the Home Rule Crisis, before the First World War crowded out all else, was of the Irish Volunteers as an infant child. Crawling out of his crib, and leaving aside 'Westminster damp blankets' and 'Liberal soothing promise syrup', the tot exclaimed, 'Here! I've grown too big for this meaningless rocking. I want arms!'[91]

Notes of censure

The autumn 1913 intervention of Lord Loreburn, former Liberal Lord Chancellor, calling for a conference of the parties and floating the exclusion of Ulster was received coldly by Liberal commentators. *Reynolds's Newspaper* asserted that to bypass the House of Commons would hand victory to the forces of oligarchy behind the Ulster insurgency and subvert the democratic process.[92] No conference, Tom Kettle complained, was suggested for tariff reform or disestablishment of the Anglican Church in Wales, yet apparently 'anything is good enough for Ireland. As for her, if she loses, she loses; if she wins, somebody lifts his voice and shakes his fist, and the win is to be disallowed.'[93] Like Kettle, *The Daily Citizen* counselled against conferences unless agreement upon a parliament for all Ireland was the starting point.[94] *Reynolds's Newspaper* warned of Unionist bad faith and a trap being set.[95]

Though calls for conciliation persisted in the Liberal press, notes of censure began to be sounded. O'Connor, in his *Reynolds's* column, railed against the proposition of Ulster's exclusion, asserting that the Liberal rank and file were 'fiercely and unanimously against even the contemplation of compromise in any shape or form whatsoever', especially one that would not 'settle the Irish question, but … unsettle it more than ever' by crystallising sectarian divisions.[96] *The Nation* professed itself mystified by Asquith's raising of the possibility of exclusion when the Parliament Act meant that the government held all the cards. Indignant correspondents to the newspaper urged the adoption of a strong line. One chastised ministers for their uneven response to Orangemen versus nationalists, charging that indifference and failure to uphold the law were bearing bitter fruit; another demanded 'an end of wobbly talk'; while a third contended that the Carson bluff had all along been taken too seriously, with the result that the Ulster Volunteers believed that ministers were afraid of them.[97]

The inconsistency of the government's actions troubled many commentators. How, when it was expedient to turn a blind eye to rebellion in Ulster, could the government imprison striking trade union leaders without a qualm? Why, the socialist *Clarion* newspaper asked, did the government shrink from acting against 'shrieking misfits in trousers' while locking up others clad in petticoats?[98] *The Methodist Times* and *The Catholic Times* both contrasted the swift response to Jim Larkin's intemperate speeches, in fighting against actual evils, to the passivity that greeted Carson's treasonous language about imaginary ones.[99] Larkin, whose only crime, *The Daily Citizen* asserted, had been to lay bare the squalidness of Dublin's sweated industries, was not to be tolerated; a Liberal government defended the interests of plutocrats by flinging him into prison. Millions of labouring men, 'suckled on the Radical faith', the *Citizen* suggested, would be soured on the party for ever by the sight of leaders so quick to lock up one of their fellows for asserting working-class grievances.[100] Militant suffragettes, Larkinists and the 'hooligan class' of labour agitators, wrote *The Methodist Times*, were taking note of the government's weak response to the Carsonite agitation.[101]

In thinking that curbing the power of the House of Lords had emasculated the forces of reaction, *The Nation* asserted, Home Rulers had been mistaken.[102] The army and other powers of authority in the state were still in Tory hands, and were ranged against the government in support of the Ulster rebellion.

Tory intrigues, claimed *The Catholic Times*, had succeeded in bringing royal pressure to bear against the bill's enactment.[103] Outside wealth, *The Nation* asserted, was pouring into Ulster for reasons quite unconnected with its struggle.[104] The Asquith ministry's unwillingness to bring military men to heel further piqued Liberal irritation. Newspapers questioned why pensioned officers serving in the UVF, 'like the grotesque Gen. Richardson', should not be struck off the Army List and stripped of civil honours.[105]

Many Liberal writers suggested that the status of the Ulster leaders, as peers and Privy Councillors, rendered them immune from prosecution: a government pledged against wealth and privilege was, in fact, kowtowing to it. Liberal ministers, argued *Reynolds's Newspaper*, ought to enforce 'the law of the land against aristocrats plotting rebellion as strongly as against Irish Nationalists fighting for land and liberty, or British workers ground down by monopoly'.[106]

The English working man, it claimed, was 'a volcano of passionate resentment' over such blatant inequality before the law.[107] Carson and his followers, *The Daily Citizen* asserted, could utter any disloyal oath, even arm themselves openly, and the government would become ever more pliable.[108] Ulster defiance had become a real danger, Liberal critics charged, because ministerial dithering had allowed it to grow to such menacing proportions. This pandering to class privilege, *The Nation* wrote, was causing indignation in the progressive ranks at a time perilous to the cause of Liberalism.[109]

In February 1914 *The Nation* published a mock column from a hundred years in the future that stressed to its supposed 'readers' of 2014 that the mystification felt by the twenty-first-century historian studying Liberal tolerance of insurrection was shared by observers in 1914:

> Subsequent history has endeavoured to explain the Government's motives in regarding Carson's immense preparations for rebellion with apparent acquiescence; but to contemporaries ... their inaction in this case must have sometimes appeared a little puzzling, when contrasted with their vigorous measures of suppression in other directions.[110]

The Daily Citizen and *The Catholic Times* agreed that the government's baffling weakness in dealing with Ulster was tantamount to giving in to blackmail.[111] *The Daily Citizen* claimed that large sections of the Liberal Party were growing impatient with 'endless olive branches'.[112] *The Nation* expressed exasperation that the Liberal administration persisted in 'raining concessions' on Ulster

only to see them scorned.[113] Professor J.H. Morgan argued that offering concessions unacceptable to Unionists was alienating friends without conciliating
enemies, and warned that the Liberal rank-and-file's patience with the party's
leaders was not inexhaustible.[114]

Leaders of causes allied to the Liberal and Labour 'coalition' – suffragists
and striking workers – were attacked and imprisoned; yet a Liberal administration remained apathetic in the face of threatened sedition led by lawyers and
peers. It was a shocking failure of nerve, or of sense, it seemed to many, that a
Liberal government came down hard on the ordinary men and women whose
interests it was pledged to defend while winking at the follies of Liberalism's
mortal opponents.[115]

Home Rule and democracy

Home Rule propagandists argued that the most significant division in Ireland
was not between two creeds or races but between two classes. The essence of
Unionist opposition, Liberal writers asserted, was an effort to preserve oligarchy, while Home Rule was a struggle to assert democratic rights. Home Rulers
were confident that they would win the fight, because resisting democracy,
they insisted, ran against the trend of modern industrial society. Resistance
to Home Rule was merely a continuation of the battle over the Parliament
Bill, many Liberal journals held, with the question of 'peers or people' still
the central issue.[116] The Tories fought so desperately to turn the government
out, *Reynolds's Newspaper* maintained, not because they cared for Ulster but
because they knew that they were fighting for their political life.[117]

Public tussles between back-bench radicals and Cabinet moderates,
however, indicated that all was not well with Liberalism. The progressive press
pondered the causes of ministerial rudderlessness. *The Daily Citizen* believed
that the struggle with the House of Lords had left the government weary
and dispirited. Asquith, it said, showed a firm grip of neither principles nor
men.[118] There was a widespread sense that ministerial ambivalence about New
Liberal collectivism, redistributive taxation, and working-class representation
was clouding the party's fortunes. Disillusionment, particularly among the
working classes, was rife, commentators asserted, and Liberals were losing
fresh recruits to the banners of Labour and other movements.

'Liberals have paltered with social reform', *The Catholic Times* wrote, but
'while they were filling the cisterns with hope … Whigs draw off the waters
of charity' by increasing expenditure on armaments.[119] H.W. Massingham,

writing in the *Daily News and Leader*, bemoaned the Cabinet's failure to keep in touch with the rank and file, or to build bridges with Labour, or to improve international relations. The Liberal government was disappointing its most ardent friends. The wave of popular enthusiasm that had swept in the Liberal ministry of 1906, he claimed, was rapidly receding from the government of 1912.[120] The passage of Irish Home Rule was so critical to the Liberal Party's survival, *The Daily Citizen* argued, because it would convince British electors that a party bold enough to free Ireland would be up to the task of tackling economic disparity and injustice.[121]

Journalists expressed reservations about the capacity of the Liberal Party to adapt to the changing political landscape. Almost the only important social fact facing the traditional parties of government, *The Catholic Times* claimed, was that most voters had lost faith in representatives other than those drawn from among their own class. Even under a Liberal government, it maintained, the doors of Downing Street remained closed to all but the wealthy.[122] *The Daily Citizen* bluntly asserted that 'the aim of both parties is to dodge Democracy – to frustrate in practice what cannot be denied in doctrine', and that, in the face of socialist pressure, hunger for office would one day force the Liberals and Tories to merge.[123] The Larkin episode prompted *The Nation* to reflect on the shifting sands beneath the Liberal Party. 'Everything else in politics is either dead or dying', the newspaper wrote, 'or as yet unready to be born. But if Liberalism falls back into scepticism about popular movements or irrational fear of their proper, rational, and inevitable expression, it will die too.'[124]

'Noble Syndicalists and Wreckers … who do not care a rap about Ulster', wrote *Reynolds's Newspaper*, were mounting 'a last desperate stand against the new Democracy which has crippled the power of the House of Lords'.[125] British democrats, *The Catholic Times* claimed, wanted only to see the passage of Home Rule, the operation of the Parliament Act of 1911, and the humiliation of the House of Lords. Upon delivery of these expectations, the government's fate would rest on a general election in 1915.[126] The House of Lords, one pamphleteer insisted, still believed and behaved as if it were its right to decide what Liberal legislation should pass and what should be struck down. The Parliament Act, secured after the verdict of two general elections, faced determined opposition from those who hoped to restore the veto power of the Lords. The real question for Liberals at the 1915 general election, it was asserted, would be whether the Parliament Act was to be sustained and their work of the preceding decade preserved.[127]

To stray from the course commanded by the electorate and give in to demands for a general election, *The Nation* asserted, would be to wreck the Parliament Act upon its first trial.[128] Yet the prospect remained, as the newspaper put it, of a Liberal government 'unbeaten in argument or the division lobby, reduced to … the voluntary surrender of the weapon with which it had armed Democracy against the House of Lords'.[129] What, *Reynolds's Newspaper* asked, would the people say if the weapon of the Parliament Act was cast aside? Was the instrument unused because it was defective, or had it been placed in an impotent hand? If the latter were true, the newspaper claimed, the British people would react with disgust, and reject Liberalism.[130] *The Catholic Times* agreed that to shrink from operation of the Parliament Act would rightly earn the Liberal Party the electorate's contempt.[131] To break faith with the people in such an inexplicable way, the newspaper said, would bring dishonour and also punishment at the ballot box among progressive constituencies, particularly the Irish in Britain.[132] Home Rule's passage, *The Nation* claimed, would mean, by contrast, 'not the dawn, but the full sun blaze of the day of British Democracy', and open the way for a fairer distribution of wealth and for political equality.[133]

The proposal to exclude Ulster was criticised in sharp terms as undermining a policy arrived at by democratic and constitutional means. 'Better to throw this Liberal government out', *The Catholic Times* stormed, 'which would mean the complete destruction of Liberalism and the quick emergence of a fresh and true democratic party – than trifle with the unity of Ireland.'[134] *The Nation* suggested that if a policy of partition were adopted, 'Mr Redmond might well pray to be delivered from Liberalism and all its works, and Liberalism, in its turn, would be driven to ask where its leaders had led it'.[135] If Liberal leaders remained unwilling to crush defiance of the authority of the House of Commons, the newspaper wrote, the party 'must meet the ruin it will have deserved, and give place to some organisation of the people's will that has more courage and more competency'.[136] In *Reynolds's Newspaper*, O'Connor claimed that if ministers contemplated further concessions to Ulster, they would find 'the whole rank and file of the Liberal Party in the country in revolt against them', and lose every seat in the north of England.[137]

A scathing critique of the government's handling of Ulster arrived in June 1914 with the publication of J.A. Hobson's *Traffic in Treason: A study of political parties*. Hobson denounced British Unionists for cynically manipulating Ulster Protestants as a proxy in the struggle of 'property against poverty, mastery against servitude, privilege against equality'.[138] With the House of

Lords emasculated, the Tories, asserted Hobson, dreaded the prospect of redistributive taxation summoning up 'an everlasting Lloyd George, who will leave them no peace, living or dead', exacting ever-larger tolls on their incomes and inheritances. In reaction the oligarchy was mobilising the influential classes, the army and the Crown. The Ulster challenge, he argued, represented the actuation of these subterranean levers of Toryism to bring the government to its knees, to 'recapture the Constitution', and to fortify themselves against 'levelling' collectivist reforms.[139] Yet Hobson damningly attributed the success of this retrograde enterprise chiefly to the complacency of Asquith and his colleagues.

Unlike the Tory Party, Hobson asserted, which the Home Rule Crisis demonstrated had become 'thoroughly alive to the meaning of real politik [*sic*]', the middle-class leadership of the Liberal Party shrank from challenging foes to whom it instinctively, and fatally, deferred. Hobson argued that for Asquith and his colleagues to treat men of high social standing (whom they secretly admired) as they would delinquents of the lower orders was quite inconceivable. Middle-class timidity, he feared, could cost Liberalism Ireland, the constitution, and the longer struggle for democracy. With Liberalism supine before Unionist resistance, and with the Labour Party unready to pick up the reins, the only hope, in Hobson's eyes, was for organised working people and their trade unions to 'stiffen and ... direct' Liberalism from within. The Liberal Party, he wrote, must urgently reconstitute itself with the 'active assistance of the people whom it ... professed to "trust", but ... always sought to "manage"'.[140]

Exasperation with ministerial pusillanimity boiled over in the Liberal press in July 1914. Moderate Liberals were no less incensed than Labourites or radicals, claimed *The Westminster Gazette*, and would resist government attempts to pressure Redmond.[141] To yield to Tory threats now, wrote *The Nation*, would result in the Liberal Party being 'torn to pieces from within and massacred from without'.[142] *The Catholic Times* agreed that the government would be 'smashed like an ... eggshell' if it surrendered to Carsonism, and rather wildly suggested that, in that event, the working men of Britain, instructed in the efficacy of force, would immediately begin drilling and arming themselves.[143] At the Home Rule Bill's eleventh hour, O'Connor warned that if ministers 'departed one hair's breadth from the straight and the loyal course to Ireland', the government would face a solid combination of every Liberal, Labour and nationalist vote in the House of Commons against it, and it would be forced to break up by condemnation of its own supporters.[144]

The dissonance between the demand of popular Liberalism, as expressed by Liberal journalists, and its practical delivery could hardly have been starker. In contrast to 1905/06, when Asquith had taken the lead in mounting the defence of free-trade principles, the Liberal rank and file looked in vain for leadership against a Unionist assault on the core of Liberal belief. There was outrage against Tory intrigues, but also against the hesitancy and expediency at the head of the Liberal Party. For a great many supporters, Liberalism was nothing if not the politics of conviction; detachment from ideology was causing a fissure to open up between leaders and led.

4

Tug of War

With the adoption of amended financial clauses in the autumn of 1912, the Home Rule Bill escaped what was anticipated to be the principal threat it faced. The measure passed the House of Commons on 16 January 1913, only to be heavily defeated in the House of Lords two weeks later. Under the 1911 Parliament Act, the Upper Chamber's veto was now merely suspensory; if the Home Rule Bill passed the Commons in its original form twice more in successive parliamentary sessions, it would become law. A drawback of the Parliament Act meant that any amendment of the Home Rule Bill to accommodate the demands of north-east Ulster was dependent upon Unionist consent.[1] The new year, 1913, brought the Liberals little relief from the troubles that had plagued them in the year just ended, with 'Marconi playing the devil', as O'Connor reported to Dillon, 'and the Insurance volcano ablaze, worse than Etna'. The Liberal Party at large, he wrote, was 'very despondent'.[2]

The Marconi scandal erupted after the disclosure of Lloyd George's purchase of shares in the American Marconi subsidiary just as a large wireless telegraphy contract was being awarded to its British parent company. The heated controversy compounded a sense of ministerial overload borne of a succession of crises roiling British society. As J.A. Spender recounted, the years leading to the outbreak of war in 1914 were 'a time of extraordinary bitterness … when the most venerable institutions seemed to be tottering'.[3] The 'great unrest' of British industry that began in 1910 showed little sign of abating. For the first time, government intervened directly in industrial disputes, for the most part effectively, but the innovation seems only to have encouraged militancy and direct action. The strain of negotiation told on ministers: at the dispatch box of the House of Commons during the 1911 coalminers' strike, Asquith, after weeks engaged in talks, became so overcome that he could not continue.[4] The Dublin Lockout of 1913 (discussed in this chapter) was among the longest and most bitter strikes of the era, and the incidence of industrial disputes in Britain continued to rise, doubling in number in 1913/14 from the figure recorded in 1910. Membership of the Miners' Federation soared to 900,000, while small rail unions amalgamated into the National Union of Railwaymen; these bodies aligned in 1914 with the National Transport Workers' Federation to form a menacing triple alliance of labour, representing millions of British workers.

The year 1913 marked the peak of violent suffragette agitation, with intensifying arson and bomb attacks on public and private property, including Lloyd George's Surrey home. The shocking death of Emily Davison, trampled by the king's horse at the Epsom Derby, made headlines around the world. Uproar over the forcible feeding of imprisoned suffragettes on hunger strike led to the introduction that year of the so-called 'Cat and Mouse Act', under which hunger strikers were released but remained liable to rearrest. The militancy of Emmeline and Christabel Pankhurst's Women's Social and Political Union was a source of disquiet for many, and arguably alienated public opinion from the cause of votes for women.[5]

In some ways these discordant developments in England validated the revolutionary philosophy of the advanced nationalists of Ireland. The resort to violent direct action arising from a failure of parliamentary initiative to redress social and political grievances was viewed by a minority in Britain, as in Ireland, as a legitimate response to provocation and neglect. For the political class it was a worrying portent. The fixation of British Tories upon Ulster, and their support for extreme and unconstitutional forms of defiance, must be understood in the context of this generalised anxiety, as must the hesitancy of Liberal ministers' response to the Unionist challenge.

Courting the opposition

The House of Lords rejected the Home Rule Bill again on 15 July 1913 during its second parliamentary circuit under the terms of the Parliament Act. Liberal belief, however, that 'Ulsteria' had failed to catch fire in the British constituencies led some to conclude that the Tories had blundered in committing themselves so deeply to the Ulstermen, and to form the view that they might eventually change tack.[6] Margot Asquith, the prime minister's wife, noted in her diary in the summer of 1913 that the Orange movement seemed to be running out of steam. She wondered whether Carson's campaign in Ulster would be remembered by history at all.[7] In comparison to the many pressing issues besetting the government, the prospect of Ulster unrest seemed a remote and none-too-troubling contingency.

Unionists, however, were harrying George V with the bogey of civil war if an attempt were made to coerce the northern counties. Bonar Law and his colleagues relentlessly urged the sovereign to dissolve Parliament, asserting that public support for the government's Irish policy was doubtful.[8] The king was dismayed when the Unionist leader, under the pretence of deploring the position in which the controversy was placing the Crown, publicly declared that once the bill passed its parliamentary stages, it would be for the monarch to decide whether to grant royal assent.[9] *Spectator* editor John St Loe Strachey expressed sympathy for George V's position and disgust at fellow Unionist 'gamblers' seeking to blackmail the king for party advantage.[10]

The beleaguered king raised the issue of Ulster repeatedly with Irish Chief Secretary Augustine Birrell over the spring and summer of 1913. Birrell concealed his private misgivings, assuring the monarch that the drama being played out in Ulster was 'very artificial'.[11] Though Orange protests were not mere bluff, he said, they would not amount to civil war. The Ulstermen knew that any action to set up a provisional government would be commercially suicidal, he told the king in July. Before the Ulster Unionist leaders took any drastic step, he said, they should put forward proposals for the future administration of matters like police and education while remaining outside a Dublin parliament.[12] Lord Stamfordham, the king's private secretary, recorded the Irish chief secretary's regret that no Unionist proposal to temporarily exclude Ulster was forthcoming; in such an eventuality, Birrell suggested, Liberal Nonconformist pressure to accept such an accommodation would be irresistible.[13]

The chief secretary's outlook was darkened by RIC reports over the summer that the Ulster situation was grave, and would certainly require a military response. In August Birrell urged Asquith to signal, perhaps in the King's Speech, the government's willingness to receive proposals to exclude Ulster from the operation of Home Rule or to make special provision for its administration. Such a gesture, he suggested, would not involve a change of course for the moment, but it would assuage the consciences of Cabinet waverers not entirely out of sympathy with those who objected to a 'Papist Parliament' in Dublin and a 'Peasant proletariat in command of the Till'.[14]

If, as seems likely, Birrell had used the king as a medium of communication, the message was underlined by Sir Edward Grey a few weeks later when he told George V that if Redmond refused a scheme of 'contracting out' for

Ulster, ministers might request a dissolution and go to the country.[15] The king told Lord Lansdowne, the Unionist leader in the House of Lords, that Asquith had indicated that he was open to the possibility of separate treatment for Ulster, allowing her to be excluded for a period of five years, with a referendum on entry upon expiry of the term.[16] The premier also confided to Churchill his readiness to consider a temporary opt-out, and reportedly deputed him to speak to Bonar Law.[17] The option of temporary exclusion, in hazy terms, thus emerged in the summer of 1913 as the government's preferred formula to deal with Ulster agitation.

Lord Loreburn sought to revive the Unionist groundswell for Home Rule all round of 1910. His much commented upon letter to *The Times* on 11 September, calling for a conference on the Home Rule question, intensified demands for talks.[18] The chief secretary dismissed the letter to Dillon as 'a douche of cowardly nonsense' likely to harden radical feeling against compromise.[19] To his chief, however, Birrell repeated his fears that Home Rule would be accompanied by violence, and recommended that a dissolution prior to the bill receiving the royal assent be considered.[20] A memorandum for the Cabinet from Sir Louis Dane, former lieutenant governor of the Punjab, diagnosed serious troubles. From a fact-finding tour of Ireland, Dane concluded that a general election might not be enough to satisfy opinion in Ulster, and foresaw the sectarian divide deepening, splitting the police and army.[21]

In answer to the king, who was pressing Asquith to obtain a popular mandate for Home Rule, the prime minister supplied masterful arguments against dissolution or a conference on tactical and constitutional grounds. The government, he maintained, was entirely open to discussion of additional safeguards for Ulster provided Unionists would concede a parliament in Dublin with an executive responsible to it. The monarch's preoccupation with Ulster, Asquith warned, risked his overlooking the much more formidable threat of disorder in the rest of Ireland should the Home Rule Bill be rejected.[22]

In an informal conversation with Churchill, Bonar Law indicated a willingness to compromise along exclusionary lines signalled by leading Liberals. The opposition leader opened up the possibility of federal Home Rule and an imperial assembly contingent upon the exclusion of Ulster from a Dublin parliament. He submitted that exclusion need not be permanent, and that provision for the voluntary accession of Ulster could be retained. Bonar Law suggested to Churchill that discussions might be broadened to cover a range of subjects, holding out the possibility of a revival of Lloyd George's 1910 coalition scheme.[23]

Asquith showed no interest in reviving improbable coalition talks, and remained sceptical of conference proposals.[24] Redmond publicly responded to the Loreburn initiative at Cahersiveen, County Kerry on 28 September, offering to discuss any detail of the Home Rule Bill with Sir Edward Carson. The acceptance of the principle of a subordinate parliament with an executive responsible to it was, however, a prerequisite to any discussion. Redmond insisted that a wholesale reopening of the question of Home Rule was out of the question.[25]

Tentative consensus

Lloyd George received intelligence from a *Daily Chronicle* correspondent in September 1913 that the Ulster Unionist movement was on the verge of collapse and that given 'sufficient rope ... they will hang themselves'.[26] From the same source he learned of Erskine Childers' view that the Orange movement was 'on its very last legs'.[27] Birrell, too, was receiving reports that enthusiasm for resistance in north-east Ulster was cooling, particularly in rural areas.[28] Amid perceptions that Unionist momentum was slowing, the advice in Cabinet of the former war secretary, Lord Haldane, that troops should be sent to Ulster in a precautionary display of force may have seemed a provocative overreaction.[29]

In Dublin, a bitter lockout of the city's tramway workers was sidelining the Irish Party and the Home Rule Bill. *The Irish Times* gleefully repeated Jim Larkin's pronouncement that 'Home Rule does not put a loaf of bread in anybody's pocket.'[30] Dillon privately expressed the wish that William Martin Murphy of the Dublin United Tramways Company and Larkin of the Irish Transport and General Workers' Union would annihilate one another. He thought, however, that any intervention in the dispute by the party could only do harm.[31] The reluctance of the senior figures of the Irish Party to intervene was probably due to their unfamiliarity with industrial disputes, and to their uneasiness about the deterioration of labour relations more generally.[32] Birrell reported to Asquith that the labour dispute had uncovered 'depths below Nationalism and the Home Rule Movement' that might sweep the constitutional nationalists away in Dublin were an election held any time soon.[33] The chief secretary contrasted the chaos in Dublin with the orderliness of Belfast in a report of conditions in the latter to Asquith, characterising the city as

... a great Protestant effort, with a Town Hall as fine as Glasgow or

Manchester and shrewd level-headed business men managing its affairs, you realise what a thing it is you are asking these conceited, unimaginative Protestant citizens to do, when you expect them to throw in their lot with such a place as Dublin, with its fatuous and scandalous Corporation and senseless disputes about the Irish language![34]

In London, Unionist leaders continued to signal a desire to compromise. F.E. Smith raised the prospect of a wider field of cooperation to Lloyd George, and to his friend Winston Churchill, if Ulster exclusion were conceded. 'Do not attach too much importance to our speeches at the moment', Smith confided to the Chancellor, suggesting that Unionist claims were being set high in anticipation of negotiations.[35] Meeting F. Harcourt Kitchin, editor of the *Glasgow Herald* and an intimate of Bonar Law's, Lloyd George expressed willingness to let Ulster vote itself out of Home Rule if the Unionists proposed an exclusion amendment.[36] To Smith, the Chancellor of the Exchequer responded with cautious warmth, referring to the possibilities of a conference to broaden Liberal/Unionist cooperation: 'You know how anxious I have been for years to work with you & a few others on your side. I have always realised that our differences have been very artificial & do not reach the "realities".'[37] Whatever else remained indistinct, the overtures of the early autumn of 1913 signalled to the Unionist leaders that ministers intended exclusion of 'Ulster', in some form, to serve as the basis for a settlement.

To clarify where the nationalist leaders stood, Asquith deputed Lloyd George to communicate the gist of what was cast as Unionist intimations to O'Connor, whom the Chancellor met on 7 October. Lloyd George affected to be unenthusiastic for a conference, and professed to have proposed giving the option of exclusion to Ulster at the start in the expectation that the offer would be refused. He indicated that he still felt it would have been a good tactic. Acting on his own initiative, O'Connor gave the Chancellor a memorandum pointing out the 'absolute impossibility' of the nationalists supporting Ulster exclusion, and stating that they would oppose the government if it were to be contemplated.[38]

O'Connor wrote to Devlin that, from what he had gathered, Carson was 'ready to accept almost anything that would save his face', and that the Irish Party leaders ought to prepare a compromise formula for the four Protestant-majority counties, such as an offer of control over education, in order to ease a climbdown. For the moment, he said, 'the best policy is to allow these gentlemen to stew a little longer in their own juice'. He urged Redmond to wire

Asquith immediately to 'put a bridle' on Churchill, due to speak in Dundee the following day, for fear that he might publicly propose exclusion.[39] Dillon reassured O'Connor that the nationalist position was strong; he believed, he said, that Carsonism was played out, and that the 'Ulster campaign has done us a great deal of good'.[40] 'Our policy', Dillon had written earlier, 'is clearly to sit tight.'[41] 'My judgment', he wrote, 'goes with Redmond in not committing ourselves beforehand'; to do more risked being misconstrued or opening the door to terms beyond limits acceptable to nationalists.[42]

Churchill indeed gave the first public hint of the substance of the private discussions with Unionists. His speech in Dundee on 8 October indicated receptivity, in a vague way, to temporary exclusion for north-east Ulster. T.P. O'Connor complained to Dillon that 'ministers were left without guidance as to what Redmond's views were and wobbled'. The Chancellor, dining with O'Connor a few days later, dissembled shamelessly. He affected that the Cabinet's rejection of his exclusionary proposal in February 1912 had disposed of the idea, but that Redmond's prolonged silence left the impression that his opposition to exclusion was merely perfunctory. He dismissed Churchill as longing for the society of his former 'pals'.[43] Lloyd George insisted that the Liberal rank and file would stand by Home Rule as it stood, telling O'Connor, 'Redmond represents the views of Radicals today.' O'Connor may have detected flattery, and he contradicted this view, saying that radicals whom he had met feared that all would be lost unless something was conceded, while 'Lib-Tories' were hot for action against Carson.[44]

Redmond expanded upon his position in a speech at Limerick on 12 October. Calling Ulster exclusion impracticable, and a mutilation of Ireland to which nationalists would never assent, he pledged that there were few lengths to meet northern objections to which he would not go to secure a united Ireland.[45] Dillon thought the speech rendered the idea of exclusion 'dead beyond all possibility of resurrection', going so far as to place Ulster behind the Dublin labour conflict, a Cork by-election, and by-elections in Britain on a list of threats to Home Rule.[46] As this confident prediction was being made, O'Connor reported that Lloyd George had suggested a plan to him to temporarily exclude Ulster for a period of five years, with automatic entry to the Dublin parliament at its end.[47] Meeting Birrell, however, Redmond indicated that he was inclined to concede an autonomous administrative body for Ulster. Birrell derived the impression that 'Devlin &c.' – usually used by the Liberal leaders to refer to the Irish Party's advanced nationalist rivals, whom Devlin was mistakenly thought to represent – were on Redmond's mind, but despite the ongoing labour dispute in Dublin, he found the Irish Party chairman quite cheerful.[48]

Asquith, meanwhile, initiated a series of secret discussions with Bonar Law and Carson, meeting them individually at sporadic intervals over the course of three months. At the first of the meetings, on 14 October, Bonar Law admitted the utility of Ulster as an electoral card, and predicted that his diehards would go to great lengths – even to the point of tampering with the army – to push the issue to the limit. He suggested that a compromise might be found in temporarily excluding Ulster from the operation of Home Rule while granting it to the rest of Ireland. Asquith rejoined that all leaders in Ireland were against this solution, but he did not dissent from the opposition leader's assertion that they were all '(more or less) bluffing'. The two men discussed the geographical area that might, hypothetically, be excluded, with the Unionist leader noncommittal, but Asquith making it clear that he had in mind the four north-eastern counties only.[49]

The Cabinet was in confident mood. Its meeting on Ulster strategy on 17 October was friendly and harmonious and its decisions unanimous. The prime minister was 'emphatic that no concession was due to Ulster threats, and none should be given', but it was agreed by all present that if the Tories would consent to offer 'a permanent settlement based on an Irish Parliament and Executive, we [the Cabinet] would go [to] any lengths to meet them'.[50] This resolution was made public in Asquith's speech at Ladybank in Fife on 25 October. This apparent determination of the Cabinet was in fact no clearer than Churchill's conciliatory plea, and was considerably less so than Redmond's unequivocal demand for a united Ireland. The incoherence of government policy was further advertised by Sir Edward Grey floating the idea of Home Rule within Home Rule (a scheme to grant a degree of autonomy to Ulster) in a speech at Berwick.[51] O'Connor was satisfied, however, that as long as ministers knew that the Irish members 'mean business about the four counties' and would sooner accept the postponement of Home Rule than a policy of exclusion, their cause was safe.[52]

Asquith received confused reports from Ulster. Meeting a northern Presbyterian minister, the prime minister heard that Carsonism was in decline, and that its landlord and capitalist leaders were 'laughed at' by working men.[53] At the same time, Birrell's advice was becoming more consistently alarmist. At the beginning of October, he wrote to Asquith of the earnestness of the Ulstermen's intent, asserting that the government must be prepared to put down the threat or seek an electoral mandate.[54] By month's end he was convinced of the urgency of finding a solution while Protestant and Catholic leaders still exercised control of their respective mobs. The situation could be contained up to the passage of the bill, he wrote to Asquith, but

> *Then* – if so much as a single Papist dog barks triumph – *blood will flow*. At the *bottom* the moving passion is *hatred* & *contempt* for the *Papist* as a *Papist*; at the top, it is *contempt* & *fear* of the Papist as a *man of business*. I don't think it is possible to *exaggerate* the *strength* of these top & bottom emotions, & if the Protestants *don't* fight, it will simply be because they can't … they will do whatever hatred can.[55]

This report informed the prime minister's position at his second private interview with Bonar Law on 6 November. Both men acknowledged that they could speak neither for their colleagues nor their adherents. The Irish nationalists, Asquith noted, had 'new and bolder spirits of whom Devlin is the type' hanging on their flank.[56] The premier dismissed the Unionist leader's suggestion of a general election on the grounds that an embittered campaign would create more bad blood than already existed. He suggested, however, that discussion might proceed on the hypothetical basis of a Dublin legislature and executive 'minus' an area to be excluded temporarily. Asquith minimised the administrative and financial difficulties attendant upon exclusion. Bonar Law suggested that a plebiscite of the whole of the excluded area (in which, he thought, Carson would insist upon including the counties of Tyrone and Fermanagh) might determine its future after a prescribed time.[57] He firmly ruled out automatic inclusion or any form of Home Rule within Home Rule.[58]

Asquith, meeting Lord Stamfordham later the same day (6 November 1913), reported that 'a tolerably clear basis has been agreed upon … an Irish Parliament and Executive in Dublin with the temporary exclusion of Ulster'.[59] To the king, the prime minister wrote that he had undertaken to report the substance of the discussion to the Cabinet and, subject to his colleagues' approval, 'confidential steps might be taken by Mr Birrell to sound out the nationalist leaders'.[60] Given the apparently categorical terms of Asquith's own accounts of the meeting, and the fact that his inclination to temporarily exclude Ulster was well known to senior Unionists, Bonar Law can hardly be blamed for expecting that an offer along these lines was shortly to be forthcoming.

For the Unionist leader, a presumptive deal was not politically advantageous: its consummation would be a triumph for the government, while it would deprive his party of its principal electioneering issue. On the other hand, Bonar Law felt sure that Asquith would have to concede a general election if the nationalists baulked at a settlement. If the Unionists won, he intended that their first act upon assuming office would be the passing of legislation cutting Irish representation at Westminster by almost half. Then, he confidently predicted to Stamfordham, 'we should hear no more of Home Rule'.[61]

Asquith revealed the fact and content of his conversations with Bonar Law to the Cabinet on 12 November. J.A. Pease complained that angry constituents had heckled him over the imprisonment of Jim Larkin while Carsonites went unpunished. Charles Hobhouse, supported by Reginald McKenna, Walter Runciman and John Burns, demanded action to deal with Carson.[62] Ministers agreed that the temper of the Liberal Party was increasingly opposed to compromise: the consensus was that 'the rank and file wholly disbelieves in the reality of Ulster threats'.[63] Birrell undertook to distribute a memorandum from the Attorney General for Ireland regarding statutory powers to deal with incipient rebellion.[64]

Despite the uncompromising mood of Liberals in the country, Lloyd George attempted to sway his senior colleagues in the opposite direction that evening. He hosted Asquith, Haldane, Grey and Crewe to dinner at 11 Downing Street: all the invitees were friends and former Liberal Imperialist colleagues of the prime minister. Birrell was notably absent. The Chancellor, brushing aside Grey's preference for an offer of Home Rule within Home Rule, pressed his scheme for the temporary exclusion of Ulster with automatic inclusion at the end of an unspecified term. Such an offer, he insisted, would deny the Ulstermen moral justification for rebellion, and stand the Liberals in good stead with British opinion. Lloyd George noted that the gathering assented to the plan, to Asquith's satisfaction.[65]

The Chancellor reintroduced the formula of exclusion of the 'Protestant counties' of Ulster in Cabinet the following day, proposing automatically terminable exclusion of five or six years. He emphasised the potential of such an offer to defuse violent rebellion and to give the British electorate two opportunities to register its verdict on exclusion. After a grant of Home Rule to the rest of Ireland, he suggested, Ulster might swiftly become a stale issue. Birrell objected that exclusion was desired by no section of opinion in Ireland and would be unworkable; Morley countered that Home Rule could not be inaugurated in bloodshed. The Chancellor's proposal met with support, and ministers agreed that discussions should be opened with Redmond.[66] Deeply unhappy with the decision to exchange *pourparlers* with the Irish Party chairman, Birrell pleaded with Asquith to be released from his office, which, he said, 'all of a sudden has become extraordinarily distasteful to me'.[67] The premier persuaded him to withdraw his resignation, and wrote to Redmond, inviting him to a meeting.[68]

'Redmond was the obstacle'

Redmond called at 10 Downing Street on 17 November. The situation in Ulster, Asquith told him, was serious and likely to worsen. He claimed, untruthfully, that Bonar Law was demanding 'total and permanent exclusion'.[69] The premier asked Redmond to consider a settlement by consent with a view towards 'the prevention, or at any rate the postponement, of the bloody prologue'. It was to this latter point, Asquith told the nationalist leader, that the plan to exclude Ulster for a fixed period was directed. Redmond replied that if the proposal were put forward at the last moment, as the price of an agreed settlement, he would consider it, but that he could not contemplate it at the present stage. Asked how far he would go to conciliate Ulster feeling, the Irish Party chairman replied (in Asquith's account) that he would concede a local legislative council, additional representation in both houses of the Irish parliament, and broadened powers for the senate.[70] This, more or less, amounted to the already rejected proposal of Home Rule within Home Rule.

Redmond omitted mention of these possible concessions in his record of the meeting, and interpreted Asquith's motives rather differently. The prime minister, he recorded, would not countenance Bonar Law's request for the total and permanent exclusion of Ulster, and he wrote that the Cabinet had discussed the five-year exclusion plan not in the expectation that it would be accepted but as a means of forestalling violence. Asquith, Redmond noted, said that he did not favour a temporary exclusion amendment, because he expected the Irish and Labour members would abstain and that twenty to thirty Liberals would vote against it. The premier assured him, he recorded, that he would 'make no proposal without consulting the nationalists and would not dream of making any proposal before next June'.[71]

Lloyd George met Dillon twice the same day, and was intrigued to discern that Dillon's chief objection to a temporary exclusion offer was one of timing, not principle. Dillon, he noted, considered that the concession might be tactically helpful if it were proposed as the bill was completing its parliamentary circuit; the nationalist leaders could then point to Home Rule as an established fact, with Ulster only temporarily excluded. The Chancellor agreed, but countered that if the intention to offer a concession was announced, 'Unionist rowdyism' would be made more difficult until the nature of the proposals were known.[72]

Asquith continued to receive visitors from Ulster. One told him that 'Ulster [was] full of men who want a [*sic*] honourable excuse for getting out of an impossible position', but that to concede anything too soon might do harm.[73] A deputation from Belfast, led by the chairman of the local trades council, presented the premier with a memorial attesting that working men had been pressured to sign the Ulster Covenant, and that only ten to twenty thousand of the signatories were seriously committed to the Unionist cause.[74]

Redmond sent a memorandum to the prime minister on 24 November affirming support for the Ladybank position: inviting opposition proposals while advancing none. The letter argued exhaustively against putting forward proposals that, he said, would imply weakness and create party difficulties for Liberals and nationalists. In the absence of a Liberal overture, Redmond foresaw that Bonar Law would be forced to name his price for peace. All the party difficulties that would attend a concession by the government, he wrote, would fall upon the opposition leader's head. The memorandum strongly urged that the seriousness of Ulster resistance was exaggerated, and claimed that, but for the boost it had received from conciliatory interventions such as Lord Loreburn's, agitation would have subsided altogether. Redmond expressed the conviction that concession before the stark choice of some form of compromise or enactment of the bill was confronted would only strengthen Unionist obstinacy.[75]

The prime minister read the Irish Party chairman's memorandum to the Cabinet the following week. Given that the letter made no reference to limited autonomy for Ulster or other concessions, the inference was erroneously drawn that Redmond had been overborne by his colleagues. Lord Morley said he would meet Dillon to warn him of the danger that the nationalists might face defeat of an unamended bill or its passage made impossible by violence. Ministers turned to consider the interdiction of arms bound for Ulster. Sir John Simon, the Attorney General, argued that there was no legal basis for such seizures, but Hobhouse, Churchill, McKenna and Runciman demanded that weapons should be seized with or without legal basis.[76]

Morley found that Dillon would not be moved, insisting that the moment for compromise had not arrived.[77] Lloyd George decided to press the matter vigorously with the apparently more pliable Redmond the following day. He maintained the fiction that Bonar Law had offered to accept the permanent exclusion of Ulster, and that this demanded a counter-offer. A planned seizure of ammunition in Ulster required a balancing concession, the Chancellor asserted, and he told him that the Cabinet supported temporary exclusion of four counties.[78] Redmond, in his record of the meeting, bluntly contradicted this. Lloyd George suggested that to withhold an offer when coercion was contemplated would lead to disaster for Home Rule, and for Redmond personally, because Grey, Haldane and Churchill would resign. The nationalist leader, according to his account, replied to the Chancellor that 'the consequences would not be nearly so serious as they would be for him [Lloyd George] personally – that the debacle would mean the end of his career and the end of the Liberal Party for a generation – perhaps, indeed, forever'. Lloyd George, Redmond recorded, did not challenge this:

> The disquieting thing about my interview was the impression left upon my mind that L.G. thought that, in the last resort, we would agree to anything rather than face the break-up of the Government. In view of this, I spoke to him more strongly and more frankly than, perhaps, was absolutely necessary. But I think I made an impression upon him.[79]

Redmond was satisfied that any Liberal proposal depended on nationalist support in the House of Commons. The Tories, he was sure, would oppose an exclusion amendment limited to only four counties. If the Irish Party voted against it, it would be joined by Labour, O'Brien's independent nationalists, and, as the prime minister had himself acknowledged, a section of Liberals. This relative invulnerability to ministerial pressure was, O'Connor wrote to Dillon, 'a nice situation for us'. Redmond, O'Connor related, judged that *in extremis* temporary exclusion would be better than losing the bill, but it would be very difficult to get the party at large to support it. The Irish Party chairman was prepared to take responsibility for such a decision, but only at the right time. Redmond, O'Connor told Dillon, 'thinks if Home Rule be now defeated, it is the end of the present party and of all its old leaders ... I think [he] is probably right'.[80]

Birrell, either shielding or deceiving his friend, discounted most of what the Chancellor had said when Redmond called on him. He denied that the Cabinet had discussed temporary exclusion, which could not, he maintained, be a basis for settlement. The prime minister, he said, had determined not to make a proposal. The chief secretary insisted that the Cabinet had not decided to seize arms, but only that something must be done, and he disputed the suggestion that action against the Ulster Unionists had to be accompanied by an offer. Relieved, Redmond emerged from the meeting describing the general situation as 'excellent'.[81]

In the face of nationalist stonewalling, the Cabinet opted to temporise. After a lengthy discussion on 25 November, it was decided that Asquith should inform Redmond that the government, while not making offers, would not shut the door to compromise. Ministers resolved, however, that before they took the responsibility of using force, they 'must be free to make such suggestions in regard to Ulster ... as seem to us to be advisable'.[82] Discussion turned to drilling in Ulster, and to the Attorney General for Ireland's report, which pronounced the loyalists' armed demonstrations illegal.[83] Following Birrell's disclosure of the detection of a shipment of 95,000 rounds of ammunition to Belfast, the Cabinet decided to ban the importation of arms to Ireland.[84] Sit John Simon submitted a memorandum on the legislative means to give this effect the following day, and a further discussion paper on 29 November outlined the legal basis upon which weapons and ammunition would be interdicted.[85] The importation of arms was proclaimed under the Customs and Inland Revenue Act 1879 on 5 December, but ministers decided that no action would be taken against the UVF until overt acts of violence were committed.[86]

Many nationalists were convinced that the government's ban on the importation of arms was a response to the formation of the Irish Volunteers on 25 November, a belief that has been perpetuated by historians. Redmond's biographer, Denis Gwynn, speculated that the prospect of nationalists arming themselves prompted the government to act.[87] Michael Tierney asserted that the timing of the decision indicated that ministers were more anxious about the Irish Volunteers than their loyalist counterparts.[88] Ronan Fanning opined that the Cabinet was more alarmed by the potential for nationalists to arm than the fact of Unionists already arming themselves in Ulster.[89]

The documents upon which deliberations about the arms proclamation were based, however, were concerned solely with developments in Ulster.[90] As Fanning acknowledged, the Cabinet's resolve was sealed by Birrell's report of a large quantity of ammunition bound for Belfast.[91] There had been before 25 November reports of nationalist drilling on a very small scale, but there is no evidence that ministers were aware of the inaugural meeting of the Irish Volunteers when they took their decision.[92] For their part, the Irish Party leaders initially thought of the arms ban only in terms of its application to Ulster. Dillon opposed the proclamation, seeing it as lending credence to the

Ulstermen's bluff.[93] O'Connor, on the other hand, supported action, believing that the consequences of Carsonism 'in the shape of suffragettes, Larkinism, [and] our own new corps' had infuriated Asquith, and at last spurred him to 'pounce on the ammunition'.[94]

The prime minister met Bonar Law on 10 December for further desultory talks. Irritated by Asquith's failure to follow up on the hypothetical proposals of a month earlier, the Unionist leader was disinclined to cast aside Ulster exclusion. He reaffirmed that his party considered Ulster the best electoral asset it possessed, and said that it would not give it up without a substantial concession.[95] A meeting with Carson on 16 December was somewhat more hopeful. The prime minister, who was on cordial terms with the Ulster Unionist leader, felt Carson was 'sincerely anxious for a settlement' because the business community of Ulster wished to relieve uncertainty and have the matter settled. Carson proposed that certain Ulster counties be excluded until the imperial parliament took up a broader scheme of devolution, which Asquith promised to consider.[96]

The Chancellor's persuasive efforts having proved unsuccessful with the two senior Irish Party leaders, Lloyd George turned his attention to O'Connor and Joseph Devlin. He once again argued that Home Rule might be lost in the event of a conciliatory offer not being put on the table. Devlin rejected exclusion entirely, with O'Connor's agreement, but said that Redmond's proposal of local autonomy for Ulster might be considered on a temporary basis. While disliking the setting up of structures that might prove difficult to dismantle, Lloyd George said that if this was the solution the nationalist leaders suggested, it was not for him to overrule it.[97] The result was the 'Suggestions' memorandum that Asquith sent to Carson on 23 December, which proposed administrative autonomy for an undefined area of Ulster, provision for local control of specified services, and powers of appeal to Westminster. The prime minister's covering letter informed Carson that the nationalist leaders knew nothing about the 'Suggestions'; this, while strictly true, was disingenuous as to the proposals' provenance.

Patricia Jalland's view that Asquith had no serious expectation that his proposals would be accepted is convincing. Her assertion, however, that they served as a diversionary cover for the real plan of exclusion is less so, given that the exclusion proposal had been known to Unionists since September, and had been explicitly raised by Asquith during his interview with Bonar Law on 6 November.[98] The 'Suggestions' seem to have been not so much a ruse aimed at the Unionists as an initiative conceived to undermine Redmond's position. Having spent a month preparing the ground for his exclusionary proposal with the nationalist leaders, Asquith hoped to force their hand. If a manifestly inadequate proposal elicited a Unionist counter-offer of temporary exclusion, Asquith probably calculated that his negotiating leverage with Redmond would be greatly fortified.

Yet advancing proposals would have placed the Unionist leaders at a political disadvantage, and they were well aware that the 'Suggestions' were hardly the government's last word. Bonar Law left the November meeting with Asquith with the not unwarranted impression that the prime minister would gain his colleagues' sanction for negotiation of an exclusionary scheme, and that Asquith would inform Redmond of ministerial policy. When this did not happen, and the meagre 'Suggestions' followed, the Unionist leader was annoyed, concluding, correctly, as he complained to Lord Stamfordham, that 'Redmond was the obstacle'.[99]

The nationalist leaders, not unreasonably, wanted Home Rule on the terms outlined in the bill. Redmond believed that pressure upon his opponents to concede would increase as passage of the bill grew nearer and, failing this, if the government held its resolve, a settlement could be put before the Unionists on a 'take it or leave it' basis at the last moment. The strategy was predicated upon the assumption that tensions in Ulster would ease as the inevitability of Home Rule became plain. This view was reinforced by a belief that the Unionist movement lacked broad-based support and was losing momentum, which was consistent, on balance, with the messages that Asquith was hearing from Ulster deputations.

Lloyd George, however, was not inclined to receive information from Ulster in a congenial light, and drew the opposite conclusion as to prospective conditions in the province as the bill's passage approached. He favoured a settlement, or if a basis for one could not be found, making an offer to take the wind from the Ulster Unionists' sails. Such a gesture would provide political cover, if needed, for the enactment of the bill in the face of resistance. Dillon, the pessimist among the nationalist leaders, was persuaded by the Chancellor's arguments. He appreciated the advantage of seizing the initiative from the Ulstermen, but he foresaw, too, that by-election losses might prompt the Tories to make an unacceptable offer. The Irish Party might find itself squeezed between Liberal pressure to concede to an apparently reasonable demand and Irish popular feeling that would reject it altogether. It might, he reflected, be better to have a barely acceptable offer already on the table than to have it pre-empted by a worse one.[100]

1914

'We are bound to be in for a strenuous and turbulent time', the prime minister wrote to his wife early in the new year, 'and I can see that whatever is to be done to steer & even save the ship, I shall do myself. L[loyd] George has no judgment, Winston is self-absorbed, Grey has very little outlook & Haldane's is completely obscured by mists & clouds.'[101] The Cabinet was racked by a ministerial dispute over naval expenditure that seemed for a time to threaten a break-up. Churchill was pressing for a budgetary increase of £10 million for new Dreadnought-class battleships; the Chancellor of the Exchequer, supported by many of his colleagues, objected to such extravagance. The row intertwined with and rather confused the Cabinet debate about Ulster, because the naval dispute aligned the strongest advocate of exclusion, Lloyd George, with the policy's most vocal opponents in the Cabinet.[102] A collapse was avoided when Lloyd George relented over the naval estimates in February, and persuaded the 'economists' to agree a slightly reduced sum for new warships.

Carson, having rejected Asquith's suggestion of modified Home Rule within Home Rule, met the prime minister for a second time, on 2 January. The two men were in agreement, Asquith recorded, 'that the real difference (not the less formidable on that account) was one of "sentiment"'. The problem was reconciling the sentiment of one side, which demanded, as Asquith termed it, 'veiled exclusion', with that of the other side, for which a 'veiled' arrangement would not satisfy. Though Carson offered to consider how accommodation acceptable to the nationalists might be found, both men recognised that 'the rock of "sentiment"' might not be circumnavigated.[103] Shortly thereafter the Ulster Unionist leader wrote to say that agreement on Ulster exclusion was a prerequisite to any proposal.[104]

John Dillon grew depressed over the position in which Home Rulers found themselves. Carsonism had been dying, he wrote to C.P. Scott, until Churchill at Dundee and Lord Loreburn's letter revived the Ulstermen's hopes. These interventions, Dillon wrote, had transformed Carson's policy into a complete success:

> ... the Liberal Party and its leaders were thoroughly frightened ... and there is always the danger in a game of bluff – that men who are not cowards – may find themselves so deeply committed – that they cannot decently turn back or give in. And of course Ulstermen like all other sections of the Irish people are not cowards.[105]

Lord Morley, too, was consumed by dark thoughts, and was coming to the conclusion that compromise was impossible. He had travelled to Donegal with Birrell in the closing weeks of 1913, and had come away with a conviction that the Covenanters had gone too far to back down, even if the politicians nominally at their head came to terms.[106] Morley believed that negotiation with leaders – Unionist and nationalist – who had lost control of their 'Janissaries' had become fruitless.[107] He wrote to Asquith of quarrels elsewhere in Ireland between Hibernians, Gaelic Leaguers and Sinn Féiners, with the result that Redmond was 'by no means out of the reach of physical peril, and knows it'.[108]

Morley forwarded a memorandum from Sir David Harrel, former under-secretary for Ireland, which asserted that opinion in the business community of Belfast had hardened considerably, and warned that a violent collision was unavoidable. All that could be done, Harrel counselled, was to make the elaborate police and military preparations as had been done in 1893, only more comprehensively so, since the Ulster Unionists knew this time that Home Rule would be passed.[109] Lord Haldane reiterated his view that overwhelming military force should be deployed in Ulster before trouble had the chance to arise.[110] There is no indication, however, that either man's precautionary advice was given serious consideration.

The prime minister confided to Lord Stamfordham his belief that the Cabinet would adopt a five- or six-year exclusion plan, with automatic accession upon expiry of the term. Such a measure might be carried over the opposition of the nationalists with Unionist consent, he felt, though he conceded that radical Liberals and the Labour Party might vote against the government. 'Already he has made offers to the opposition', Stamfordham recorded, 'which if known to the nationalists would drive them to exasperation.'[111]

With Asquith, Stamfordham raised private statements of military officers that they would refuse to fire on Ulstermen, and suggestions that many senior officers would resign.[112] The premier 'admitted the possibility of the latter contingency' but he did not believe that officers would refuse to obey orders, for fear of setting a deplorable precedent. 'The fact is there is not a spark of enthusiasm about Ulster or against Home Rule', he insisted. When it was pointed out that Unionists would say there was little enthusiasm the other way, the prime minister did not demur. 'The country', he said, 'is sick of the question.'[113]

The Cabinet that met on 22 January learned of the stalled discussions with Bonar Law and Carson. Grey believed that no further negotiation was possible until after the bill had passed, though he noted that the king was under heavy pressure to withhold his assent.[114] From his meeting with Devlin, the Chancellor inferred that he would take anything short of permanent exclusion; McKenna said that a source close to Redmond had told him the same. Ministers, Charles Hobhouse recorded, resolved to consult with the Irish as to timing, but to implement a conciliatory plan of their own choosing.[115]

The Cabinet was concerned that the king's state of perpetual anxiety might mean that he could be frightened into dismissing his ministers before the Home Rule Bill's third legislative circuit. Such an eventuality would defeat not just Home Rule but also Welsh disestablishment and the Plural Voting Bill. Lloyd George's strategy of offering terms so generous as to make rebellion impossible was an attempt to avoid this contingency and (what was feared would be) the rout of the Liberal Party. Haldane was despatched to Windsor to 'administer lubricants' to the king, and Asquith summoned Redmond.[116]

The 'bomb' discharged

Meeting the nationalist leader on 2 February, the prime minister summarised developments since the two had last met the previous November. The Cabinet, he claimed, was firmly against Ulster exclusion, even on a temporary basis. The general situation had deteriorated, however, owing largely to divisions over the navy estimates, which had engendered dissatisfaction on the Liberal back benches. The king had been pressing hard for a general election, and Asquith could foresee circumstances in which the monarch would dismiss his ministry and send for Bonar Law. Even if the Liberals were returned at the ensuing election, the prime minister warned, the legislative sequence required by the Parliament Act would have been broken, and Home Rule would have to start afresh. The crisis might be precipitated, he said, if the Unionists blocked the Army Annual Bill in the House of Lords. Such an extreme step might prompt the king to intervene.[117]

Such, Asquith told the nationalist leader, were the considerations that had led him to conclude that an offer to Ulster to deprive the Unionists of moral justification was essential. Further, he professed to Redmond that he felt certain that any offer short of exclusion would be rejected. The prime minister went on to outline the content of his 'Suggestions': administrative autonomy for Ulster, including control of education, and a grant of powers of appeal to Westminster by a majority of Ulster members of the Irish parliament. To these he added retention of the post office by the imperial authorities. Redmond immediately protested that the concessions would be taken as a substantial abandonment of the bill, and that the Unionist leaders could not accept the proposals any more than nationalists could. Asquith replied that all that he expected from the Irish Party was to make large concessions consistent with both a parliament and a responsible executive, and conservation of the integrity of Ireland, subject to the opposition's agreeing to allow the bill to pass by consent. Birrell, who was present, took little part in the uncomfortable interview.[118]

Given that an exclusionary settlement had already been discussed with the Unionists, and was in his sights, Asquith's 'veiling' of the already rejected proposition of Home Rule within Home Rule in the language of exclusion was a curious move. It might have been an effort to inch the nationalist leader closer to unambiguous exclusion, or, as Patricia Jalland speculated, a means of demonstrating to him the fruitlessness of his preferred formula.[119] That the prime minister's tactic was to soften up the 'Leviathan' is not in doubt, as indicated by his description of the meeting in an oft-quoted letter to Venetia Stanley:[120] 'I recouped the situation with such art as I could muster, until the psychological moment arrived for discharging my bomb. My visitor shivered visibly & was a good deal perturbed, but I think the general effect was salutary.'[121]

Having been told by the prime minister two months earlier that no proposal was contemplated until June, Redmond wasted no time in drafting a well-argued rebuttal of the bases for concession. He asserted that the proposals were sure to be rejected by the opposition. They would be used to claim that Home Rule had been so mutilated that it was dead, reinforcing efforts to wreck the bill, and emboldening violence or tampering with the Army Bill. The proposals would expose the Irish members to charges of betrayal at home and worsen Liberal demoralisation; their refusal by the Unionists, he argued, would create an impossible situation for both sets of supporters. He challenged Asquith as to what attitude, he, as Irish nationalist leader, was to take in debate in the House of Commons:

> Am I to accept them? Am I to reject them? It would be impossible for me to accept them, in view of the certainty that they would be rejected by the Tory speakers. Am I to reject them? Then I would give to the Tories the argument that the suggestion of the Government, rejected by them and by us, could not supply any basis for settlement by consent.[122]

Redmond again asserted that preparations for rebellion in the north were greatly exaggerated, and stressed that the Irish Party would place no obstacle in the way of assuaging even unreasonable fears of the Ulstermen. He registered 'the strongest objections' to making premature proposals, animated by a 'profound conviction that they will lead, not to advancing, but to preventing, the hopes of a settlement by consent'.[123]

Redmond may – or may not – have chosen this moment to set off a bomb of his own. The day after the interview, Birrell wrote cryptically to Redmond, 'I think he [Asquith] was momentarily startled at the numbers, but it was only a passing shock.'[124] Did this mean that the nationalist leader had estimated, for the prime minister's benefit, the number of Labour and Liberal members who would follow him into the 'No' division lobby against a concessionary offer if matters came to it? Whether the Irish Party chairman resorted to such a tactic is entirely speculative, but his 'rather unsatisfactory communication' was read to the Cabinet on 5 February, and the chief secretary, Redmond recorded, told him that his views would be respected.[125] Birrell, however, counselled Redmond that Asquith still favoured making a general statement of intent to grant administrative autonomy to Ulster and some form of legislative veto. He cautioned the nationalist leader that ministers would soon make up their minds about what ought to be offered to Ulster. They would insist on making an offer, he believed, not in the hope of acceptance but to ease their consciences.[126]

Carson's 11 February appeal to nationalists to win over their northern countrymen exercised a powerful effect on Liberals (and, indeed, upon John Redmond), heightening the mood for accommodation.[127] Lloyd George revived the exclusion proposal, garbed in new arguments. The government's difficulties, he argued to his colleagues, were exacerbated by the need for an amending bill so that the original bill could pass under the Parliament Act. The problem, as framed by the Chancellor, was that if the Unionists objected to an amending bill, the government would be forced to coerce Ulster into a scheme that they had already conceded ought to have been amended. What was needed, the Chancellor asserted, was a proposal, 'the rejection of which would place the other side entirely in the wrong'. County-by-county plebiscites on accession, after an interval sufficient to allow for a general election, would extend an opportunity for Unionists, if they won, to make exclusion permanent. The Ulstermen, Lloyd George reasoned, would not 'rise up in rebellion against future oppression which a Unionist general election win might prevent anyway'. Rejection of such an offer, the Chancellor argued, would shift responsibility for any subsequent disorder onto Unionists.[128]

Devlin circulated a memorandum asserting that the threats of the Ulster

Volunteers were 'grossly exaggerated' and that Home Rulers in the north were 'astonished that anyone outside Belfast' took them seriously.[129] Lloyd George, in reply, claimed that intelligence reports in his possession indicated that the nationalists understated the risk of civil strife. Whether there would be riots or something worse, he argued, the government faced the prospect of bloodshed if it proceeded with the bill as it stood. This 'was so obviously to the advantage of the Unionist Party', he wrote, 'that I cannot imagine their missing any opportunity of fomenting it.' The county option proposal, with plebiscites after a period of exclusion, the Chancellor insisted, promised a means to escape rioting or insurrection by deferring the realisation of Ulster Protestant fears. It would have the additional virtue, Lloyd George asserted, of allowing the Irish parliament to overcome its early difficulties and to establish itself without rancour.[130]

In Dublin, T.P. Gill belatedly recognised the seriousness of the threat that Ulster posed to the bill, and resumed his behind-the-scenes influencing efforts. He wrote to Canadian premier Robert Borden, suggesting that a conference of imperial leaders might calm the situation, and that Canada's example of unity under self-government might be offered as a model to the empire.[131] Borden replied with a memorandum about minority rights in Quebec.[132] Gill sought the advice of W.G.S. Adams. Adams considered that the greatest safeguard that could be extended was a veto to exclude Ulster from any legislation enacted by the Irish parliament. He suggested amendments to water down provisions for control over the police and judiciary and customs-varying powers, and to provide for retention of full Irish representation at Westminster, both because it might be argued that Ulster's rights were being diminished, and because the Irish parliament's purview would be so curtailed.[133] Gill wrote to Redmond endorsing these suggestions as workable and preservative of the integrity of Ireland and of the Irish Party's position, both of which were under threat.[134] His advice, however, was overtaken by events.

Lloyd George and Birrell met Redmond, Dillon and Devlin on 27 February to press the nationalist leaders to accept county option of temporary exclusion. The ministers again predicted that the House of Lords would amend the Army Bill to forbid the use of troops in Ulster, resulting in disruption of the armed forces across the empire. This would precipitate a general election, and the Home Rule Bill would be lost. Lloyd George and Birrell insisted that permanent exclusion was desired in neither Ireland nor England, and that the government proposed temporary exclusion for three years, by county poll, *conditional* upon acceptance of Home Rule for the rest of Ireland. Concessions on the judiciary and post office were also contemplated. The Cabinet believed, they said, that the Unionists would reject the offer for domestic political reasons. The Chancellor and the chief secretary assured the nationalist leaders that this was the limit of what they were prepared to offer, and that they would not ask them to go further. With extreme reluctance, Redmond conceded that if the Unionists accepted the offer, the Irish Party might yield under protest. However, he warned that if it were rejected, his party could not be expected to vote for it.[135] The Chancellor, Redmond noted, assured the Irishmen that the scheme 'would be the last word of the Government; and that, if it were rejected, they were prepared and determined to proceed with the Bill as it stands forthwith, and to face any consequences in Ulster that might result'.[136] Lloyd George told Margot Asquith that Redmond 'all but wept' when he realised the magnitude of the concession, so odious was it to nationalists.[137]

The ministers conveyed this information to the Cabinet, and met the nationalist leaders again a few days later, this time joined by O'Connor. Lloyd George and Birrell said that the prime minister agreed with the nationalist leader's reservations from their previous meeting, and stressed that the Irish Party would not in any circumstance be expected to vote for a temporary partition of Ireland. As the offer was conditional upon Unionist consent to the rest of the bill, the amendment would involve no division in the House of Commons. Redmond was, not surprisingly, particularly insistent that the offer would be a final one, and recorded Lloyd George's undertaking in this regard: 'He gave us the most emphatic assurance, saying he had "placed his life upon the table & would stand or fall by the agreement come to". He assured us also that this was the attitude of the P.M.'[138]

The Cabinet, doubtless with some relief, adopted the county option scheme. Birrell, dissatisfied with the decision, again tendered his resignation to Asquith, which was once again refused.[139] Redmond wrote to the prime minister outlining his conditions. The nationalists, he said, insisted that the Unionists must bear full responsibility for the offer's acceptance. The Irish Party's agreement was also conditional on its being the government's last word; if the offer were rejected, he said, they should pass the bill as it stood, and face the consequences in Ulster.[140] Asquith replied that the Cabinet agreed to the conditions stipulated without tying its hands with regard to 'details' in negotiation.[141]

Redmond despatched Devlin to canvass views and secure support in Ulster. Devlin reported that Home Rulers in Belfast would probably submit, but 'not with the best grace'.[142] He had satisfactory meetings with the bishops of Derry and Letterkenny, and on 6 March he met twenty prominent men of the four counties at the Linen Hall Hotel.[143] The national president of the AOH, executives of the UIL, county councillors, JPs and clergy were represented. There was unanimity of opinion, Devlin reported, that everything that could be done had been done. The Irish Party, he wrote, would have behind it not the grudging acquiescence of these influential men but their 'unqualified approval and support'. 'I am quite certain that, wherever else trouble may arise', Devlin assured his chief, 'none will come from the northeast corner.' MacVeagh met with Cardinal Logue, the archbishop of Armagh, to explain the situation.[144] Though temporary exclusion may have been accepted in the expectation of its refusal, the party's leaders were carefully preparing the ground in the event that it should come to pass.

The Chancellor's extravagant protestations of fidelity notwithstanding, Asquith and Lloyd George had no intention of being bound by their promises to Redmond, and set about prying his terms apart. The three-year exclusion period was swiftly extended to six years on the pretext that the need for two general elections to intervene had only just occurred to Asquith.[145] A six-year term had in fact been discussed in Cabinet since the autumn, and was anticipated by Bonar Law in December.[146] The exclusionary offer was thus being prepared not in anticipation of rejection, as Lloyd George had claimed, but to conform to the Unionist leader's demands. Even as he gave assurances to Redmond, the prime minister confided to Lord Stamfordham that if the Tories held out for exclusion of six counties and wished to dispense with plebiscites, 'no doubt the Government would be prepared to bargain on these terms'.[147] Asquith appears to have had few qualms about carving up Ireland to appease the Unionists, or about leaving Redmond and his colleagues to the tender mercies of their political rivals in Ireland.

Asquith's emollient manner and affectation of frankness concealed his less than honourable intentions from the nationalist leader. Redmond's biographer asserted that the Irish Party chairman had absolute confidence in Asquith's integrity, a conviction to which, if Margot Asquith is to be believed, he tearfully attested on one occasion.[148] Such faith was, with hindsight, misplaced; and it is difficult to escape the conclusion that Asquith exploited Redmond's trust and sense of honour in order to deceive him. The nationalist leader's dignity, and the political leverage that he wielded, may have led him to believe that he enjoyed a relationship of mutual respect with Asquith where, it appears, none existed.

As the character of Asquith's relations with Redmond became increasingly adversarial, the premier's attitude towards the Unionist leaders remained collegial. Doubtless social class and national identity played a part in this. Asquith was condescending towards those whom he regarded as social or intellectual inferiors – he had private nicknames for Edwin Montagu, Bonar Law and Redmond, but none for Grey, Balfour or Crewe.[149] To Crewe, the prime minister confided that he felt no great warmth for Redmond, but it is unknown if he shared his wife's mild distaste for the Irish themselves.[150] Asquith was on congenial terms with Carson. Though an Irishman, Sir Edward Carson, a prominent London barrister and solidly middle class, was representative of the type of man with whom the premier was accustomed to dealing.[151] By contrast, Redmond was the leader of a party resented by the British establishment, and even by some of Asquith's ministerial colleagues, as an alien band of parliamentary upstarts.

Historians have levelled charges of naivety at the Irish Party leaders for conceding temporary exclusion at all. Patrick Maume argued that by agreeing to temporary exclusion that might easily have become permanent, Redmond and Dillon unwittingly conceded permanent partition at this juncture.[152] Such judgements must be tempered by consideration of the Irish Party leaders' thinking as to the result of county plebiscites. The decision to accept county polls was predicated on the assumption that nationalist majorities in counties Tyrone and Fermanagh would prevail, and Redmond maintained to Asquith that he considered it by no means certain that all four Protestant-majority counties would opt out.[153] The smaller the territory to which Ulster resistance could be reduced, the nationalist leaders reasoned, the less practicable its continuation would become. Limitation of the geographical area to be excluded, based on majoritarian calculation, was to be the safeguard of impermanence.[154]

This reckoning did not consider the passions of Ulster Protestants, nor the extent of their determination to resist. The notable absence of discussion of Ulster in the correspondence of the nationalist leaders (save for rosy reports from Devlin, and more cautious, but still optimistic, assessments from Gill) underlines their dismissive attitude. The notion of conflicting identities in Ireland was one that was privately rejected and publicly ridiculed by the Irish Party leaders as an instrument to wreck Home Rule. Such complacency is indicative of the nationalist leaders' entrenched assumptions: of the righteousness of their cause, a belief that no challenge to a unitary polity of Ireland could be legitimate, and faith in the pre-eminent rights of majorities.

These convictions served the nationalists' political ends, and could also be conceptually justified; their justice in practice, however, relied upon the unassailability of the concepts of a unitary Irish nation and majoritarian democracy. Such assumptions were contested by Unionists, who disputed the government's right to forcibly deprive a minority community in Ireland of their settled and consensual form of government. In the context of the Irish-Ireland parochialism of the first decades of the twentieth century, with its implication that Protestants must accept subordination and absorption in a Catholic-nationalist Ireland, the fears of Protestant Ulster were real enough.[155] Richard Bourke argued that the inherent injustice of coercing the Protestants of north-east Ulster, however democratic the method of their compulsion might appear to be, was a fundamental obstacle in the way of Irish self-government. Its circumnavigation, he asserted, demanded a settlement by consent.[156]

Paul Bew and Alvin Jackson, echoing Stephen Gwynn, both highlighted the placatory effect upon Ulster that an early offer of indefinite exclusion might have had, had the nationalist leaders grasped the nettle. While Bew ascribed Redmond's failure of vision principally to concern for the rights of northern Catholics, Jackson acknowledged both the idea's merits in principle and its impossibility as a matter of practical politics.[157] The sensitivity of nationalist feeling in the spring of 1914 was emphasised by T.P. Gill, who wrote urging that Redmond, in his desire to pacify Ulster, should not forget the depth and volatility of passion on his own side:

> Everything in the present situation is provocative of the old Adam within the Nationalist breast. I feel it myself so strongly that I have to use force with myself to examine this problem in a conciliatory and constructive frame of mind. In this I am only typical of the ordinary Southern Nationalist, and this [strength] of feeling is significant and a factor in the [situation]. It constitutes a temptation and a danger.[158]

It is perhaps understandable that a broad-minded solution, however commendable it might appear with hindsight, did not present itself to leaders facing a nationalist constituency they knew to be in no mood for overly generous proposals.

In any event, the preoccupation on all sides in late 1913 and early 1914 was the area to be excluded, not its duration. The consensus of ministerial opinion had swung to exclusion of the four Protestant-majority counties of Ulster in November 1913, and Asquith's subsequent manoeuvres seem to have been aimed at inducing Redmond to concede this. Exploitation of the concession, however, hinged upon expanding the excluded area from four counties to six, the minimum acceptable to Unionists, but a proposition intolerable to the nationalists.

The prospect of imposing Ulster exclusion on terms more or less dictated by the Unionists concentrated ministerial minds on the vulnerability of their Commons majority. A sharply circumscribed measure of Home Rule might be enacted with Unionist support, but the furious indignation of radical Liberals and Irish MPs that such perfidy would unleash would render the government's viability doubtful. A forced dissolution of Parliament in such circumstances seemed probable, and Liberal reliance upon an electoral pact with the Labour Party (to avoid three-cornered contests that would advantage the Tories) suddenly loomed large. Lloyd George sought to shore up the alliance, meeting Ramsay MacDonald, the Labour Party leader, on 3 March.[159]

The Chancellor affected to believe that the contemplated conciliatory offer to Ulster would be rejected, and that the Tories would resort to tampering with the Army Annual Bill. In anticipation of a general election to decide the Home Rule issue once and for all, he told MacDonald, ministers desired a more robust electoral understanding with the Labour Party. The Chancellor stressed the danger to progressives of a Tory victory and a restoration of the veto powers of the House of Lords. He offered the Labour leader a substantial increase in members, by standing down Liberal candidates in constituencies that Labour would be likely to win. Lloyd George indicated that a legislative programme would be agreed, and he offered the Labour leaders representation in the Cabinet, if it was desired.[160]

The senior Liberals' desire for a formal coalition with Labour is suggestive of their view of their party as the senior partner in the relationship for the foreseeable future, but also of a wish to contain their would-be rivals. The promise of a joint legislative programme implied the ideological triumph of New Liberal collectivism over the laissez-faire Liberalism of old, a transition to which, Peter Clarke asserted, the introduction of old-age pensions had unmistakably pointed the way.[161] If Lloyd George's offer indeed represented the view of his colleagues, it suggested that moderates like Asquith and Grey were bowing to a reconstruction of progressive politics, if not of the Liberal Party itself, on more proletarian lines. The prospective departure foretold a generational and ideological succession, raising the possibility that one day, perhaps at the end of the next parliament in 1920, Lloyd George would take his place as Liberal leader, at the head of an ambitiously reforming progressive alliance.

The initiative also indicated the seriousness of ministers' intent to break with the nationalists, if necessary. The episode, like Lloyd George's abortive coalition scheme of 1910, is illustrative of their readiness to throw their Irish allies over in ruthless fashion. In this context, consolidation of the compact with Labour and an ideological tack to the left might have seemed an expedient means of limiting damage from the fallout. With a progressive legislative programme in view, radical Liberal disaffection might be limited to protests, rather than defections to Labour or some new grouping of the left. With the passage of the Army Annual Bill in April, however, the prospect of a general election receded, and hopes faded for a merger of radical Liberal and Labour forces, longed for by MacDonald, and by New Liberals like L.T. Hobhouse.[162]

The county option concession, so laboriously extracted from Redmond, was announced in sketchy terms before a packed and anxious House of Commons on 9 March. The proposal was rejected by the Unionist leaders in peremptory fashion, with Carson denouncing it as a 'hypocritical sham'. The reality was that all parties recognised that only the four Protestant-majority counties of Antrim, Down, Derry and Armagh were likely to vote for exclusion, which would have left the Ulster Unionists in a precariously isolated position. Asquith could hardly have hoped to have surprised the Unionists, as Jalland suggested, with a proposition that had already been privately dismissed, and Bonar Law still had no incentive to give up the issue upon which he had staked great political capital by stating Unionist terms in response.[163] Within days, Asquith confessed to Stanley that 'it looks as if the thing had broken down'.[164]

Gill advised Redmond that rejection of the exclusion offer should be made irrevocable at all costs. The nationalists, he counselled, should indicate their willingness to consider the options that remained: Home Rule within Home Rule or the Plunkett plan of exclusion by county after a trial period.[165] The former was no more palatable to Unionists than it was to the Irish Party, he said; the latter required only minor modification of the bill. The choice, Gill wrote, should be presented as the option of exclusion after a period or accepting the bill as it stood. The real value of the Liberals' short-lived offer, Gill asserted, was that it had put the bona fides of the exclusion demand to the test, and it had failed.[166]

Liberal and nationalist spirits were buoyed by a bullish speech by Churchill in Bradford in which he coupled the finality of the offer with the government's preparedness to coerce Ulster if necessary. Asquith and other observers felt that the speech's enthusiastic reception, and that accorded to Churchill himself when he next appeared in the House of Commons, was proof that the mood of the party was to see the law upheld.[167] There was near-unanimous praise for Churchill's bellicosity in Cabinet.[168] Lord Morley, however, deplored such talk, even if it did have a bracing effect on the party. 'You may talk of bloodshed', he claimed to have admonished the prime minister, 'but I venture to say that the first blood shed in Ireland … in conflict between the Ulster Volunteers and the forces of the Crown, will mean the end of Home Rule.'[169]

Proposals for compromise circulated fitfully. In the House of Commons, Bonar Law answered the county option offer with a call for a United Kingdom referendum on Home Rule, and pledged to abide by the result. Asquith, Grey and Churchill were initially attracted to the idea, but J.A. Spender of *The Westminster Gazette* rejected it as a design to subvert the Parliament Act.[170] James Douglas, editor of *The Star*, wrote to Asquith supporting a referendum, insisting that the force of objections to the idea was diminished by the fact that the principle of a plebiscite had been conceded for Ulster. Alternatively, he submitted, the government might substitute a proposal excluding Ulster pending a federal organisation of the United Kingdom. Carson, Douglas asserted, had already virtually acceded to such an arrangement.[171] The substance of these proposals was published, apparently with Asquith's blessing, in a letter to *The Times* on 25 March.[172]

The prime minister, meanwhile, volunteered to Austen Chamberlain, Bonar Law and Carson that the six-year exclusion plan could be extended to an area of six counties, with a plebiscite to be held only at the end of the exclusion term.[173] Such a scheme, with further stipulations, Bonar Law intimated to the Archbishop of Canterbury, could be accepted if it were publicly offered by the government.[174] The problem for the Cabinet, as the Unionist leaders saw it, would be inducing the nationalists to accept. They bluntly informed ministers of their belief that, had the government been 'willing or able to exercise so much pressure, they would have done so long ago'.[175]

Having signalled his willingness to exclude six Ulster counties and abandon the elective principle upon which his proposal of a fortnight earlier had been founded, the prime minister appeared ready to do what the Tories doubted that he could, and try to overbear the nationalist leader. However, there could be little disguising the fact that an attempt to impose six-county exclusion would be nothing less than outright betrayal. If Redmond exposed the duplicity, a revolt in the Liberal and Labour ranks was certain, as was an explosion of resentment in Ireland. An unlikely Liberal/Tory combination to pass Home Rule in abridged form might easily have split both parties. With Redmond humiliated, just who would carry the policy forward in Ireland it was impossible to say. For the moment, however, such questions were academic, as the Home Rule Crisis began in earnest with the 'mutiny' at the Curragh barracks.

The Curragh Incident and afterwards

Ministers continued to receive conflicting reports of conditions in Ulster throughout the spring of 1914. At the beginning of March, Asquith told his colleagues that the leaders of the Ulster movement had grown so alarmed by the fury they had whipped up that they were keen to settle.[176] Birrell asserted that the prospect of civil war in Ulster was overshadowed by the conviction of ordinary Unionists that it would never happen.[177] This complacent view was reinforced by the emboldened mood of Liberals after refusal of the conciliation offer.

A Cabinet committee was appointed on 11 March to study potential responses to Ulster Volunteer Force action.[178] The committee determined that the police in the province should be brought under a single command in Belfast, and that in the event of organised rebellion, forces would be concentrated in five or six important centres. On 14 March the Cabinet sanctioned an order to move troops north to safeguard arms depots in Armagh, Omagh, Carrickfergus and Enniskillen, which was issued to Lieutenant General Sir Arthur Paget, commander-in-chief of troops in Ireland.[179] Paget at first refused to carry out the troop movements for fear of precipitating disorder. Summoned to London by Secretary for War J.E.B. Seely for conferences at the War Office on 18 and 19 March, Paget received clearer orders as to the reinforcement of troops guarding depots. His instructions about a response to possible contingent developments, however, were more ambiguous. Paget's anxieties were deepened by Seely's hypothetical discussion of future deployments and maladroit guidance in the event of outbreaks of disorder in Ulster. In such an eventuality, Paget was told, officers domiciled in the province should be allowed to remain at their posts rather than take part in operations, but any others who refused orders, or who sought to resign, should be discharged without pensions.[180]

Paget appears to have returned to Dublin in a state of great confusion. On 20 March he addressed his seven brigade commanders in a manner that could scarcely have been more inept or at variance with his instructions. Neglecting his orders for a limited movement of troops to secure arms depots, Paget created the impression that large-scale deployments against the UVF were being commenced. Ireland, he told the assembled commanders, would be a theatre of operations the following day. He went on to state that officers who refused to obey orders would be dismissed, and that any who felt unable to comply should make this clear. This was taken by four of his seven subordinates to have been a directive that this choice should be put before their officers.[181]

Presented with this fatuous and wholly unnecessary ultimatum, most of the subordinate officers accepted their duty, whatever it might be, but fifty-eight officers under Brigadier General Hubert Gough's command at the Curragh barracks indicated that they would prefer dismissal to leading active operations against Ulster loyalists. Efforts to smooth over the affair as a misunderstanding did not placate Gough, who demanded a written pledge that his brigade would not be used to force Home Rule on Ulster. On 23 March the Cabinet authorised an assurance to the officers that Paget's questions sought only to ensure compliance with lawful orders. Under pressure from a dissatisfied Gough, however, Seely, on his own initiative, added a statement that the army would not be used to crush opposition to Home Rule. Taking the amended statement as having the Cabinet's authority, Sir John French, chief of the imperial general staff, made it categorical, and signed it on behalf of the army council.[182]

Asquith at once appreciated the scale of the debacle. The permanent secretary to the Treasury, who was with him on the weekend that the news broke, related that he had never seen the prime minister, celebrated for his sang-froid, so overcome.[183] As information filtered in, Asquith wrote to Stanley:

> The military situation has developed, as might have been expected, and there is no doubt if we were to order a march on Ulster that about half of the officers in Kilkenny – the navy is more uncertain – would strike. The immediate difficulty in the Curragh can, I think, be arranged, but that is the permanent situation, and it is not a pleasant one.[184]

Not the least of the premier's cares, as he attempted to take charge of the situation, was mollifying the king, greatly distressed by the embroilment of the army in the political controversy.[185] Though Asquith minimised the incident to his wife as 'the silliest bolt from the silliest blue', the reality of things was that he had failed to mitigate a contingency that he had admitted was not altogether unexpected.[186]

Much was made, at the time, of the 'mutiny' at the Curragh, a term that has been much debated by historians but is not generally used.[187] The opposition gleefully seized upon the public humiliation of the government, alleging a sinister plot to provoke the UVF into action in order to wipe it out.[188] The chief effect of the incident, as Birrell later conceded, was to render the reliability of the armed forces to enforce Home Rule 'somewhat dubious', but since coercion of Ulster was not contemplated except in the last resort, the exposure of this fact was less important than it seemed.[189] The troop movements sanctioned by the Cabinet were, in the event, executed without incident, and no orders were disobeyed.[190]

The development diminished the government's practical leverage over Ulster agitation, and revealed the intense hostility of army officers to their democratically elected political masters.[191] The pledges demanded by Gough seeking to limit the government's legitimate freedom of action were viewed by many Liberals as a tactic of political sabotage by the officer class. What was a matter of speculation for contemporaries has been confirmed by historians through revelation of the outrageously partisan plottings of Major General Henry Wilson to undermine the government and even his superior officers.[192] If mutiny there was, it was the shadowy mutiny of senior generals in London and Aldershot that was surely of the greatest significance, as Liberals and their progressive allies were coming to realise.

The following Monday, 23 March, a 'red hot House' heard allegations of plots and countercharges, most energetically argued from the government benches by John Ward, Lib-Lab MP.[193] Seely's statement that the army would not be used to coerce Ulster was swiftly repudiated by the prime minister, resulting in the resignations of Seely, French and his adjutant, Ewart. The situation was steadied by Asquith's assumption of the War Office portfolio. Despite the fiasco, the premier was satisfied with the results of the political skirmishes. The Tories had luckily made a bad fist of the scandal, he wrote to Stanley. Liberals, he said, were energised 'more than they have [been] for a long time … we are going to score out of what seemed an almost impossible situation. So true is it – according to my favourite axiom, of which by this time you must be getting tired – that the Expected does not happen.'[194]

Gill wrote to Redmond cautioning him against any attack on the army or the king, and urging him instead to stress the Irish stock of Generals Gough, French and Roberts, and to recall the gallantry of the Munster Fusiliers in the South African War. He urged the nationalist leader to tack away from the controversy by speaking of the value of Ireland to the empire, and of the readiness of her people to be reconciled and loyal. He should, Gill said, flatter the king, and invite him to open an Irish parliament where north and south could seal their allegiance to the Crown and empire.[195] Gill's advice to be circumspect arose from larger concerns, which Gill expressed in a letter to Adams: 'The enigma, the dangerous enigma in this is the King and his entourage', he wrote; 'Even bigger issues, bigger internal issues for England than Irish Home Rule may loom up out of it.'[196]

Gill warned Redmond of the danger that the crisis could spin out of control into a collision of classes and masses in Britain,

> … bringing about in its course a foreign war and God knows what confusions out of which we might, or might not, pick profit or reap calamity, but in the midst of which Home Rule, as we are looking at it now, would get swallowed up for the time being like a piece of wreckage. Now as the practical problem immediately to hand, you want Home Rule *at once*.[197]

This prophetic assessment goes far to explain the nationalists' strategy henceforward: to get the bill on the statute book at all costs. With the formidable powers of the British establishment ranged against them, nothing could be trusted any longer to the buffets of fortune; much might be risked for the imperative of securing the bill.

Federalism revived

'While the Government is recovering consciousness', Sir Francis Hopwood observed, he pondered whether the time was right for a royal initiative to bring together the opposing sides on the Ulster question.[198] George V was clearly receptive to such counsels, burdened as he was with 'the terrible responsibility from which he could not escape, no matter how much … ministers were prepared to accept it, if Civil War broke out'. The monarch was weighed down by the sense of his historical position, and irritated by accusations by the Liberal press of partiality and pressurising ministers.[199]

Asquith admitted to the king that he might be thought overly optimistic, but he professed that 'if he was alive in a year's time, his majesty would be reminded by him of his now expressed belief that the Irish question could be settled without shedding a drop of blood'.[200] The source of this imperturbable confidence was divined by Lord Morley, who told an intimate, 'You may take it from me, as a family secret, the Carsonites will get everything they ask for.'[201] As the five-year term of Parliament was to end in 1915, the ticking of the electoral clock seemed to urge settlement on both sides. Ministers did not want to go to the polls with Ulster unsettled, and neither did they relish the prospect of coercing the province by force if they were returned to office. Doubtless they reasoned that Unionists were grappling with similar considerations.

It seems, rather, that the attention of the Unionist leaders was fixed on forcing a general election before enactment of the bill abolishing plural voting.[202] Plural voting, giving wealthy electors a vote in each constituency in which they owned a residence or business, was a privilege exercised assiduously by Tories. Under a franchise limited to about sixty per cent of adult males, this gave the Unionists a substantial advantage in many constituencies. In East Grinstead in January 1910, it was reckoned that there was a ninety-per-cent turnout of plural voters; in Lewes the local Liberal association believed that 2,500 plural votes went to the Unionists in the constituency.[203] The Liberal and Unionist central offices independently calculated that plural votes had swung twenty-nine seats to the Unionists in the December 1910 election.[204] With the removal of the peers' veto by the Parliament Act, passage of the 1913 Plural Voting Bill promised another serious blow to the Tories' power, depriving them of half a million votes cast in multiple constituencies.[205] Thwarting the loss of this huge electoral advantage was a key objective of senior Unionists in the prospective tampering with the Army Annual Bill.[206]

The Unionist Round Table Movement, dedicated to the establishment of a visionary federation of the British Empire, sought to recapture the cooperative spirit of 1910. F.S. Oliver urged public endorsement of a federal system of governance for the United Kingdom by the Unionist leaders, with a view towards convening an inter-party conference. Such a conclave, he suggested, could settle the Irish question, reform the composition of the House of Lords, and decide questions of the franchise and a redistribution of seats.[207] Asquith fastened on the idea of Ulster exclusion pending a federal settlement, which Carson had proposed the preceding December, as one that might be carried by consent.[208] The revival of talk about a collaborative policy on a range of questions naturally attracted Churchill and F.E. Smith, strong supporters of Lloyd George's 1910 coalition scheme. The two men roughly drafted a petition calling for leaders of all parties to make a federal settlement 'paramount ... to avoid the National and Imperial misfortunes with which we are now threatened'.[209]

A petition, substantially similar to that devised by Churchill and Smith, was presented to Asquith demanding the exclusion of six Ulster counties and calling for a conference.[210] Though no conference was convened, discussions, which appear to have included Asquith, Lloyd George and Churchill for the government, and Smith, Austen Chamberlain and Carson for the opposition, produced a compromise formula. The proposal called for the enactment of Home Rule with six-county exclusion for Ulster as the first stage of an elaborate scheme of federalism for the United Kingdom. An Irish Commission, it suggested, could be convened alongside the new Irish legislature to consider how Ireland might be constituted as a single self-governing unit within the broader scheme of federal devolution. Towards this end the commission might elect an all-Ireland provisional assembly to preserve nominal national unity, with the fate of the indefinitely excluded counties of Ulster dependent upon the consent of both parts of Ireland.[211] Redmond, to whom the proposals were sent in a Cabinet memorandum on 6 April, was appalled by the scheme, noting on his copy: 'What would become of the *Irish Parliament*?'[212]

Redmond rightly feared that after the Curragh affair, members of the Cabinet were prepared to concede practically anything. The Ulster Volunteers' gunrunning exploits at Larne on the night of 24 April, when the UVF landed thousands of rifles and great quantities of ammunition, appeared likely only to worsen this tendency.[213] Redmond and Dillon had hitherto argued against interference with the UVF, believing that any action against the Ulster leaders, such as expelling Carson from the Privy Council, would strengthen the Unionists' hand and diminish the possibility of an eventual reconciliation.[214] The nationalist leaders now let it be known to ministers that they supported moving troops to Belfast, though they were still strongly against prosecutions. Lloyd George, Burns and Hobhouse favoured ordering additional troops to Dublin and the Curragh, but the suggestion that units should be sent to Belfast was resisted, for fear of fraternisation.[215]

Asquith recorded that the Cabinet was unanimous for 'instant and effective action' following the spectacular coup at Larne. Ministers considered three potential avenues of prosecution: proceedings for unlawful assembly, incitement to treason or felony, or proclamation of the UVF as a treasonable conspiracy. Each of these was rejected, in turn, as 'inadequate, excessive, or inexpedient'. It was decided instead that the Attorney General of Ireland should take injunctive action against the leaders of the conspiracy, threatening them with prosecution for any *future* efforts to obstruct officers of the law.[216] What no one appears to have pointed out is that by demonstrating ministerial unwillingness to act against lawbreakers, a *quo warranto* action against continuation of lawlessness was neither instant nor effective. Meeting three days later, the Cabinet, influenced by the pleas of the nationalist leaders not to prosecute the offenders, rescinded even this feeble sanction.[217]

As in October 1910, federalist speculation in the British press once again surged.[218] The efforts of Round Table intermediaries bore fruit in the shape of public statements from Lansdowne and Carson giving qualified support to the federal proposition, provided there was separate treatment of Ulster.[219] The 'dodge' behind exclusion until the enactment of a federal scheme, as Sir Francis Hopwood put it to Lord Stamfordham, was to persuade the nationalists that Ulster was not excluded for ever, while delivering to Unionists exclusion without a time limit.[220]

There were private indications of nationalist willingness to engage with the federal plan. Gill tried to recruit Hopwood to chair Asquith's proposed Irish Commission, telling him that he was Redmond's choice to bring Irish self-government into force.[221] Hopwood, seeking intelligence for Lord Stamfordham, engineered a 'chance' meeting with Sir Thomas Esmonde, nationalist MP for North Wexford; Esmonde claimed that Redmond had told him that he could settle with Carson within hours on the basis of Ulster exclusion 'until a satisfactory scheme of Federalism is settled', and said nothing about a time limit. Redmond, he related to Hopwood, was afraid that Carson would refuse, and was nervous about the reaction of his followers.[222]

This confidence to a colleague was consonant with Redmond's attitude to federalism four years previously, but at variance with the memory of the public outcry that forced a retraction of his sympathetic statements in 1910. It also stood in contrast to his contemporaneous insistence to Asquith that the Irish Party's leadership would be repudiated if he conceded anything beyond six-year exclusion for (what he assumed would be) four counties.[223] The inconsistency of Redmond's position may reflect the tension between the deal-making instinct of a Westminster veteran and his awareness of the growing volume of disaffection emanating from Ireland. However, if the nationalist leader was tempted to entertain federal proposals afresh, he appears to have been nettled out of his complacency by a characteristically caustic speech by T.M. Healy, reported early in May.

Redmond decisively pricked the federalist *ballons d'essai*, reminding Asquith of his pledge to abide by the nationalists' limitations on concessions. In a memorandum for the Cabinet, the nationalist leader pronounced the six-county exclusion plan as 'absolutely unacceptable'. To meet the offer of exclusion for Unionist-majority counties with a demand that nationalist majorities in Fermanagh and Tyrone be excluded without a vote, he said, was 'absurd and intolerable'. Redmond claimed that Liberal dalliance with federal schemes had aroused great alarm in Ireland, and he enclosed a newspaper extract of Healy's speech to indicate the criticism to which he was subjected in the country. If, like his letter, the following passage was read to the Cabinet, it would have saved Redmond the trouble of issuing a bald threat himself:[224]

Mr Redmond ought to address the Government as follows:– 'I voted for your Budget: Deliver the goods. I voted for the Insurance Act: Deliver the goods ... I voted for Dreadnoughts and increased taxation: Deliver the goods'. If Mr Redmond got no satisfactory answer to this demand he could say, 'If by tomorrow morning you don't put Home Rule through intact I will deliver the goods. I will deliver you to the cold shades of Opposition'.[225]

Asquith replied to this glacial note on 6 May, assuring the nationalist leader that the points he raised were 'not being overlooked'.[226] There was no further Liberal talk of federalism.

Ambiguous signals

Asquith had a further meeting with Bonar Law and Carson on 5 May. Bonar Law responded favourably to the idea that Ulster counties might be subdivided for purposes of exclusion from the operation of Home Rule; Carson was doubtful of its viability. Both men insisted that the nationalists, Asquith reported to the king, 'should be brought to see that the alternative [to exclusion] is the forcible coercion of Ulster which no British party is prepared to carry through'.[227] That Asquith appears to have offered no demur confirmed that his government's policy was, in essence, one of finding political cover for indefinite exclusion of an area demanded by the Unionists. He had reportedly already told ministers that the army could not be used in Ulster.[228]

Despite the strain on relations, Asquith recorded a 'fairly satisfactory interview' with Redmond and Dillon on 7 May, as the Cabinet considered the amending bill.[229] A majority of ministers, speculated one well-placed observer, would be willing to settle on Carson's terms, 'but both in the Cabinet and in the party there is an uncompromising section which would prefer to stand by Redmond' and proceed with the Home Rule Bill come what may.[230] The intention to introduce an amending bill, giving no indication as to its content, was announced on 12 May. Rising in the House of Commons to respond to the announcement, Redmond was greeted with lively jeers from the opposition; but when he sat down after predicting that Irish hopes were approaching triumph, he was cheered by the government benches for two or three minutes.[231]

The support of the Liberal back benches was the source of Redmond's strength and the reason he was able to restrain the government from surrendering to the Unionists. The suggestion that ministers were subject to Irish dictation – a claim asserted by many Tories at the time, and a theme that historians of the Conservative Party have perpetuated – ignores the nature of Redmond's appeal to the broader Liberal Party. Redmond's speeches expressed, in a straightforward manner, the desire of many Liberal supporters: for a Liberal ministry to ignore Tory efforts to subvert democratic government and do what it had pledged to do. Above all, this meant the passage of obstructed legislation by means of the Parliament Act, and the historic final humiliation of the House of Lords. This was Redmond's power over the vitality and unity of Liberalism, and he used it to remind ministers that he was capable of triggering a party split. The dictation, if it can be called that, to which Asquith was responding, was coming from his own dissatisfied supporters.[232]

In the dark as to precisely what was contemplated for the amending bill, Redmond wrote to Birrell making clear his presumption that there was no intent to press the nationalists beyond the concessions already agreed. As for Ulster, he repeated his assurance that nationalists there would exercise restraint, and he remained convinced, he said, that there was no danger of civil war.[233] To Percy Illingworth, Redmond professed that even if the Covenanters started to riot, northern nationalists, under Devlin's leadership, would remain quiet in their homes. The bishop of Raphoe, he said, had assured him that nationalists understood the situation, and knew that they could honourably refrain from a fight, for Ireland's sake.[234] Nonetheless, the nationalist leader recommended to Birrell that garrisons in Ulster should be strengthened and police forces reinforced where local outbreaks of violence might be anticipated.[235]

Redmond maintained to Birrell that if a provisional government was declared, it could easily be brought to heel, bloodlessly, by closing ports and cutting communications. The business community of the north, he asserted, 'already alarmed and secretly hostile to the Carson movement, would bring down the provisional government'.[236] While the anecdotal evidence of the attitude of Ulster businessmen to a prospective rising is mixed, what is not in doubt is that there was solid cause for powerful northern industrialists to have second thoughts in the spring and summer of 1914.[237]

Birrell had doubtless seen intelligence reports of commercial disruption in Ulster. Fears that a provisional government might lead to an annulment of contracts resulted in a tightening of credit across the province. In March linen mills in Armagh and Tyrone were put on short time.[238] From Antrim, in May, it was reported that 'goods were being offered to American firms at cost price to get ready money' and that London discount houses were refusing to extend financing even to the big industrial firms, resulting in 'serious loss and inconvenience'. The effects of 'a general reluctance to invest money in Ulster' cascaded across the province, as larger enterprises conserved their capital and reduced purchases from smaller firms. Shopkeepers were hit by a withdrawal of credit, and tradespeople were reportedly finding it hard to collect debts.[239]

In Belfast, shipbuilding and engineering remained steady, but the linen and building trades, as elsewhere in the province, were 'gravely' affected by the uncertainty.[240] *The Times'* correspondent in Derry reported that large quantities of scrip, bearer bonds and other securities were being transferred to England, and insurance underwriters doubled their rates to insure against credit risk in Ulster.[241] English suppliers were reportedly refusing credit, and industrial firms resorted to borrowing from Belfast banks for short-term financing at interest rates higher than those quoted in London.[242] By June several Belfast linen mills were said to be on the brink of insolvency; tourism in Donegal had almost completely dried up.[243] The Irish Party chairman was almost certainly aware of such a widespread dislocation of trade, given the intelligence he received from Gill, who travelled to the north regularly and mixed freely with prominent Unionists.

The business community of the rest of Ireland was on Carson's mind for very different reasons. Carson suggested to Asquith and Lloyd George that Redmond should be urged to summon a meeting of Protestant businessmen in the south and west to reassure them about the policies of a Home Rule government. In other words, as the Chancellor related it, Redmond should 'invoke their aid to secure good government for Ireland – If he would do this, Sir E. Carson, who is leader of the Unionists in other parts of Ireland than Ulster, would urge his followers to accept this invitation'.[244] This suggestion of a conciliatory move by Redmond appears to have been offered to give practical expression to Carson's February appeal for the nationalists to win over their fellow countrymen, but it also suggested that the Ulster Unionist leader's desire for harmonious coexistence was not merely rhetorical. Conspicuously, however, it relied on the nationalists taking the initiative; this no doubt reflected the tightness of the corner into which Carson had backed himself with his supporters. Redmond's reaction to this pacific proposal, or whether it was conveyed to him at all, is unknown.

Given the ministerial inclination to surrender, it was scarcely surprising that Asquith found Redmond and Dillon 'rather panicky'.[245] Hearing a rumour that a statement of some sort was to be made, the Irish Party chairman wrote to Birrell that if proposals went any further than the nationalists' conditions laid down in March, 'our position will instantly become an impossible one, and we should be compelled to make a public protest on the spot'.[246] Birrell replied that if pressed to say anything, he would state only that the government would introduce county plebiscite proposals.[247] After fiery exchanges between Asquith and Bonar Law, the Home Rule Bill passed the House of Commons for a third time on 25 May. Little enthusiasm greeted the bill's final Commons passage, however, so clouded was its fate by uncertain amendments.[248]

With Parliament in recess, and Asquith holidaying in Anglesey, greatly relieved 'to be beyond the reach of telephones and callers', a curiously optimistic Birrell embarked on a fact-finding tour of Ulster.[249] Gill, meanwhile, was surveying the mood at a technical-instruction conference in Killarney. He reported to Redmond that the northerners he had met were reconciled to Home Rule and vehemently against exclusion. Gill counselled that, given sufficient time, Ulster would settle down. No doubt, he said, there would be a skirmish or two around the 'Glorious Twelfth' (Ulster Day), but there was little fear among the people to whom he spoke of anything worse.[250] He sensed that the real trouble was that the Covenant oath had made a climbdown difficult. The crux of the problem, Gill said, was how to amend the Home Rule Bill so as to allow its opponents to save face.[251]

As if to reinforce this intelligence, Alec Wilson, son of Harland and Wolff director Walter Wilson, wrote to Redmond representing himself as an emissary of the Ulster Unionist leadership. Strongly implying that he wrote on behalf of Carson, Wilson asserted that if autonomy for the whole of Ulster were granted, the Ulster Unionist leaders would pledge to bring about the province's accession to the Irish parliament with as little delay as possible.[252] The proposal was cast as a formula to cover the adoption of a policy of harmonisation with the Dublin parliament. If Wilson's claim to speak for the Ulster Unionist leaders was true, this marked the debut of a conciliatory initiative that Carson was to advance privately in July.[253] No record of a reply to Wilson survives, but the overture may have served to sustain the nationalist leader's confidence that Unionist rhetoric was overblown and a belief, shared by Gill, that if presented with Home Rule as a fait accompli, the Ulster Unionist leaders would bow to the inevitable.[254]

Lloyd George, meanwhile, oscillated between confidence and disbelief as to the chances of settlement.[255] Lord Stamfordham was amused when the Chancellor remarked to him that '"We lawyers" – as if he were one of the leaders of the Bar – "know perfectly well that the most critical cases are often settled out of court at the last moment."'[256] The prime minister, Stamfordham related, was constant in his assurances to George V that a solution would be found, but, disquietingly, the king indicated to Crewe and Morley his strong view that having decided upon the necessity of introducing an amending bill, ministers could hardly expect him to assent to the Home Rule Bill without its companion measure.[257]

Birrell returned from Donegal, his confidence diminished, but with a clearer view of the 'unheroic imbroglio' facing the government in Ulster.[258] He reported to the Cabinet that the conviction in Ulster was that a general election was needed, and that opinion there expected its result would dispose of Home Rule. The legal profession, bankers and businessmen small and large, he said, had come to the view that 'however bad Home Rule may prove to be, exclusion is and must always be worse'. Thus the proposals intended for the amending bill, he said, while useful proof of the government's desire not to coerce Ulster, were of no value at all in placating Protestant fears. The Ulster Volunteers, in Birrell's view, were 'sick to death of drilling ... Their leaders are perceiving that their men must either fight soon or ... dwindle away and disappear'. The notable change, he wrote, was the formation of the Irish Volunteers, which had made a great impression on all Irishmen. However, he believed that the Carsonite leaders would be compelled to 'raise the flag somehow or another in Belfast' once the bill received royal assent.[259] The Irish chief secretary made no prediction as to the consequences flowing from this.

With the Home Rule Bill near the end of its parliamentary circuits under the provisions of the Parliament Act, ministers considered their next crucial steps. If disaster were to be avoided, the situation required sure-footed leadership and the utmost delicacy of handling; but in Sir Francis Hopwood's judgement, this was too much to hope for of Asquith's administration: 'I fancy a crisis is coming very fast', he predicted to Gill; 'the Government, which never has any stomach for governing, will fumble at the eleventh hour.'[260]

5

Home Rule in Liberal Britain

Twentieth-century Liberal attitudes to Home Rule were shaped, in the main, by electoral considerations, the relation of the Irish cause to other constitutional reforms, and its impact on competing priorities, such as social reform. Given the strong ideological convictions of many of the Liberal Party's followers, enthusiasm for Home Rule was also a measure of the effectiveness with which the issue was communicated as an embodiment of Liberal doctrine. As has been seen, Home Rule propagandists deployed a variety of arguments to assert that self-rule for Ireland advanced the Liberal agenda, with the core principle of democracy to the fore.

This chapter is the first of two that will chart the dynamic character of Home Rulers' responses to the revival of the Irish question, and to the political tribulations that the third Home Rule Bill faced. Public sentiment is notoriously difficult to approximate or quantify, but this chapter and the next aim to sketch a picture of the evolving popular mood. Chapter 5 considers Home Rule sentiment in the Liberal heartlands of Britain, while Chapter 6 recounts the evolution of attitudes to the new bill in nationalist Ireland, and to the challenges that its passage faced.

To understand the state of popular political sentiment at the climax of the crisis in the summer of 1914 – when the volatility of feelings heavily influenced political decisions – it is necessary to depart momentarily from the chronology established in the book thus far, and look backwards and, more problematically from the point of view of clarity, *forward* in time in this chapter and the next. This perspective will help to establish the extraordinary atmosphere of popular feeling in Britain and Ireland as the crisis deepened, and set the stage for the unfolding of Home Rule's final act in Chapter 7. For clarity, in instances where reference is made to events that prefigure their appearance in Chapter 7, the reader will be signposted to their later and fuller discussion.

When Home Rule was restored to the Liberal Party's agenda in 1910, the sensibilities of a distinct set of internal constituencies had to be considered. Ministers worried, for instance, that Nonconformist hostility to Home Rule would be a critical obstacle to be overcome.[1] The issue of denominational education preoccupied the Nonconformist Churches, whose leaders were impatient for legislation to replace the Liberals' Education Bill of 1906, withdrawn after a mangling by the House of Lords. Free Church hierarchies were nominally in favour of Home Rule, though the attitude of their congregations was judged to be more doubtful. Torn between traditional loyalty to Liberalism and sympathy for their co-religionists in Ireland under threat from Roman Catholicism, many Nonconformists found it difficult to enthusiastically embrace Home Rule. They were, however, susceptible to appeals to reason, justice and religious liberty, and it was to these themes that the Home Rule Council's comprehensive catalogue of publications was directed.

The restoration of Home Rule as a flagship policy was somewhat problematic for collectivist New Liberals, as the persistence of the hoary Irish question retarded the advancement of social-reform legislation.[2] Home Rule's dominance of national debates, and the congestion of business in the House of Commons that it caused, frustrated reformist zeal. Yet New Liberal support for Irish self-government arose not just from impatience to clear the path for progressive legislation but also from attraction to its democratising symbolism. The vision of self-government for Ireland was consistent with the ideals of individual liberty and self-realisation, and was capable of translation by New Liberal theorists into a model for liberation of the British working classes through widened enfranchisement, redistributive taxation, and other 'levelling' reforms.

Traditional radicals showed themselves to be the most faithful of Home Rule's supporters. Self-government for Ireland was so intimately associated with the Gladstonian legacy that the issue took its place in the pantheon of cherished ideals beside disestablishment of the Welsh Church and the abolition of plural voting. Redmond's instrumentality in annulling the absolute veto of the House of Lords – the high-water mark of Liberal democracy in the eyes of many – won him the admiration of followers of the radical tradition, and ensured their firm support for the Irish cause when it was needed.

Though the Irish question was, in 1910, regarded warily from the top of the party and with a degree of apathy from below, by 1914 Liberal propaganda (largely a creation of Irish nationalists) had successfully communicated to supporters that opposition to Home Rule was a challenge to their fundamental beliefs. Enthusiasm for Home Rule grew in response to the threat posed to Liberals' core democratising ideology, coalescing all sections of the party in defence of Liberalism. For a brief, and arguably, last time, the Unionist challenge to Home Rule united the Liberal Party's rank and file. The growing awareness of the endangerment of democratic principles impelled a wave of support for Home Rule that swept Liberal Britain in 1914. Yet it was also becoming clear to many Liberals that Asquith and his colleagues, governed as they were by political expediency, were indifferent to these feelings. The dissonance of principle and pragmatism undermined confidence in the Liberal leadership, and called into question the future of Liberalism.

The electoral climate

Home Rule's perceived unpopularity accounted for its virtual elision from Liberal election appeals in 1910, and for the establishment, a year later, of the Home Rule Council propaganda organisation with the intention of combating Liberal apathy. Some observers feared that the lack of enthusiasm for Home Rule was symptomatic of a farther-reaching lack of interest. 'Whether it be the Parliament Act', reported a disheartened Liberal activist from Plymouth in the summer of 1913, 'or whether the man in the street is content that "all's well", there is no denying the fact that there has been a general listlessness on the part of the British public.'[3] Campaigning in Blackburn, Labour MP Philip Snowden claimed that England was heartily sick of the Home Rule question, and wanted to be done with the matter.[4]

Even Liberal constituency agents were seen to be lacking in passion for the Irish cause. Percy Illingworth, the chief whip, addressed a special message to agents attending the 1913 National Liberal Federation meeting. If Home Rule did not appear to them 'so absolutely vital and exigent' as it did to their nationalist allies, Illingworth admonished those attending, they must remember the prospect of Irish support for future social and political reforms and, in particular, for the bill to abolish plural voting, which would remain the 'first and vital consideration of the Liberal Party'.[5] Given that abolition of plural voting would deprive the Tories of half a million votes nationally, it is not surprising that the measure was so highly prized by salaried Liberal Party agents.

In by-election contests, the unpopularity of the 1911 National Insurance Act was the main issue with which Liberal candidates had to contend. It was hoped that working-class voters would come to realise the wisdom of the 'ninepence for fourpence' slogan once they had cause to claim benefits for sickness or unemployment, but the drag of the insurance issue on Liberal fortunes did not abate, even by 1914. The *Daily Mail* fanned the embers of controversy with a 'Free Insurance Slaves' campaign, which distributed 'huge posters and tonnes of literature' to contested constituencies. The Unionist appeal to household economy connected with voters. 'Old age pensions, Free Trade, the coming franchise reform, the danger of Tariff Reform, and Conscription', lamented one Liberal agent, 'all counted for nothing against 4d. per week' in National Insurance levies.[6]

Liberal activists in the constituencies refused to believe that the spectre of Irish Home Rule much perturbed the British electorate. In Taunton, Home Rule and Welsh disestablishment were thought to have indirectly contributed to a Liberal by-election defeat, but only by mobilising Protestant clergy and local eminences to come out in support of the Tories.[7] The Unionist call was to 'get this Government out' at Altrincham, but Home Rule played no greater part in the debate than did the Welsh Church issue, National Insurance, or the Marconi scandal.[8] In north-west Norfolk, the 'Home Rule bogey was paraded' by the Unionist campaign, but voters, the local agent reported, 'were not at all alarmed that anybody would be the worse for Home Rule or Church Disestablishment'.[9]

The perceived electoral utility of the Irish question was illustrated by where the Unionists chose to wheel it into battle. In the safe Tory seat of South Buckinghamshire in March 1914, Home Rule was the chief issue in an appeal to 'give the Government a knock-down blow'. Unionist 'tap room missionaries' misrepresented the National Insurance Act to working-class voters and prophesied the end of the empire if the Liberals remained in power.[10] By contrast, Charles Masterman, the Liberal candidate at Bethnal Green, defeated that same month, noted that while the Tory cry in the House of Commons was for a general election on Home Rule, little or nothing had been heard of it in the East End by-election campaign.[11] At Ipswich in April (a contest which Masterman also lost), insurance was again the Unionists' principal thrust, though anti-Catholic handbills were distributed in the district, appealing to Nonconformist prejudices.[12] There was no denying that the tide of by-election results was flowing against the Liberals, but agents ascribed the adverse electoral trend not to Home Rule but to the unpopularity of National Insurance and superior Unionist organisation.[13]

Contrasting this judgement, *The Times* reported in October 1913 that eighteen Home Rule meetings had been held in Britain the previous day, and ruefully observed that Unionists had no comparable organisation in the country to match the Home Rulers.[14] The Liberal Party's Home Rule Council was a formidable propaganda machine, sending speakers and canvassers to English and Scottish by-elections, and organising an exhaustive programme of meetings. The Irish Press Agency supplied speakers for a joint propaganda campaign in Britain with its Liberal counterpart. The two organisations mounted a claimed two to three thousand engagements over three years, drafting the services of forty to fifty Irish Party MPs for the purpose. Leading Ulster Protestants, such as Thomas Shillington, David Hogg MP and W.H. Davey of *The Ulster Guardian*, were also recruited to speak.[15]

Sympathetic journals reported intensive campaigning activity and great enthusiasm at Home Rule demonstrations. In February 1912 *Reynolds's Newspaper* recounted a meeting in Trafalgar Square organised by the National Radical League and the United Irish League of Great Britain, attended by an estimated 20,000 people.[16] A 'monster' rally in Liverpool in November 1912, reported *The Manchester Guardian*, attracted as many as 100,000 people, mainly Irish, from as far as Birkenhead and Bootle.[17] In the autumn of 1913 the Home Rule Council published a schedule of forthcoming Home Rule demonstrations in the Liberal heartlands. John Redmond was to address meetings in Northampton, Birmingham and Alloa; his brother Willie was engaged to speak in Ashton-under-Lyne, Southport and Rochdale; T.P. O'Connor was to appear in Bradford; Dillon at Devonport, Newton Abbot and Dewsbury; and Devlin was to address rallies in Rossendale, Eccles, Devon and Cornwall. Home Rule Council staff and members of the Ulster Liberal Association and the Women's Liberal Federation (WLF) were to address meetings in smaller towns.[18] By the end of 1913, the Home Rule Council claimed that 250,000 Britons, in aggregate, had attended its meetings.[19]

St Patrick's Day celebrations for 1914 were marked by the lord mayor of Dublin attending a banquet in Liverpool, and by great assemblies at the Queen's Theatre in Leeds and Woodside Hall in Glasgow. The Theatre Royal in Cardiff saw one of the largest and most enthusiastic demonstrations in local memory, or so *The Freeman's Journal* claimed.[20] Speeches at the gatherings invoked the spirit of Gladstone, pronounced the Ulster threat a bluff, and emphasised Irish fitness for self-government. Home Rule supporters did not, however, confine their enthusiasm to Liberal meetings. Anti-Home Rule meetings were disrupted, such as at an assembly in Bermondsey addressed by six Ulster working men, who faced a 'very hostile reception' from a mainly Catholic audience, who cheered Redmond and Lloyd George, and sang 'God Save Ireland'.[21] *The Observer* reported that another meeting in Leeds was stormed by a jeering band of Irishmen led by a girl waving a Union Jack.[22]

The annual meetings of the National Liberal Federation offered another opportunity to express enthusiasm for Home Rule. Before sympathetic conference audiences, Asquith showed some sensitivity towards Unionist allegations of a 'corrupt bargain' with the 'Dollar dictator', telling the 1910 assembly, to laughter, that he did 'not in the least grudge the Tory party any electioneering capital that they can extract from Mr Redmond's American dollars'. Whether such contributions were subscribed by Irish-Americans or Canadian fellow subjects, he said, they attested to the sympathy of the dominions and the wider world to Irish Home Rule.[23] Referring to Redmond's presence on the stage at the 1912 conference, Asquith gently turned Tory jibes against them by pointing out that the question of who was subservient to whom, prompted by his invitation to the nationalist leader, would find different answers from critics in Britain and Ireland.[24] In 1913 Home Rule dominated his party-leader's address. He rebutted charges that Liberals had concealed their intentions in 1910, and maintained that Liberal faithfulness to the cause of Irish self-government had never wavered. Irish loyalty, he told an audience of 4,000, would not be betrayed. With ironic prescience, Asquith asked delegates whether, if the Irish demand 'were to be indefinitely postponed or mocked by some half-hearted and unsatisfying compromise, does anyone suppose you would have got rid of the Irish difficulty? But there would remain the difficulty in a form more menacing and formidable than ever.'[25] Asquith's failure to prosecute a resolute policy forced him to seek just such an unsatisfactory and discreditable transaction. The 'Irish difficulty' revived, in due course, with all the vengeance that he had prophesied.

The Home Rule finance controversy

The Liberal leaders knew that Ireland's precarious finances and huge land-purchase liabilities meant that the Home Rule Bill's financial arrangements would inevitably be a focus of criticism.[26] Herbert Samuel's elaborate scheme of finance, intended to overcome these objections, created problems of its own. Critics attacked the complexity of the bill's financial clauses, and the consequent difficulty of modifying its structure. The magnitude of the transitional annual grant intended to get the new Irish administration on its feet (over and above the transferred sum for devolved services), the power to vary rates of duty, and the body to be set up to oversee financial relations all came under Liberal and Unionist fire in the House of Commons.

Thomas Agar-Robartes (Liberal mover of the failed Ulster-exclusion amendment) echoed Tory criticisms of the retention of Irish members in the House of Commons as a means of extorting financial concessions from the English taxpayer in perpetuity. Liberals more often objected on free-trade grounds. The bill, they argued, left the door open to the erection of tariffs to protect Irish trade, to the potential detriment of British industries. They speculated that protection could be disguised by establishing subsidies on production for certain industries. It was also suspected that the Irish Exchequer might protect infant industries by offsetting the customs duties paid on raw materials against excise duties levied on the manufactured goods for which they were used. Despite repeated assurances by ministers that any reduction of Irish rates of duty would correspondingly reduce the transferred sum, Liberal MPs continued to grumble about the threat to free trade, and about the possibility that a reduction in revenues would be at the Imperial Exchequer's expense.[27]

Ministers defended the provisions, arguing that any self-governing nation would have an interest in providing financial incentives for developing industries. To charges that Ireland promised to be a costly and perpetual drain on the Imperial Exchequer, they replied that the Tories' proposals for Ireland amounted to a lavish and never-ending ransom for the preservation of the Union.[28] With not a little hypocrisy, Unionists attacked the financial arrangements for being too meek and too restrictive. Austen Chamberlain argued that accepting the Primrose recommendation of fiscal autonomy would have been preferable. Walter Long charged that the financial arrangements 'breathed distrust of the Irish people' in every line.[29] Sir Edward Carson, in comments that might have applied equally to the whole of the 1912 bill, characterised its financial aspects as a ramshackle halfway house between Union and full separation.[30]

The proposed Joint Exchequer Board came in for criticism from all sides. It was claimed that the board would usurp the authority of the House of Commons, since no provision for appeal of its decisions had been made in the bill. The board's establishment, *The Nation* argued, diluted the Irish parliament's authority and diminished its incentive for financial responsibility.[31] William O'Brien attacked the whole concept of 'true revenue', which was the elusive figure that the Joint Exchequer Board was to be charged with identifying. O'Brien argued that if revenues actually collected in Ireland were counted, the apparent budgetary deficit would disappear. Tea drinkers in Ireland, he claimed, were the real payers of the tea duty, even if the tax had been levied in Liverpool.[32] Unionists, and some Liberals, worried that in the absence of

machinery to determine revenue generated from the trade of dutiable com-
modities between Britain and Ireland (as existed for imports to the United
Kingdom in custom houses), the determination of Irish solvency rested solely
in the 'Frankenstein' or 'Star Chamber' of the Joint Exchequer Board.[33] In
response, Liberal ministers asserted, not without some difficulty, that as the
board's role would not entail the formulation of policy, merely the checking
of figures, the concerns raised would not materialise.

Liberal backbenchers continued to express dissatisfaction with the power to
vary duty in the bill. Claiming to speak for seventy or eighty Liberal members,
pro-federal MP Lewis Haslam asserted that variable rates of duty within the
United Kingdom were inconsistent with the principle of federalism. The
knowledge that Irishmen might enjoy cheaper tobacco, he claimed, would
breed discontent among Britons, and encourage smuggling.[34] The prospect of
a sizeable back-bench revolt induced ministers to amend the bill, eliminating
the power of the Irish parliament to reduce customs duties, and restricting
its scope to increase them. Given that indirect taxation accounted for a huge
proportion of Irish revenues, this amendment, as Redmond well knew, practically amounted to a nullification of the fiscal powers of the Irish parliament.
Despite his keen appreciation of such a blow, Redmond acknowledged that
the widespread feeling on the Liberal benches could not be resisted. The government was thereafter condemned by its opponents for inconsistency, and
nationalist rivals accused the Irish Party, with some justice, of desiring to pass
a bad bill at any cost.

The Irish Party and women's suffrage

The Irish Party's stance on the issue of votes for women sorely tried the
patience of its progressive allies. The party's parliamentary delegation was
said to be, after that of the Labour Party, the most consistently favourable
to an extension of the franchise to women. Prominent supporters among its
members included Willie Redmond, T.P. O'Connor, Joseph Devlin, J.G. Swift
MacNeill and Tom Kettle.[35] The well-known sympathy of many nationalist
members made the withholding of their votes when the question came before
the House of Commons in 1912/13 all the more inexplicable.

A private member's bill, the Parliamentary Franchise (Women) Bill of
1910, passed its second reading in the House of Commons by a large majority
on a free vote. Liberal members voted nearly three to one in favour; twenty
Irish nationalists supported the measure, against fourteen who voted against;

about half of their number abstained. Though the majority of the Cabinet supported women's suffrage, Asquith, in perhaps the starkest example of his failure of vision, notoriously did not. Over the protests of suffragists, the bill was consigned to a committee of the whole House, effectively shelving the issue for the parliamentary session.

The Conciliation Bill of 1911, so called because it enjoyed broad cross-party support, offered suffragists new cause for optimism. Though passed as a private member's bill by a majority of 187, Asquith rescinded an undertaking to give the bill parliamentary time, and the legislation was dropped in favour of a more comprehensive manhood-enfranchisement measure, to which a women's-suffrage amendment might be appended. Despite this second government dodge, great hopes were attached to the Parliamentary Franchise (Women) Bill of 1912, which proposed to extend the vote to around one million property-owning women. Suffragette militancy intensified in anticipation of the vote, and a campaign of organised window-breaking began in London's West End. Perpetrators of these acts of vandalism were prosecuted harshly, and some imprisoned women went on hunger strike, a tactic that the government countered, highly controversially, with a policy of force-feeding. The suffragettes' recourse to violence against property alienated much moderate support. When the vote on the women's-franchise bill came in April 1912, a fortnight before the Home Rule Bill's debut, most nationalist members abstained.

Attention focused on the Irish Party's culpability for the bill's defeat, along with that of the eight ministers who voted against it. *The Freeman's Journal* sought to deflect criticism, adopting the party line that it was the actions of the suffragette window-breakers that had killed the bill.[36] It was widely believed, however, that the nationalist leadership had pressured MPs to withhold their votes so as to avoid taking up parliamentary time ahead of the Home Rule Bill.[37] The apparent abandonment of principle for political expediency outraged suffrage campaigners. Francis Sheehy-Skeffington bitterly complained that by its vote on the bill, the 'contemptible' Parliamentary Party had betrayed Irish nationalism, because no nation could be free without free women.[38]

Suffragists expressed indignation at the volte-face on the part of the nationalists, and protested that their own long-standing support for Irish liberty was not being reciprocated in the cause of women's emancipation. They attacked the Irish Party members' unprincipled conduct, which they saw as logically and morally inconsistent. The Women's Liberal Federation, a body

whose leadership was comprised largely of the wives of ministers and prominent MPs, gave voice to the suffrage demand of Liberal women. Its national
meeting in June 1912 accorded the Irish Home Rule Bill a warm welcome.
An amendment to the resolution, calling for votes for Irish women, was successfully opposed by Molly Childers, wife of Erskine Childers, who argued
that self-government for Ireland should not be encumbered with the suffrage
controversy.[39] After the WLF's self-denying stance on extending the franchise
to Irish women, the perverse voting record of the Irish Party that followed
heightened Liberal and suffragist exasperation.

In November 1912 Philip Snowden MP attempted to force another vote
on the women's question. He moved an amendment to the Home Rule Bill
to give the vote to all persons in Ireland on the local-government register,
which included female property owners.[40] Ministers opposed the alteration
of the bill, arguing that the decision on women's suffrage should be deferred
until consideration of a Franchise Bill, then in the planning stages. Redmond,
wishing to see no tampering with the Home Rule Bill, concurred with this
judgement, but promised a free vote for Irish members on the issue in the
eventual Franchise Bill division. Their position on the motion thus justified,
nationalist MPs voted unanimously against the Snowden amendment.[41]

Redmond's personal stance on women's suffrage had changed over time.
He told a meeting of the Irish Women's Franchise League in 1907 that he had
supported votes for women as a young Member of Parliament. His views had
altered, he told his suffragist audience, for reasons that he did not explain;
but he remained open, he professed, to persuasion by peaceable means. The
Irish Party chairman said he would support the jailed suffragettes' claim to be
designated as political prisoners, though he in no way condoned their extreme
actions.[42]

Redmond expressed less guarded views in an interview that same year
with Francis Sheehy-Skeffington. The Irish Party chairman opposed women's
suffrage, he said, because he felt it would inhibit bold policies and hinder the
chances of Home Rule; asked if his position would change after a grant of
self-government, when this objection would disappear, Redmond replied that
other reasons would arise.[43] In discussion with C.P. Scott in 1913, Redmond
clarified his opinion. Nothing like the entry of women into education and
public bodies in England had occurred in Ireland, he explained to Scott,
except to a small extent in cities. As a result, he said, such a radical change
as the granting of the vote was inimical to traditions of propriety and reserve
among Catholic womanhood.[44]

John Dillon told Scott that he supported women's suffrage as a democrat and opposed it as a Catholic. The decision to oppose suffrage measures, he claimed, sprang from loyalty to Asquith, whom the Irish leaders had no wish to harm. Maintenance of the premier's standing and authority, Dillon argued, was vital to the prospects of Home Rule. It was in the interest of the Irish Party to spare him an embarrassing defeat on an issue that he had publicly opposed. Scott subsequently put it to Redmond that it would be said that freedom for Irishmen had been obtained at the expense of liberty for English women. The Irish Party chairman admitted as much, but countered that since the prime minister had declared emphatically against votes for women, to be compelled against his inclinations to push a suffrage measure through would put Asquith in an impossible position, and potentially result in his, or the government's, resignation.[45] By such private admissions, the Irish Party leaders substantially validated the suffragists' public criticisms of political expediency.

The leaders' attitudes towards women paralleled their indifference to recruiting support from organisations promoting cultural nationalism. The Irish Party offered little to attract women, who were very sparsely represented in the party organisation, even at local level. Only a handful of ladies' branches of the UIL managed to sustain their existence. Women of progressive views were even less likely to be enthusiastic supporters, being alienated by the leaders' attitude to votes for women, and by their tolerance of AOH violence against suffragists. Though Hanna Sheehy-Skeffington, her sisters Mary and Kathleen, and Kathleen Shannon were all committee members of the Young Ireland Branch of the UIL, their views on women's political participation were more advanced than those of some of their supposedly progressive male colleagues.[46]

Asquith's promised Franchise Bill, abolishing plural voting and university representation, and extending the vote to a further two million male electors, was introduced in June 1912. The measure left the door open to women's-suffrage amendments, which were moved, as expected, in the debates that autumn. A ruling by the Speaker, however, that such amendments effectively rendered the bill a new piece of legislation led to its withdrawal in January 1913. The abortive Franchise Bill was replaced by a shorter bill to abolish plural voting, which was introduced in the House of Commons in April.

In anticipation of a renewed effort to force a vote on women's suffrage, the officers of the WLF appealed to the better instincts of Irish nationalist members. They wrote to each Irish Party MP noting that suffrage measures before 1912 had enjoyed the support of an average majority of twelve of the

nationalist parliamentary delegation. The WLF leaders expressed sympathy
with the anxiety not to endanger Home Rule, but stressed the reinforcement
of Liberal strength that they saw the body of newly enfranchised women
lending to a new Irish administration in its crucial first months. They also
emphasised the moral obligation of nationalists to Liberal women, reminding
them that the WLF had remained faithful to Home Rule in the 1890s 'at a
time when there was danger of Liberals faltering in their fidelity to that cause
from motives of Party interest'.[47]

An opportunity for the nationalists to prove the reciprocity of their principles arose in June 1913 when W.H. Dickinson MP introduced another private
member's bill that would have had the effect of enfranchising six million
women. Rosalind Howard (Lady Carlisle), president of the WLF, recognised
the Irish Party's desire to avoid embroilment in the suffrage controversy, and
met Redmond to urge him to order nationalist members to abstain.[48] Despite
the Liberal women's lobbying efforts, however, fifty-five nationalists voted
against Dickinson's bill in the Commons division, against seven who voted
for it, and the measure was defeated by 269 votes to 221.

Delegates attending the annual council of the WLF, meeting the morning
after the bill's rejection, furiously denounced the '55 members who had
betrayed them last night'. A further instance of tactical voting by a sympathetic majority of Irish Party members convinced many of the women present
that the nationalist MPs had been overborne by their leader under pressure
from the hostile Asquith. Lady Carlisle, defending her 'very severe' efforts
to influence Redmond to withdraw or allow a free vote, faced a sceptical
assembly. Unable to quieten dissenting interventions, she left the podium
calling, 'If you prefer to look upon them [the Irish nationalists] as the pawns
of the Prime Minister, so be it!'[49]

Rebecca West, writing in the socialist *Clarion* newspaper, derided the Irish
Party's perfidious attitude to women's suffrage. Redmond's ignorant and single-
minded pursuit of Home Rule, at the expense of liberty for women, she
wrote, had shown the Irish Party's democratic posturing to be a fraud.[50] The
nationalists' efforts to duck the controversy earned them the enmity of British
suffragists for blocking progress on what many saw as a question of liberty
no less important than Irish self-rule. Though nationalist MP Hugh Law's
plea that Irish suffragists desired the party to put Home Rule first probably
spoke for the majority of their number in Ireland, in the context of the British
progressive alliance, held together by a democratising impulse, the Irish Party's
self-serving tactics left it looking rather dishonourable.[51] Disillusionment with

the nationalists' lack of principle placed a serious strain on the sympathy of many British progressives and suffragists, but ultimately did not break their loyalty to Home Rule.[52]

Revelation and rededication

The dawning of the possibility, early in 1914, of the army being used to subvert the will of the democratically elected House of Commons began to alter the Liberal mood. Use of the peers' power to amend the Army Annual Act threatened to trigger a fresh constitutional crisis, probably precipitating the dissolution of Parliament and the abandonment of the Home Rule Bill. The recognition of Unionist readiness to attempt to extort a retreat by obstructing the government of the country widened the dimensions of the controversy beyond the question of Ireland. The contemplated resort to extra-parliamentary means to defeat the government represented, for many Liberals, an effort to reverse hard-won democratic reforms and to reimpose aristocratic ascendancy.

The importance of overriding the veto of the House of Lords by operation of the Parliament Act had been a feature of Liberal rhetoric since that measure's introduction as a bill in 1911. The extremes to which the Tories were prepared to go to prevent the establishment of that precedent galvanised Liberal determination to see Home Rule on the statute book. The intensification of the democratic struggle in 1914, far from demoralising the rank and file, heightened combative sentiment. The reflexive stiffening of stance among back-bench Liberals was strengthened by the government's apparent preparedness to appease lawbreakers, signalled by the temporary exclusion concession extracted from the nationalists.

The hardened attitude of Liberals did not signify a surge of enthusiasm for Irish self-government so much as a realisation that the future of democracy and of Liberalism was intimately tied up with the fate of the Home Rule Bill. To permit the bill to fall before the operation of the Parliament Act would be to surrender to the forces of aristocratic privilege. To lose the contest or, worse, to capitulate in the struggle would cost Liberalism not just its claim to embody democratic principles but also its legitimacy to lead the fight for justice for the working-class people of Britain. It was this revelation of the deeper significance of the battle for Home Rule that transformed and energised Liberal sentiment.

Just as Irish nationalists had framed much of the Liberal case for Irish self-government, the new urgency for Home Rule that gripped Liberalism in 1914 was set in motion by Redmond. A dinner in the Irish Party chairman's honour at the National Liberal Club on 6 February 1914 was the occasion for a reaffirmation of Liberal support for Home Rule and a rededication of purpose. After an enthusiastic welcome from the assembled guests, Redmond paid tribute to the cooperation of the Liberal Party and Irish Party in working for the goal of 'emancipation of the democracies' of Britain and Ireland, towards which Irish Home Rule was a stride for all.[53] The resistance that Liberals were meeting, he claimed, was really a continuation of 1911, of the battle over the Parliament Act and limitation of the Lords' veto. The Irish, he declared, viewed by some as an inferior race, refused to accept a return to the status quo ante:

> 'Let it be clearly understood,' exclaimed Mr Redmond amid loud cheers, 'we will no longer in Ireland submit to this stigma. We will no longer submit to be made the pawns and playthings of the British parties. Never, never again will Ireland submit to be governed by the old rotten system of superiority and ascendancy [cheers], and I say to those who imagine that they can kill the Home Rule Bill that if they succeeded – thank God we know they will not succeed [cheers] – Ireland will never again submit to, Ireland would be absolutely ungovernable, under the old regime [cheers].'[54]

The warmth of the Irish Party chairman's reception in the spiritual home of Liberalism attested to his popularity among radicals, but it also evinced receptivity to a hardened stance on Ulster. Redmond's demand of the government, if Unionists refused to compromise, was met by the loudest and most prolonged enthusiasm of the evening: 'If no agreement is come to', he declared, 'the Bill must go through as it stands [loud cheers].'[55] *The Daily Chronicle*, reporting the event, judged that Redmond's insistence that concessions be made only in exchange for the passage of Home Rule by consent reflected the opinion of the bulk of the Liberal Party.[56]

Evidence that this sentiment was percolating up from the Liberal grassroots was offered by Richard Holt, MP for Hexham. Late in February, Holt gave notice of an amendment to the Home Rule Bill that was intended, he said, to give voice to the opinion of back-bench members and Liberal supporters. The amendment affirmed the House of Commons' twice-recorded decision to pass the bill into law, and called upon the government to take steps to protect the lives and property of the majority in Ireland.[57] In the event Holt did not move the amendment; he had tabled the motion, he explained in a Commons speech, in order to speak for ordinary Liberals. He attacked Unionist support for a policy of lawlessness, even to the point of civil war, and insisted that the Liberal Party must resist the violent course proposed by the party's opponents. The Liberals would proceed with their policy, Holt told the House, and pass the Home Rule Bill under the Parliament Act. The Liberal Party, Holt contended, would not relinquish the constitutional parity with the Tories that the Parliament Act had conferred:

> We know that what it really all means is that hon. Gentlemen opposite wish to destroy the Parliament Act … The present position is one which we mean to maintain at whatever cost. If hon. Members wish to live under a peaceful constitution in this country they will have to recognise that we are honest, that we are not cowards and that we intend to have the same rights in the State as they have themselves.[58]

The rallying call to the defence of Liberalism and democracy was used to mobilise supporters and stiffen the backs of ministers. Dillon spoke of the ill-concealed Tory attack on the Parliament Act at York; P.J. Brady, in Cardiff, claimed a defeat on the question of democracy would so dishonour Liberals as to banish them from power for a generation.[59] Feeling for Home Rule was thought to be particularly strong in the West Riding of Yorkshire;[60] Liberal MP Edward Shortt told a meeting in Leeds in March that the limit of concessions had been reached, and that no Liberal seat in the country would be safe if the party's leaders retreated from principle.[61] The defiant spirit of Churchill's well-publicised Bradford speech the same month, calling for unrepentant Orangemen to be taught a lesson, captured the mood, ministers believed, of the party in the country.[62]

A new cry

Amid this state of heightened Liberal feeling, news of the Curragh affair broke. Ferocious Unionist attacks on apparent ministerial bungling failed to hit their mark. The intensity of Liberal sentiment about the wider issues of principle raised by the affair blunted the impact of what might have been a debacle for Asquith's government. The exposure of the army's actuation as a political lever of the Tory establishment demanded a reassertion of democratic principle and the supremacy of the House of Commons. Liberals found their champion in trade unionist and Lib-Lab MP John Ward.[63] Ward's speeches in the Curragh debates in the House of Commons frankly addressed the conflict of classes behind the effort to block Home Rule. His attacks on alleged aristocratic efforts to use the army and the king to preserve the influence of the House of Lords caused a sensation among Liberals.

Refusing to be cowed by taunts from the opposition, Ward asserted that the incident had shown working men like him that the law and force were to be directed against them only; workers' representation in Parliament was meaningless, he said, if authority was to remain solely the sphere of the privileged classes.[64] Ward argued for recognition of the true question under debate:

> We have here and now unquestionably to decide … whether for the future this House, when elected by the people, must go to a committee of officers and ask that military junta whether this is a subject that will be allowed to be put into execution or carried into law if so decided by the House, or whether it is a subject with which they, as officers of the Army, think that we, as representing the people, are not entitled to interfere.[65]

This received loud Liberal acclamation, but Ward's peroration, calling upon members to consider whether they would acquiesce in a new form of absolutism or assert their right 'to make the laws of the country absolutely without interference either from King or Army' drew thunderous cheers from the Liberal, Labour and Irish benches for three minutes.[66]

The Times called Ward's 'new Liberal cry' a 'parliamentary portent – a rare phenomenon', and reported that 'the National Liberal Club gave three cheers for the navvies' member "for saying what we all think"'.[67] Unionists mocked him, but Ward's exposure of a facet of the democratic struggle concealed in the battle for the Home Rule Bill made a great impression on progressive thinking. 'A storm', *The Nation* wrote, would be an inadequate term to describe what the Liberal Party had been through: 'convulsion' would be a more accurate word. Outrage over army interference in constitutional government had kindled a fire, the newspaper claimed, that had engulfed Liberal Britain, especially in the north.[68] *The Westminster Gazette* held that Ward's impassioned speech accurately represented the inflamed feelings of the working classes. The issues of adherence to law and the supremacy of the Commons, it said, had unified progressive opinion as no others had in recent years.[69] Determination to see the trinity of Liberal legislation – Home Rule, Welsh disestablishment, and the abolition of plural voting – enacted without interference suddenly solidified.

Ward's portent pointed to the increasing cleavage of politics on class lines, and the growing demands for the redress of economic inequality. Though Ward was firmly in the Liberal camp, his intervention resonated with Labour's impatience to advance beyond constitutional issues to the settlement of pressing economic ones. Labour's position on Irish Home Rule was one of support on its own merits and for clearance of an old issue blocking social reform; but the party also had self-serving reasons. Like many other observers, Labour leaders foresaw the breakdown of traditional party divisions in Ireland once the long-held demand for Home Rule was satisfied. The emergence of a strong Irish Labour Party, it was hoped, would attach many Irish in Britain more firmly to the British Labour Party, thus fortifying it throughout the United Kingdom.[70] Labour members particularly resented the reassertion of the powers of privilege behind the Ulster controversy that Ward's speeches exposed, and their opposition to a government cave-in steadily intensified.

Ward's lead was taken up by a meeting of the National Liberal Club on 31 March, which passed a resolution condemning 'unpatriotic attempts of the Tory Party to corrupt the Army and use it as an instrument for the defeat of Parliamentary government'.[71] A similar memorial was addressed to the prime minister by the London Young Liberal Federation.[72] Several local Liberal associations passed resolutions calling on ministers to take vigorous action to discharge disloyal officers, disarm the Ulster rebels, and put the UVF leaders on trial for treasonable conspiracy.[73] On 3 April the General Committee of the National Liberal Federation condemned the Unionist tactics as subversive and unpatriotic, and called upon the government to 'preserve unimpaired the constitutional rights of the people … to have their laws settled for them in Parliament without any military interference'. The Liberal ministry, a speaker told the gathering,

> … was not going to be bullied into compromise. They were not going to be dictated to by the Army or browbeaten by rebels, and they were determined, if they had to smash no matter what ancient institutions, that the people should be masters in their own house [loud cheers].[74]

The Freeman's Journal claimed that, amid the swell of feeling that arose after the Curragh episode, it would be difficult to find a Liberal who would support the principle of an amending bill. It speculated that, just as in 1910, when in deciding the precedence of the budget or veto proposals Liberal backbenchers had been swayed by the views of the Irish Party, the proposed amending bill's fate would be similarly determined.[75]

Emboldened backbenchers had two objectives: to pressure ministers to cease pandering to lawlessness in Ulster, and to defeat Unionist anti-democratic designs by passing Home Rule under the Parliament Act. A group of forty Liberal MPs met to express their dissatisfaction with the government's failure to prosecute Ulster gunrunners, and to give voice to the strong feeling in the country about the impunity extended to Carson.[76] The meeting, which the *Daily News and Leader* regretfully noted had been characterised by a degree of timidity, resulted in a resolution eventually signed by sixty Liberal members.[77] Neil Primrose MP led a deputation of dissentient Liberals to 10 Downing Street that included fellow members Eustace Fiennes, Arthur Sherwell, Colonel James Greig, James Hogge and Walter Roch.[78] The import of the deputation's personnel was probably as great as the message it bore, indicating, as it did, dissatisfaction from all sections of the party: Sherwell and Hogge were social-reforming radicals, as was Primrose; military men Greig and Fiennes, with Roch, were from the party's right wing. The grass-roots origin of the discontent was emphasised by the Liberal Central Association, which, in May 1914, offered reassurance of the certainty of the passage of the 'trinity' of Liberal bills, which 'the rank and file of the party in the constituencies rightly expect the Government to pass ... before another General Election takes place'.[79]

A group of prominent Irish men and women sought to reinforce Liberal opinion against Ulster exclusion in a letter published in the *Daily News and Leader*, *The Manchester Guardian*, and *The Irish Times*. Signed by Sir Roger Casement, Eoin MacNeill, Darrell Figgis, Alice Stopford Green, George Russell (Æ), Alec Wilson and others, the letter declared that partition of Ireland would be a calamity for Ireland and Britain. The trade and banking interests of north-east Ulster would suffer, the writers warned, and the Irish question would remain in British politics, worsened by raw feeling and by unpunished threats of violent disorder that would ignite trouble in Britain and the empire. The writers suggested a conference of Redmond, Carson and independent Irish leaders to consider an alternative to the dismemberment of the island, an evil for which, they wrote, all parts of the nation would be the poorer.[80] The appeal for all-Ireland talks recalled earlier initiatives, such as the fruitful 1902 Land Conference, and for the advanced nationalists among the letter's signatories the proposal was consistent with the creed of strict Irish self-reliance.

Lloyd George, a keen observer of the barometer of Liberal opinion, addressed a gathering of a thousand members of the Bristol Radical Operative Association on a day's holiday in Criccieth. The Liberal Party, he said, was in the final stages of a struggle to make democracy predominant. He affirmed that the progressive 'coalition' was united in desiring to see the Parliament Act a 'living law', and that 'the Government were not going to give up until they had reaped the harvest which had been sown at the command of the people'. There might be a 'little temporary trouble in the North-East of Ireland', he told the assembly, but 'he had no doubt at all [it] would settle down'.[81] *The Manchester Guardian* thought the Chancellor over-optimistic about the prospects for Ulster but right regarding the Parliament Act. Liberal disaffection, it asserted, had played a part in the string of recent by-election defeats, but it was not owing to any swing to the Unionists; it was, rather, discontent with the slow pace of progress of social reforms, and a lack of vigour in applying Liberal principles.[82]

Calls for greater government forthrightness came from many quarters. John Ward, who published expanded arguments against army interference in civil society in *The Soldier and the Citizen* in July, demanded revision of the Parliament Act to ensure fair play for Liberals.[83] The WLF council, meeting in June, passed both a resolution 'rejoicing' that Home Rule would soon be law, and a rider proposed by Molly Childers urging the government to make no further concessions to the Ulstermen.[84] In the House of Commons, Arthur Sherwell questioned Birrell about police orders to deal with Ulster Unionists openly carrying arms. The chief secretary's evasive reply that discretion would be exercised drew a supplementary question from Neil Primrose asking how the Irish government showed any sign of life at all.[85] Giving ominous testimony to the depth of generalised back-bench dissatisfaction, twenty-two Liberal MPs abstained in the vote on the budget on 7 July. While many of the abstainers objected to new taxation and expenditures in the bill, others, such as Sherwell, Roch and Baron DeForest, ostentatiously remained in their seats during the division in protest against the Cabinet's supine response to Ulster gunrunning.[86]

Sensing the growing militancy of opinion, speeches at Liberal meetings emphasised the democratic aspect of the struggle. At Oldham, Liberal candidate W.H. Somervall's speech to his local association called for Home Rule on majoritarian grounds, and warned that its defeat would shake British democracy to its foundations.[87] In Batley, Walter Runciman, president of the Board of Agriculture, vowed that there would be no surrender of the Parliament Act, and professed that the ministry would be unworthy of support were it to do so.[88] Addressing a WLF garden party in Halifax, junior minister C.P. Trevelyan acknowledged Liberal criticism of the prime minister and the anxiety in certain quarters that the party might be diverted from enacting the bills that the electorate expected it to pass. F.D. Acland MP and Lord Beauchamp appealed to Liberal demonstrations at Steyning and Northampton to trust the party's leadership, and pledged that the Parliament Act would not be subverted.[89] Liberal associations in Huddersfield, Blackpool and Didsbury passed resolutions against further concessions to Ulster, and demanded that the Parliament Act should operate.[90]

The announcement of the Buckingham Palace conference (which is discussed more fully in Chapter 7) caused disquiet among Liberal MPs owing to their concern about the apparent infringement of the rights of the House of Commons. A meeting was called by members incensed by the king's action, but the whips caught wind of the move and ensured the attendance of compliant Liberal members with a view to stifling dissent.[91] On 21 July 112 Liberal MPs, representing forty per cent of the party's parliamentary delegation, met in the Grand Committee Room of the House of Commons.[92] Speakers denied that they objected to the conference, but urged that no attempt be made to force a settlement upon the nationalists.[93] The demand of the meeting's co-sponsor, Sir Thomas Whittaker, that the prime minister should insist upon dismissal by the king rather than advise the dissolution of Parliament, aroused enthusiasm, but Leo Chiozza Money's motion protesting against the king's intrusion was defeated.[94] The meeting unanimously affirmed its

> … unswerving support for the claims of Ireland as put forward by the Nationalist members and embodied in the Government of Ireland Bill and renews its determination to stand by them till their cause was won … [the Liberal members'] most emphatic opinion was that it is the imperative duty of the Government to complete the whole of their programme under the Parliament Act before a further appeal is made to the constituencies.[95]

Whittaker and Sir Henry Dalziel MP delivered the meeting's resolution to the prime minister.[96] Though the backbenchers denied that the message they carried was in any way a censure, it was a public expression of exasperation with ministerial backsliding, and a veiled threat of revolt to Asquith.[97] *The Westminster Gazette*, with marvellous understatement, admitted that matters had taken an unconventional turn, but insisted that the resolution was unnecessary because ministers had no intention of calling an election or forcing a settlement on the nationalists.[98] *The Freeman's Journal* portrayed the development as a sign of strength, signifying that Liberalism was responding to an assault on the British people's right to govern themselves.[99] This optimistic interpretation ignored what was plainly a disagreement with ministers, but the back-bench protest did attest to the transformation of Irish Home Rule into an issue symbolic of the vindication of British democracy and to its electrifying effect on Liberals.

Criticism of the inter-party conference abounded. Independent nationalist MP Laurence Ginnell defied the Speaker in asking the prime minister what authority he had to advise the king to place himself at the head of a conspiracy to defeat the House of Commons.[100] Dr John Clifford wrote sternly to the *Daily News and Leader* deploring the initiative. Drawing inspiration from J.A. Hobson, Clifford described as 'traffic in treason' the Tories' risking the destruction of every institution of the state in order to deny to the people the power to govern themselves.[101] Implicit in his criticism was a judgement upon Asquith for trafficking of the same dishonourable kind at the conference table. A Labour Party resolution condemned 'undue interference on the part of the Crown … calculated to defeat the purposes of the Parliament Act', noting its 'surprise that two of the representatives are practically rebels under arms against constitutional authority'.[102] An anonymous Liberal MP, writing in the *Daily News and Leader*, denounced the conference as another attempt to sabotage the mechanism of the Parliament Act. Asking whether the Cabinet realised the attitude of the Liberal rank and file, the writer asserted that if Parliament were dissolved before the bills were passed, the Liberal Party would go into a general election utterly discredited and deserving of defeat.[103]

Liberal MPs interviewed by the *Daily News and Leader* were divided as to the wisdom of a conference, but they were uniformly against the dissolution of Parliament. Some wished to see the Home Rule Bill passed intact if the amending bill was rejected; others defended the principle of temporary exclusion. Thomas Lough said the crisis was artificial, and that the only talk of civil war was in the London Tory press. Russell Rea asserted that even if talk of disturbances in Ulster were true, 'we have come to the point that we have got to risk it. I cannot conceive that Parliament should be dissolved as part of a bargain in the face of the opinion of the party.' Neil Primrose insisted that the 'Liberal Die-Hards' represented the view of the majority in the country. Gordon Harvey claimed his constituents in Rochdale were 'very disinclined to make further concessions, and they are indignant at the suggestion that there should be an appeal to the country on the Irish question again'. Radical MP J.W. Logan wired the prime minister threatening to resign his seat if further concessions were made. Arthur Sherwell declared that a Cabinet cave-in to demands for a dissolution 'would be to abdicate democratic government, and to imperil the whole theory and practice of representative government'.[104] The executive committee of the National Liberal Federation, meanwhile, with Liberal grandee Sir John Brunner in the chair, resolved unanimously on behalf of the Liberal associations of Britain to declare that the rank and file in the country was unwavering in its determination to see the three crucial bills enacted under the provisions of the Parliament Act.[105]

Forceful statements of Liberal feeling in the country to see the Parliament Act vindicated were accompanied by displays of appreciation for the Irish Party chairman. *The Freeman's Journal's* parliamentary sketch writer described how, when Redmond rose to respond to the announcement of the conference in a humble, almost meek manner, he was greeted with hearty and sustained cheering from the radical Liberal, Labour and nationalist benches.[106] Days later, as spectators waited for the Buckingham Palace conferees to emerge, cheers went up when the crowd spied Carson and Bonar Law. Redmond and Dillon, leaving on foot shortly thereafter, were pursued by boisterous crowds down Birdcage Walk. As the Irishmen progressed on their way to Westminster, the crowd grew dense, shouting its support for Redmond and Home Rule. When the noisy procession passed Wellington Barracks, off duty Irish Guards flocked to the windows, waving caps and cheering on the nationalist leaders.[107] The guardsmen's political enthusiasm provoked adverse comment in the evening newspapers, and the following day the soldiers were confined to barracks and the nationalist leaders left the Palace in a taxi.[108] Redmond's appearance in the House of Commons after the conference's failure prompted another vocal effusion from the government benches. Not since John Ward's speech of 25 March roused the House of Commons, commented the *Westmeath Examiner*, had Parliament witnessed such a demonstration of devotion and enthusiasm from the Liberal and Labour benches.[109]

Protest at the eleventh hour

Sir Henry Dalziel chaired a grand public demonstration attended by 5,000 people at the London Opera House on Kingsway on the evening of 29 July 1914. *The Times* reported that 50,000 applications for tickets had been received in the week following the meeting's announcement, prompting an equally large overflow meeting to be improvised at the Aldwych Skating Rink.[110] Liberal, Labour and nationalist MPs were in attendance, as was, commented *The Freeman's Journal*, the cream of the capital's progressive political thinkers and a large London-Irish contingent.[111] The occasion was, said *Reynolds's Newspaper*, 'the most remarkable manifestation of enthusiastic Liberalism that London has seen for many a day'.[112] A band played radical protest anthems; when it struck up 'God Save Ireland', the assembly rose as one in song.[113] 'Democracy before the Army', called a stentorian voice a little later, and 'Three cheers for John Ward!' The crowd warmly obliged the invitation.

Dalziel spoke of 'open and avowed war against the fabric of the State', while Joseph Devlin MP claimed that 'The issue was not between the Tory Party and Ireland, but between the Tory Party and democracy.'[114] Ulster, he told the gathering, was merely a proxy in a larger conflict between privilege and progress. If the government were to fall before the trinity of Liberal legislation was secured, he told the crowd to an outburst of cheers, the Parliament Act would be a dead letter.[115] Rising in response to cries from the audience, John Ward stressed the determination of progressive forces to see Home Rule through, and repeated his warning that to submit to intimidation or violence would spell the end of representative government.[116] Neil Primrose moved the demonstration's sole resolution: 'That this meeting demands that the Government shall complete its legislative programme and thus secure the effective operation of the Parliament Act.'[117] Arthur Sherwell stressed the instrumentality of Irish Home Rule as a test of the mettle of Liberalism, and the key to its life or death:

> We say ... that so long as the government sets itself to discharge the mandate from the electorate, 'Stand firm, go ahead with your work, justify and vindicate the Parliament Act, we as Liberals will be behind you to a man'. [Cheers] But we also say to the Government: 'Waver and hesitate, yield to attempted pressure or influence, and we will do our best to overthrow you as a Government – [renewed cheers] – and to recreate and re-establish Liberalism in this country on a sound and Democratic basis [Great enthusiasm]'.[118]

As the meetings ended, crowds spilled into the streets, clogging the roads as far as Wellington Street, cheering and singing for Ireland and for democracy. The acute political crisis, whose uncertain climax seemed so imminent, faded imperceptibly with the voices of the revellers into the cool summer night. A half-mile away, at the War Office in Whitehall, the electric lights were burning. With black clouds gathering on the European horizon, the department's War Book had been opened that afternoon.

6

The Ferment of Nationalism

The meteoric rise of the Irish Volunteers in 1914 was a development apprehended by many contemporaries as a remarkable and momentous event in Irish history. Given impetus by the example of the Ulster Volunteer Force and propelled by anger at the government's feeble response to Ulster resistance, the emergence of a nationalist paramilitary movement offered discontented strands of nationalist opinion – variegated advanced nationalists, a dwindling band of Sinn Féiners, and labour agitators – an opportunity to press for a more assertive modus operandi. Notwithstanding the vast preponderance of Irish Party supporters among the Irish Volunteers' membership, its inception, ethos and popular appeal constituted a criticism of, and challenge to, Redmondism.[1]

The existence of a nationalist paramilitary force further complicated the issue of Ulster, confirming northern prejudices and appearing to vindicate Unionist attacks on Home Rule. The Irish Party's adoption of militant rhetoric in emulation of the Volunteers deprived it of the gloss of generous moderation towards Ulster that the constitutionalists had hitherto affected, and crystallised an adversarial posture that the orthodox leaders had been anxious to avoid. Despite the care taken by the Volunteers' founders to stress the non-sectarian and non-factional character of the movement, it embodied a political impulse that lent credence to the possibility of a severance of the union with Britain.[2] Its spread hardened attitudes against exclusion in nationalist Ireland and, as the Irish Party leaders well understood, exacerbated the intractability of an already vexed situation. This danger was underestimated by the Volunteers' founders, many of whom acted out of naive idealism; others appear to have been motivated by a reckless philosophy of creative destruction.

A rival doctrine of physical force, whether or not such force was actually to be wielded or should remain implicit, intensified the Irish Party's difficulties with its own constituency. The radicalisation of public discourse threatened its hold over popular nationalism. Military posturing and assertions of manliness gave vent to pent-up nationalist frustrations, and particularly appealed to the young. The Volunteers' leaders promised that the force would be an enduring presence, come what may, and at its zenith the movement seemed almost to become self-propagating. This raised the prospect of a powerful, permanent rival to the Irish Party's political hegemony, and an ever-present threat to an Irish government. Such a militia might exercise influence to restrain or command the actions of a nascent administration, or potentially curtail its existence.[3]

The question of whether Ulster would fight when Home Rule was enacted dominated police reports and preoccupied ministers, and has subsequently been much debated by historians.[4] Yet a survey of resident magistrates in the summer of 1914 revealed them to be much more concerned about the intentions of the nationalist Volunteers. It was not the formation of a provisional government in Ulster, nor the possibility of sectarian bloodletting, alarming though these prospects were, that most worried magistrates in the counties; it was the seeming inescapability of violent revolt in the rest of Ireland, if the Irish Volunteers succeeded in arming themselves, that riveted provincial officials charged with maintaining order.

This chapter draws on Bureau of Military History (BMH) witness statements of members and observers of the Irish Volunteer movement in 1913/14, recorded between 1947 and 1957. Since BMH testimony was solicited from participants in the events of Easter 1916 and afterwards, it necessarily reflects an advanced nationalist bias. A recounting of thoughts and events thirty to forty years in the past also raises obvious questions as to the accuracy of the testimony provided. In addition, witnesses' concern for their reputations, together with their awareness of the potential political impact of their testimony and the possibility that they might have internalised a received historical narrative, undermine the reliability of the recorded evidence. In view of the complex factors affecting its veracity, where BMH testimony is cited it will be made clear that the views expressed were recollections recorded well after the events.

Founding principles

The Irish Volunteer militia, as conceived by the organisation's principal founder, Eoin MacNeill, was an instrument designed to secure and defend Home Rule. MacNeill feared that the Irish Party leaders underestimated the lengths to which Home Rule's Unionist opponents might go to wreck it. He asserted that Tory subversion of the constitutional path to Home Rule amounted to a nullification of the franchise of the Irish people and the removal of what few rights the Act of Union had left them.[5] MacNeill's objective was not to undermine the constitutional effort, nor to contest the Irish Party's authority; he sought, rather, to demonstrate to British Tories that the denial of Home Rule would necessitate coercion of a kind they had never imagined.[6]

At the same time, MacNeill hoped to bring about the spiritual restoration of nationalism. The nationalist-militia's formation was a development not simply in emulation of the Ulster Volunteers but one that sought to combat the impression in Britain and Ireland that Irish nationalists were a beaten people. The Volunteers, MacNeill asserted, were brought into being to prevent despondency by showing that nationalists refused to be treated with contempt.[7]

Ideas of a restoration of Irish self-respect and manliness echoed the discourse of Fenianism, a nineteenth-century revolutionary philosophy aimed at establishing an independent Irish republic. In the wake of a failed Fenian rising in 1867, radical-nationalist energies were largely dissipated by engagement with constitutional nationalism and increasing land agitation. The revolutionary flame still flickered, however, for a hard-line fringe in the secret Irish Republican Brotherhood (IRB), which sustained a shadowy existence through lean years in the early twentieth century. With the collapse of support for Sinn Féin in 1908, the IRB's militant creed gained renewed appeal, and by 1910 a younger and unambiguously insurrectionist group of men had assumed the secret society's leadership. The possibilities of a nationalist paramilitary force as a vessel for radicalisation were obvious to these would-be armed revolutionaries, and it was no coincidence that twelve of the thirty original Volunteer organisers were, or were shortly to become, members of the IRB.[8]

The physical-force men among the Volunteers' founders had ambitions beyond MacNeill's aim of creating a deterrent force to safeguard the granting of Home Rule. Joseph Plunkett, writing in the first issue of *The Irish Volunteer* newspaper, proclaimed that the awakening of the Volunteer spirit represented the material and symbolic reassertion of Irish manhood, so long suppressed and humiliated.[9] Catholic-nationalist visionary Patrick Pearse, who believed that redemption required the ultimate test of Irish manliness, asserted that only armed struggle could attain meaningful nationhood.[10] Thomas MacDonagh, another of the Volunteers' advanced nationalist founders (though, like Plunkett, one not yet sworn into the IRB), was far-sighted and pragmatic but no less idealistic than his colleagues. MacDonagh aspired to use the might of the new national 'army' to wrest political control from the orthodox nationalist leaders and forever change the relationship of Ireland to England. MacDonagh's vision implied an Ireland independent of the British Empire, with sovereignty residing not in Crown and Parliament but in the Irish people. As Matthew Kelly asserted, ideas such as these were incompatible with a Home Rule settlement that sought to restore the legitimacy of British governance by a modification of the Union.[11]

Like MacNeill's dual purposes of moral reinvigoration and deterrence, the philosophy of the physical-force men of the Irish Volunteers' provisional committee also cloaked pragmatic ends. It was a short step from extolling the manly spirit of volunteering to cultivating the ground for armed resistance to British rule. Manipulating the movement for revolutionary purposes was clearly in the minds of the IRB men among the Volunteers' organisers from the outset, and this conspiratorial clique dominated the organisation's life.

MacNeill did not share the disruptive aims of his more extreme provisional committee colleagues, and was anxious to do nothing to harm the chances of Home Rule. He and Bulmer Hobson (another IRB man) were careful to install Irish Party members in prominent positions at the organisation's inception, and ensured that constitutionalists were well represented among the speakers at the movement's inaugural meeting at the Rotunda in Dublin on 25 November 1913. However, an equivocal speech of welcome at the meeting by Michael Davitt, namesake of his agrarian-agitator father, voiced the ambivalence of the Irish Party men. It contrasted starkly with Pearse's dramatic heralding of the awakening of a spirit of self-reliance to secure freedom for the Irish people.[12] One of those present on the Rotunda dais reflected later that deep divisions in the organisation were evident from its first meeting.[13]

MacNeill was equally concerned that the movement's all-inclusive character be seen to embrace differences of party or sect. He extended a hand of comradeship to dissenting Ulstermen with a call for cheers for Sir Edward Carson at an early Volunteer meeting in Galway. The surprising flourish, a ploy to disarm charges of nationalist malice, was warmly received. However, AOH men in Cork, at a Volunteer meeting in the city days later, took MacNeill's repetition of the call as a cue to rush the stage and assault the organisers.[14] Despite the mayhem, Liam de Róiste recalled that by the meeting's end, hundreds of men had been enrolled as Volunteers.[15]

The infant-movement's potential to upset the delicate work of the Irish Party leaders elicited their immediate hostility. Redmond believed Sir Roger Casement, co-author of the Volunteers' manifesto, to be a 'dangerous revolutionary', while Dillon's view that the paramilitary movement was unhelpful and unnecessary was expounded over the winter and spring of 1913/14 by MPs Thomas Lundon and Richard Hazleton.[16] MacNeill sought to calm anxieties, writing to a nationalist MP of his belief that Home Rule was far from secure, and reiterating the value of a Volunteer force to render Ireland ungovernable by a Tory administration if it succeeded in disrupting the bill's implementation.[17]

The spread of disaffection

The formation of a nationalist militia coincided with the arms proclamation of 5 December 1913. What appeared to be a disproportionate response to the inception of a nationalist Volunteer corps aggravated suspicions of double standards. One advanced nationalist later reflected that the apparent blatant inconsistency confirmed that the British, 'Tory or Radical, obscurantist or progressive, were, as the separatist press was constantly telling us, all the same'.[18] Redmond's concession of temporary exclusion of Ulster in March 1914 excited bafflement and disappointment, even among moderate nationalists, and elicited fresh manifestations of discontent. The Clonbroney, County Longford branch of the UIL adopted a resolution asserting that the Home Rule Bill as introduced was the minimum acceptable; if the bill was mutilated, its fate would be, as for the Council Bill in 1907, a humiliating rejection by the Irish people.[19] IRB member Ernest Blythe was sent to Belfast to agitate against exclusion, particularly through Sinn Féin and organised-labour channels. Through the IRB's 'Freedom Club' propaganda organisation, he demanded that nothing short of a national convention could sanction a scheme of exclusion that might become indefinite.[20] The Irish Party, however, resisted such demands, arguing that the 1912 Irish Convention had expressly given its leadership full authority to deal with amendments.

The Irish Citizen Army, organised by Jim Larkin to defend striking workers against the police in the Dublin Lockout, was reorganised in November 1913. The 'army', however, as even friendly observers recalled, could muster only scant numbers before the war.[21] Its membership in 1913/14 never appears to have amounted to more than a few hundred.[22] Nonetheless, what it lacked in numerical strength it made up for in pluck, disrupting Laurence J. Kettle's reading of the manifesto at the inaugural meeting of the Irish Volunteers. His speech, a witness recorded, was rendered entirely inaudible by a 'pandemonium ... [of] shouts, yells, cat-calls, interspersed with explosions', owing to

Kettle's supposed sympathy with the employers during the strike.[23] Racked by infighting, the Irish Citizen Army had nothing but spite for the more successful Volunteer movement, which it attacked unceasingly in *The Irish Worker*.

On 22 March 1914 the National Council of Sinn Féin met to debate the option of temporary exclusion for Ulster counties. Arthur Griffith, presiding, told the meeting that the arrangement amounted to the perpetual dismemberment of Ireland, and asserted that it was the first time in European history that disintegration of a country was proposed under the guise of freedom. Alderman Thomas Kelly claimed that it was obvious that the Tories were using the people of Ulster as pawns in the British party game.[24] A resolution supported by Jennie Wyse-Power, one of Sinn Féin's founders, Countess Constance Markievicz of the Irish Citizen Army, and union leader Seán Milroy, and unanimously adopted, asserted 'That the territorial integrity of Ireland, and the essential unity of its people, are the basis of Irish Nationalism, and any proposals antagonistic to them, temporarily or permanently, no matter how, or wherever put forward, must be condemned and resisted.'[25]

The Sinn Féin resolution was circulated to all representative bodies in Ireland with an invitation to nominate delegates to a national convention in Dublin to consider steps for giving it practical effect. At a meeting of Cavan Urban Council, its proposer argued that demands for blind loyalty to the Irish Party were suffocating the instinctive national impulse of the Irish people.[26] In Abbeyleix, no decision on the Sinn Féin measure was taken, but even a local UIL representative spoke in favour of sending Redmond a pointed loyal message to stiffen his resolve.[27]

The parliamentary committee of the Irish Trades Union Congress mounted a demonstration in Sackville Street on 5 April 1914. Placards proclaimed that the meeting's objective was to resist the severance of Ulster from the rest of Ireland and to defeat the efforts of a privileged class of army officers to frustrate the will of the majority.[28] Crowds large enough to stop the trams in Dublin's main thoroughfare heard speeches from William O'Brien, chairman of the Dublin branch of the Independent Labour Party, and other labour activists condemning exclusion proposals. Honoured guests Countess Markievicz, Hanna Sheehy-Skeffington and Bulmer Hobson observed the proceedings from a wagonette. P.T. Daly, an advanced nationalist and secretary of the Irish Trades Union Congress, told the crowd that northern Unionists would be taught a lesson by those whom they arrogantly held in contempt. D.R. Campbell of the Belfast Trades Council asserted that John Redmond – whose name was greeted by groans – had overreached his authority in conceding county option of exclusion. He commended, instead, Sir Horace Plunkett's plan of an opt-out for individual Ulster counties after a trial period.[29]

In the first weeks of April, the Sinn Féin anti-exclusion resolution was adopted by more than a dozen public bodies. In the north of the island it was approved by Lisnaskea, Ardee and Inishowen district councils, by Clones Urban Council, and by the Dromore West Board of Guardians. In the west, guardians in Oughterard and Dingle adopted the resolution, as did Tuam Town Commissioners and Glenamaddy and Ballinasloe councils. Elsewhere, Gorey, Edenderry and Celbridge district councils endorsed the Sinn Féin demand, as did Sligo, Limerick and Clonakilty boards of guardians.[30] A counter-insurgency by local Irish Party politicians charged the dissentients with damaging factionalism, which was answered by countercharges of attempts to stifle dissent. Seán Milroy, writing to *The Freeman's Journal*, denied that the resolution was directed against the Parliamentary Party, and asserted that the issue was a grave one, dealing as it did with the question of whether the Irish nation could work as one to secure freedom and well-being for its people.[31] *The Freeman's Journal* noted that resolutions of support for the Irish Party outnumbered adoptions of the dissident programme, and that votes for the Sinn Féin resolution had been rescinded in many places.[32] Still, the rash of declarations against exclusion demonstrated Sinn Féin's capacity to influence the political agenda, and raised the party's credibility to its highest level in years.

Sinn Féin followed up its widely debated motion with a detailed programme. Calling Ulster's claim to a right greater than Ireland's right of national destiny illogical, its proposals advanced increased representation for the northern counties and additional safeguards for the minority population, while maintaining democratic principles.[33] The compromise formula, launched by Arthur Griffith and W.T. Cosgrave at a meeting of the National Council of Sinn Féin on 29 April, failed to gain traction and soon disappeared from view.[34] However, Sinn Féin's willingness to engage with Home Rule set it apart from the intransigent attitude of the IRB. The abstentionist party took a pragmatic view of the orthodox nationalists' much-derided strategy of incremental progress towards autonomy when it was seen that it might be of advantage to Sinn Féin.

An uneasy union

With the failure of Sinn Féin's initiative and of the labour-activists' efforts to mount an effective challenge to exclusion proposals, the Irish Volunteers remained the principal channel for expressions of discontent. One Volunteer recalled that the Curragh Incident rendered it 'crystal clear to the Irish man-in-the-street that no matter what challenge a "Tory-Orange confederacy"' would put up, Asquith's government lacked the stomach for a fight.[35] This realisation added force to the Volunteers' message of self-reliance, and led, another claimed, to a jump in the numbers joining local corps.[36] From its origins as a small and largely Dublin-centred movement, by the end of April 1914 the RIC reported that the Irish Volunteers had assembled 123 battalions with 19,206 members outside the Dublin Metropolitan Police district, and 1,370 Volunteers organised into ten battalions within the city. The police believed that rifles were possessed only in negligible numbers.[37]

Adverse developments for Home Rule were reported with a mixture of alarm and despondency in the orthodox nationalist press.[38] By May, facing headwinds in public opinion at home and concerned that ministers might seek to press them into making further concessions, the Irish Party leaders came to the decision that they must take control of the Volunteers. Redmond, incredulous at the spread of the movement, told Darrell Figgis that he would not countenance forming a government with so large an organisation in existence capable of disputing his authority.[39] The party opened negotiations with the Volunteer leaders in a peremptory fashion, souring an already difficult prospective union. While protracted and disagreeable bargaining was underway, the IRB men of the Volunteers' provisional committee initiated secret efforts to obtain rifles.[40]

T.P. Gill sought to smooth the path for the Irish Party's assumption of control of the Volunteers, advising Redmond, after meeting MacNeill, that the Volunteers' chief of staff could be treated with 'perfect candour. He is absolutely straight and loyal and of good judgment.'[41] Stephen Gwynn was courting the Volunteer leader, confessing that he thought the party had been mistaken in not associating itself with the movement from the outset.[42] For his part, MacNeill stressed that he wished to see harmony, citing the Volunteers' capacity to unite the young and the nationalist old guard as its greatest success.[43]

Advanced nationalists, Laurence Nugent recalled, perceived the Irish Party's move as a craven effort to retain its hold over increasingly disaffected supporters. Some, he claimed, believed that British ministers instigated Redmond's action.[44] Many deplored the nullification of a non-party, non-sectarian ethos that a takeover by the party would bring, while the IRB men of the organisation feared that Joseph Devlin and J.D. Nugent of the hated Ancient Order of

Hibernians would try to swallow the Volunteers whole.[45] Amid this atmosphere of suspicion and indignation, Redmond's heavy-handed efforts to overbear the provisional committee only alienated the advanced nationalists further, ensuring that the merger of party and militia was never more than grudging and incomplete.

Gill was doing his best to gloss over the 'little exuberances and eccentricities' of the extremists of the provisional committee with the Irish Party chairman.[46] He advised the appointment of a general officer for the Volunteers so as to avoid the organisation creating 'mischief of all sorts' and becoming 'a peril instead of a magnificent source of moral and physical strength'.[47] Gill suggested General Sir Thomas Kelly-Kenny, Irish hero of the South African War, whom he believed Asquith would favour, as

> ... from the Imperial point of view as well as from the general Irish
> and British point of view there is nothing more necessary now than
> to get the Nationalist Volunteers effectively organised from above ...
> It is the surest road to peace between north and south – and, indeed,
> to creating an Imperial as well as a national asset.[48]

Gill's observation provides an insight into a loyalist-nationalist state of mind that he shared with Redmond, a phenomenon admirably explored by James McConnel and Alvin Jackson.[49] Gill was a nationalist of no little passion, proud of the resurgence of Irish manhood, who, as has been seen, occasionally had to master his emotions at slights and provocations to the national cause. Yet he saw nothing incompatible between Irish nationality and imperial patriotism. Gill, like Redmond, wanted a self-governing Ireland to play a prominent role in the affairs of the empire along the lines of the overseas white-settler dominions, and felt genuine concern for its welfare. This peculiarly unionist form of nationalism, with its strongly British as well as Irish sense of identity and its embrace of imperialism, intensely antagonised the Irish Party's detractors. What to old parliamentary warriors like Redmond and Gill was instinctive and patriotic was to advanced nationalists obsequiously West British and utterly repugnant.

Redmond's list of nominees to the provisional committee aroused great antipathy. The list of three MPs, four clergymen and a collection of provincial mayors bore a greater resemblance to a charitable board than to the organising committee of a fighting force. The party's nominations of Joseph Devlin, J.D. Nugent and Michael Davitt were particularly objectionable. For the IRB men of the provisional committee, Devlin and Nugent personified the AOH, while the youthful Davitt's tepid enthusiasm at the Rotunda meeting had marked him out as an agent of Devlin's benefactor, John Dillon.[50] Joseph Plunkett saw that Redmond's demand for control of the Volunteers placed its founders in an impossible situation. In the absence of arms, any action the movement might take to resist the party's overture risked its becoming 'merely political'. While Plunkett accepted that the majority of the provisional committee was unwilling to risk responsibility for the loss of Home Rule that a breach with the Irish Party might precipitate, he believed that an open rupture would soon become unavoidable.[51]

With Redmond's publication of humiliating terms for the absorption of the Volunteers in a letter on 13 June, a decision was forced upon the provisional committee. The committee's public statement made no attempt to hide its divisions or difficulties. Redmond's demand for twenty-five delegates to the committee, it said, rendered the pretence of the Volunteers' non-party character untenable. The committee's majority had decided, however, that in the interest of national unity, and in furtherance of the aim of establishing a permanent, armed force of Volunteers, the lesser evil was to accede to the Irish Party's demands. The capitulation thereafter rendered MacNeill and Bulmer Hobson, who threw their weight behind this line, figures of suspicion among the IRB faction in the Volunteers' leadership. Signifying the rift created by the decision, the dissenting minority on the committee published a letter of protest.[52]

That the Irish Volunteers fell some way short of being the national asset that Gill desired was observed by Maurice Headlam, a senior British civil servant travelling in the south of Ireland in the summer of 1914. Unionist friends in the country, he recorded, were anxious that, once the Volunteers were armed, their 'natural instinct' would be to mount a guerrilla campaign against the police. Fishing at Knocklofty, County Tipperary, Headlam's party came upon a squad of men being drilled by an old man. The tourists tried to act as naturally as possible, but as soon as they were noticed, the elderly instructor called his squad to attention and shouted, 'Prisint arms, ye devils, prisint arms to the gintry.' Doubtless uncertain of whether this acknowledgement of their presence was deferential or ironic, the gentlemen touched their hats and hurried on.[53] Exasperation with the disorganised and ill-equipped state of the Volunteers was felt by those leading them. Thomas MacDonagh received a report of poor turnout for a drill. The small unit had borne the taunts of watching soldiers well, his correspondent recorded, but the conductor of the fife-and-drum band had been drunk, and refused to leave the procession when asked to do so.[54]

The Volunteer zenith

As Michael Wheatley persuasively argued, the Irish Party's assimilation of the Irish Volunteers was more of a reverse process, with Volunteer corps displacing many of the functions of the UIL and AOH.[55] Irish Party and AOH endorsement of the Volunteers caused enrolments to soar. Ex-army men were signing up, Liam de Róiste recalled, and money was coming in from wealthy men who had hitherto shunned the movement.[56] The RIC estimated the Irish Volunteers outside of Dublin to number 78,000 at the beginning of June, nearly 114,000 by month's end, and 132,000 early in July.[57] This remarkable rate of growth was reported in somewhat exaggerated terms in the British press, and prompted Unionist questions in Parliament.[58]

The organisation had already attracted support from all classes of nationalists, but the party's sanction gave the Volunteers a new respectability. It could count among its prominent members Roman Catholic clergy, county and district councillors, magistrates, ex-military men, and a few Protestant notables. The mayor of Waterford took an active interest in his local force, and the master of the Tipperary foxhounds pledged £100 for uniforms for the county corps. In Queen's County (County Laois), the nationalist militia had the blessing of the Protestant rector of Coolbanagher, and the Kildare Volunteers had on their rolls two justices of the peace, one Church of Ireland and the other Presbyterian.[59]

The excitement at developments in the south of Ireland paradoxically bred a sense of fraternity with the Ulstermen. Many observers commented on the mutual respect that the opposing bodies of Volunteers, north and south, had for one another. At New Ross, 200 Irish Volunteers paid tribute to Carson for showing them the meaning of physical force.[60] A northern correspondent of Redmond's wrote that the men of the UVF were flattered by the imitation, and that a sense that both corps existed to stop outrages and riot was having a wholesome effect on the Protestant community of Ulster.[61] Birrell believed that the Larne gunrunning had been admired by nationalists almost as warmly as by Ulster Unionists; conversely, he speculated that the drilling of 'tens of thousands of the finest young fellows in the south and west makes many a pious Presbyterian in Antrim and Down more than half inclined to whisper the prayer: "Would that once more we could all be united

Irishmen.'"[62] Despite the danger that the opposing armies might one day soon be fighting one another, the widely reported respect that the two corps had for one another seemed proof, to some, of a proud and inextinguishable national spirit.

A women's counterpart to the Irish Volunteers, Cumann na mBan (Irishwomen's Council), was established in May. Like the Volunteers, the organisation stressed its non-partisan credentials, but six of the eight founder members of its provisional committee were advanced nationalists. Cumann na mBan's constitution was dedicated to organising Irish women in defence of liberty and in support of the Irish Volunteers. Yet it sought to be more than a ladies' auxiliary, lending the Irish Volunteers material support by fund-raising for the acquisition of arms and equipment.[63] Perhaps inevitably, the suffragist leanings of Cumann na mBan's progressive leaders came into conflict with the organisation's own constitution, which firmly subordinated all other questions to the national cause.[64]

Irish shopkeepers sought to cash in on the popularity of the Volunteers and the new-found unanimity of nationalist support. Signs advertising military gear appeared, and stocks of Irish-made bandoliers, haversacks and water bottles were offered, as were belts with an Irish harp design.[65] Under a banner hailing the irrepressible advance of the Irish Volunteers, tailors and outfitters Thomas Fallon of Dublin advertised made-to-measure uniforms, touting the bargain price of '45/-' (£2 5*s*).[66] Booksellers M.H. Gill & Son and Ponsonby's, both in Dublin, advertised military handbooks and musketry manuals; song-writer Felix McGlennon hawked a book of marching songs; while the Kilkee Holiday Camp invited Volunteers to spend their summer holidays under canvas.[67] Whelan & Son attested to the company's nationalist fidelity with a motto in the window of its Dublin clothing shop welcoming recruits to the coming Irish army.[68]

The party's co-option of the movement divided nationalist opinion. The O'Brienite *Cork Free Press* criticised the subordination of the movement to the AOH, while an advanced nationalist correspondent to the *Irish Independent* railed against the Volunteers' departure from their non-party roots and how they were being turned to imperial ends.[69] A 'Sinn Féin Volunteer', quoted at length in *The Scotsman*, complained of the party's impertinence in co-opting a movement that it regarded with contempt, and predicted that the new committee would soon attempt to oust some of the organisation's founders.[70] Correspondents to other journals congratulated Redmond for thwarting the subversion of the movement and for subduing the IRB men, whom they predicted would henceforth be 'meek as lambs'.[71] *The Kildare Observer* applauded the wresting of control from an irresponsible fringe of Sinn Féiners and a scattering of misfits with preposterous names.[72] *The Meath Chronicle* and the *Leitrim Observer* expressed similar satisfaction.[73]

Kevin O'Shiel recalled that the Irish Party's takeover of the Volunteers enhanced Redmond's prestige, and was greeted with relief even by some of his critics. Many felt, he recounted, that the party's moderating influence would restrain the 'wild physical force men … [who] wanted a reckless flare-up with England to avenge the Fenian fiasco'.[74] The Stradbally Volunteers expressed their wish to be known as Redmond's personal corps; the Aughrim battalion declared that the Irish Party chairman alone could command soldierly obedience with the authority of Ireland.[75] The consolidation was praised most enthusiastically in the north of the country. The committee of the Letterkenny Volunteers gave its unanimous approval to Redmond's assumption of leadership of the movement. Delegates at a large meeting of the Raphoe Volunteers expressed their full confidence in the Irish Party and Redmond's leadership, as did a similar gathering in Strabane. Ex-MP James Boyle told a meeting of 2,000 Volunteers and supporters at Castlefin, County Donegal that the Volunteers would back up the Irish Party, not for attack but for the defence of homes, altars and, most of all, the indomitable spirit of Irish nationality.[76] Loyalty to the party appears to have remained strongest in the north because of Devlin's personal popularity and also because of the refuge for Catholics offered by the AOH amid rising sectarian tensions.

Some advanced nationalists spoke in defiance of their apparent humiliation. Thomas MacDonagh dismissed the controversy as a fabrication of the press at a large meeting at Bridgetown, County Wexford, and insisted to the gathering that the Volunteers were a physical-force movement that no power could suppress.[77] Patrick Pearse, at Tralee, proclaimed that it would be remembered that this generation of Irishmen had answered a call of destiny. It was no exaggeration, he professed, to say that Ireland's future lay in the Irish Volunteers' hands.[78] Speaking to a crowd of 5,000 at a Volunteers meeting at the Curragh on 7 June, Michael (The) O'Rahilly denied that the movement was hostile to the Irish Party or Home Rule, though he confessed that he was among a small number on the provisional committee who desired something more.[79] The Volunteer movement, he claimed, was a *permanent* force that would secure an Irish government, preserve its position, and possibly expand its powers if called upon to do so by the Irish people.[80] Before a large meeting of Volunteers in Ballycanow, County Wexford, Seán Etchingham vowed that the nationalist militia would not become the tool of English parties, and that, once armed, its members would never lay down their rifles, no matter who told them to.[81] Recalling the demise of the original Irish Volunteers of 1782, the physical-force men of the provisional committee promised recruits that the historic mistake of disbandment would not be repeated.

The rhetoric of headstrong nationalism bore the clear implication that the Volunteers would be used as a weapon, but just whom they were to fight remained unclear. Some speakers asserted that the Volunteers existed to defend Catholics against outrages or to subjugate the Orangemen; others said the militia would expel the British army. Still others said that it was a movement to cow Asquith's government. Some hinted, darkly, that the force would be used to intimidate a future Irish government. Although these desires were inconsistently espoused and often ambiguously stated, they roughly demarcated the division between party supporters and advanced nationalists of various stripes.

Still, orthodox nationalists were surprisingly outspoken in identifying the British as the enemies against whom the Volunteers would defend Ireland. Richard Hazleton MP told a crowd at Glenamaddy that 'if Home Rule is defeated by the methods of Carson … it would be their duty to take such measures as would make British government impossible in Ireland'. In May Thomas Lundon MP declared that '200,000 Volunteers would parade the streets of Dublin and show the government, Liberal or Tory, that they would not allow that measure of justice so dearly won to be withdrawn'.[82] The secretary of the Cavan branch of the UIL veered slightly off-message in suggesting higher ambitions: to not only prevent a Tory administration from reversing Home Rule, but also to leverage self-government for something more.[83]

Colonel Maurice Moore, inspector-general of the Irish Volunteers, claimed principles of unity and inclusivity for the organisation, but warned that the movement would resist the exclusion claims of northern counties. Any government intending to deny Ulster nationalists their right to self-government, he declared, would have to render an account to the Volunteers.[84] At a large meeting in Derry, Rev. William O'Doherty proclaimed that the only thing to stop exclusion 'was a loud, angry protest of Nationalists, backed up by the steady tramp of Irish Volunteers [cheers]. They in the north had yielded enough in the way of exclusion. They would yield no more [renewed cheers].'[85]

Northern speakers made intimate appeals calling on their followers to prepare for a defensive struggle. Joseph Devlin also invoked the defence of homes, altars and liberties. He called on all men over the age of sixteen to join the Belfast regiment of the Irish Volunteers so as to fight for their homeland and, if need be, give their lives for it.[86] The consciousness of northern nationalists of the vulnerability of their position at the front line of the sectarian conflict simplified their view of the Volunteers' purpose.

Devlin's rhetoric seemed to confirm that he viewed the Volunteers as a Home Rule army to coerce defiant northern counties, a sentiment echoed in the speeches of others. Michael Judge told a contingent of Roscommon Volunteers that if the Ulstermen would not accept Home Rule, they should be forced to do so, implying that the men assembled before him should be prepared for the task. Arthur Clery, a proponent of a distinctive Ulster identity, told a gathering of Volunteers in May that no body of men would be permitted to take away nationalists' hard-won rights.[87]

Nowhere was the conflict of aims between orthodox nationalists and physical-force men clearer than when it came to distributing the few rifles that the Irish Volunteers possessed. Pearse intensely resented Devlin's channelling of Volunteer rifles to arm his northern AOH adherents.[88] For some separatists on the provisional committee, the haste to acquire arms and ammunition was not to be in readiness to answer whatever Ulster might do, but to be used to harass the British authorities at an early date. This fundamental inconsistency of purpose was a fault line along which many Volunteer leaders believed a split must one day come.[89]

Divisions at the top of the movement remained hidden from public view. Each weekend, thousands of Irish Volunteers drilled in gatherings, small and large, all over Ireland. The Roman Catholic clergy endorsed the movement, and one Volunteer remembered improvised arrangements for men on exercises to hear Mass.[90] The Cumann na mBan's Defence of Ireland Fund collected donations at church doors.[91] Clerical interventions were sometimes of a robustly unecclesiastical character, as when Rev. C.D. O'Brien admonished a Volunteer rally in Wicklow town: 'People talk about uniforms. The coats you have are good enough to fight and die in. Put all your money into your rifles and your leaden bullets.'[92]

Pride in the vigorous, masculine spirit of nationalism was felt even by moderates like Gill. In contrast to the soothing messages he sent to Redmond, Gill appears to have been privately much less guarded in celebrating what his old friend Walter D'Alton called 'the glorious thrilling Fenianism of which your letter speaks'.[93] D'Alton wrote to him in wonder at the sudden casting off of furtiveness:

It was slavery everywhere in Ireland: we drank, we lied, we fawned, we feared, we yielded basely, we hid our thoughts, we whispered – and it is all over now. It is a thing to bring tears to our eyes and exultation to our hearts and prayers to God … for Ireland resurgent – and we have seen the miracle … As you say, God's hand is in it – I don't deny the value of Home Rule, but what was the statute[?] – a miserable catalogue of phrases.[94]

The view from the counties

With the 'prairie fire' spread of the Irish Volunteers, and the Home Rule Bill nearing the end of its parliamentary circuits, the undersecretary for Ireland, Sir James Dougherty, commissioned a survey of the state of the country. At the end of June he issued a circular to resident magistrates seeking intelligence as to the disposition of the people in their districts, the dangers to peace, and the precautions that might be advisable to maintain order.[95] Their returns provide a glimpse of the state of Ireland in the summer of 1914 from a uniquely informed, though biased, perspective. The provincial eyes and ears of the British authorities outside Ulster were less fixated on sectarian conflict in the north-east than were their superiors in Dublin and London, and saw much the greater danger coming from a possible nationalist revolt against British rule.

Newton Brady, resident magistrate (RM) for Belfast, reported that in his opinion the Ulster Volunteer Force, hitherto a stabilising influence, would declare a provisional government if the Home Rule Bill were passed. A military force of 50,000, he suggested, would be required to deal with the situation. Captain Gosselin, in Omagh, concurred, saying that 'overwhelming force' would be required 'to overawe the Ulster Volunteers or if not overawed [to] wipe them out'. The alternative, standing aside, he noted tartly, 'seems like eating humble pie but it is the outcome of having allowed the Ulster Volunteers to become the force they are'.[96]

A preponderance of magistrates urged the imperative of preventing the Irish Volunteers from arming. Captain Gosselin foresaw 'pandemonium' in Omagh if the nationalists obtained rifles.[97] A.G.W. Harrel, in Bandon, reported that the real aim of the Irish Volunteers was to

… establish an Irish republic by force of arms. So far they are not very strong nor are they armed, but they are progressing and may be a very formidable body to deal with later on … however troublesome the task of interference may look now the situation will be getting worse with every week's delay.[98]

From Sligo, the resident magistrate, Captain Fitzpatrick, advised that

> The National Volunteers here – as no doubt they now do all over Ireland – look upon themselves as the coming national army of Ireland – a force to act – and help to make 'Ireland a Nation' – and no one seeing them – speaking to them or seeing their local papers – could suggest for a moment that they are – or ever were – or ever intend to be – loyal to our Crown and constitution.[99]

Magistrate A. Bell in Ballinrobe offered the clearest vision of the implications for a Home Rule government taking office in the then turbulent conditions:

> I believe it to be a menace to peace in the near future and later on when a new regime comes into being in this country, it will form a strong physical force party which may make good government founded on fair dealing, justice and conciliation impossible ... when disturbance begins to establish a kind of martial law ... it will mean that the Imperial troops will be brought into collision with what could be considered in the country the National force – and that would only accentuate the differences which unhappily exist and increase the difficulties of the situation.[100]

Magistrates were divided as to what should be done. A slim majority of respondents advised that no precautions be taken, though in many instances this was because it was feared that any intervention would do more harm than good. An almost equal number of RMs recommended that the prohibition on the importation of arms be enforced at all costs. As for dangers to public peace, the magistrates overwhelmingly identified the nationalist force as the primary menace to the interests of the state rather than the better-armed and better-disciplined Ulster Volunteers.[101]

A synopsis of the magistrates' responses was prepared for Dougherty on 14 July. The summary for the undersecretary reflected the inconsistency of the district returns in advising no course of action, but downplayed the alarming content of the underlying reports.[102] Though referring to the 'dangerous possibilities' of a nationalist Volunteer organisation intent on 'subversion of

British rule', the Dublin Castle digest did not convey the immediacy with which many of the county magistrates expressed concern.[103] Neither did the summary, sent on to Birrell, carry the conviction of some of them that the Volunteer leaders were in earnest about mounting an armed rebellion at the earliest opportunity.

In a pattern to be repeated until 1916, the magnitude of the danger perceived by officials in Ireland does not appear to have been communicated to London. Ministers, preoccupied with Ulster and deprived of intelligence as to the intentions of the physical-force men of the south, did not fully apprehend the tumultuous state of nationalist Ireland. This reinforced a belief that Redmond's concerns about bruised nationalist sentiment were exaggerated. For his part, the Irish Party chairman appreciated the perils of the situation, but he may have been unwilling to reveal their full extent to ministers for fear of undermining confidence in the stability of a new Irish government. The magistrates' reports, however, render somewhat problematic Catriona Pennell's assertions that Ireland was firmly united to Britain at the start of the First World War, and that British fears of advanced nationalist dissidence were insubstantial.[104]

It is nonetheless important not to overstate the Irish Volunteers' capacity to undertake any kind of coordinated operations. British army officers viewed the nationalist militia with contempt.[105] Despite efforts to improve its organisation, command of the Irish Volunteers remained ineffective. Diarmuid Coffey, a young lawyer charged with assisting the organisation of the Volunteers into military units, found a confused and chaotic administration at headquarters in South Frederick Street, Dublin. Matters were even worse at the Volunteer office in Kildare Street, which was mostly occupied by the IRB men of the provisional committee. Colonel Edmond Cotter, Colonel Moore's chief of staff, griped incessantly about his superior, while county inspecting officers nursed petty rivalries, and local units refused to work with county organisations.[106] Lacking competent leadership and coherent organisation, the Irish Volunteers' potential to acquire arms, still more to use them effectively in coordinated operations against the instruments of British rule, was doubtful. Yet it was this very lack of control, in the view of the commanding officer of British forces in Belfast, General MacCready, that made the enormous nationalist corps such a dangerous and unpredictable factor.[107]

Disquiet and division

Exultation and outrage were added to the already charged emotions of nationalists after the Howth arms landings and the shootings at Bachelor's Walk. Liam de Róiste recalled feelings of pride among some of the Irish he encountered in London, where he received both congratulations and expressions of sympathy. A fellow Irishman, he recounted, who attended Redmond's speech at the House of Commons on 27 July described it as 'painful' and 'tantamount to an apology for what had occurred and an excuse for the soldiers who had shot the people' on the banks of the Liffey.[108] A Meath County Council resolution condemned the inconsistent application of laws in Dublin and Belfast, while Borrisokane District Council urged public bodies throughout the country to encourage Volunteer corps to arm themselves for defence against further outrages. In Thurles, the formation of a nationalist provisional government was urged if Home Rule did not come to pass.[109] Sligo County Council unanimously called upon Redmond to demand the unamended bill and, if enactment were refused, to return to Ireland and lead the Irish Volunteers, who, it claimed, could overwhelm the Orange forces.[110]

Public pledges of support were issued from the United States. The treasurer of the United Irish League of America announced that he was sending $10,000 to Redmond; meeting in Providence, Rhode Island, the general convention of the AOH promised $25,000 for the Irish Volunteers.[111] Another AOH meeting in Norfolk, Virginia addressed a memorial to Redmond, saying that the organisation's 200,000 members in the United States pledged their assistance to preserve the integrity of Ireland.[112]

At a meeting of the Gaelic League, Douglas Hyde vowed that the one thing the country would not stand for was harsher application of the law to nationalists than to Unionists.[113] Patrick Pearse welcomed the intense resentment at the shootings; the first blood shed for Ireland, he claimed, had hardened public opinion in a desirable way.[114] Wilfrid Scawen Blunt, a correspondent of both Dillon and Sir Roger Casement, saw a salutary lesson for the government in the public revulsion, in that it now knew that there was at least as much danger in disappointing the nationalists of Ireland as in displeasing Ulster.[115]

Four weekly newspapers, *The Irish Volunteer*, *Sinn Féin*, *The Irish Worker* and the IRB's *Irish Freedom*, published sustained criticisms of the British government and its Irish Party 'accomplices' in Ulster exclusion and the coercion of northern nationalists. Though the circulation of these journals was small (*Irish Freedom* claimed a circulation of 7,000 but, by comparison, only 1,000 copies of *Sinn Féin* per week were sold by Eason and Son in 1914), their messages were influential.[116] Radical newspapers appealed to young national-ists disheartened by the delay to Home Rule and susceptible to ideas and emotions churned up by the political turmoil. Kevin O'Shiel recalled the effect of the 'fringe' nationalist press in 1914: 'subtly, clearly and constantly they appealed to and drew out the latent and nationalistic separatism inherent in nearly every young Irishman.'[117]

The febrile state of the country seemed to bring fulfilment of advanced nationalists' hopes nearer. Patrick Pearse believed that the Dublin Volunteers were ready to support a *coup d'état* but could not act for want of arms.[118] Sir Roger Casement predicted to Blunt that the amending bill would 'kill Home Rule. If we had 10,000 rifles in the rest of Ireland we'd kill the British Empire. The young men in the Volunteers are out for one thing only – to revive the Fenian spirit, and please God will do it.'[119] In reply to similarly extravagant claims, Colonel Moore reminded Casement that, unlike the Irish Volunteers, the Ulster Volunteers were armed. They were also backed by a British army more than prepared to shoot nationalists, arrest their leaders, and hang them. In the Irish Volunteers' unarmed state, he told Casement, they could not withstand sustained attack.[120] Nonetheless, the attraction of romanticised Fenianism for nationalists of political convictions as varied as those of Gill and Casement marked a significant departure from the earlier resigned acqui-escence to the parliamentary approach. 'Fenianism', a term that would have been an anachronism a few years before, was acquiring new resonance in the changed conditions of Ireland, and inspiring dynamism in nationalist hearts and minds.

The outbreak of the First World War and Redmond's pledge of nationalist loyalty convinced many separatists that the time for the Volunteers to split had arrived. Seán O'Kelly remembered that war was 'welcomed with real joy' by the IRB men, and that there was relief that Redmond's pledge at last 'cleared the air', enabling the physical-force men to adopt a policy of active opposi-tion.[121] Francis Sheehy-Skeffington, grossly exaggerating, professed to former Labour MP and fellow suffragist George Lansbury that nationalist opinion was solidly on the side of Germany. British power, Sheehy-Skeffington hoped, would be sufficiently weakened by war to enable the Volunteers to insist on more than a 'discredited Home Rule Bill'.[122] Though Liam de Róiste later recorded that his expectation at this time was that Home Rule would be put into operation, he recalled that he and Seán Milroy agreed that the political situation would sooner or later force the Volunteers to intervene by a *coup de main*.[123]

Yet recollections of the early days of the conflict also attest to nationalist support for the war. Some who classed themselves as 'dissenters', such as Kevin O'Shiel, believed that Redmond's committal of the Volunteers to home defence reflected the 'feelings of the vast majority of Nationalists of all schools … England had the country, for the first time in the co-history of the two nations, psychologically in the hollow of her hand.'[124] Anti-German feeling ran high. Following news of the destruction of the library and cathedral of St Pierre in Louvain, Dublin mobs looted German butchers' shops.[125] The wartime spirit temporarily healed divisions in Cork, with O'Brienites, advanced nationalists and the Irish Party all backing a drive to equip the local Volunteer corps.[126] The impulse to support Redmond's pledge of loyal self-defence, believed Cahir Davitt, represented the firm majority of opinion in Ireland. Detractors of his war policy were judged, he recalled, to be cowards, pro-German or factionists derided as 'Sinn Féiners'.[127]

The Lisnaskea, Carrick-on-Shannon and Aughrim companies of Volunteers loyally offered their services to Dublin Castle for home defence or foreign posting.[128] Castle authorities received numerous letters from companies of Irish Volunteers and Ulster Volunteers proposing the formation of new units for civil service and public-utility workers, or suggesting sporting corps to be led by cricket or football captains.[129] Redmond's pledge of Irish self-defence in wartime reconciled many southern Unionists to the Irish Volunteers. Lords Gormanston and Powerscourt and Sir Horace Plunkett attended a meeting at Volunteer headquarters to discuss the appointment of county inspectors-general, for which posts prominent Unionist landlords such as George Taaffe and Lord Dunsany were recruited.[130] Many of these newcomers of high standing assumed that the Volunteers would become a reserve force of the British army.

The loyalties of Volunteer corps were torn in many places. A dispute erupted in Cork between the local committee and Captain Talbot Crosbie over the disposition of the corps for wartime service. The committee accused the officer of overstepping his authority in offering men to the War Office, to which he responded with charges of inconsistency and dishonesty.[131] A similar struggle between Redmondites and 'Sinn Féiners' erupted in the Limerick corps.[132] Francis Sheehy-Skeffington believed that the Volunteer 'rank and file are bewildered, the "leaders" seem helpless – their morale has been sapped by their cowardly surrender to Redmond', who, he wrote, on the strength of a flimsy promise intended to remould them as 'Irish Territorials'.[133]

A 'glass bowl and a false note'

The manifest indecision of Asquith's Cabinet and the interruption of the progress of Home Rule, coupled with a suspicion that the war might be used as an excuse to shelve the bill altogether, soured the public mood in Ireland. Michael Wheatley described the pervasive sense of exasperation in the provincial press in August and September 1914. Even the most orthodox of nationalist newspapers, he asserted, adopted a sceptical editorial policy, with less inhibited journals giving voice to charges of English perfidy and expressing pro-German sentiments.[134] Particular criticism was directed at Irish recruiting without a compensating grant of Home Rule. Though press criticism was mostly reserved for English targets, speakers at public meetings were sometimes less circumspect. *The Freeman's Journal* reported the warning of a priest to the Volunteers on parade in Killeshandra

> … to be on their guard against the destructive weakness of Irishmen, viz., their too great generosity and trustfulness in belief with new friends who have been old and dishonourable enemies … when England has made use of us in her days of trial to avert disaster she may soon forget her oily promise and repay us with betrayal and contempt.[135]

That such ill-concealed criticism of Redmond appeared in the Irish Party's press organ spoke to the extent of dissatisfaction in the country and the widespread anxiety that nationalist loyalty should not be sold at too small a price.

At the dismal Volunteer headquarters, Colonel Cotter sensed that the nationalist corps was stagnating in a hopelessly divided state. Cotter proposed that Redmond should mount a '*coup d'état*' and purge the provisional committee. Eoin MacNeill, Diarmuid Coffey recorded, backed the scheme for several days.[136] Joseph Devlin, meeting Cotter, agreed that establishment of a strong central authority and expulsion of the extremists were desirable, but he was doubtful of their practicality. The scheme was abandoned when MacNeill cooled on the idea, as his cooperation was deemed as essential cover for any overt move against the physical-force men.[137] MacNeill's biographer claimed that, at this time, he appealed to Devlin on behalf of the parliamentary leaders to unilaterally declare their authority over the affairs of Ireland. Devlin, in this account, demurred, insisting that the responsibility was too great.[138]

Diarmuid Coffey privately ridiculed the strutting incompetence of the physical-force men. He suspected that Hobson and The O'Rahilly – 'a pretty pair of conspirators' – were purposely withholding information.[139] Suspicious of British intentions and troubled by Redmond's imperialist effusions, Coffey and Colonel Moore nonetheless viewed the War Office as the only agency capable of organising the Volunteers into a force to safeguard the operation of Home Rule at war's end. The swift adoption of the Ulster Volunteers into the British army, transforming them into a battle-hardened force, increased the urgency for nationalists to organise.[140]

MacNeill warned Redmond that a split threatened if the nationalist attitude towards the war was misconstrued. He believed that the War Office intended to direct the defence of Ireland and reduce the Irish Volunteers to an adjunct of the British army. He urged Redmond to reassert the independence of the Volunteers, and to stick to the terms of his purely defensive original offer.[141]

The extreme sensitivity of nationalist feeling dominated Gill's thoughts. He foresaw that Irish recruitment would be the next hurdle to be cleared, but he was more immediately concerned by the pervasive mood of anxiety and disaffection he found in the country. He sought to convey to Robert Donald, editor of the London *Daily Chronicle*, 'how touch-and-go the situation is at the moment', demanding from the government bold and emphatic action on the Home Rule Bill. Asquith, he insisted to Donald, must be made to understand that the fragility of nationalist sentiment was like a 'glass bowl and [a] false note', the shattering of which would result in irrevocable consequences for Ireland and for Britain's fortunes in the war.[142]

On Sunday 6 September 10,000 Volunteers marched in two columns through Dundrum and Rathfarnham, converging at Three Rock Mountain for a sham battle. The procession was impressive, but order broke down when skirmishing began, and the exercise rapidly dissolved in confusion. Volunteer officer James Crean, present at the day's chaotic climax, ascribed the collapse of discipline to the arrogance and ineptitude of the exercise's extremist sponsors.[143] Dublin Castle authorities took the manoeuvres as a show of force. The *Sinn Féin* newspaper accused Irish Party municipal politicians of acting as police informants.[144]

Gill alerted Redmond to the vigorous activities of the advanced nationalist element. 'Sinn Féiners', he said, had sent a deputation to the German emperor via Holland, and despatched envoys to America in the hope of recruiting revolutionary republican Clan-na-Gael men to lead the Volunteers. The Irish-American judge Daniel Cohalan, a senior Clan-na-Gael figure, he reported, was in Ireland. Gill warned the party chairman that the separatist threat was serious and had to be confronted:

In my opinion a systematic propaganda both here and in the U.S. will
have to be organised against some of the proceedings that are going on
… I meet the rank and file and know how far the *inoculation* has gone.
The Leader (well-meaning) had lost its head. But I have taken hold of
[editor D.P.] Moran and put him right … You will have to suppress
that provisional committee.[145]

A meeting of the Young Ireland Branch of the UIL the following week
anticipated the direction of travel of Redmondite policy. The meeting resolved
that a German victory would be disastrous for the spread of Celtic influence
and the cause of democracy. Francis Cruise O'Brien moved that the Irish
Volunteers should join Lord Kitchener's 'Second Army' for the sake of Irish
unity. Speakers told the meeting that men who mistook hatred of England for
patriotism endangered the national interest, and called on Redmond to demonstrate to the world that Irishmen were not pro-German.[146] These pro-war
declarations were contested by others present, including Coffey.[147]

Redmond heeded Gill's advice to act against advanced nationalist incur-
sions on the party's support in the country. Volunteer company commander
Laurence Nugent claimed many years later that he was leading a parade of
troops in the Wicklow Mountains on Sunday 20 September when Redmond
motored into the village. Nugent claimed that he and his men ignored the
nationalist leader's conspicuous presence and marched past, denying an
angry Redmond the opportunity of addressing them.[148] Whether this is true
or not, the Irish Party chairman came upon a body of men marching at
Woodenbridge, and it was there that he made his fateful speech, calling on
Volunteers to enlist in the British army. In doing so, Redmond sounded the
false note that fractured the uneasy coalescence of nationalists that the Irish
Volunteers had briefly brought together.

The men and women of Volunteer headquarters were incensed when news
of Redmond's speech reached them, but Colonel Moore decided to remain
neutral in the 'accursed muddle' that ensued. MacNeill advised Moore that a
split was inevitable, and within days the IRB faction seized the Kildare Street
office.[149] Dissident members of the provisional committee, one of their number
recalled, timed the rupture with the Redmondites for the eve of Asquith's
recruiting visit to Dublin on 25 September.[150] The dissenting faction's public
memorandum to the Irish Volunteers reaffirmed the manifesto of December
1913, and asserted that Redmond's call for enlistment was fundamentally at
variance with it. The statement repudiated Redmond's authority to consent to

the dismemberment of Ireland, or to 'offer up the blood and lives of the sons of Irishmen and Irishwomen to the service of the British Empire'.[151]

The Round Room of the Mansion House was packed for the prime minister's recruiting meeting; according to *The Times*, Redmond received a thunderous welcome and roused the meeting with a pledge that Irishmen would avenge Louvain, fighting as an autonomous nation at last.[152] Heavy police precautions were in place against anti-English and anti-war protestors. Away from the meeting, dissident Volunteers paraded in the streets, to the cheers of spectators.[153]

Redmond's gamble appeared, momentarily, to have paid off. The Dublin press roundly condemned the insurgent Volunteers' declaration. The Irish Party's captive organs of the press, *The Freeman's Journal* and *Evening Herald*, immediately labelled the breakaway faction the 'Sinn Féin volunteers', as Sinn Féin, one observer recalled, was regarded as a discredited and spent force at this time.[154] The Navan Board of Guardians endorsed recruitment for the front, also using 'Sinn Féin' as a term of disparagement, denouncing the dissentient policy as one that would earn Ireland the world's shame. Anti-recruiting posters were put up by groups of Volunteers in Thurles, only for them to be torn down by a larger crowd of their fellows. The local corps split, with the largest section, as was overwhelmingly the case elsewhere in Ireland, remaining loyal to the Irish Party.[155] In abhorrence at the unpatriotic attitude of the dissident Volunteers, some parents withdrew their sons from Patrick Pearse's St Enda's School.[156]

Despite surviving the schism as much the larger entity, the endorsement of recruitment condemned the 'National Volunteers', as the Redmondite wing of the movement was now known, to a lingering death. Coffey concluded that the War Office thought Redmond could secure them recruits without the need to offer support to the nationalist militia. He resignedly resolved to use the Volunteer organisation 'to go on working quietly & to discourage enlistment as far as we can without openly preaching anti enlistment'.[157]

At University College, Dublin, debates of the Literary and Historical Society divided students between orthodox and dissenter nationalists. Denis Gwynn and Patrick Hogan, representing the majority who supported the Irish Party, penned articles in the *National Student* supporting the Redmondite policy of 'burying the hatchet' while deprecating both sycophancy to English parties and what it called 'narrow nationalism'.[158] Feelings about German outrages against Catholic Belgium remained strong, but one observer recalled that enthusiasm for the war was dampened by the postponement of Home

Rule, the tacit consent to partition, and by the British failure to reconstitute the Irish Volunteers as an Irish army corps.[159] War dissipated the passions of the summer, but the challenge to the constitutional movement's hegemony that the Irish Volunteers represented had shaken its authority. The Irish Parliamentary Party's claim to speak for Irish nationalism would never again go uncontested.

7

Impasse: Summer 1914

Having passed the House of Commons in three successive parliamentary sessions under the terms of the Parliament Act, the Home Rule Bill could no longer be blocked by the House of Lords. However, the unresolved fate of the government's promised amending bill, offering Ulster counties the option of temporary exclusion, still stood in the way of its becoming law. John Redmond's political strategy in the final stage of the Home Rule Crisis had to attempt to disarm a complex of interrelated threats. The most obvious of these was the intransigence of Ulster Unionists, who were demanding the indefinite exclusion of the whole of the province, or, at a minimum, of the four Protestant-majority counties plus counties Tyrone and Fermanagh, where Catholics were in the majority. The Ulster Unionist leaders were threatening violent rebellion if their demands were not met, but there was also a risk that temporary exclusion, already conceded in principle, might be modified to a permanent partition of Ireland; this was desired by some, though by no means all, of the recalcitrant Ulstermen.

The second and related threat stemmed from the preponderance of senior Cabinet ministers intent on conceding an exclusionary settlement and seemingly prepared to go to almost any lengths to meet the Unionists' terms. Although the extent of this ministerial desire to collude with Unionists was only a matter of suspicion for Redmond, it was a tendency that had to be vigorously combated because of the third serious challenge that the constitutional nationalists had to face: the hostile forces advancing on their flank in Ireland. A rival philosophy of physical force was gaining traction in the country, and Redmond was cognisant that the survival of the Irish Party depended on his delivering Home Rule and resolutely resisting pressures to yield to Ulster concessions beyond the plebiscite formula to which he and Dillon had reluctantly acquiesced in February.

The few analyses of the Liberal/Irish nationalist dynamic of the third

Home Rule Bill's final dispensation have followed a convention of casting Redmond as a hapless supplicant to a capricious premier.[1] Dermot Meleady's *John Redmond: The national leader* at least credits the Irish Party chairman with having a strategy, as opposed to being almost entirely reactive to events, but the source of the nationalist leader's political leverage to constrain Asquith from settling on Unionist terms is unexplained.[2] Ronan Fanning's *Fatal Path* briefly discussed the wartime disposition of the Home Rule controversy, concluding that Redmond persisted in a delusional belief that partition could somehow be avoided.[3]

This chapter, by contrast, argues that the summer of 1914 saw a dawning of comprehension – ministerial and Tory – of the strength of Redmond's position. On the one hand, Asquith and his colleagues came to understand that to defy the parliamentary bloc of radical Liberals, Labour and nationalists, for whom Redmond spoke, would precipitate a shattering of the Liberal Party. For the Unionists, the prospect of having to deal with the 130,000-strong Irish Volunteer organisation – which from June 1914 was under Redmond's control – suddenly loomed large.

In contradistinction to a near-ubiquitous narrative of imminent civil war, this chapter presents evidence casting doubt on the likelihood of a rising in Ulster in summer 1914. With Unionist reservations about the wisdom of declaring a provisional government being expressed, and northern counties already experiencing serious commercial disruption, Ulster Unionist leader Sir Edward Carson privately advanced (with apparent sincerity) exclusion as a face-saving transitional arrangement. This chapter argues that despite, or perhaps because of, the perils swirling in Ireland in the summer of 1914, the possibilities of compromise were not exhausted when the First World War broke out, and the Irish controversy was swallowed up by the cataclysm.

The underappreciated logic of Redmond's ultimately disastrous wartime strategy is also explored here. The need to repulse separatist encroachments on the Irish Party's political hegemony provided a powerful incentive for casting Ireland's lot with Britain in the First World War. Redmond's 'long war' recruiting strategy depended upon Irish nationalist loyalty being met with a spirit of reciprocal generosity by the British authorities. In the event, the spurning of a nationalist army corps by hostile British generals lent force to the anti-war and anti-English messages of advanced nationalists, grievously undermining the rationale of the parliamentary movement. Redmond's perilous gamble proved to have been misjudged, but neither delusion, complacency nor exhaustion accounted for its failure. The thinking behind Redmond's strategy over the summer and early autumn of 1914 will be shown to have been a matter of deliberate political calculation.

The last card

The government's amending bill offering county option of exclusion was moved in the House of Lords on 22 June. The bill provided that any county in Ulster could petition for a poll to exclude itself from the rest of Ireland for six years. Upon expiry of that period, during which time the British electorate would twice deliver its verdict on Home Rule in general elections, excluded counties would automatically accede to the authority of the Dublin parliament.[4]

Unionist peers with Irish landholdings were inclined to amend the amending bill to curb the powers of the Irish parliament. Two of these, Lord Lansdowne, the Unionist leader in the House of Lords, and Lord Midleton, were apprehensive about the consequences for their class if nationalists assumed power in Dublin. Midleton believed that the temptation for an Irish government to enact popular measures to tax the wealthy would be irresistible, and he feared that it might even seek to tax Irish landowners on their property outside Ireland.[5] Despite such alarming prognostications, Bonar Law saw danger in either attempting to make Home Rule workable or wrecking it altogether. Still intent upon securing a general election (which his party managers deemed 'absolutely essential' in order to halt the abolition of plural voting), he recommended that Unionist peers should alter the amending bill only in such ways as would be seen to avoid civil war.[6]

Margot Asquith believed that the amending bill's chief merit would be to absolve her husband of guilt if violence broke out. She hoped that electors would know that, if the worst happened, the prime minister was blameless, having been met by unrelenting Unionist intransigence and hostility, and having risked the loss of 'masses of his own supporters' in advancing a compromise.[7] John Dillon thought Lord Crewe's invitation of amendments and praise for Carson in his speech moving the bill in the Lords to be excessive; but he recounted to C.P. Scott that Lord Morley had told him that the Ulstermen had won, and that the government would be bound to acknowledge this fact.[8]

Sir Francis Hopwood continued his political angling. He happened upon Morley before a Cabinet meeting and, as he related the news to Stamfordham, 'gave it to him "hot and strong"'. He claimed to have asserted to Morley that many Liberals 'would rather have civil war in Ireland than give up the Plural Voting Bill', and that if the government refused a general election in order to secure its passage, 'it will be truly said that you dare not face the country until you have jerrymandered the constituencies'.⁹ Dining with Morley, Seely and J.A. Spender, editor of *The Westminster Gazette*, a few days later, Hopwood found his companions at sixes and sevens. Morley asserted that the only honourable course for the government would be to resign if the amending bill were lost. Ministers, he insisted, could not throw their responsibilities on the monarch by presenting an unamended Home Rule Bill for royal assent. Spender vehemently disagreed, and Seely predicted that the Liberal Party faced ruin if the government fell before passing Home Rule and the Plural Voting Bill. It was all the fault, he said, of that 'cursed Parliament Act'. Hopwood related to Stamfordham that he 'stoked the fire all I could'.¹⁰

There was near unanimity among senior ministers that six-county exclusion, with the power to continue to contract out of the Irish parliament for as long as desired, should be offered. This seemed to be the minimum acceptable to Unionists, but any effort to coerce the nationalists into a settlement risked splitting the Liberal ranks. Irritatingly (for ministers), but seemingly immovably, Redmond held the key to the situation.

Asquith charged the resourceful Lord Murray, the newly ennobled former chief whip, with continuing mediation efforts. Murray paired with Edwin Montagu, the financial secretary to the Treasury, to act as intermediaries with the Unionist leaders, while Lloyd George and *Daily Mail* proprietor Lord Rothermere negotiated with the nationalists.¹¹ Montagu found Carson worried about losing control of the UVF men on Ulster Day (12 July), and believed him keen to settle.¹² Murray reported to Asquith that Redmond and Dillon reacted favourably to Bonar Law's offer of a cantonal arrangement for Ulster, which would split counties along sectarian lines in exchange for Unionist support for Home Rule in the south.¹³ Redmond recorded that Murray told him that Carson and Bonar Law had acknowledged the inevitability of Home Rule, and that the two men believed that Ulster was certain to join the new legislature after a short period of time.¹⁴ Redmond, Asquith later told the king, was prepared to concede indefinite exclusion for the four counties, the city of Derry, and the greater part of Fermanagh; but he refused all entreaties to give up County Tyrone.¹⁵

Tyrone occupied a position of importance to both sides in the controversy because of its fine sectarian balance, and the strength and organisation of the Volunteers in the county. Fermanagh and Tyrone were majority-Catholic counties, but Tyrone was only so by a relatively narrow margin: 55.4% Catholic to 44.6% Protestant.[16] Three of the county's four parliamentary constituencies were held by nationalists. Home Rulers felt that the democratic principle demanded that the Catholic pluralities of Tyrone and Fermanagh see their desire for Dublin rule fulfilled; overruling the wishes of the majority, in order to appease a discontented minority, was offensive to justice.

Twenty battalions of Irish Volunteers in County Tyrone (reputedly a stronghold of the IRB) had recruited 8,000–10,000 men by the summer of 1914, and were making rapid progress in organisation and drilling.[17] Early in July, a packed meeting of Irish Volunteers at Cookstown was told that the Volunteers' presence in the county assured that the homeland of the O'Neills would never be separated from Ireland, and that no matter what the future held, the force would not be disbanded.[18] Prominent local nationalists criticised the Irish Party leaders: at a meeting of the East Tyrone executive of the UIL, the consent to a policy of exclusion by Devlin's spring conclave of northern nationalist eminences was denounced.[19]

The numerical preponderance of nationalists in the county was, however, counterbalanced by the wealth of its propertied Protestant population, and by the presence of a large and well-disciplined force of Ulster Volunteers. The Ulster Volunteers of Tyrone were respected by the police in the county, and feared (so the resident magistrate believed) by the local Irish Volunteers. Commanded by Captain A. St Q. Ricardo DSO, the corps was led by ex-army men who modelled themselves on the 'puritans of old', the magistrate recorded, and manned by recruits 'drawn from the best classes'.[20] Tyrone's Ulster Volunteers were estimated to number between 4,300 and 10,000 men in July 1914, and were said to have as many as a hundred rounds of ammunition per man.[21] Such a body of men could not easily be abandoned if Carson hoped to remain in control of the movement in Ulster. It was the collision of these two forces – the sentiment of the majority of the population and the formidable reputation of its Unionist 'army' – that placed County Tyrone at the epicentre of the Ulster dilemma.

Lloyd George's efforts to press further concessions on Redmond were in vain, but Murray held out hope that the Irish Party leaders would be persuaded to bargain, albeit possibly only after 'veiled menaces and ginger' were applied.[22] Montagu suggested that the premier should approach Bonar Law with the object of persuading him to, separately, pressure the nationalists into giving up Tyrone.[23] On reflection, Asquith decided not to, fearing 'we might both have been tempted to say things which we should afterwards wish unsaid', and in so doing reveal to the opposition leader how feeble ministers' commitment to their nationalist allies had grown.[24]

A memorandum prepared for the Cabinet by the military members of the army council on 7 July confirmed just how dire had been the consequences of ministerial inaction in Ireland. Two opposing forces amounting to approximately 200,000 men, it reported, were now training and arming in the country. The War Office, lacking any guidance as to the policy envisaged in the event of generalised disorder in Ireland, had neither prepared nor considered plans for military operations. In view of the potential scale of serious unrest, the generals believed that deployment of the whole of the Expeditionary Force might be required to restore order, that rebellion might spread to Egypt and India, and that unnamed powers in Europe might take advantage of British disarray.[25] The culmination of government policy, they concluded, meant that Britain might be denuded of forces to repel an invasion, the Expeditionary Force might be unavailable to assist colonial authorities, and the country might not be able to meet its external obligations.[26] This wholly unappealing document, written with ill-concealed contempt of the military men for their political masters, could only have added to ministerial perplexity and despair.

As miserable as the prospects looked, ministers could at least console themselves with the thought that their opponents' predicament was no less acute. Bonar Law professed to the king's private secretary his disbelief that Asquith could ask for the royal assent without an amending measure. Having pressed the monarch for months to demand an appeal to the electorate, the Unionist leader now insisted that a 'General Election at the present time would not make things easier no matter which Party was returned to Power', and suggested that George V's abdication would be preferable to granting assent.[27]

Bonar Law's ignoble and, indeed, incredible suggestion that the king should shake the monarchy to its foundations in order to block Home Rule is, without doubt, reflective of the Tory leader's desire to evade responsibility for a predicament that he had done much to create. Sharper minds than Bonar Law's, however, saw danger in triggering a constitutional earthquake. To Hopwood's surprise, he found Lords Milner and Peel, with whom he dined on 8 July, firmly opposed to any action by the king. By acting to impede his ministers, they said, the sovereign could well provoke a nationalist insurrection with which a Unionist administration might have to deal. Nothing but a settlement, they maintained, could avoid the eruption of violence in Ireland. Hopwood was gratified to note 'an awakening of some sanity', but such pusillanimous political triangulation betokened no alteration of the Unionists' cynical irresponsibility.[28]

Hopwood found that Liberals apprehended the Unionists' change of heart. T.J. Macnamara, junior minister at the Admiralty, told him,

> Redmond is not only our Dictator, as they call it, he is the Dictator to the other side … It does not matter to him which side is in power, so if he does not like our terms he will vote us out … The Tories have woke up to it that they cannot put down Redmond any more than we can put down Ulster.[29]

Lord Devonport told Hopwood that Redmond was 'on velvet' in parliamentary terms, because neither side could refuse his demands. Lloyd George, he recounted, told him that the government had been relying on being able to coerce Redmond into a deal at the last moment, but that the growth of the Irish Volunteers had altered that assumption. The nationalist leader's hand could no longer be forced. The likely outcome, as Devonport saw it, would be a staged ministerial offer to Redmond, which would be refused. Home Rule would be placed on the statute book pro forma, with a dissolution and a general election to follow.[30]

An unexpected front in the negotiations was opened up, apparently on her own initiative, by Margot Asquith, the prime minister's wife. Taking tea on the House of Commons terrace on 6 July, Mrs Asquith, spotting Redmond, discreetly asked him to meet her, at a secret location, the following day. In an extraordinary account, made more vivid by her description of Redmond, in 'hideous pale grey hat & clothes, his little parrot eye looking for the number of the door', the prime minister's wife claimed to have challenged the nationalist leader as to whether he intended to push Ireland to the brink of war over County Tyrone. Redmond replied that he had been cursed in Ireland for conceding exclusion at all, and that if he or Carson went against their respective supporters over Tyrone, neither man's life would be safe; 'the old Fenian lot', he told her, 'would turn up & kill me.' He expressed concern that a deal might be done behind his back, but also spoke of his confidence that nationalist restraint would prevent anything more serious than rioting in Ulster. Once the bill was on the statute book, he assured her, he and Carson would find a path to settlement.[31]

Redmond's admission of the potential for serious violence in Ireland is difficult to reconcile with his confidence that disorder could be contained. It was an acknowledgement that the nominal political leaders in Ireland were not in control of events. Though he headed the dominant political party, and a few weeks earlier had assumed control of the Irish Volunteers, Redmond possessed no overt coercive power. He had confided to T.P. O'Connor in 1913 his belief that the loss of the Home Rule Bill would spell the end of the Irish Party; he was aware now that a concession too far might cost him his life. He was cognisant, too, that his opponent was barred from retreat by the same mortal danger. Despite the apparent inextricability of his position, the Irish Party chairman seems to have been banking on his leverage over the Liberals to get the bill enacted, and upon the anxieties of the business community of north-east Ulster to inhibit serious disorder.

On 8 July, after a long and dreary Cabinet meeting spent trying to solve, as Asquith put it to Stanley, the 'old problem of trying to get a quart into a pint', the prime minister met Carson.[32] The Ulster Unionist leader told Asquith of 'a strong party who wish for perpetual exclusion' in the northern province, which would prefer exclusion of the six heavily Protestant counties to that of the whole of Ulster on the basis that a larger, heterogeneous unit might be inclined to accede to Dublin rule before long. Nonetheless, Carson made the case for exclusion of the *whole* of Ulster on the grounds that it offered the best hope for a united Ireland. Asquith confided to the king that he agreed with this assessment; he doubted, however, that Redmond could withstand the opposition of Roman Catholic majorities in counties Cavan, Donegal and Monaghan.[33] In an interview with Lord Stamfordham the same day, Carson went further, asserting that six-county exclusion might be easier for the government, 'But total exclusion means a quicker united Ireland. Indeed he believes in that case Ulster would come in *before* the 6 years expire: she will come in *if she is not coerced.*'[34] Carson's remarkable stance, at dramatic variance with his defiant public orations, suggests that he hoped to thwart the partitionist ambitions of his more intransigent adherents. The leader of Ulster Unionism, now resigned to the inevitability of Home Rule, appears to have been more concerned for the unity of Ireland than for the sacrifice of the Union that passage of the Government of Ireland Act 1914 would entail. Amid all the talk of civil war and Ulster irreconcilability, Edward Carson's private view may reveal him to have been, first and foremost, an Irishman.

It might be argued that this conclusion relies upon an overly credulous reading of the evidence: a barrister of Carson's shrewdness would have been quite capable of a disingenuous feint to wreck the whole of the Home Rule project. From this outlook, it is conceivable that Carson calculated that to persuade Asquith to surrender the whole of Ulster would detach the nationalists, split the Liberals, and topple his government before Home Rule could be enacted. Armed Ulster would be insulated from the turmoil in the rest of Ireland that would be sure to follow, and she would soon be likely to have the protection of a Unionist ministry at Westminster. It would have taken a man of exceptional effrontery, however, to convincingly affect such a pose and to deceive in this way even the king's private secretary. The sceptical view of Carson's sincerity also neglects the evidence suggesting that the Tories had lost their appetite for a general election by July 1914. The Unionist leaders had no wish to assume responsibility for putting down a rebellion in the south and west of Ireland that might dwarf that threatened by Ulster. Even Unionist hardliners such as Lord Milner knew that a settlement was the only route out of danger; thus the bona fides of Carson's initiative must be judged in the context of the Unionists' curious aversion to office in the summer of 1914.

Carson's proposition, however, as he would have known, came at the price of giving the Ulster Unionists the appearance of total victory and the utter humiliation of the nationalists. Given the righteous outrage that betrayal of Redmond would ignite on the Liberal benches, it is not clear how Carson thought Asquith could possibly concede, though he believed (correctly) that, left to himself, the prime minister would agree to total exclusion.[35] Yet a settlement might leave the Tories in no better shape than their opponents. One senior Tory worried that even if Asquith 'threw over Redmond, relying on the Unionist vote', for Bonar Law to ask his backbenchers to vote for Home Rule in the south of Ireland – a vote that would keep Asquith and Lloyd George in office – would be a contingency that would tear the Unionist Party apart.[36] Yet Bonar Law allegedly told Lord Rothermere that he would risk even this in preference to facing the electorate after a precipitate coup in Ulster. Sensible of divisions in the Liberal ranks, the Tory leader hinted (Rothermere reported to Montagu) that he would see the government through on any settlement with Carson, even if it split his own party.[37]

The substance of Carson's proposal for the indefinite exclusion of the whole of Ulster was advocated by Thomas Shillington, a prominent Ulster Protestant Home Ruler, in a letter to Redmond, a letter purportedly already seen by Asquith. To the nationalist leader's consternation, *The Daily Telegraph* that day reported something similar as a probable basis for settlement. Such proposals, Redmond protested to Asquith, created great unease in Ireland, and, if they were advanced publicly, would be instantly denounced by him. Despite arguments that such a scheme was 'likely to lead to the earliest union of the whole of Ireland', Redmond wrote that to entertain it for a moment 'would at a blow destroy our power and our party'.[38]

Asquith's serene optimism in the face of an increasingly perilous situation was causing concern. Lord Stamfordham, raising the gravity of the political situation at an interview, was disconcerted when the prime minister mistook him to be referring to a Commons vote on the Finance Bill.[39] Asquith confessed to Stamfordham that he was pleased by the rapid proliferation of the Irish Volunteers, in the apparent belief that their existence would inhibit action by the UVF.[40] Lord Morley believed the premier to be 'constitutionally disinclined to anticipate events' and to have been taught by experience that decisions were, in most instances, best deferred until the last moment.[41] Lloyd George and J.A. Spender were unsettled by Asquith's imperturbable belief that a compromise would be found. The Chancellor urged Redmond to see the prime minister immediately, because, O'Connor wrote, 'Asquith is quite capable of not realising the situation as we see it'. He must be made to understand, O'Connor told his chief, that the issue was not merely Tyrone but the 'impossibility of going beyond the four counties'.[42] Thus when Asquith met Dillon and Redmond on 13 July, he found the two men 'in a decidedly impracticable mood'.[43] With Unionist peers mauling the amending bill in the House of Lords, Redmond recorded that he warned the prime minister that if the government announced concessions to which he did not agree, it would find itself reliant on Tory votes in the Commons, for 'the great bulk of the Liberal Party and the whole of the Labour Party' would vote with him in opposing the second reading of the amending bill. Asquith, Redmond claimed, acknowledged that such a position would be intolerable, and that he could not and would not allow it to arise.[44]

The nationalist leaders' hope, as expressed by Dillon to J.A. Spender, was for the government to hold firm if the amending bill were rejected and to put the original bill on the statute book. This, Dillon believed, would force the Tories to come to a reasonable accommodation. Spender challenged Dillon's assumption that the constitutional machinery would operate normally if an attempt were made to force Home Rule through over Tory opposition. The king, he said, might refuse to sign the unamended bill, or grant royal assent only on condition that an appeal to the electorate followed immediately. If the nationalists were seen to have unreasonably made the status of Tyrone paramount, baffled British opinion might turn against them. Dillon confessed that the need to preserve a route back to a united Ireland had reconciled him to the possibility of exclusion without a time limit. This, commented Spender, reporting the conversation to Asquith, meant that the 'last card' – intervention by the king – might not be unavailing.[45]

Privately, Dillon told Lord Granard that he would accept indefinite six-county exclusion. Dillon's brother-in-law, Theobald Mathew, confided to Hopwood his belief that Redmond would concede exclusion of the whole of Ulster if he could, but that he did not dare.[46] The Irish Party leaders knew that they were captives to their long-standing appeals to majoritarian justice. They could no more escape the logic of their arguments than they could the outraged wrath of nationalist Ireland that would descend upon them if the exclusion of the whole of Ulster were contemplated.

On 14 July the House of Lords stripped the amending bill of county option, and altered it to make the exclusion of all nine Ulster counties permanent.[47] With the amending measure hopelessly mutilated, Asquith attempted to conclude the sort of separate peace that so worried the nationalist leaders. He instructed Murray to ascertain 'whether Carson & his friends would *definitely* treat' if Antrim, Derry, Down (except for the Catholic parts of the south), north Armagh and north Fermanagh were excluded, with the possibility of partitioning Tyrone; Protestants and Catholics who wished to migrate, he suggested, might be relocated at state expense. The prime minister 'could not *guarantee* that Redmond would assent', he wrote to Stanley, 'but if C[arson] falls in, I shall have to put on the screw to R[edmond].'[48]

In a week of intense activity, Murray – occasionally joined by Lord Rothermere – saw Redmond, Carson, Bonar Law, Asquith, Lloyd George and Hopwood.[49] Carson, who days earlier at Drumbeg, County Down had dramatically declared 'give us a clean cut of Ulster or come and fight us', was insistent that he could not give up an inch of Tyrone. Asquith found Redmond and Dillon 'dead against' partition of the county or a ministerial 'parade ... of possible concessions' in the coming amending bill debate. Bonar Law admitted, the prime minister recounted to the king, that the differences had narrowed to a point where they might settle between themselves, 'but the Irish ... for the moment dominate the situation, and control the votes of the rank and file of both parties here'.[50] An attempt by the government and opposition to impose a settlement upon the Irish parties, Asquith told Stamfordham,

> ... would probably result in a large number of the members of the Government & opposition going over to the Irish who would unite & defeat the Government – he fancied Mr Bonar Law's position is

not a very strong one & he may have difficulties in keeping his party together.[51]

In other words, the Irish were in effective command of English politics. After all Bonar Law's imprudent braggadocio, reactionary Tories would not permit a volte-face on Home Rule at any price, while a ministerial betrayal of Redmond promised to result in the wholesale rejection of Asquith's leadership by Liberals.

As fraught with difficulties as the political situation was in England, political authority in Ireland had been corroded even more deeply. Rival armies filled the vacuum left by Asquith's virtual abdication of governance in Ulster, a policy of impunity fully supported by Redmond. Surrender on either side promised to precipitate a repudiation, of unknown scale, of the moderate Irish leaders. What power to act that Redmond and Carson possessed, if pushed too far, was wholly negative in character. Carson could lead his loyalist paramilitaries over the threshold of political violence, while Redmond could smash the Liberal Party and bring down the government, in the process losing Home Rule and destroying his own party. Thus was the terminal point of the Unionists' tactic of exploiting Ulster for party political advantage, and of Asquith's policy of appeasement: the prospect of bloodshed, or an atomisation of politics in Britain and Ireland.

The prime minister faced the reality that to debate the amending bill in the prevailing circumstances would only exacerbate differences, perhaps irreparably. Less in the hope of finding a solution than of postponing violence in Ireland, Asquith advised George V to summon a conference of the party leaders.[52] The Irish on both sides, the prime minister told Lord Stamfordham, required a summons in the king's name to save face before their more extreme supporters.[53]

With a conference by royal command in the offing, Lloyd George took stock of the possible outcome of the talks.[54] It was likely, he thought, that settlement by conference would be conditional upon an early dissolution of Parliament. The outlook for Home Rule under these circumstances, he concluded, was dismal. An early dissolution would amount to a refusal to use the Parliament Act, and would spark a revolt of large sections of the Liberal Party, particularly in the industrial north of England. Liberal electors, he argued, would demand to know why the programme they had authorised the government to carry out had been abandoned.

It cannot be emphasised too strongly that the great desire of the Liberal Party in the country is to see the Parliament Act work. They care, indeed, more for this than for the intrinsic merits of the three Bills which they desire to see passed under the Parliament Act ... After a struggle lasting thirty years they insist that under the Parliament Act the opposition of the House of Lords and the Tory Party should be beaten and broken down.[55]

If a dissolution after the passage of Home Rule would be damaging in England, the Chancellor suggested, the consequences would be disastrous in Ireland. Home Rule might, in such circumstances, be placed on the statute book, but after an election its fate as an operative measure might be in the hands of its enemies. The Irish nationalists 'would say that with a condition approaching civil war in Ireland, that the Liberal administration had run away' instead of protecting their interests. This view, he predicted, would be supported by the Labour members and *three-quarters* of the Liberal Party. Foreshadowing the fate of the Liberal Party four years in the future, Lloyd George asserted that the prime minister would be left in the position of dissolving and appealing to the country on behalf of himself and a remnant of the former governing party.[56]

To royal displeasure, and to the consternation of ministers, leaked news of the conference (by Bonar Law, as Asquith subsequently learned) was published in *The Times* and the *Daily Mail* on 20 July.[57] Labour members immediately tabled a resolution condemning royal interference in the business of the House of Commons, but more alarming, the Liberal chief whip reported to the premier, was a 'wide spread feeling among our own rank and file' that the conference was a prelude to a general election.[58] Just as the Chancellor warned, the party was reacting with indignation to what it saw as an effort to circumvent the Parliament Act.

Detailed accounts of the Buckingham Palace conference have been published elsewhere.[59] The briefest of summaries of the three days of talks will suffice to advance the analysis here. Asquith suggested that discussions should turn first to the area to be excluded. Carson made a strong appeal for the total exclusion of Ulster in the interests of securing unity at an early date.[60] Redmond ruled this out, and maintained that county option was the only defensible way to proceed, as majorities would choose for or against exclusion.[61] The Unionist delegation refused to consider this. Asquith suggested that existing Poor Law divisions be used to separate Catholic and Protestant districts in Ulster. Carson altered his demand to six-county exclusion, but maintained that no part of Tyrone or Fermanagh could come under the jurisdiction of the Dublin parliament.[62] Redmond and Carson both insisted on having the whole of Tyrone, but each said that he understood the other's position. Asquith wrote to Stanley of having reached 'an impasse, with unspeakable consequences, for a matter which to English eyes seems inconceivably small, and to Irish eyes immeasurably big'.[63]

Privately, Bonar Law asked Redmond to agree to an election and suspension of the unamended bill until after the ballot. If the Tories were returned with a modest majority, he undertook to settle on Home Rule at once.[64] Lloyd George submitted a plan to reconcile the differences by proposing the exclusion of six counties, which would still send representatives to the Irish parliament.[65] Neither of these initiatives influenced the course of the conference's third and final day on 24 July. Carson elaborated his 'clean cut' proposal for Ulster autonomy – arranged so as to facilitate accession to the Irish parliament after a brief period – but the matter was dropped. The discussion turned to the status of Tyrone, and once again ground to a halt. Speaker James Lowther, who chaired the meetings, tried to close the gap by asking whether a face-saving proposal for the temporary exclusion of the county offered a way out. Both Irish leaders dissented. Redmond enquired formally whether any concessions other than exclusion would satisfy Ulster, and Carson answered in the negative.[66] The conference ended in utter failure.

The 'malignity of fortune'[67]

Amid the sobering implications of the conference's breakdown, its end was suffused with bathos. Redmond and Carson parted in tears, and Captain Craig of the Ulster Unionists seized Redmond's hand to pay him a heartfelt tribute. The contrast of public excoriation, private cordiality, absolute irreconcilability, and perfect understanding brought to Margot Asquith's mind an epigram of Louis Philippe: 'Irlande est une maladie incurable mais jamais mortelle.'[68] 'Aren't they a remarkable people?' Asquith wrote, 'And the folly of thinking that we can understand, let alone govern them!'[69] The Liberal and nationalist leaders reconvened at 10 Downing Street, where the prime minister told the Irishmen that he intended to proceed with the amending bill offering county option of exclusion without a time limit. With considerable reluctance, Redmond and Dillon agreed to try to persuade the Irish Party to accept the change. A Cabinet meeting later that day confirmed the decision, and went on to discuss the situation in Ulster in desultory fashion; the European crisis had grabbed ministers' attention. The Austrian ultimatum to Serbia had been delivered the previous evening, and the spectre of a general European war suddenly loomed. The situation threatened, as Asquith reported to Stanley, 'a real Armageddon, which would dwarf the Ulster & Nationalist Volunteers to their true proportions. Happily there seems to be no reason why we should be anything more than spectators. But it is a blood-curdling prospect – is it not?'[70]

The grave situation in continental Europe remained momentarily distant. Asquith advised the king that the amending bill would be proceeded with, substituting a second county poll on inclusion at the expiry of an undefined term.[71] Asquith confided to Stanley that he doubted whether an amending bill could be agreed by the two Houses, in which event he believed it quite possible that the king would assent to the passage of Home Rule only on condition that an immediate dissolution would follow. If this was refused, the prime minister speculated that the monarch would dismiss the government and send for ministers who would agree. Given the feelings of rank and file Liberals about upholding the Parliament Act, Asquith believed that a general election at such a juncture 'would be one of the worst things that could happen to the country, or (I suspect) to the Liberal Party'.[72]

A dire situation was made worse by the news from Dublin that evening. The Bachelor's Walk shootings, the most 'inopportune coup' the premier could imagine, occurred on the eve of the second reading of the amending bill.[73] The incident aroused great indignation among nationalists, and convinced many that differential treatment of Unionists and nationalists was a bloody reality. Birrell and Asquith met Dillon and Redmond the following day. The nationalist leaders asserted that voting for the amending bill, a difficult enough matter for them before the slayings, was now quite impossible, and demanded that its consideration be put off. Asquith replied that he feared that if the Irish abstained on the amending bill they would be followed (just as the Chancellor predicted) by the whole of the Labour Party and many Liberals. The government, the prime minister told the nationalist leaders, would be imperilled by such a protest vote.[74] Redmond requested that consideration of the amending bill be deferred for a week, until Monday 3 August.[75] The Irish leaders were, not unnaturally, anxious; Dillon, in particular, was worried about the nationalist reaction to a scheme of indefinite exclusion.[76] Asquith, however, sensed that the opposition was also 'in a funk' over the apparent deadlock, making settlement more likely.[77]

The political situation was on a knife-edge. Inflamed feelings in Ireland prevented the Irish Party from voting for the amending bill except at the risk of repudiation by the party's infuriated supporters, who wished to see it killed altogether. Ramsay MacDonald threatened that the Labour members would unseat the government should they bow to what he characterised as royal pressure to defeat the House of Commons. Over a hundred Liberal MPs resolved to stand by the Irish nationalists until their cause was won, and demanded that the government complete its programme under the Parliament Act before consenting to a dissolution. The king, however, might insist that just such a dissolution of Parliament would be the price of royal assent.[78] Revolt in Ulster seemed a serious possibility, and, after Bachelor's Walk, the danger of nationalist unrest, if expectations of Home Rule were frustrated, came into menacing focus. The situation looked so bleak that Wilfrid Scawen Blunt thought the prime minister might simply 'throw up his cards and resign'.[79]

Despite the dangers attendant upon a step in any direction, and his reputed penchant for delay, Asquith resisted Redmond's 'idiotic proposal' of a week's deferral of the amending bill. It would, he told Stanley, 'have made everyone say that we were drifting on, not having yet made up our own minds, and waiting for our Irish "Master" to make them up for us'. Instead, he announced that the House of Commons would consider the measure on Thursday 30 July.[80]

The European situation, which first entered the minds of ministers days earlier, was looking increasingly ominous. Talk of civil war in Ireland receded into the background. On 29 July Asquith wrote to Venetia Stanley that 'the Amending Bill & the whole Irish situation are of course put in the shade by the coming war – "coming" for it seems nothing but a miracle could avert it'.[81] Though precautionary military measures were put into effect the following day, British participation was still not a certainty.[82]

On the morning of 30 July, as the prime minister was preparing his speech for that day's amending bill debate, he received a telephone call from Bonar Law inviting him to meet at the opposition leader's Kensington flat. There he found Carson waiting with the Unionist leader, who proposed delaying the second reading of the amending bill and that a party truce be called. Asquith recounted the morning's events to Stanley with a whiff of cynicism as to the men's motives:

> He [Bonar Law] thought that to advertise our domestic dissensions
> at this moment would weaken our influence in the world for peace,
> &c. Carson said that at first he had thought it impossible to agree, as

it would strain further the well-known and much tried 'tensions' of his Ulstermen, but that now he had come to see that it was a patriotic duty, &c. I of course welcomed their attitude, but said I would consult some colleagues before giving a definite answer.[83]

Asquith read the two men the latest telegrams from Berlin, which, he judged, indicated that the German government was calculating that internal disarray would disrupt British foreign policy.[84]

Returning to Downing Street, the premier sought the counsels of Grey and Lloyd George, who urged acceptance of the truce. Redmond was preparing a never-to-be-delivered speech announcing his reluctant support for an offer of indefinite exclusion by county polls when he was summoned by Asquith.[85] The prime minister reported to Stanley that the Irish Party chairman

> ... thought it an excellent chance of putting off the Amending Bill, and for the first time in my experience of him made a really useful suggestion: namely, that if we put off the Amending Bill till the next session, he would agree that the operation of the Home Rule Bill (to be put on the Statute Book now) should be suspended until the Amending Bill became law. He said that under those conditions he could make much larger concessions than he can now.[86]

Asquith recorded for Lord Stamfordham that at the meeting Redmond 'remarked that, in case of emergency, it would be easy to withdraw all the regular troops from Ireland, which would be rendered perfectly safe by the combined, or reciprocal efforts of the Ulster and the National Volunteers'.[87] In the House of Commons that afternoon, Asquith announced the postponement of the amending bill owing to the gravity of the international situation.

It might be asserted that with the inevitable postponement of the amending bill, the Irish Party chairman was simply making the best of a bad situation. It has not been widely recognised, however, that the suggestion to suspend Home Rule's operation originated with Redmond.[88] The nationalist leader's intervention bears closer examination than Ronan Fanning's dismissal of it as a ploy merely to delay inevitable partition.[89] This anachronistic judgement does not consider the tactical advantages that Redmond's move might have presented. The shelving of the amending bill, even at the price of a temporary suspension of self-government, offered an escape from more repugnant proposals that might be advanced. The enactment of the Home Rule Bill in suspended form also promised to be more than just a moral victory for the nationalists. As Patricia Jalland and John Stubbs pointed out, its placement on the statute book, coupled with the deferral of an amending bill, would have amounted to a loss *de jure* of the principle of exclusion and dealt a real blow to the Unionists' position.[90]

Redmond's suggestion was also predicated on the assumption that once the Government of Ireland Act was in being, the situation would be transformed. The Ulster Unionists would be unlikely, nationalists reasoned, to revolt against an Act in suspense. They hoped that a tranquil interlude in Ireland before an amending bill was considered in the winter session would calm rebellious spirits. Vitally, Home Rulers such as T.W. Russell judged, if exclusion by county plebiscite were offered when negotiations resumed, the vote would no longer be on the political question of self-government – the Act being on the statute book would have settled that. The question would be largely an economic one, concerning the partition of Ireland; and however much Ulstermen disliked Home Rule, it was improbable that they would be able to muster support for the retrospective erection of administrative and commercial barriers to a self-governing Ireland.[91] In such circumstances, Russell believed, the Unionists might carry exclusion in Antrim and Down, but this would scarcely be a viable unit for resisting accession to the Dublin parliament for long.[92]

Nationalist hopes that the Orange powder keg might be dampened were reflected in the anxieties of Unionist leaders, some of whom sensed a loss of momentum in the summer of 1914. As the reality of commercial disruption attendant upon exclusion affected Ulster, the reactionary peer Lord Milner feared that Unionist determination was crumbling. A despairing Milner, who *wanted* the Ulstermen to rebel, sensed that their resolve had already been broken, as he wrote to Bonar Law on 15 July:

> I don't believe the Ulster *coup* will be any *coup* at all if it is much longer deferred. In fact I doubt whether it will be attempted. If they think – & after all it is their business – that it is too great a risk to rise *now*, I can't conceive why they should run it later when there will be much less to gain by it.[93]

The seizing up of credit in Ulster – causing, as one of Milner's correspondents noted the same month, a 'severe depression of business' – lent powerful force to this belief.[94]

H.A. Gwynne, editor of the rabidly Unionist *Morning Post*, was getting cold feet about the whole enterprise. He insisted to Carson that plans to finance the provisional government by seizure of the Custom House in Belfast and confiscation of duties were fantastical:

> What will result is that owing to the uncertainty and the confusion ... *shippers will refuse to ship* and you may have a food famine on you in a week ... you would have to feed, if not pay, your rank and file, your force would be mobilised, work would be at a standstill, there would be a panic in the city here—and then?[95]

Gwynne warned that a collapse of the provisional government would be a victory for the 'arch traitor' Asquith, and that for Unionists, British and Irish, it would 'mean ridicule and ridicule would kill us all'.[96]

Territorial considerations, too, occupied the minds of Unionists, though from the opposite perspective from those of the nationalist leaders. The Unionist Lord Crawford noted on 25 June that much of the value of six-county exclusion was the demoralising blow it would deal to Redmond's power over the nationalist ranks.[97] By the same token, a diminution of 'defiant Ulster' that Redmond's strategy sought to bring about promised to sow disunity among the Unionist leaders. Measured against Unionists' opposing objectives, and their private fears for the sustainability of the Ulster campaign, there was much to commend the nationalist strategy of passing Home Rule in suspended form.

Though Britain's entry to the European conflict was looking probable, there was considerable disagreement in the Cabinet and more widely over the question of going to war. On 31 July Asquith reported to Stanley that 'things look almost as bad as can be'. Lord Kitchener and Churchill were strongly for backing France to preserve the honour of the empire, he wrote, but 'the general opinion at present – particularly strong in the City – is to keep out at almost all costs'.[98] Redmond would have shared the uncertainty about the war and, doubtless, the belief of the political class in England that if war came, its issue would be decided quickly.[99] He thus would have had little reason to think that the suspension of Home Rule might extend past the winter, and could have been reasonably confident that in making his offer, he could avert bloodshed in Ireland and secure self-government for nine-tenths of the island early in 1915. The Irish Party chairman's improvisation to extricate Home Rule from the mortal danger it was in might well have seemed a coup to his colleagues. Barring a breakdown of the party truce, which remained a threat if the bill was proceeded with, the culmination of nationalist hopes must have seemed within grasp.

With war seemingly inescapable, Redmond was being pulled in opposite directions. Margot Asquith wrote urging him to follow his instincts and offer the services of his Volunteers in the moment of crisis.[100] By contrast, Colonel Moore of the Irish Volunteers suggested that Irish reservists should refuse to mobilise unless Home Rule became operative immediately.[101] The Irish Party chairman met the prime minister on 3 August, and pressed him to commit to placing the Home Rule Bill on the statute book. Redmond stressed the perils of the situation in Ireland if it were not done immediately. Although Asquith agreed that Home Rule should be acted on without delay, he was transfixed by the imminent prospect of war, unable to say what would be the course of the parliamentary session or how long the House would sit. 'He is simply living from hour to hour', Redmond recounted to Dillon, 'his mind filled with one thing only.'[102]

War

Redmond's eve-of-war speech in the House of Commons on 3 August pledged that every British soldier could be withdrawn from Ireland. The nation, he declared, would be defended by her armed sons, the Volunteers of the south locking arms with their brethren in the north. Redmond's words and moving delivery electrified the House. Margot Asquith observed 'old crusted Tories' raving about the speech; some listening on the opposition benches, she wrote, had tears in their eyes.[103] If the move was calculated to diminish the possibility of upsetting the party truce, it had its desired effect, as Christopher Addison recorded:

> Redmond's speech was a masterpiece. It was a striking example of political genius; of a man grasping a great opportunity with both hands. His speech snuffed out Ulsterism and the anti-Home Rule movement as one snuffs out a candle. Everybody felt this. One could see that even Carson, who looked as miserable as the rest of us, realised it too.[104]

O'Connor advised that the remarkable atmosphere created by the speech should be immediately capitalised upon, and used to force a settlement on the Unionists. Opinion in Ireland, however, was not so enthralled by the new departure as that in Britain. 'Sinn Féiners', O'Connor wrote to Dillon, were already damning Asquith for treachery, and openly calling for a German victory. Devlin intimated to O'Connor his intention to denounce the government, since without Home Rule in being to mollify embittered nationalist feeling, he believed the Irish Party's position would be an impossible one.[105] Redmond cabled Dillon in Dublin asking him to attend a meeting of the Volunteers' provisional committee to head off any embarrassing declaration it might make.[106]

Contrary to Paul Bew's assertion, the nationalist leader extracted no commitment to place the Home Rule Bill on the statute book prior to making his pledge, as evinced by his actions in the days that followed.[107] Perhaps it was Horace Plunkett's letter to *The Times* calling for the deferment of Home Rule's passage until the winter session of Parliament, but Redmond immediately became convinced that ministers intended to delay royal assent for the bill.[108] He wrote to the prime minister and the Chancellor of the Exchequer the day after his dramatic intervention, emphasising the risk he had taken among his supporters in making the pledge. He appealed to Asquith urgently 'in the midst of this crisis and perhaps *because* of this crisis' not to jeopardise his position in Ireland. If, after making such an offer as he had, he went back to Ireland empty-handed, Redmond wrote, 'my people will consider themselves sold and deplorable things will be said and done which may perhaps wreck the Irish cause'.[109] 'Surely, surely', he wrote to Lloyd George, 'we are entitled to this ... I cannot go back to Ireland if Royal Assent is postponed for two or three months. Don't fail us now.'[110]

War was declared on 4 August 1914. The prime minister received appeals in its first hectic days from Bonar Law and Carson seeking assurances that the status quo would be maintained.[111] The opposition leader had caught wind of Redmond's idea to prorogue and not adjourn the parliamentary session, which would have had the effect of annulling the amending bill while merely suspending progress of the Home Rule Bill, which was ready for royal assent.[112] Redmond met Carson in the Speaker's library on 5 August, but the nationalist leader found Carson in an 'irreconcilable mood', threatening to obstruct the wartime Appropriations Bill if Home Rule was put on the statute book. Redmond implored Asquith not to be deflected by such threats, which would, he said, ruin the Unionists in the court of English opinion.[113] The premier assured the Irish Party chairman that the party detente left Home Rule in no danger, and that his determination to see the bill on the statute book in the current parliamentary session was unchanged.[114]

The frayed tempers on both sides meant there was no rest for the prime minister. He was called to the Cabinet room late one evening to attempt to placate Bonar Law, perhaps suspicious that a prorogation was being contemplated. It was difficult to know who was being more 'foolish and unreasonable', Asquith complained to his wife, the Unionist leader or the Irish. An earlier long discussion between the Irish Party chairman and the Chancellor of the Exchequer, he related, 'ended up with them both being so furious that Redmond went out and banged the door & Ll.G. [Lloyd George] went out by the window'.[115] Asquith offered Bonar Law resumption of the debate on the amending bill after an adjournment, or a one-clause bill suspending the operation of the Government of Ireland Act until an amending bill had been passed.[116] The Unionist leader responded by threatening to issue a manifesto in the newspapers denouncing the decision to proceed with Home Rule.[117]

Redmond and Dillon were further unsettled by a meeting with Lord Kitchener on 8 August. The newly installed war secretary made it clear that he had no interest in taking up the Irish Party chairman's pledge, nor in utilising the Irish Volunteers as a unit in any form. Dillon, who abhorred the war, pointed out that the nationalist leaders had not come in the expectation of being enlisted as recruiting sergeants, but, as F.S.L. Lyons concluded, it is likely that this was precisely the role Kitchener had in mind for them.[118] Redmond did not abandon hope of War Office assistance for the Volunteers, urging Dillon to do everything in his power to induce the provisional committee to give a fair hearing to General Bryan Mahon of the new 10th (Irish) Division during his visit to Dublin the following week.[119] When he himself met Mahon, however, Redmond reportedly attached two conditions to the use of the Volunteers: that they should not be required to swear allegiance to the king, and that they should serve only on Irish soil. Despite Mahon's protests regarding the gravity of the situation on the Western Front, the nationalist leader remained adamant that there should be adherence to his terms.[120]

The Cabinet that met on 10 August was scarcely less deadlocked about what to do about the Home Rule Bill than were the nationalist and Unionist adversaries. Churchill was all for settlement; Kitchener feared that the setting up of a provisional government in Ulster would damage the war effort; and Grey, who had received a letter from Bonar Law appealing to his sense of honour, felt bound to resign if the Home Rule controversy flared anew.[121] The Chancellor, evidently having been persuaded by at least some of Redmond's arguments, joined Reginald McKenna in pressing for the Home Rule Bill to be placed on the statute book immediately.[122] With his colleagues at loggerheads,

Asquith announced a fortnight's adjournment in the House of Commons later that day, expressing the hope that, in the interval, ministers would come up with proposals that might meet with broad acceptance.

Having returned to Augavanagh, Redmond became more alarmed than ever that negotiations were taking place behind his back. He cannot have been comforted by Birrell's news that an immovable faction in the Cabinet cared less for majorities in Tyrone and Fermanagh than for what might be done to appease Carson.[123] Sir Edward Grey's position was critical. Given Asquith's personal loyalty to the foreign secretary, and the esteem in which Grey was held in the Liberal Party, Grey's resignation might precipitate the fall of the government. To the dismay of Unionists to whom Grey spoke, however, it seemed he, together with the colonial secretary Lewis Harcourt and Lord Haldane, were coming around to the idea of suspending Home Rule's operation for the duration of the war.[124] The prime minister was anxious to impress upon the Irish Party chairman that coming to an arrangement before Parliament would reconvene on 25 August was 'absolutely imperative'; he discussed with Birrell, he told Stanley, 'how best to put an effective pistol at the head of Redmond'.[125]

Asquith still gravitated towards a more definitive resolution of the Irish question than its simple deferral. He proposed, he wrote to Stanley, to offer the nationalist leader a choice between three courses. The first, provisional 'exclusion of six counties or thereabouts', was favoured by Asquith, as despite 'its logical drawbacks ... so far as Great Britain is concerned it clears the whole damned business out of the way'. Redmond's option to enact the Home Rule Bill with a suspensory clause for one year would, he thought, be rejected by the Tories as insufficient surety against the bill's eventual operation in Ulster. As for the third option – of hanging up the bill until the winter parliamentary session with a provision that it be taken up in precisely the same position in which it was left with respect to the Parliament Act – he expected 'Redmond will jib at it, because it does not give him his Bill on the Statute Book now, and leaves *him* more or less at the mercy of fortune'.[126]

The prime minister summoned the nationalist leader to London. Redmond, doubtless suspecting the pressure that awaited him in the capital, did not hurry back, to Asquith's annoyance. The prime minister instructed Birrell to write to the Irish Party chairman advising him of the three proposals to be offered, and asking him to be prepared to choose one.[127] This Birrell did on 19 August, in a letter expanding upon Asquith's ideas. The chief secretary wrote that he believed the Grey faction supported 'an agreement as to acreage' in Ulster, and that the prime minister was inclined to an arrangement like the Speaker's suggestion of the temporary exclusion of Tyrone for expediency's sake. There was no certainty, Birrell wrote, in Redmond's proposal to enact and suspend Home Rule for the duration of the war. Such a suspension would, he anticipated, bring them close to the general election due in 1915, and the nearer this date drew, the louder would be the demand to extend the suspension of Home Rule's operation until after the electorate had given its verdict. Neither could the quiescence of the two bodies of Volunteers in Ireland be guaranteed if a suspended bill were to be passed. This, he said, was the greatest anxiety of the ministers insistent upon settlement. Birrell once again assured Redmond that no official negotiations with the opposition were taking place, and closed by commenting that the latest military opinion was that the war was going to be 'a long job that will tax all our resources in men and money'.[128]

Redmond seems to have believed that once the bill was enacted, he could continue to exercise leverage over the Liberal and Labour backbenchers in the House of Commons to block implementation of any exclusion proposals. So confident was he of obtaining his end in this way, he wrote to Gill, that he regarded exclusion as dead.[129] Such a strategy, however, presumed a speedy end to the war and a resumption of normal parliamentary business. Redmond's optimistic letter to Gill of 19 August crossed with Birrell's to him, of the same date, warning of a long and arduous struggle ahead.

With the war two weeks old, T.P. Gill believed that Churchill and Kitchener had taken charge, and were in danger of fatally misjudging the state of feeling in Ireland.[130] O'Connor shared the view that there were men in the Cabinet more in sympathy with the Ulster Unionists than with nationalists, and that Asquith, despising ministerial disputes, was vacillating.[131] Redmond was irritated by Asquith's indecision; he believed the prime minister would place Home Rule on the statute book were it not for the possibility of Grey's resignation.[132]

Asquith found the Irish Party chairman 'disposed to be exorbitant' when the two men met on 21 August.[133] The nationalist leader agreed that settlement on areas to be excluded would, if practicable, be best; but, Asquith recorded, Tyrone 'and those infernal snippets of Fermanagh and Derry popped up again', with no more prospect of reaching agreement on them than three weeks previously at Buckingham Palace. Redmond ruled out hanging up the bill until the winter session, and advanced his plan of enactment and suspension. Meeting Bonar Law directly afterwards, the prime minister, not for the first time, found the situation reversed. The Unionists would not agree to a suspended Act at any price, but would concede a three-year time limit on Ulster exclusion, provided the area was extended to six counties. This possibility intrigued Asquith, though he could not see how the difference could be reconciled in the few days remaining before Parliament next sat.[134]

George V, with whom Asquith had an audience that day, was 'full of appreciation for his ministry and of flattery', encouraging his first minister to exercise his enhanced wartime authority to impose a settlement upon the Irish disputants. Asquith emerged from the meeting inclined, he told Stanley, to 'declare that they *must all* take' a settlement of his design as 'a sort of ultimatum'.[135] Redmond was unaware of this line of thinking when expressing his views to Asquith in a long letter stressing the advantages of suspension of the Act. He forwarded a copy to Grey.[136] The Irish Party would pledge (he wrote) that ample time should be given for discussion and 'if possible passage by agreement of an Amending Bill if such an Amending Bill were still required'. He warned, however, that should enactment be postponed, 'small but loud' forces would break free from his control in Ireland and the United States.[137] The contingent nature of Redmond's undertaking hinted at a strategy of obstructing exclusion after Home Rule was on the statute book.

Asquith mused on the possibilities of settlement. In a handwritten note dated 22 August, he put on record, 'in case of accident', his view of 'the fairest and most equitable way of dealing with the Irish situation' in the circumstances created by the war. The prime minister's plan was a hybrid of the government's county option proposal and Bonar Law's latest suggestion, heavily weighted in favour of the Unionists. The Home Rule Bill, he wrote, should at once be placed on the statute book, though suspended for a few months. Before prorogation of Parliament, however, a new bill, or an amended amending bill, should be passed to provide for a plebiscite of the electors of Ulster, voting en bloc, for the exclusion of six counties for three years. At the expiry of this period, a poll by county on the question of exclusion would determine the fate of each.[138]

Asquith, fortified on 25 August by a letter from the king urging settlement for the sake of national unity, was braced to actuate his 'contemplated *coup d'état*'. The 'ghastly possibilities' of the situation, he felt, left him with little choice. He met Bonar Law to explain the initiative, and found the Unionist leader receptive; he undertook to transmit its terms to Carson. At the same time the premier sent Birrell to tell the nationalist leaders that, with bad news coming in from the Western Front, areas and time limits were 'not the urgent matters of the moment ... and they must be content with further delay'.

Asquith gave George V's plea to the chief secretary to 'use as a fly for Redmond and Dillon' in the hope that they would be influenced by a letter from the sovereign.[139] The two men, however, were unimpressed by its implication that they should be the ones to concede, and they coolly suggested to Birrell that His Majesty 'might well see Carson and put pressure on him'. As for the plan to impose a settlement, undisclosed as yet to the nationalists, Birrell advised his chief that he thought it gave away too much; McKenna told the prime minister that if Redmond were to demur and protest in the House of Commons, he would 'carry the bulk' of the Liberal Party with him.[140]

This intelligence dampened the premier's brief enthusiasm for a heavy-handed approach to Redmond, and the ultimatum was quietly shelved.[141] In response to a plea from Robert Donald, editor of *The Daily Chronicle* (and Lloyd George's golfing partner), for help to stiffen ministerial resolve, Gill wrote of a choice between risks. The danger of alienating nationalist senti-ment, he argued, was more serious than any threat from Ulster:

> ... the thing risked in mishandling the Nationalist sentiment now is immeasurable ... I wish I could convey to you an idea of what it means – what the Nationalists could do if a revulsion of feeling were provoked (for instance, holding up Irish food supply, stopping recruit-ing, to say nothing of things to be done in the U.S. and Colonies).[142]

Gill doubted, he wrote, if even Redmond realised the level of suspicion that was abroad in the country that Irish loyalty was to be repaid with betrayal. He subsequently forwarded his 'Special Correspondent' articles for *The Daily Chronicle* to Redmond to equip him with arguments to counter ministers.[143]

The chief secretary endeavoured to give Redmond a 'photograph of the Prime Minister's mind' after talking with him on 28 August. Asquith, he said, keenly felt the 'gravity' of pressures – implying royal pressures – to pass an amending bill excluding a part of Ulster before Home Rule's enactment. Such action would find favour among certain Liberal MPs, 'which though scanty in numbers are powerful in personalities' – that is, the adherents of Grey – though it would expose ministers, he wrote, to 'grave dangers in certain authoritative and really populated quarters of the House'. Asquith, Birrell said, was coming to the view that if the immediate prospect of exclusion was to be avoided, 'the passage into law of some Amending Bill should be the condi-tion for terminating the suspensory period of the Home Rule Bill'. Radicals would object, he acknowledged, that the House of Lords could sabotage or delay such a bill. However, Birrell gave this little credence, saying that in six months' time the war would have obliterated the Ulster controversy, and that he was in no doubt that a better amending bill could be obtained then than when passions were at their height.[144]

That the prime minister was coming around to the idea of suspension would have come as heartening news to the nationalist leader. He had no wish to hasten an amending bill, believing, like Birrell, that the longer it could be delayed, the more its *raison d'être* would diminish. It was now clear, though, that the European conflict was going to be a longer struggle than was first appreciated. Redmond, initially believing that the war worked to the advantage of the nationalists, had not yet formed a strategy to sustain enthusiasm for a suspended measure of Home Rule through a prolonged war.[145]

Donald of *The Daily Chronicle*, whom Lloyd George had consulted as to the state of opinion in America, advised the Chancellor (along lines suggested by Gill) that the delay to Home Rule was strengthening the hand of Clan-na-Gael in the United States, which would work assiduously against British interests there.[146] The impact of Home Rule's enactment in the United States, with its potential to favourably sway Irish-American politicians and counteract German-American agitation, was, Donald counselled, an even more important consideration than its effect in Ireland.[147] Arguments such as these were persuasive: opinion in the United States was to prove the crucial factor in winning Grey's support for enactment in suspended form.[148]

Donald enclosed the latest report from his 'Special Correspondent' (presumably Gill) for the Chancellor, which argued that settlement was impossible under present conditions. Carson, it claimed, had promised his followers exclusion of the whole province; if the Unionist leader recanted now, he faced a split in the Ulster Volunteers. The placing of the bill on the statute book, the article asserted, with its operation suspended and an amending bill left to the winter session, would ease tensions in Ulster and find her much more amenable when negotiations resumed. 'The really momentous trouble', the report concluded, lay in playing the Irish nationalists false, for on their goodwill was staked 'the winning or losing of Ireland, and her military and political strength throughout the English-speaking world.'[149]

Writing privately to Donald, a pessimistic Gill complained that Asquith, anxious to exhaust the possibilities of settlement, had squandered a golden opportunity. Had the prime minister met Redmond's speech of 3 August with an unequivocal pledge to enact Home Rule, Gill said, 'all England and the Empire would have applauded him and there *would have been* settlement by consent'. Redmond could have returned to Ireland and called upon the Volunteers to send 40,000 or 50,000 men to the front. Instead, he had been muzzled by Asquith's inaction:

> Instead of Redmond – who came forward at the first moment of the war, making no bargain, only relying on the bargain that was made being kept – being enabled to do this, it is Carson who gets the chance. If Asquith does then keep the plighted word of a British Government – which Grey thought it worthwhile entering a European war to do – it will be, I fear, after the Act has been deprived of three fourths of its grace and after nine-tenths of the possibilities have been missed, and after God knows what mischiefs have been set afoot here.[150]

He urged Donald to speak to Lloyd George or Churchill, and to induce them to take action at once

> ... which will enable Redmond to call upon the Nationalists to rally to the war levy and which will at the same time put things right – before the country and the World – as regards Ulster ... Incidentally if this chance is missed, away go the fruits of Liberalism and democratic power. Kitchener takes control and Mr Asquith and the rest may be allowed a seat in the ambulance wagon until it is time to send them off the scene altogether.[151]

The road to Woodenbridge

Carson duly received the patriotic adulation that Gill felt should have been Redmond's. The Ulster Unionist leader called, unconditionally, for Ulster Volunteers to enlist in Lord Kitchener's New Army on 3 September.[152] John Dillon recognised Carson's astute move to bolster his position in England while the Irish Party was 'disheartened and bewildered' in Ireland. The country, he wrote to O'Connor, was 'seething with suspicion and disappointment' after 'the shilly-shallying and delays of Asquith &c.'; his great fear was that any announcement the government might make would be coldly received. Dillon noted with alarm the political capital being made by advanced nationalists – principally members of the provisional committee of the Irish Volunteers – whom he conflated with adherents of the Sinn Féin movement. This 'Sinn Féin' element, he told O'Connor, was preparing the ground, giving notice of anti-recruiting resolutions for the next committee meeting of the Irish Volunteers, and embarking on 'an extremely active propaganda campaign'.[153]

Gill worried that the marked upsurge in separatist activity, combined with the lack of leadership from London, was inducing Redmond to 'lose his bearings' and play dangerously to the '"Hungarian" gallery'; a move, he thought, that would alienate British support after Carson's loyal turnabout.[154] The anti-English, pro-German content of newspapers like *Sinn Féin* and *Irish Freedom*, Gill believed, would scandalise British public opinion; to have any whiff of it linger around moderate nationalism would be ruinous.[155] Having hastily discussed the dangers of the situation with Redmond, Gill took soundings from prominent nationalists, who appear to have included Denis Kelly, bishop of Ross; Colonel Maurice Moore; Walter D'Alton, a Tipperary veteran of the Land War; and Gill's brother, Robert.[156] The view emerging, he wrote to his chief,

> ... is that assuming that Asquith [pays] up ... the more boldly and clearly you call on the country to recruit into the Expeditionary Army the better. The country is ready to support you on this line – provided you take a few precautions to put the thing tactfully and considerately as regards the Volunteers. A prompt and whole-hearted announcement too will check the proceedings of the Sinn Feiners in good time.[157]

This advice prefigured the call that Redmond was to make at Woodenbridge, County Wicklow nearly a fortnight later. His full-throated backing for recruitment, which ultimately proved disastrous, has sometimes been portrayed as spontaneous and ill-considered, but it appears, rather, to have been a reasoned and deliberate strategy sanctioned by at least some of the party old guard.[158]

The call for nationalists to enlist in the British army, to serve not in Ireland but to fight on the Western Front, was not dangled before Asquith as an inducement to place Home Rule on the statute book, though it was contingent upon his honouring his pledge. Redmond's decision to emphatically support the British war effort was a strategic move with three objects in mind. The first, as Paul Bew asserted, was to cement Home Rule by uniting Ireland in military service, shouldering the wartime burden under what was hoped would be the banner of a national brigade. Secondly, as Bew observed, it would permit nationalists to level the field with the Ulster Unionists and demonstrate that they were no less loyal to king and country.[159] It was through conspicuous sacrifice for the empire that nationalists would win British hearts, as disunion in Ireland was being mended. As Gill's canvassing of opinion indicated, however, backing for recruitment was also intended as a thrust in a political counteroffensive against the advanced nationalists. Rallying to the colours (among which, it was intended, green should figure prominently) appears to have been viewed as a 'long war' strategy to reclaim the political initiative from the physical-force men, and to submerge separatist and anti-war agitation under a tide of martial patriotism. Reconstituting the Irish Volunteers into a distinctive national army corps, Gill believed, was the master stroke that could sweep away the separatists.[160]

Gill followed up his recommendation to Redmond with an appeal for help to Hopwood, begging him to do everything in his power to stress the importance of Ireland to American opinion. As for ill feeling created by ministerial inaction, and Lord Kitchener's much-publicised dissatisfaction with Irish recruitment levels, Gill wrote:

> ... something has to be written off for the harm of these five weeks. And don't expect miracles from Mr Redmond. Especially when you don't play up to him. You have left him – after he took his plunge – and the constitutional Nationalists behind him in a plight something like that of the Belgians after the first weeks of the war when they began to ask 'where are the Allies?'[161]

Gill complained that no overtures had been extended to the Irish Volunteers, despite the efforts of their inspector-general, Colonel Moore. The impression created among Volunteers, Gill asserted, was that 'Lord Kitchener regards them with contempt and distrust'. He argued that bold action alone could transform the situation in Ireland, and suggested a royal proclamation to pool the Ulster and Irish Volunteer corps, and to reorganise them as new Irish armies, territorial and expeditionary.[162]

The protracted dilemma for Asquith's administration over what to do about Ireland was at last coming to its conclusion. The chief secretary wrote to Redmond on 8 September that a committee of the Cabinet had concluded that, subject to the Irish Party chairman's assent, the Home Rule Bill would be enacted at once, together with a short measure postponing its operation for a defined period. Assurances would also be given that an amending bill would be passed before its operation. However, he said, Asquith was still 'firmly persuaded' that 'certain proposals of his own might with great advantage to the Home Rule cause' be embodied in an amending bill that could be passed by consent, and, Birrell reported, he had convinced both McKenna and Lloyd George of his case. Enactment and suspension, Birrell said, would not be consented to by the opposition; Carson would denounce it, and there was no telling 'how far their fury would carry them … When the war is over, Ulster will once again be found ready to exclude Home Rule by force from her boundaries.' On the other hand, the chief secretary wrote, the prime minister's proposal would probably be reluctantly accepted, because it involved the exclusion of parts of the six counties, even if only for a short period.[163]

This iteration of Asquith's thinking (which appears to have been an elaboration of Bonar Law's cantonal plan of June) offered nationalists immediate operation of the Government of Ireland Act at the cost of modified six-county exclusion for an indefinite term. The proposal envisaged that the Home Rule Bill would be enacted and take effect; a second bill would be passed excluding Antrim, Armagh, Down, Derry, Fermanagh and Tyrone, but *including* parliamentary districts in Belfast, Derry and Newry, and making careful legislative and judicial arrangements to preserve legal continuity throughout Ireland. The amending bill would remain in force for the duration of the war and for twelve months afterwards, but if no permanent provision for the government of Ireland had been found in the interval, its operation might be extended. The memorandum suggested that in the event that no solution presented itself, an imperial conference, bringing the dominions into closer cooperation with the governance of the empire, would consider the permanent settlement of Ireland at the end of the war.[164]

The proposal represented little advance on what Cabinet waverers had desired almost from the outbreak of war, and was only a modest alteration of Carson's final demand at the Buckingham Palace conference. From Asquith's perspective, bringing Home Rule into operation for part of Ireland would enable him to proclaim a triumph to his supporters. It also would have commended itself as a means of pacifying Ulster and leaving open a path to reconciliation. However, Asquith's thinking was as blind to nationalist feeling as it had ever been. The outrage at Bachelor's Walk had exposed a rich seam of Anglophobic sentiment in Ireland that anti-war agitators were exploiting to the full. As Redmond feared, in the five weeks of delay the idea that the Irish Party had been 'sold' embedded itself in nationalist minds, and raw feelings rendered further territorial concessions utterly inadmissible. Yet ministers in London, absorbed in the war effort, remained mostly ignorant of developments in Ireland, and were irritated by the 'exorbitance' of the Irish Party chairman's demands.

Not surprisingly, Bonar Law preferred the prime minister's alternative proposal to passage of Home Rule in suspended form, though Asquith warned him that the 'great bulk' of Liberal supporters might find it unacceptable.[165] The king, too, expressed a preference for exclusion.[166] Redmond, however, rejected Asquith's proposal when he and Dillon met the premier on 9 September. The exclusion of six counties was cited, as it had been all along, as the insurmountable obstacle. The leaders agreed to suspend the Government of Ireland Act's operation for twelve months or for the duration of the war, whichever was the longer; and they would undertake, in the meantime, to pass an amending bill.[167] Despite last-minute royal intimations that the decision should be reconsidered, ministers unanimously ratified the suspensory formula on 12 September.[168]

The Unionist leaders professed to be 'amazed and disgusted' when the prime minister informed them of the decision to enact Home Rule in suspended form, alleging that it was a violation of an honourable truce. Asquith doubted there was much reality in their indignation, which he believed would 'fizzle out'.[169] The premier came to share Redmond's view, or perhaps was able to convince himself, that simply having the bill enacted into law was 'everything'. The majority in the House of Commons, he wrote to Stanley, would have nothing less.[170] The course belatedly adopted by Asquith had been urged upon him by the Irish Party leader since the eve of war.

A displeased George V wrote to Asquith on 13 September reminding his first minister of the terms of the political truce, under which a promise had been given to prosecute no matters of a controversial character. As recently as the previous week, the sovereign asserted, the government had confirmed its intention to introduce an amending bill, and such a bill had been before Parliament when the truce was agreed:

> It is possible that you and your colleagues have found themselves unable to carry their supporters with them up to the point of giving full effect to the truce. If so the Government must defend that situation. Meanwhile I grieve to feel that Irish politics will continue to stand in the way of the solid front which the whole Empire should otherwise present to the common enemy.[171]

While Asquith could dismiss Unionist protests as overblown, he could not lightly disregard a royal rebuke. He reassured the king that an amending bill would be passed before Home Rule came into operation, and that he would declare, in order to placate Unionist anxieties, that ministers would not attempt to coerce Ulster in the circumstances of the war.[172]

The prime minister, Birrell wrote to Redmond, was anxious that there should be 'no "crowing" over the victory', to which the chief secretary replied that he saw 'very little to crow over'. Asquith would 'doubtless refer to his elusive Amending Bill' in his speech introducing the suspending measure, but, Birrell assured Redmond, the placing of the Home Rule Bill on the statute book weighted negotiations over its modification in the nationalists' favour.[173] On 15 September Asquith introduced bills in the House of Commons to suspend the operation of the Government of Ireland Act and the Established Church (Wales) Act. In line with his assurances to the king, he coupled the undertaking to pass an amending bill with a pledge that

> ... the employment of force, any kind of force, for what you call the coercion of Ulster, is an absolutely unthinkable thing so far as I am concerned, and so far as my colleagues are concerned – I speak for them, for I know their unanimous feeling – that is a thing which we would never countenance or consent to.[174]

Redmond, in his reply, said that he desired no county of Ireland to be forced into a national parliament against its will.[175] The Tories staged a walkout; in their absence, the suspensory bills were passed. 'The whole House rose and cheered wildly', Asquith recorded for Stanley's benefit, 'for it was the end of the Home Rule controversy, and a really historic moment ... history will record [it] as a really great achievement.'[176] As the Home Rule Bill was put on the statute book as the Government of Ireland Act 1914, the prime minister expressed satisfaction that 'all the bluffing and outrageous manoeuvring of the Tories has been frustrated'.[177] The Irish chief secretary was also very gratified, though he wrote to Redmond, in reference to the king, that 'an Illustrious Person will be more interested in the Recruiting aspect of the question than any man'.[178]

Recruitment was also on the mind of T.P. Gill, who offered insistent counsels to Redmond, urging, on 12 September:

> I hope you are going to come out with a plead [*sic*]; and whole-heartedly, for Ireland joining in the war, and recruiting for the front (in an *Irish* army formed on mine – or some such – scheme). If you do Ireland is saved (and saved no matter what Asquith does). Otherwise she is lost and eternally disgraced. She has no alternative.[179]

Gill outlined arguments for such a policy for the Irish Party chairman.

Parliament's faith having been kept with Ireland, Gill wrote, she could at last stand with the free peoples of the British Empire in a fight for liberty and democracy. Ireland was in natural solidarity with the peoples of Belgium and Poland, and those of France, a historical friend and champion of liberty. Ireland should make, Gill suggested, but one stipulation: that her sons joining an expeditionary force be kept together as a unit, so that their bravery and sacrifice might stand to the credit of the nation.[180]

Gill was convinced of the necessity of nationalists matching the patriotism of Carson lest, in the supreme crisis, their loyalty be impugned. He judged that the upsurge of anti-English feeling demanded also that Redmond identify the European conflict with Irish interests. He wanted the Irish Volunteers, serving gallantly as a unit, to become a symbol of national pride, obliterating the disloyal influence of separatists in nationalist hearts. Thus, Gill believed, could advanced nationalist opposition be quelled, Ulster reconciled, and an Irish army created to back up a Dublin parliament when the Government of Ireland Act 1914 came into force at war's end. The impression that the Irish Party was out of sympathy with the Volunteer movement, Gill insisted to Redmond, must be corrected if nationalist pride was to be realigned towards war service.[181]

Redmond's manifesto, published on 17 September, and his speech at Woodenbridge on the twentieth calling for Irish Volunteers to serve on the Western Front, struck many of the notes suggested by Gill: of pride in the Volunteers, expressions of solidarity with small nations, and the call for the formation of an Irish army corps. At Woodenbridge the Irish Party chairman echoed Gill's words about the 'eternal disgrace' that would be Ireland's if she stood aloof:

> The war is undertaken in the defence of the highest principles of religion and morality and right and it would be a disgrace for ever to our country, and a reproach to her manhood, and a denial of the lessons of her history, if young Ireland confined their efforts to remaining at home to defend the shores of Ireland from an unlikely invasion.[182]

This speech, coming only days after the Home Rule Bill's enactment, was to rebound heavily upon Redmond as the war ground on. It must be remembered, however, that from the perspective of the early autumn of 1914, the most important tasks in view for the nationalist leaders were the negotiation, or preferably, obviation of an amending bill, and the consolidation of the

Irish Party's threatened position at home. In the latter respect, success hinged upon the speedy formation of an Irish army corps around which party politicians could weave a narrative of nationalist patriotism to counteract separatist anti-war agitation. However wrong-headed it may appear with hindsight, Redmond's move to throw his full weight behind the war was a bold effort to stop the rot and recast Irish patriotism in a martial mould. Despite an Ulster division being instantly brought into being, however, and plans being drawn up, apparently at the behest of Gill, to make the Irish Volunteers subject to mobilisation under the Territorial and Reserve Forces Act of 1907, Kitchener and the War Office were unrelenting in their refusal to recognise the Irish Volunteers.[183] The military men regarded Irish nationalists as disloyal, and were doubtless anxious about what a trained and battle-hardened corps might do once the war was over. Gill wrote to Hopwood protesting that the obstruction of a nationalist division out of 'political and social animus ... with the intended effect of deterring Nationalist recruitment' was nothing short of treasonous.[184]

The chilling effects of disappointment over a belated and inert measure of Home Rule and the failure of hostile British generals to give effect to Redmond's call for a nationalist army corps were felt almost immediately.[185] Scarcely three weeks after Woodenbridge, Redmond reported to O'Connor that 'the Sinn Feiners are putting up a big fight and we will have trouble in America, but the country at home is on the whole sound'.[186] Birrell was not so sure, however, worrying about a 'catastrophe' when the prime minister visited Dublin to recruit in October. 'The violence and folly of some of their [separatist] newspapers', he wrote to Dillon, 'are beyond conception.'[187] Irish Party funds tightened. UIL receipts for 1914 were down thirty-five per cent from the previous year, and thirty-seven league branches closed from June to December, with the loss of 5,800 members.[188] In New York *The Irish World* newspaper denounced the party and endorsed the 'Sinn Féin' separatist agenda, seizing United Irish League of America funds in its care.[189] At the end of the year the national treasurer of the league in the United States reported that 'no money whatsoever' was coming in.[190] Long before the sanguinary toll of war truly began to bite, Redmond's strategy of fusing Irish and imperial patriotism was disintegrating, and exasperation with the Irish Party was making itself felt, even if this did not immediately translate into results at parliamentary by-elections.[191] As weeks turned to months, and more and more Irish blood was spilled in the trenches and fields of Flanders, public sympathy for the war gradually deadened. Muddled principles, naive hopes, and knee-jerk patriotism all faded; the promise of Irish nationhood remained unfulfilled.

8

Auguries

On a rainy evening in November 1914, the Dublin Metropolitan Police (DMP) were deployed in large numbers on the streets of the city in anticipation of a protest. The chief superintendent of the DMP was in attendance. Inspectors issued orders that notes be taken to aid subsequent prosecutions. The RIC had 100 men in reserve; General Hill had 120 cavalry and 250 infantrymen in readiness at Beggars Bush and Portobello barracks. Magistrates were standing by to accompany troops if their use was deemed necessary.

At around 8.30 p.m., what the police termed a 'Socialist-Sinn Fein Demonstration of Protest' progressed over O'Connell Bridge to Westmoreland Street and up Grafton Street. A column of about 400 marchers, led by James Connolly, was accompanied by fifty armed men of the Irish Citizen Army. The procession halted at the north-west gate of St Stephen's Green, where a swell of spectators blocked the exit of trams. Police estimated the crowd at 700, noting that heavy rain had diminished the turnout for the meeting. The assembly was more representative of the Irish Transport and General Workers' Union than of the Irish Volunteers, except for the presence of The O'Rahilly.

Echoing the message of a banner recently unfurled across the frontage of Liberty Hall, Seán Milroy told the gathering, 'We have no King but Ireland … the British Empire, let it go to hell in its own ungodly fashion.' Then, referring to Germany, he proclaimed, 'Gloria in excelsis Deo that that empire has met at last an opponent that can give back blow for blow.'[1]

P.T. Daly professed to the crowd that he had two sons eligible for service, but 'by the living God I would put a bullet in them if I thought they would join the Army'. Ireland's parliamentary leaders, he railed, 'the wise men who came out of the East, must have forgotten the past because Home Rule is on the Statute Book'. Two shots were fired as Countess Markievicz gave a short address, concluding with the words, 'Christ died to make men holy, we will die to make men free.'[2]

James Connolly asserted that if Lancers or the DMP were turned loose on protesters in Dublin, within a week every Irish soldier in the army would know it, and none could be counted on again:

> Sooner or later the Government would be forced to believe that this is a hostile country as much as Germany is … the British government is tottering to its destruction, then instead of standing by, say for God's sake boys let us give it one great kick to help it on its road.[3]

The O'Rahilly promised that there were Irishmen ready to administer the blow: 'A good deal of the country is in the hands of men who were willing to sell it, but there is a force of Volunteers of which you will hear some more, and Europe will hear more before the War is over.'[4] A resolution pledging the assembly to fight unceasingly for the establishment of 'an Independent Republic in Ireland' closed the proceedings. As the meeting dispersed, there was more rifle fire. Crowds sang 'A Nation Once Again'; some paused outside the recruiting office on Grafton Street to cheer the Kaiser.[5]

Sir Matthew Nathan, the newly appointed undersecretary for Ireland, remained at Dublin Castle receiving news until 10.30 p.m. The following day he sent digests of the police reports to the Attorney General, Sir John Simon, asking what action should be taken.[6] In conformity with the pattern of government complacency exhibited over matters Irish, it took Simon a full three months to reply. His letter indicated that the military had the power to try the offenders, but he advised against police intervention. 'That is exactly what these people are playing for', Simon wrote. 'The speeches are reeking with sedition and treason. The country is fighting for its existence and these people are endeavouring to weaken the hands of the military authorities. The Army should act and the sooner the better.'[7]

Concerned but, like his colleague in London, evidently seeing no urgent threat from the speakers beyond fomenting public disaffection, Nathan dutifully consigned the matter to his files.

Conclusion:
An 'endless legacy of trouble'

There was, in the third Home Rule Crisis, a foretaste of the 1915 wartime coalition, which pitted, as A.J.P. Taylor observed, the Liberal and Conservative front benches in the House of Commons against their supporters at the back.[1] There were fascinating undercurrents of compromise between the British parties that revealed deep disquiet about the growth of working-class political consciousness. Liberal elites had long feared that expanding democracy through universal manhood suffrage would split the electorate along class lines, resulting in, as Lord Rosebery had foretold in 1895, the obsolescence of Liberalism in the confrontation between socialism and reaction.[2] Avoidance of this prospect appears to have been the lure that Lloyd George used to attract his Liberal colleagues to his proposed 'National Efficiency' coalition in 1910. The issue of Ireland, however, scuttled the official and unofficial cross-party negotiations of that year, and stood in the way of a Liberal/Unionist combination that still appeared to some to be both desirable and within reach.[3] It is no accident that the earliest proposers of Ulster exclusion, Lloyd George and Churchill, were also the keenest ministerial advocates of finding a political accommodation with the Unionists.

Influential members of the Cabinet, such as Crewe and Grey, felt that Liberalism was at the end of its tether in the field of social reform, and feared the political forces that further democratisation would unleash.[4] A striking aspect of Lloyd George's 1910 coalition plan was the lack of protest elicited from his Liberal colleagues against the coercive methods it prescribed. The readiness of leading Liberals to accede to an undemocratic and highly statist proposal was an indication of just how detached from ideology they had become. The ministerial impulse to collude with the Tories was in stark contrast to what many in the ranks of Liberalism saw as its future direction. New Liberals saw the Liberal Party's twentieth-century mission as one of redressing the political and economic inequities affecting the working classes.

Some of the party's middle-class leaders, however, shared Tory anxieties about the erosion of the social order (and, possibly, the extension of redistributive taxation) under an electorate based on universal suffrage. This left the Liberal Party's uneasy leadership increasingly out of step with progressive opinion-formers and swathes of Liberal supporters, a trend accelerated by the crisis brought about by the third Home Rule Bill.

The Curragh Incident was a significant moment of realisation that Irish Home Rule had become an issue of British democracy. Historians have widely (and correctly) viewed the resignation of army officers as the event that effectively neutered the option of coercing Ulster, but arguably the 'mutiny' also had lasting implications for the Liberal and Labour parties. J.A. Hobson's *Traffic in Treason* articulated the deep Liberal discontent arising from the controversy. The intrusion of the army into a political controversy, with strong suggestions of the hidden hand of royal and aristocratic influences, brought into sharp focus the issues at stake. Ministerial pusillanimity, about which Hobson wrote witheringly in the summer of 1914, incensed a strong segment of Liberal opinion that viewed the Parliament Act as the legislative weapon of democracy. The abolition of plural voting and the humiliation of the House of Lords by the enactment of Irish Home Rule under the provisions of the Parliament Act were viewed as critical to the establishment of constitutional parity for progressive political parties. The cause of Irish self-government was thus the catalyst and crucial instrument for the advance of British democracy.

In persisting with a policy of appeasement of the Unionists, Asquith, Liberalism's brilliant but laggardly leader, led his Cabinet into a position of virtual opposition to its followers. The groundswell of democratic conviction in the Liberal ranks against the contemplated surrender of the principle of the Parliament Act left ministers almost entirely unmoved, except with regard to its electoral implications. To the consternation of many of his supporters, the prime minister elected to ignore an assault on democracy that dwarfed the question of Home Rule, and sought, with the Unionist leaders, to impose a pragmatic resolution of the Ulster difficulty upon Redmond.

Liberal patience had worn thin with leaders who had repeatedly proved that, though they might hold office, they would not wield power.[5] The disaffection of an estimated three-quarters of the parliamentary party by the summer of 1914 was the source of John Redmond's leverage over Asquith and his colleagues. If it was improbable that Redmond would unseat the government, his capacity to actuate the disintegration of the Liberal Party was taken sufficiently seriously to prevent an outright capitulation to the Unionists.

This political phenomenon renders problematic Peter Clarke's argument in *Lancashire and the New Liberalism* that the Liberal Party entered the First World War in robust condition. In arriving at his diagnosis, Clarke asserted that Liberalism remained ideologically vibrant, having synthesised Liberalism and socialism into a coherent progressive ideology. The questions of popular politics, he argued, had become fundamentally economic ones, which both the New Liberal legislative programme and the Tories' dismal policy of tariff reform aimed to address.[6] The pre-war rally to the defence of outraged democracy lends credence to Clarke's assertion that New Liberalism's shortcomings were more to do with political democracy than with social democracy, though in a manner not discerned in his analysis.[7]

The data upon which Clarke's assessment was based, an analysis of by-election results in the north-west of England to May 1913, may be a less-than-reliable indicator of the Liberal Party's state of health in August 1914. The eventful final fifteen months of peace, during which the Home Rule controversy raged, may hold one of the keys to the demise of Liberalism. The evidence presented here suggests that just before the outbreak of war, the Liberal Party leadership was racked by an acute crisis of confidence. Many Liberals were disillusioned and ideologically at odds with leaders seemingly more in sympathy with their opponents than with the tens of thousands of supporters clamouring for the vindication of the party's core democratic doctrine. It seems probable that, for many in the movement, this was a moment of realisation that Asquith and his colleagues were ready to sell Liberalism's soul.

The Liberal Party – whose mission ceased if it failed to 'voice the wishes of the Democracy', its chief whip wrote in the spring of 1914 – may have reached the end of its road by that summer.[8] The embrace of authoritarianism and militarism in the first weeks of the war, epitomised by the enactment of the Defence of the Realm Act 1914 on 8 August, arguably hastened an intellectual migration already begun. Liberal MPs Arthur Ponsonby, C.P. Trevelyan and Joseph King, all critics of ministerial abandonment of principle before the war, became, with Labour's Philip Snowden and Ramsay MacDonald, leading figures of the Union of Democratic Control, an organisation protesting against the conflict's undemocratic instigation and direction.[9] The Union of Democratic Control remained a fringe movement, but its emphasis on democracy was significant, and contiguous with the pre-war agitation for the execution of the principle of the Parliament Act.

As the war's remorseless bloody course demanded ever-more illiberal measures from an ostensibly Liberal government, many progressive thinkers began to look to the Labour Party as a movement more invested in the establishment of democratic institutions. As C.P. Scott's *Manchester Guardian* observed just before the war's outbreak, once confidence in the ideals of Liberalism was lost, a 'democratic movement, never more keenly alive nor more alert to new impressions than it is at this moment, turns to new men and still newer methods'.[10] New men would be found in Britain; new methods would be tried in Ireland.

In a sense, the constitutional nationalist leaders were engaged in their own revolt of officers against the ranks by persisting in a strategy of gradualism. It is probably too much to say (as did Margaret O'Callaghan) that constitutional nationalism was dead before Parnell's fall in 1890, but the spread of a bolder mood of Irish nationalism meant that constitutionalism faced an increasingly difficult task.[11] The cultural ferment of the 1890s had seen an efflorescence of Irish cultural and literary forms and the popularisation of the Irish language. Racial conceptions of the Gael, to whom the 'alien' – that is, Protestants – must be subordinated, were embedded in the popular mind by the nationalist press and through a multiplicity of Irish-Ireland organisations. A headstrong, chauvinistic Gaelicism, hostile to Anglo-Irish culture, pointed to a nationalism inseparable from Roman Catholicism, and one that placed self-righteous cultural and religious purity above inclusivity.[12]

The reorientation of nationalism did not leave the Irish Party unaffected. The constitutional nationalist movement, once led by Isaac Butt and Charles Stewart Parnell, both Protestants, became increasingly identified with Catholicism. Dillon's backing of the Ancient Order of Hibernians, apparently to queer the pitch for O'Brienite conciliation, was a calamitously short-sighted move, with damaging implications for Irish unity. The association of mainstream nationalism with an aggressively sectarian mass movement arguably did more to alienate communities in Ireland from one another than did any other factor. It is important to note that many of these divisive cultural and political phenomena were developments within orthodox, constitutional nationalism, though the cult of the Gael strongly influenced advanced nationalist ideology, as articulated by Patrick Pearse after 1913.[13]

At the same time, the Irish Party's immersion in British radical and anti-imperialist politics, argued Philip Bull, undermined its political rationale by subordinating the Irish national demand to a broader British crusade against privilege.[14] James McConnel similarly identified a cultural duality among Irish Party MPs, borne of long exposure to life in London, which distanced them from the concerns of their constituents.[15] Dissatisfaction with the perceived apathy of the parliamentary delegation found expression in the Irish Convention's rejection of the Irish Council Bill in 1907, the initial political successes of Sinn Féin, and the endurance of William O'Brien's All-for-Ireland League. The demand of the Young Ireland Branch of the UIL for no minor measures also betokened growing impatience among moderate nationalists.

Fears for the Irish Party's political hegemony led its leaders to neglect burgeoning strands of Irish nationalism. The varying degrees of indifference or antipathy shown towards Gaelic Leaguers, the Young Ireland Branch, nationalist women, and cultural nationalism in general cost the party a credit of sympathy against which it could have usefully drawn in 1914. Bridges might even have been built with Sinn Féin, which showed signs of willingness to engage with Home Rule, but the Irish Party's reflexive response was to attempt to strangle its potential rival at birth.

The Home Rule Bill of 1912 did not quieten restive nationalist sentiment. The Irish Party leaders' welcome of legislation seemingly designed to make Ireland at once a colony and a province gave proof of the circumscribed ambitions of Redmondite nationalism. In the anxiety to ease British fears, the wishes of the nationalist majority in Ireland, whose urgent demand the Home Rule Bill was intended to satisfy, seemed almost to disappear from view. Yet even this scant measure faced a treacherous navigation through Westminster. Herbert Samuel's unstated intention to withhold fiscal autonomy in perpetuity revealed just how distant conceptions of self-government among moderate Liberals were from those of constitutional nationalists. The severe limitations on what could be obtained from sympathetic British politicians tended to vindicate advanced nationalist critiques of the impossibility of benign British rule.

Still, Redmond placed much faith in the symbolic power of the Home Rule nomenclature to mask the flaws of the 1912 bill. It seems plain that he viewed it in the same light as he had the 1907 Council Bill, as an intermediate measure capable of passage through Westminster. The nationalist leaders were confident that, once in being, an Irish parliament could revise the settlement to expand the boundaries of its legislative domain. Redmond corrected those inadequacies in the bill he could influence, and overlooked, for the moment, those that he could not. He cared only for getting a Home Rule Bill, of almost any description, on the statute book, and was content to leave its flaws to be rectified later. The irony was that Home Rule's most ardent supporters and steadfast opponents could agree that passage of even a modest measure would open the door to ever-greater autonomy.[16]

The contradictions inherent within Parnellism – accommodating imperialism and a looser form of union, and separatism, with partition of Ireland as its consequence – were confronted when Home Rule once again assumed centre stage.[17] Redmond perhaps felt that he could manage frustrated nationalist ambitions until after the measure was on the statute book, but the unexpected violence of the Ulster Protestant reaction upset all calculations. When, in due course, the Irish Party chairman was forced to concede the principle of Ulster exclusion, many nationalists interpreted this as acquiescence to the dismemberment of Ireland and the ultimate betrayal of the national ideal. Widespread revulsion at this prospect undermined confidence in Home Rule and intensified fissiparous pressures within nationalism.

As for the attitude of Redmond and his colleagues toward Ulster, the artificiality of British Unionist posturing made it difficult to discern what was a credible threat and what was political theatre. Yet there was an equal measure of unreality about the Irish Party leaders' ignorant disregard for the legitimate concerns of the Ulstermen and their obstinate insistence that majoritarian arithmetic was all that mattered. To the extent that Ulster Unionist menaces were believed at all, civil disorder was viewed, with startling complacency, as a remote and manageable risk. It is difficult to resist the conclusion that the nationalist leaders' almost wilful incomprehension of Ulster, and their apparent confidence that Unionist opposition could be steamrolled in the Irish Party's customary fashion, were a measure of the arrogance borne of thirty years' political dominance in the rest of Ireland.

British Unionists cynically churned the waters in Ulster, and the answering swell of nationalist indignation unwittingly drove Ireland towards partition. 'What the north began' reverberated from north to south and back again, exacerbating tensions. Advanced nationalists found fertile ground for the dissemination of Anglophobic rhetoric among the ranks of the Irish Volunteers. With the revival of separatism as a credible possibility, Ulster Protestant dread of Dublin rule intensified, and the demand for exclusion from Home Rule began to give way to a demand for the partition of Ireland. The Irish Party leaders foresaw the divisive effect of advanced nationalist militancy, which accounted, in part, for their unease with the Volunteer movement. From the perspective of national unity, their efforts to contain what they apprehended as the physical-force men's nihilism might have been prudent.

Redmond's insistence on plebiscites to decide the fate of Ulster counties was consistent with the democratic ideals of his radical Liberal allies, but it was also a strategy designed to isolate Ulster resistance and to hasten the day that excluded counties would opt to join their self-governing southern neighbours. His readiness to accede to county option of indefinite exclusion at the end of July 1914 indicated that the area to be excluded, not the duration of its exclusion, was the critical factor in his thinking. This huge concession – never announced owing to the outbreak of war – was consistent with Redmond's expectation that only four counties would opt for exclusion, and his calculation as to the doubtful viability of a defiant Ulster rump.

If the success of Redmond's strategy seems improbable against the Ulster Unionists' promised armed rebellion, one must guard against subscribing to a partitionist fatalism under which neither side laboured in 1914. Far from signifying an irresistible impulse to partition, Sir Edward Carson's nine-county-exclusion proposal behind the conference doors of Buckingham Palace was suggested (seemingly not disingenuously) as a formula for Irish unity. It could be argued that this was not really a peace offer at all, because it was one that was patently impossible for the nationalists to accept, and its contemplation might have brought down Asquith's government. However, as has been asserted in these pages, even Tory hardliners such as Milner had come to realise that driving the Liberals from office would leave the Unionist Party in the very undesirable position of having to pacify nationalist Ireland. Bonar Law, having badgered the king for over a year to dissolve Parliament, notably lost his stomach for a general election in July 1914, and acknowledged that Home Rule was inevitable. The existence of huge numbers of Irish Volunteers was, it seems, the factor that persuaded the Unionist leaders that a compromise formula must be found. The impact of the nationalist paramilitary force in 1914 was, perhaps, not as wholly negative for Redmondism as it is so often perceived to have been.

Whether the ultimate extent of Unionist concession had been reached in the summer of 1914 can never be known, but the anachronistic assumption that the exclusion of Ulster counties would inevitably become permanent cannot be supported by what is known of Carson's views. The Ulster Unionist leader's ultimately unitarian vision was affirmed early in 1915 when he privately expressed his openness to 'government of Ulster as a Home Rule province' provided the predominance of its Protestant population was reflected in its make-up. He welcomed the prospect of Catholic participation in the transitional government of the northern counties, and foretold that the reopening of the exclusion question, after six years, 'might see either a fusion between the two Home Rule Governments of Ireland, or in the case of a financial break down of the Home Rule system a reversion to the union'.[18]

These comments reveal the inclusive character of Carson's outlook and the essentially pragmatic nature of his objection to Home Rule by 1915.

What might have happened if war had not stopped the clock on Home Rule and Redmond had announced his support for a policy of indefinite exclusion by county plebiscites? Declaration of an Ulster provisional government was possible, as was a revolt against Redmond's or Carson's leadership; or there might have been spontaneous outbreaks of violence in the north. The siren call of old hatreds might well have overcome the reason of the two denominational populations in the province.[19] Yet Carson's reconciliation to the inevitability of Home Rule, together with the dislocation of trade already affecting Ulster, and Bonar Law's fears that an Orange revolt would torpedo the Tories' electoral prospects, all point to a wavering of resolve at the head of the Unionist leadership. (Viewed from this perspective, the fact that it was Bonar Law and Carson who proffered the flag of truce to Asquith is surely not insignificant.) In the circumstances of the high summer of 1914, one may fairly conclude that a grudging acceptance of indefinite exclusion by county polls was not the least likely of all possible outcomes.

This interpretation, sceptics may argue, relies too much on the personal antipathy of Dublin-born Carson to the idea of Irish partition, and fails to take into account the seriousness of intent of the Ulster Volunteer Force in the summer of 1914. The credulity with which historians have viewed Unionist determination has, doubtless, been influenced by a century of solemn commemorations of the UVF together with tales – often embellished – of Unionists' dour determination. In his study of the mythology fabricated for Ulster Unionism in 1912–14, Alvin Jackson asserted that the elaborately constructed edifice of Unionist inflexibility in fact concealed doubts and divisions between political leaders and businessmen providing finance.[20] The UVF, Jackson contended, did not, in 1914, warrant the reputation for military potency that it later acquired in Unionist folklore. The Larne gunrunning, he asserted, had equipped the force with an inadequate number of weapons of incompatible types, leaving the UVF capable of mounting only guerrilla warfare. Carson, Jackson argued, recognised that an Ulster rising would be suicidal folly, even if some of his followers had not come to that realisation.[21]

Timothy Bowman, author of a comprehensive study of the Ulster Volunteers, opined that the UVF certainly had the capability to overawe or overwhelm the RIC or Irish Volunteers in the province.[22] There seems little doubt that the UVF had the capacity to disrupt British authority in north-east Ulster, but who was to issue the order to seize strategic positions? The ultimate decision-making power over the force's deployment, in Bowman's judgement, lay with Carson.[23] Yet it seems that the man who had the ultimate authority to mobilise the UVF was disinclined to take that responsibility.

There is reason to believe that James Craig, unlike Carson, felt that north-east Ulster should go her own way, but his readiness to use force to achieve this end is unclear.[24] The nominal commander of the UVF, General Sir George Richardson, whose hesitancy irritated some of his officers, was unlikely to take the lead.[25] Chief among the militants was Major Frederick Crawford, the architect of the Larne gunrunning enterprise, who assiduously sought to acquire automatic weapons (and even field guns) for the UVF right up to the outbreak of war.[26] Crawford's zeal arose from his fierce anti-Catholicism, but also, at least in part, out of a conviction that the Protestants of Ulster were the king's most loyal subjects, and he appears to have felt deep respect for Carson's leadership.[27]

Crawford reflected, shortly after the events of summer 1914, that, given a few more weeks, the crisis 'would have been settled by leaving Ulster out and giving Tyrone … in with Ulster' – a result, significantly, that he believed could have been achieved by the *threat* of violence, as opposed to actual insurrection.[28] Had Carson backed an offer of indefinite exclusion for those Ulster counties voting themselves out of Home Rule, would the prospect of ceding Tyrone have been sufficient cause for hawks such as Crawford to revolt against the leadership that had sustained the UVF through a proud, and broadly successful, campaign? Perhaps so; and Carson was certainly aware of that danger. Yet Carson's biographer, Alvin Jackson, emphasised his barrister's instinct to risk all, even to the point of schism; it is not altogether implausible that the Ulster Unionist leader was prepared to gamble on retaining the loyalty of his followers.[29]

The unquestioning compliance of local UVF commanders, on whom, Bowman argued, decision-making would have rapidly devolved, was far from assured.[30] Even if UVF units complied with an order to stand down, militant factions could still have resorted to civil disobedience or violence over the months-long period of uncertainty that county plebiscites would have entailed. The forced expulsion of Catholics from Fermanagh or Tyrone, or a sectarian lockout from workplaces, might have precipitated a violent response, allowing Unionists to frame nationalists as the aggressors. With tempers running high, and with rifles in abundance (at least in Unionist hands), there was great potential for violence in Ulster. All responsible leaders, however, had an interest in curtailing riot and bloodshed. The point of this counterfactual speculation is not to attempt to lay odds on what might have happened but to underline that an Ulster revolt in the summer of 1914 was by no means certain, and to emphasise that, had the war not broken out when it did, exclusion of four or more Ulster counties for a transitional period was, at the least, a credible possibility.

If serious violence was averted, there was a possibility that demands for perpetual exclusion might predominate in the four or more heavily Protestant counties that voted to exclude themselves from Home Rule. The siege men-tality that grew up in Northern Ireland in the 1920s might have taken hold against the Dublin government in 1915/16. Yet conditions would not have been the same as those that saw James Craig establish a state of virtual Protestant despotism in Northern Ireland after partition. Both parts of Ireland would still have been under the Crown and represented at Westminster; the failure of the anticipated horrors of self-government to materialise might have sapped British support for the Ulstermen; and if Home Rule obviated the need for a nationalist 'blood sacrifice' south of the border, the spectre of separation might not have driven the north-eastern counties to seek their permanent severance from the rest of Ireland.

Yet unitary Home Rule might have faced another threat. Had no European conflict interrupted access to rifles, and with funds supplied from the United States, the IRB men of the Irish Volunteers' provisional committee might have attempted to mount a guerrilla campaign against a 'collaborationist' Redmondite regime-in-waiting. The dissentient Volunteers' lack of organi-sation and training, however, would probably have limited such disruptive activities to a small scale. With an operative Irish government for the great majority of the country in immediate prospect, the popular appeal of separa-tism must be considered doubtful. This was the view of Eoin MacNeill, who wrote, a decade earlier, that although he considered himself a separatist, had a meaningful measure of autonomy been granted to Ireland, he, like the vast majority of nationalists, probably would have accepted it.[31]

Of course, the First World War *did* intervene, and the opportunity for a transitional arrangement for Ulster was lost; but there is cause to believe that British adoption of Redmond and Gill's wartime strategy might have slowed the advance of separatism. Kevin O'Shiel recorded his belief, years after the events, that had the War Office established a really distinctive Irish army corps, led by Irishmen and with its own uniform and colours, an overwhelming impression would have been made. O'Shiel and all his friends critical of the Irish Party, he claimed, would have joined up.[32] Within months, however, it was apparent that the hostility of the generals had crippled Redmond's initiative. The failure of the plan to equip and train the nationalist militia was regretted by the unlikely figure of Edward Carson. Early in 1915 Carson told a Liberal interlocutor that he regarded it as

> … a great misfortune that the Volunteers had not been supplied with rifles after Redmond's great speech … had the Southern Volunteers been able to get guns in the same way [as the UVF] it would have made them respond much more readily to Redmond's appeal that they should volunteer for the war.[33]

The War Office's attitude was all the more deplorable, the Ulster Unionist leader asserted, 'now that Home Rule is assured in one form or another'.[34] While implementation of Redmond and Gill's long-war plan of an Irish army corps and martial 'green flaggery' might have bolstered the Irish Party's support and impeded the separatists, it probably would not have arrested grinding war weariness, forestalled the looming conscription controversy, nor altered the Irish Party's path to eventual displacement.

As Matthew Kelly pointed out, Redmond's calamitous miscalculation in backing Irish recruitment gave advanced nationalism an opposing force to push against, and sharpened still further the contrast between Parnell's boundless march of a nation and Redmond's tethered and subordinate brand of nationalism. The imperial dimension of Redmondism, especially when its dreadful implications became inescapable in the context of the war, was the last straw for advanced nationalists, enabling them to repudiate the constitutional project once and for all.[35] Redmond did not anticipate how discordant, in wartime, his imperial notes could be made to sound to Irish ears.

A *Times* memorial published upon Redmond's death in 1918 (over Augustine Birrell's initials) said of him that 'English people as their wont is, gushed over him as an English patriot and flouted him as an Irish statesman … He took the curve too sharply and did not carry the train with him.'[36] Yet it seems, rather, that the outbreak of war changed the points before the Redmondite locomotive reached the bend. The unexpected cataclysm, usually seen as averting the eruption of civil war in Ireland, may have served to dash a life's work on the cusp of its culmination. The personal tragedy of the final years of John Redmond's life is of little consequence in the context of a conflict that claimed millions of lives, but the snuffing out of the possibility of a peaceful settlement of the Home Rule Crisis in 1914 deepens a sense of the First World War as a turning point in Irish history.[37]

For many Irish nationalists, Redmond's decision to back recruitment to the British army in the First World War remains his unpardonable sin. The decision unquestionably added to the toll of the 30,000 Irish lives lost in the war, but, as J.J. Lee observed, no constitutional leader hoping to secure a united Ireland in the circumstances of the summer of 1914 could have acted differently.[38] With less justice, Redmond's memory is denigrated for his consent to the exclusion of Ulster. Yet while the Irish Party chairman is condemned for contemplating the exclusion of four or more Ulster counties by a democratic process, his political successors largely escape judgement for the arbitrary, actual partition of Ireland. Notions of preordination usefully shield their reputations from questions of culpability. Popular memory might elide over this inconsistency, but it was a point that did not go unremarked upon by some contemporaries. In 1921 Redmond's old enemy T.M. Healy castigated the Sinn Féin leaders for entering talks with the British government, with Ulster's exclusion a fait accompli:

> In 1914 Mr Redmond and Mr Dillon at the Buckingham Palace conference with Messrs. Carson and Craig, on the eve of the war, refused to purchase Home Rule by any such surrender, yet 7 years later Sinn Feiners are expected to crawl down to a tamer position than that of the dethroned parliamentarians and go forth to history as signatories to a pact in Downing Street which Mr Redmond refused to make in a Royal Palace.[39]

Historical perceptions of the Irish Free State leaders are less clouded by the taint of failure than the lens through which John Redmond is viewed. Paul Bew asserted that, despite the overthrow of all that Redmond worked for, his achievements grow in stature when considered in the proper context of the events in the decades following his death: Redmond came closer than any other political figure of the twentieth century to becoming leader of all of Ireland.[40]

Yet even this may be an understatement. If this volume achieves its aim, it will stimulate an appreciation of Redmond's decisive role in securing a historic stride for British democracy, the forcefulness with which he stood up to ostensible friends and foes of Irish nationalism, and the nearness to which his project of an autonomous, united Ireland may have come to fruition.

It is an inevitable task for the Irish historian to attempt to locate his or her work in the debate over revisionism in Irish history. Briefly, revisionist historians challenge the received canon of nationalist history, a body of work sometimes crafted, wittingly or unwittingly, with the aim of constructing a legitimising past for the Irish Republic. A lengthening perspective should make possible both a dispassionate reappraisal of the *ancien régime* and a critical approach to the new dispensation that followed it. However, the revisionism debate in Ireland, and even more so among the Irish diaspora, retains a strong emotional charge from the burden of Irish history, a history that, while by no means uniquely tragic, was characterised by centuries of oppression, brutality and human misery under British rule.[41]

In the context of Home Rule, Irish historical revisionism questions, as Roy Foster (famously or notoriously) did, whether the degree of autonomy achieved by the Irish Free State in the early decades of the twentieth century could have been attained without the need for the bloody struggles of 1919–23.[42] In suggesting that the Redmondite strategy of gradualism could conceivably have neutralised Unionist resistance and culminated in unitary self-rule, this book will undoubtedly be placed, by those sensitive to the distinction, in the revisionist corner. Indeed, for its admission of the possibility of an Ulster capitulation, and its reflection upon the role of nationalism, orthodox and advanced, in adding impulse to the partition of Ireland, the extent of its revisionism may be obnoxious to nationalists and Unionists alike. Yet it is hoped that the foregoing analysis in no way downplays the perfidy of Asquith and his colleagues, nor the root cause of the acute crisis in 1914: British Conservatives' cynical exploitation of Ulster as an electoral card in the game of domestic politics. But for the words and acts of Bonar Law, F.E. Smith and virtually the entire Tory leadership, old hatreds would not have been so bitterly revived nor their force have been so amplified. But for the financial, and probably logistical, support of British Unionists, the UVF was unlikely to have acquired arms in the numbers that it did. The Tories' wildly disproportionate resistance to Home Rule prompted the emergence of the Irish Volunteers, further polarising estranged communities in Ireland, and adding impetus to the case for partition. Popular memory of the Tory 'lunacy' of the Edwardian era may have faded, but Ireland lives still with what C.P. Scott called its 'endless legacy of trouble'.[43]

No history is free of bias, any more than the historian who writes it can be. In the context of the counterterrorism culture of the early twenty-first century, and a revulsion, however hypocritical, towards political violence in the West, a historical analysis stressing the possibilities of peace may reflect the anxieties of its time. Hopes that the reduction of tensions in Northern Ireland represents a permanent subsidence of 'the Troubles' may also reinforce a pacific interpretation. With the recent centenary of the Easter Rising of 1916, and the desire of many professional historians to avoid the politicisation of history or the perpetuation of a nationalist martyrology, this book may be seen to exhibit an excess of zeal to disavow a nationalist usable past. Its analysis, too, may be influenced by the 'otherness' of its author, being neither Irish nor British, nor possessing, unlike my forebears, a particularly strong sense of identity as an Irish-American. It may be felt that an unhealthy degree of emotional detachment arises from a lack of 'skin in the game'.

There may be detected in these pages a wistfulness for the era when democracy was advancing and social protections were being introduced. Writing at a time when a wholesale dismantling of the social contract is underway, questions of democracy, oligarchy and privilege remain pertinent, if subdued, owing to the depoliticising effect of pervasive consumer culture and the debasement of journalistic enquiry and public discourse. The decline of ideology and political identity, coupled with rising economic insecurity and inequality, is prompting many in the West, at the time of writing, to reject a political process they feel is bankrupt and has abandoned them.

The historical arc of the late twentieth and early twenty-first centuries may one day come to be seen as a sort of plutocratic counteroffensive against social democracy. Yet while some developments (not least, technological ones) point towards a further curtailment of liberties, encouragement may be drawn from the example of the events of the first decades of the 1900s. Fighting against challenges no less severe than those our contemporaries and succeeding generations may face, popular political agitation established social democracy, and a consensus on an equitable social contract, as the dominant political philosophy in the Western world. The forces behind that historical development may have been suppressed, but they have not gone away. Looking back to earlier struggles for workers' rights, women's rights and civil rights for black people may inspire a new generation to confront our latter-day 'caricature of democracy', and remind them that securing fairer and fuller democracy will always remain unfinished business.

Notes

Introduction: The Liberals and Ireland reconsidered

1 The Orange Order was established in 1795 to defend Protestant civil and religious liberties. Its name is derived from the Protestant king, William of Orange, who deposed the Catholic James II of England in the Glorious Revolution, and defeated his army at the Battle of the Boyne in 1690.

2 Alvin Jackson, 'Unionist Myths, 1914–1985', *Past & Present*, no. 136 (August 1992), pp. 164–85.

3 The view is shared by many academic historians. A 2016 panel of distinguished Irish historians assented to a questioner's assertion that the failed Protestant-led rebellion of 1798 was probably the last opportunity for securing an non-partitioned Ireland. Rebellion and Reaction: Perspectives on 1916 conference, Queen Mary University of London, 27 May 2016.

4 For example, Alvin Jackson, *Judging Redmond and Carson: Comparative Irish lives* (Dublin: Prism, 2018), pp. 115, 117–18, 125.

5 Ibid. p. 136.

6 Ronan Fanning, *Fatal Path: British government and Irish revolution, 1910–1922* (London: Faber & Faber, 2013), pp. 54, 74, 91, 124, 134.

7 David Brooks, *The Age of Upheaval: Edwardian politics, 1899–1914* (Manchester: Manchester University Press, 1995), pp. 158–9. Syndicalism is a political philosophy that aims to topple capitalism by means of general strikes and sabotage.

8 The term 'middle class' herein is used in its British historical sense – that is, to describe a propertied stratum of society comprised largely of professionals, industrialists and investors. This stands in distinction from the term's American sense, which, more or less, describes the skilled working class.

9 P.F. Clarke, *Lancashire and the New Liberalism* (Cambridge: Cambridge University Press, 1971), p. 6.

10 Trevor Wilson, *The Downfall of the Liberal Party, 1914–1935* (London: Faber & Faber, 1966), p. 18.

11 J.A. Thompson, 'Historians and the Decline of the Liberal Party', *Albion: A Quarterly Journal Concerned with British Studies*, vol. 22, no. 1 (spring 1990), pp. 66, 70, 81.

12 Alvin Jackson, *Home Rule: An Irish history, 1800–2000* (London: Weidenfeld & Nicolson, 2004), pp. 138–9, 154–5.

13 Maurice Bonham Carter to Roy Jenkins, n.d. (Bodl., MS Bonham Carter 737).

14 Clarke, *Lancashire and the New Liberalism*; Wilson, *Downfall of the Liberal Party*; Michael Bentley, *The Climax of Liberal Politics: British Liberalism in theory and practice, 1868–1918* (London: Edward Arnold, 1987).

15 Eugenio F. Biagini, *British Democracy and Irish Nationalism, 1876–1906* (Cambridge: Cambridge University Press, 2007), pp. 3–7, 317–31, 353–61.

16 G.K. Peatling, *British Opinion and Irish Self-government, 1865–1925: From Unionism to Liberal Commonwealth* (Dublin: Irish Academic Press, 2001), p. 79.

17 Richard Bourke, *Peace in Ireland: The war of ideas* (London: Pimlico, 2003), pp. 269–70; Paul Bew, *Ideology and the Irish Question: Ulster Unionism and Irish nationalism, 1912–1916* (Oxford: Clarendon Press, 1994), p. 53.

18 Patricia Jalland, *The Liberals and Ireland: The Ulster question in British politics to 1914* (Brighton: Harvester Press, 1980), p. 176. Alvin Jackson's 2018 work not only affirmed the thesis of a purposely dilatory policy, but also asserted that Redmond appeared to support it. Jackson, *Judging Redmond and Carson*, p. 119.

19 Jalland, *Liberals and Ireland*, p. 15.

20 Nicholas Mansergh, *The Irish Question, 1840–1921* (London: Allen & Unwin, 1965), p. 176.

21 The letters of Prime Minister H.H. Asquith to Venetia Stanley might have been counted among these had they not been extensively quoted in several recent studies. Venetia Stanley (1887–1948) was the object of Asquith's ardent obsession for several years. The prime minister wrote to her daily, or sometimes several times a day, mostly on political matters, from 1912 until her marriage to Edwin Montagu in 1915. Asquith's letters to Stanley constitute a unique historical record of Cabinet discussions, and provide a revealing account of the latter stages of the crisis.

22 Thomas Patrick Gill (1858–1931) organised agrarian agitation in the 1880s and served as nationalist MP for Louth from 1885 to 1892. Retiring from politics, Gill began a fruitful partnership with the Anglo-Irish visionary Sir Horace Plunkett. Seeking to expand the ethos of agricultural cooperation embodied in Plunkett's Irish Agricultural Organisation Society, the two men successfully lobbied for state support for agricultural development. Gill was appointed secretary of the Department of Agriculture and Technical Instruction in 1900. Gill's opaque loyalties rendered him a figure of suspicion for many: Unionist opposition blocked his nomination to the Irish Convention of 1917. Marie-Louise Legg, 'Gill, Thomas Patrick (1858–1931)', *Oxford Dictionary of National Biography* (Oxford: Oxford University Press, 2004).

23 A speculative element must be acknowledged about the evidence from Gill's papers. Scant correspondence from Gill survives in Redmond's manuscripts, though the Irish Party leader is known to have destroyed letters. Since receipt of Gill's letters cannot be verified, there is no certainty that their content, quoted here, represents a final version, nor even that they were sent to Redmond at all. What correspondence that survives between the two men, however, is consistent with an interpretation of a close advisory relationship, and the content of Gill's letters is treated here as indicative, in general terms, of a shared philosophy and strategy.

24 Francis Hopwood, first Lord Southborough (1860–1947), rose through the ranks first at the Board of Trade, then the Colonial Office, becoming permanent undersecretary for the colonies in 1907. It was in this capacity that he accompanied the Prince of Wales (the future George V) on a visit to Canada in 1908. He became Additional Civil Lord of the Admiralty in 1912. He served as secretary to the (ultimately unsuccessful) Irish Convention in 1917, and was created Baron Southborough in the same year. Upon his retirement from the civil service in 1926, Hopwood assumed the chairmanship of armaments firm Armstrong, Whitworth & Co., and also served on the committee of the National Physical Laboratory. H.M. Palmer, 'Hopwood, Francis John Stephens, first Baron Southborough (1860–1947)', rev. Mark Pottle, *Oxford Dictionary of National Biography* (Oxford: Oxford University Press, 2004).

Chapter 1: The Case for Irish Self-government, 1909–12

1   The physical unsuitability of recruits for the South African War seemed incontrovertible proof of British national decline. 'National Efficiency' became the slogan for policy proposals to arrest this perceived degeneracy, involving interventionist social reforms, economic planning and varying degrees of compulsion. See G.R. Searle, *The Quest for National Efficiency: A study in British politics and British political thought, 1899–1914* (Oxford: Blackwell, 1971).

2   The original political philosophy of radicalism that emerged in Britain in the eighteenth century argued for fundamental change in existing institutions by means of widening enfranchisement, abolishing aristocratic privilege, and securing press freedoms. Some of its proponents also espoused redistribution of wealth and republicanism.

3   L.T. Hobhouse, *Democracy and Reaction*, ed. P.F. Clarke (New York: Barnes & Noble Books, 1972), p. 219.

4   Plural voting enabled property owners to vote multiple times, both where they resided and in each constituency in which their properties or businesses were situated. Graduates of universities could also vote in university constituencies. Plural voting benefited the Unionist Party electorally, and its abolition was anticipated by Liberals as another stride for democracy and erosion of privilege.

5   Clarke, *Lancashire and the New Liberalism*, pp. 154–5; Stephen Koss, *The Rise and Fall of the Political Press in Britain*, vol. ii (London: Hamish Hamilton, 1984), pp. 540, 612.

6   Neal Blewett, *The Peers, the Parties and the People: The general elections of 1910* (London: Macmillan, 1972), p. 311.

7   H.A. Taylor, *Robert Donald: Being the authorised biography of Robert Donald, G.B.E., Ll.B., journalist, editor and friend of statesmen, etc.* (London: Stanley Paul & Co., 1934), p. 41.

8   Clarke, *Lancashire and the New Liberalism*, p. 156.

9   Koss, *Rise and Fall of the Political Press*, vol. ii, pp. 577, 648–9.

10 Beazley was the father of Piaras Béaslaí (né Pierce Beazley), who was to fight in the 1916 Easter Rising and would later serve as a Sinn Féin TD in Dáil Éireann.

11 Ibid. pp. 612, 673.

12 Taylor, *Robert Donald*, p. 77.

13 Koss, *Rise and Fall of the Political Press*, vol. ii, pp. 673–4.

14 Alexander Murray to John Redmond, 8 September 1911 (NLI, Redmond Papers, MS 15253). In striking testimony to the high level of public engagement with electoral politics, the Liberal Publications Department distributed a claimed forty-one million pieces of electioneering material during the January 1910 election campaign: copies of over a hundred different leaflets and booklets to local Liberal associations, 600,000 posters, a million *Liberal Song Sheets*, and 900,000 copies of the election numbers of the *Liberal Monthly Magazine* to the general public. Liberal Publications Department, *Proceedings in Connection with the Thirty-second Annual Meeting of the National Liberal Federation, London, November 1910* (London: Liberal Publications Department, 1910), p. 17.

15 *Proceedings in Connection with the Thirty-fifth Annual Meeting of the National Liberal Federation* (London: Liberal Publications Department, 1913), p. 16.

16 *Southern Star*, 17 October 1914.

17 Edward Harvey to Francis Sheehy-Skeffington, 29 January, 14 February 1912 (NLI, Francis Sheehy-Skeffington Papers, MS 33611 (3)).

18 Anon., *The Home Rule Library (No. 1)* (London: Home Rule Council, 1912), pp. 6–9; Anon., *Home Rule ?s Answered* (London: Home Rule Council, 1912), p. 61.

19 Anon., *Home Rule ?s Answered*, p. 64; *East Hants Liberal Monthly Magazine*, October 1911, p. 6.

20 Anon., *Home Rule ?s Answered*, p. 60.

21 Ibid. pp. 58, 62.

22 *Daily News and Leader*, 12 April 1912.

23 Ibid. May 1912.

24 Ibid.

25 T.M. Kettle, *The Open Secret of Ireland*, ed. Senia Pašeta (Dublin: University College Dublin Press, 2007), p. 45.

26 *Daily News and Leader*, 15 April 1912.

27 Kettle, *Open Secret*, p. 103.

28 Erskine Childers, *The Framework of Home Rule* (London: Edward Arnold, 1911), p. 144.

29 *East Hants Liberal Monthly Magazine*, June 1912, p. 6.

30 William Palmer, *Under Home Rule: A novel* (London: Baines & Scarsbrook, 1912).

31 Childers, *Framework*, p. 147.

32 *Daily News and Leader*, 9 February 1912.

33 Anon., *What the Home Rule Bill Will Do* (London: Home Rule Council, 1912), p. 29.

34 Ibid. pp. 31–3.

35 Ibid. p. 31. This figure was an extrapolation of the 1898 Royal Commission's finding that Ireland was over-taxed by nearly £3 million annually. *Hansard*, 4 July 1898.

36 Anon., *What the Home Rule Bill Will Do*, p. 31.

37 T.M. Kettle, *Home Rule Finance: An experiment in justice* (Dublin: Maunsel & Co., 1911), p. 60.

38 Ibid. pp. 63–5.

39 Ibid. p. 43.

40 Ibid.

41 T.M. Kettle, 'The Financial Aspect of Home Rule', *English Review*, January 1912, p. 344.

42 Kettle, *Home Rule Finance*, p. 43.

43 Kettle, 'Financial Aspect', p. 343.

44 Jeremiah MacVeagh, *Home Rule in a Nutshell* (London: Home Rule Council, 1911), p. 10; Kettle, *Open Secret*, p. 103.

45 *Daily News and Leader*, 22 April 1912.

46 Anon., *Home Rule ?s Answered*, pp. 10–11. Costs of administration in Ireland in 1911 were £2 4s per head of population, versus 23s 3d in Scotland.

47 Kettle, *Home Rule Finance*, p. 51.

48 Anon., *Home Rule ?s Answered*, p. 9.

49 *Catholic Times*, 29 March 1912.

50 Anon., *Home Rule ?s Answered*, pp. 17–19.

51 *East Hants Liberal Monthly Magazine*, November 1911, p. 8.

52 C.R. Buxton (ed.), *The ABC Home Rule Handbook* (London: Home Rule Council, 1912), p. 101.

53 Fred W. Evans, *A Workman's Views of the Irish Question* (London: National Press Agency, 1887).

54   *Catholic Times*, 15 March 1912.
55   Ibid. 5 July 1912.
56   Ibid. 2 August 1912.
57   *Daily Citizen*, 18 January 1913.
58   Ibid. 7 August 1913.
59   *Lepracaun Cartoon Monthly*, December 1910, p. 93.
60   *Reynolds's Newspaper*, 26 February 1913.
61   Ibid. The established status of the (Anglican) Church of Wales, which linked it to the state, was anomalous in a principality whose population was overwhelmingly Nonconformist. Disestablishment of the Welsh Church was viewed as an important symbol of religious liberty.
62   *Daily News and Leader*, 19 June 1912.
63   *Catholic Times*, 22 November 1912.
64   *Clarion*, 14 June 1907.
65   Harold Begbie, *The Lady Next Door* (London: Hodder & Stoughton, 1912), p. 320.
66   Ibid. p. 24.
67   *Catholic Times*, 2 August 1912.
68   *Nation*, 12 October 1912.
69   Begbie, *Lady Next Door*, p. 17.
70   *Clarion*, 14 June 1907.
71   'West British' was a derogatory term for Irish men or women thought to be in the thrall to English culture, or suspected of aping its ways.
72   Begbie, *Lady Next Door*, pp. 319–22.
73   *Catholic Times*, 3 January 1913. Preservation of a decentralised, agrarian and, above all, Catholic Ireland was at the heart of Fianna Fáil's social and counterproductive economic policies in the 1930s Irish Free State. R.F. Foster, *Modern Ireland, 1600–1972* (London: Allen Lane, 1988), p. 547.
74   *Nation*, 12 October 1912.
75   Sydney Brooks, 'Aspects of the Religious Question in Ireland', *Fortnightly Review*, February 1912, p. 392.
76   *Freeman's Journal*, 9 September 1912.
77   Begbie, *Lady Next Door*, p. 323.
78   Ibid. p. 325.
79   Ibid. pp. 53–5, 58–9.
80   *Baptist Times*, 14 September 1906; *Daily News and Leader*, 13 April 1912.
81   Basil Williams (ed.), *Home Rule Problems* (London: P.S. King, 1911), p. 106; *Nation*, 12 October 1912.
82   Peel's increase of a British grant to the seminary at Maynooth, County Kildare provoked a storm of anti-Catholic feeling in England.
83   Shaw's comment appeared in the preface to *John Bull's Other Island* (1904), and that of Lord Randolph Churchill in a private letter in 1885. Anon., *Home Rule ?s Answered*, p. 59.
84   Brooks, 'Aspects of the Religious Question', p. 390.
85   Ibid. p. 391.
86   Joseph Hocking, *Is Home Rule Rome Rule?* (London: Ward, Lock & Co., 1912), pp. 128, 174, 189.
87   Brooks, 'Aspects of the Religious Question', p. 392.
88   *Baptist Times*, 12 July 1912.

89 J.B. Armour, 'The Presbyterian View', in J.H. Morgan (ed.), *The New Irish Constitution* (London: Hodder & Stoughton, 1912), p. 468.
90 *Catholic Times*, 2 August 1912.
91 *Methodist Times*, 5 January 1911; *Baptist Times*, 19 April 1912.
92 W. Crawford, 'A Nonconformist View', in Morgan (ed.), *New Irish Constitution*, p. 90.
93 Hocking, *Rome Rule?*, p. 191.
94 Ironically, this also echoed 1860s Fenian discourse. Hocking, *Rome Rule?*, p. 189.
95 *Daily News and Leader*, 13 April 1912.
96 Anon., *Home Rule ?s Answered*, pp. 42–5.
97 Kettle, *Open Secret*, p. 74.
98 Ibid. p. 77.
99 Ibid. pp. 75–6.
100 *Nation*, 20 January 1912.
101 Hocking, *Rome Rule?*, pp. 184–8.
102 *Methodist Times*, 29 August 1912.
103 *Methodist Times,* 12 June 1913; *East Hants Liberal Magazine*, February 1912, p. 5.
104 *Daily Citizen*, 21 June 1913, p. 3.
105 *English Review*, May 1914, p. 275.
106 *Daily Citizen*, 17 December 1913, p. 8.
107 *Daily News and Leader*, 17 April 1912.
108 *Nation*, 6 January 1912.
109 *Baptist Times*, 4 October 1912.
110 *Methodist Times*, 18 April 1912.
111 Kettle, *Open Secret*, pp. 78–9.

Chapter 2: The Re-emergence of Home Rule

1 Clarke, *Lancashire and the New Liberalism*, pp. 220–32. Members of Parliament were unsalaried until 1911.
2 Lloyd George reportedly made this observation of Gladstone. Lucy Masterman, *C.F.G. Masterman: A biography* (London: Nicholson & Watson, 1939), p. 181.
3 T.P. O'Connor to John Dillon, 24 September 1909 (TCD, Dillon Papers, MS 6740).
4 *Daily Citizen*, 23 November 1912.
5 'Interview with Mr John E. Redmond' notes, 5 May 1907 (NLI, Francis Sheehy-Skeffington Papers, MS 40474 (5)).
6 Jackson, *Judging Redmond and Carson*, pp. 109–10. See pages 109 and 208 of this volume for accounts of Redmond's forceful exchanges with Lloyd George.
7 James McConnel, 'John Redmond and Irish Catholic Loyalism', *English Historical Review*, vol. cxxv, no. 512 (2010), pp. 84–7, 110–11; Jackson, *Judging Redmond and Carson*, pp. 136–8. Redmond called the war 'unjust and abominable' in the House of Commons, but he was less outspoken than some of his colleagues, including his brother, Willie Redmond MP. As usual, the Irish Party chairman's tongue was looser in front of North American audiences. *Hansard*, 12 February 1900.
8 J.O. Baylen, '"What Mr Redmond Thought": An unpublished interview with John Redmond, December 1906', *Irish Historical Studies*, vol. 19, no. 74 (September 1974), p. 173.

9   When confronted with the political consequences of an extended franchise in the altered circumstances of 1918, however, many Irish Party members showed themselves to be less enthusiastic democrats. James McConnel, 'The Franchise Factor in the Defeat of the Irish Parliamentary Party, 1885–1918', *Historical Journal*, vol. 47, no. 2 (June 2004), pp. 374–5.

10   The rejection of the 1906 Education Bill by the House of Lords in a landslide election year was but one exercise of 'Mr Balfour's poodle', as Lloyd George mockingly referred to the Upper Chamber.

11   Buxton (ed.), *ABC Home Rule Handbook*, p. 31.

12   A bronze bust of John Redmond in the House of Commons, arguably a finer tribute to Redmond's memory than any in Ireland, commemorated the nationalist leader's contribution to British democracy and his place in the affections of radical MPs. The memorial, commissioned by Malcolm Stewart – son of the ninety-three-year-old ex-radical MP Sir Halley Stewart – was sculpted by Francis Doyle-Jones and unveiled in 1931. *Fermanagh Herald*, 1 August 1931.

13   F.S.L. Lyons, *John Dillon: A biography* (London: Routledge & Kegan Paul, 1968), pp. 239–40.

14   *Times*, 10 August 1927.

15   Philip Bull, *Land, Politics and Nationalism: A study of the Irish land question* (Dublin: Gill & Macmillan, 1996), p. 166; Jackson, *Home Rule*, p. 107.

16   Denis Gwynn, *The Life of John Redmond* (London: George G. Harrap, 1932), p. 106. Lord Dunraven's 1904 devolution initiative aroused great controversy. Bitter condemnation and charges of perfidy by Ulster Unionists cost Irish Chief Secretary George Wyndham his job.

17   T.P. O'Connor to John Dillon, 3 March, 6 April 1904 (TCD, Dillon Papers, MS 6740). To his credit, Redmond also offered a parliamentary nomination to Jacob Eylan, a prominent member of Dublin's Jewish community, at a time when anti-Semitism was widespread in Ireland. Dermot Meleady, *John Redmond: The national leader* (Dublin: Merrion Press, 2014), p. 78.

18   Bull, *Land, Politics and Nationalism*, p. 171; Dillon reportedly engineered the 1906 expulsion of two Irish Party MPs, D.D. Sheehan and John O'Donnell, the latter a former general secretary of the UIL. Through T.P. O'Connor, Dillon also exerted influence over the United Irish League of Great Britain against what he regarded as 'servile' conciliation. Joseph V. O'Brien, *William O'Brien and the Course of Irish Politics, 1881–1918* (Berkeley, CA: University of California Press, 1976), p. 172; Patrick Maume, *The Long Gestation: Irish nationalist life, 1891–1918* (Dublin: Gill & Macmillan, 1999), p. 69.

19   Bull, *Land, Politics and Nationalism*, p. 172.

20   Paul Bew, *John Redmond* (Dundalk: Dundalgan Press, 1996), p. 48. This phenomenon can be overstated, however. Conor Mulvagh's construct of a quadripartite leadership circle of Redmond, Dillon, O'Connor and Devlin yokes evidence to a thesis, which, for the 1909–14 period at any rate, probably distorts the real nature of the interrelationship. Redmond's leadership vis-à-vis his colleagues, was, it is true, necessarily consultative, but his primacy as chairman of the Irish Party, publicly and privately, was, by 1909, firmly established. Conor Mulvagh, *The Irish Parliamentary Party at Westminster, 1900–18* (Manchester: Manchester University Press, 2016), pp. 100–18.

21   Lyons, *John Dillon*, pp. 38, 324.

22 Bull, *Land, Politics and Nationalism*, p. 173.
23 Hamilton Fyfe, *T.P. O'Connor* (London: Allen & Unwin, 1934), pp. 217–18; Lyons, *John Dillon*, p. 323.
24 *Freeman's Journal*, 13 May 1907.
25 M.J. Kelly, *The Fenian Ideal and Irish Nationalism, 1882–1916* (Woodbridge: Boydell, 2006), pp. 162–6; Maume, *Long Gestation*, pp. 85–93.
26 John E. Redmond, *Some Arguments for Home Rule: Being a series of speeches delivered in the autumn of 1907 by J.E. Redmond, M.P.* (Dublin: Sealy, Bryers & Co., 1908).
27 For example, John Redmond to Augustine Birrell, 21 June 1908 (TCD, Dillon Papers, MS 6748).
28 *Lepracaun Cartoon Monthly*, May 1909, p. 13.
29 T.P. O'Connor to John Dillon, 24 September 1909 (TCD, Dillon Papers, MS 6740); Fyfe, *T.P. O'Connor*, p. 223.
30 O'Brien, *William O'Brien*, pp. 185–7.
31 Bew, *John Redmond*, p. 48.
32 Francis Sheehy-Skeffington to J.F. Byrne, 3 January 1911 (NLI, Francis Sheehy-Skeffington Papers, MS 33612 (11)).
33 Francis Sheehy-Skeffington to Denis Johnston, 11 January 1909 (NLI, Francis Sheehy-Skeffington Papers, MS 33612 (6)).
34 *Times*, 13 February 1909.
35 Ibid. 11 March 1909.
36 John Redmond to Augustine Birrell, 22 June 1909 (NLI, John Redmond Papers, MS 15169/2).
37 John Redmond to John Dillon, 12 July 1909 (TCD, Dillon Papers, MS 6748).
38 T.P. O'Connor to John Dillon, 13 July 1909 (TCD, Dillon Papers, MS 6740).
39 John Redmond to H.H. Asquith, 2 October 1909 (TCD, Dillon Papers, MS 6796).
40 *Times*, 5 November 1909.
41 Ibid. 6, 12, 17 November, 20 December 1909.
42 John Dillon to David Lloyd George, 28 November 1909 (PA, Lloyd George Papers, LG/C/4/7/1). No such appeal was made in Ireland, but English Roman Catholic bishops issued a condemnatory manifesto in December advising Catholic voters in England to judge their choice of parliamentary candidates solely on the issue of denominational education. This was, more or less, an open instruction to vote Unionist. *Irish Times*, 27 December 1909.
43 *Times*, 19 November 1909.
44 John Redmond to Lord Morley, n.d., copy in Asquith's hand dated 1 December 1909 (Bodl., MS Asquith 36).
45 Augustine Birrell to John Redmond, 1 December 1909 (NLI, Redmond Papers, MS 15169/2).
46 John Redmond to John Dillon, 5 December 1909 (TCD, Dillon Papers, MS 6748).
47 Lord Morley to John Redmond, 6 December 1909 (NLI, Redmond Papers, MS 15207/2).
48 Unionist leader Arthur Balfour damningly accused Asquith of this in the House of Commons in the spring: 'He has bought the Irish vote for his Budget, and has bought it successfully. The price he has paid is the price of the dignity of his office, and of all the great traditions which he, of all men, ought to uphold.' *Hansard*, 14 April 1910.

49 Augustine Birrell to John Dillon, 31 January 1910 (TCD, Dillon Papers, MS 6798).
50 T.P. O'Connor to John Dillon, 7 February 1910 (TCD, Dillon Papers, MS 6740).
51 Asquith and his colleagues were all too aware of the precariousness of their new position: 'The distribution of parties in the new House of Commons', he reported to the king on 11 February, 'was felt to be such that, unless the Nationalist and Labour sections are content to forego or postpone their particular objects, a condition of permanent instability must result.' 'Prime Minister to the King' Cabinet report, 11 February 1910 (Bodl., MS Asquith 5).
52 Ronan Fanning, 'The Irish Policy of Asquith's Government and the Cabinet Crisis of 1910', in A. Cosgrove and D. MacCartney (eds), *Studies in Irish History Presented to R. Dudley Edwards* (Dublin: University College Dublin Press, 1979), pp. 284–5.
53 Roy Jenkins, *Asquith* (London: Collins, 1964), pp. 13–63.
54 Michael and Eleanor Brock (eds), *H.H. Asquith Letters to Venetia Stanley* (Oxford: Oxford University Press, 2014), p. 10.
55 Rosalind Fergusson (ed.), *Shorter Dictionary of Catch Phrases* (London: Routledge, 1994), p. 144.
56 *Quarterly Review*, July 1914, p. 276.
57 Asquith's wife recorded that her husband hated rows, and, indeed, the prime minister went to almost comical lengths to evade ministerial confrontations, locking himself in his cabin aboard the Admiralty yacht *Enchantress* on one occasion. Lord Morley agreed with an assessment of Asquith's temperamental 'reluctance … to be master in his own house'. Diary entry, n.d. (Bodl., Margot Asquith diaries, MS Eng. d. 3210); Edward David (ed.), *Inside Asquith's Cabinet: From the diaries of Charles Hobhouse* (London: J. Murray, 1977); Almeric Fitzroy, *The Memoirs of Sir Almeric Fitzroy*, vol. ii (London: Hutchinson, 1925), p. 545.
58 Despite the shocks it was dealt, Asquith's administration proved highly resilient, suffering no resignations until the outbreak of war in 1914. Asquith held the record as the longest-serving prime minister of the twentieth century until Margaret Thatcher exceeded his term of eight years and eight months in 1988.
59 A.G. Gardiner, *Pillars of Society* (London: James Nisbet & Co., 1913), pp. 81–2.
60 Yet Asquith also had a frivolous side. His son recalled his father's unflagging sense of humour. He was an early fan of the books of P.G. Wodehouse, and his letters brim with amusing political gossip. In one letter to his wife, Asquith, annoyed by copious correspondence from his colleague John Burns on the subject of a much-publicised shipwreck, wrote, 'I thought of replying to him that, short of swimming to the scene of the accident, that he had done everything possible.' *Manchester Guardian*, 13 September 1952; H.H. Asquith to Margot Asquith, 31 May 1914 (Bodl., Margot Asquith Papers, MS Eng. 6691).
61 Fitzroy, *Memoirs*, p. 432.
62 'Prime Minister to the King' Cabinet report, 10 February 1910 (Bodl., MS Asquith 5).
63 *Times*, 11 February 1910.
64 Meleady, *John Redmond*, pp. 169–70.
65 Fanning, 'Irish Policy', p. 287. One intimate observer described how unnerved Asquith was to be seen to have broken a pledge. 'He paced the room, agitated and distressed … for weeks the pall of that desolating speech hung over the sky of the new Parliament.' Gardiner, *Pillars of Society*, p. 84.
66 *Hansard*, 21 February 1910.
67 *Irish Times*, 23 February 1910.

68 *Times*, 24 February 1910.
69 *Scotsman*, 24 February 1910.
70 'Prime Minister to the King' Cabinet report, 19 February 1910 (Bodl., MS Asquith 5).
71 Fanning, 'Irish Policy', p. 288.
72 John Redmond to T.P. Gill, 20 February 1910 (NLI, Gill Papers, MS 13485).
73 *Irish Independent*, 21 February 1910; *Irish Times*, 20 December 1909.
74 *Irish Independent*, 21 February 1910; *Irish Times*, 13 November 1909, 15, 19, 23 February, 3 March 1910; *Times*, 10 February 1910.
75 'Prime Minister to the King' Cabinet report, 27 February 1910 (Bodl., MS Asquith 5).
76 Fanning, 'Irish Policy', p. 290.
77 'Prime Minister to the King' Cabinet report, 27 February 1910 (Bodl., MS Asquith 5).
78 Jenkins, *Asquith*, p. 208.
79 *Hansard*, 28 February 1910.
80 John Redmond to John Dillon, 8 March 1910 (TCD, Dillon Papers, MS 6748).
81 Fanning, 'Irish Policy', pp. 294–5.
82 Ibid. p. 295; Masterman, *C.F.G. Masterman*, p. 161.
83 David, *Hobhouse Diaries*, p. 89.
84 Masterman, *C.F.G. Masterman*, p. 161.
85 Fanning, 'Irish Policy', p. 298.
86 Masterman, *C.F.G. Masterman*, p. 161.
87 *Manchester Guardian*, 18 April 1910.
88 Despite the intense controversy over the budget in Ireland, there is reason to believe that Irish public opinion appreciated that the Irish Party's tactics were bringing Home Rule nearer. *The Manchester Guardian* reported that Irish Parliamentary Fund subscriptions were up substantially for 1910, and were projected to reach £20,000 for the year, up from £12,000 in 1909. *Manchester Guardian*, 8 April 1910.
89 J.A. Spender and Cyril Asquith, *Life of Herbert Henry Asquith, Earl of Oxford and Asquith*, vol. i (London: Hutchinson & Co., 1932), p. 261.
90 R.J. Scally, *The Origins of the Lloyd George Coalition* (London: Princeton University Press, 1975), pp. 176–8.
91 John Dillon to T.P. O'Connor, 5 June 1910 (TCD, Dillon Papers, MS 6740).
92 The delegates were Asquith, Lloyd George, Birrell and Lord Crewe for the Liberals; Arthur Balfour (leader of the opposition), Austen Chamberlain, Lord Lansdowne and Lord Cawdor for the Unionists.
93 H.H. Asquith to Arthur Balfour, 9 June 1910 (Bodl., MS Asquith 23).
94 The scheme, named after Lord Ripon, was mooted in Cabinet in 1907 but rejected in favour of a suspensory veto. C.C. Weston, 'The Liberal Leadership and the Lords Veto, 1907–1910', *Historical Journal*, vol. 11, no. 3 (1968), p. 511.
95 'Ripon Scheme' memorandum, n.d. (NLI, Redmond Papers, MS 15252/1/B; PA, Lloyd George Papers, LG/C/6/11/8).
96 *Times*, 26 July 1910. Devolution of powers in the UK in a federal system had been proposed in the 1870s; it was envisaged that parliaments for England, Scotland, Wales and Ireland would legislate domestic matters. All would be subordinate to the imperial parliament.
97 A.M. Gollin, *The Observer and J.L. Garvin* (London: Oxford University Press, 1960), pp. 201–2.
98 *Reynolds's Newspaper*, 31 July 1910.

 99   Michael Wheatley, 'John Redmond and Federalism in 1910', *Irish Historical Studies*, vol. 32, no. 127 (May 2001), p. 349.
100   'Memorandum on coalition v party government for dealing with social reform', 17 August 1910 (PA, Lloyd George Papers, MS LG/C/16/9/1).
101   Diary entries, 22 November 1910, 2 December 1910 (Bodl., Margot Asquith diaries, MS Eng. d. 3207). Margot Asquith's diaries are a somewhat problematic source. The prime minister's wife was a frenetic letter writer, fiercely defensive of her husband, and notoriously indiscreet. She was frequently bedridden with colitis, and suffered from depression and insomnia. Her diaries appear to have been written with one eye to preserving Asquith's historical reputation and the other to eventual (and, she hoped, lucrative) publication. With this scepticism in mind, the diaries nonetheless hold fascinating detail. Margot Asquith to John Burns, 25 April 1916 (BL, Burns Papers, Add. MS 46282).
102   Lord Crewe to David Lloyd George, 21 October 1910 (PA, Lloyd George Papers, MS LG/C/4/1/2).
103   Gollin, *J.L. Garvin*, pp. 210, 229.
104   Catherine B. Shannon, *Arthur J. Balfour and Ireland* (Washington DC: Catholic University of America Press, 1998), p. 151.
105   *Morning Post*, 17 October 1910.
106   Wheatley, 'John Redmond and Federalism', pp. 354–5.
107   Ibid. pp. 357–8.
108   *Times*, 10 October 1910.
109   Austen Chamberlain, *Politics from Inside: An epistolary chronicle, 1906–1914* (London: Cassell & Co., 1936), p. 287.
110   *Times*, 19 October 1910.
111   *Morning Post*, 26 October 1910.
112   Shannon, *Balfour and Ireland*, p. 155; G.R. Searle, 'A.J. Balfour's Secret Coalition Talks Memorandum, 1910', *Historical Research*, vol. 66, no. 160 (1993), p. 228.
113   Gollin, *J.L. Garvin*, p. 230. Balfour evidently spent five or six days in surreptitious discussions with the Chancellor at 11 Downing Street, 'going in by [the] garden entrance in slouched hat'. Asquith thought him 'much bitten by the idea'. Diary entry, 22 November 1910 (Bodl., Margot Asquith diaries, MS Eng. d. 3208).
114   Searle, 'Balfour's Coalition Talks', pp. 226, 228.
115   Conference notes, 19th, 20th, 21st sittings, 2–4 November 1910 (U.Birm. L., Austen Chamberlain Papers, MS AC 10/2/53, 54, 61).
116   'Ripon Scheme' memorandum, n.d. (NLI, Redmond Papers, MS 15252/1/B).
117   Fitzroy, *Memoirs*, vol. ii, pp. 395, 398.
118   Fanning, 'Irish Policy', p. 283.
119   Cameron Hazlehurst and Christine Woodland, *A Liberal Chronicle: Journals and papers of J.A. Pease, first Lord Gainford, 1908–1910* (London: Historian's Press, 1994), p. 166.
120   David, *Hobhouse Diaries*, p. 88.
121   Fitzroy, *Memoirs*, vol. ii, p. 430. John Burns, the local-government minister, was one of the first Cabinet members to come from a working-class background.
122   Anon., *Proceedings in Connection with the Thirty-second Annual Meeting of the National Liberal Federation, London, November 1910* (London: Liberal Publications Department, 1910), p. 75.
123   Meleady, *John Redmond*, p. 188. The consequence of a reduction in contributions

was the exclusion from the scheme of certain categories of workers, including agricultural labourers, as well as the elimination of medical benefits for Ireland.

124 *Times*, 4 November 1911.
125 Diary entry, 16 August 1911 (Nuffield College Library, Oxford, J.A. Pease Papers, MS Gainford C85/33/3).
126 For example, *Times*, 7 June 1911, *Manchester Guardian*, 13 March 1911.
127 Jalland, *Liberals and Ireland*, pp. 37–42.
128 Ibid. p. 40.
129 William O'Brien to H.H. Asquith, 4 November 1911 (Bodl., MS Asquith 36).
130 Jalland, *Liberals and Ireland*, pp. 42–4; Jenkins, *Asquith*, p. 274.
131 Ulsterman James Douglas, editor of the Liberal *Star* newspaper, later claimed to have laid a six-year exclusion plan before Lloyd George and Alexander Murray in January 1912. The chief whip, he claimed, asked him not to make it public because he and Lloyd George 'thought it might later prove a valuable *via media*'. James Douglas to H.H. Asquith, 21 March 1914 (Bodl., MS Asquith 36).
132 Jalland, *Liberals and Ireland*, pp. 59, 64; David, *Hobhouse Diaries*, p. 111.
133 Jalland, *Liberals and Ireland*, pp. 63–4.
134 Ibid.
135 A former legal colleague sent him a copy of the document several months after the Cabinet decision. Arthur Gwynne-James to H.H. Asquith, 21 July 1912 (Bodl., MS Asquith 36).
136 Sir David Harrel to Augustine Birrell, 8 February 1912 (Bodl., MS Asquith 38).
137 Jalland, *Liberals and Ireland*, pp. 73–5; RIC report, September 1911 (Bodl., MS Asquith 38); 'Reports with Regard to Probable Resistance to Home Rule', 14 February 1912 (PA, Lloyd George Papers, LGC 19/3/4).
138 Jalland, *Liberals and Ireland*, pp. 67–8.
139 T.P. O'Connor to John Redmond, 22 December 1910 (NLI, Redmond Papers, MS 15215/2/A).
140 *Times*, 20 April 1912, 17 May 1913.
141 Ibid. 27 May, 6 July 1911.
142 Ibid. 19 July 1911.
143 T.P. Gill to Edward Shortt, 9 October 1919 (NLI, Gill Papers, MS 13517).
144 'Committee on Irish Finance Minutes of Evidence' (PA, Lloyd George Papers, LG/C/20/1/2).
145 T.P. Gill to W.G.S. Adams, 20 September 1911 (NLI, Gill Papers, MS 13485).
146 T.P. Gill to Denis Kelly, 25 September 1911 (NLI, Gill Papers, MS 13485).
147 Denis Kelly to T.P. Gill, n.d. (NLI, Gill Papers, MS 13485).
148 'Report by the Committee on Irish Finance', 17 October 1911 (NA, CAB 37/108/132).
149 David, *Hobhouse Diaries*, p. 106.
150 Jalland, *Liberals and Ireland*, p. 45.
151 'Irish Finance III', 14 November 1911 (NA, CAB 37/108/146). Statistics compiled in preparation for the 1918 Irish Convention indicated that seventy-six per cent of Irish revenues for the year to 31 March 1914 were derived from customs and excise duties. Memorandum, n.d. (Bodl., Hopwood Papers, MS Eng. c. 7356).
152 Memorandum, 27 November 1911 (NA, CAB 37/108/161).
153 'Government of Ireland Bill Outline of Financial Provisions', 1 April 1912 (NA, CAB 37/110/57).

154 'Memorandum on Irish finance', 6 December 1911 (NLI, Redmond Papers, MS 15252/2).

155 'Memorandum on the clauses of the Home Rule Bill', 29 January 1912 (NLI, Redmond Papers, MS 15266; NA, CAB 37/109/8); Meleady, *John Redmond*, p. 151. Paul Bew asserted that costly New Liberal collectivism was prompting a retreat from economic nationalism. However, Redmond's securing (through Gill) of a recommendation for fiscal autonomy from the Primrose Committee, efforts to curtail Irish National Insurance contributions and benefits, and his apparent desire to cut the rate of old-age pensions in Ireland do not support such a conclusion. Social reforms, it seems, were subordinate to the goal of fiscal autonomy. In 1924, in what proved to be a politically costly move, the post-revolutionary inheritors of the Irish Party, Cumann na nGaedheal, cut pension entitlements. Bew, *Ideology and the Irish Question*, p. 156; Cormac Ó Gráda, '"The Greatest Blessing of All": The old age pension in Ireland', *Past & Present*, no. 175 (May 2002), p. 150.

156 'Government of Ireland Bill Outline of Financial Provisions', 1 April 1912 (NA, CAB 37/110/57).

157 'Government of Ireland [and House of Commons Devolution of Business Bill]', 4 March 1912 (NA, CAB 37/110/38); 'Memorandum on Irish finance', 6 December 1911 (NLI, Redmond Papers, MS 15252/2).

158 John Redmond to John Dillon, 12 December 1911 (TCD, Dillon Papers, MS 6748).

159 Gwynn, *John Redmond*, p. 196.

160 Jackson, *Home Rule*, pp. 127–8. The special reference to marriage was necessitated by controversy over the *Ne Temere* papal decree and the notorious McCann case arising from the break-up of a mixed marriage and the separation of a Protestant mother from her children.

161 Lyons, *John Dillon*, pp. 322–3; Meleady, *John Redmond*, p. 206.

162 Augustine Birrell to John Redmond, n.d. (NLI, Redmond Papers, MS 15169/3).

163 John Dillon to John Redmond, 14 January 1912 (NLI, Redmond Papers, MS 15182/19).

164 'Vital matters', n.d. (NLI, Redmond Papers, MS 15252/2).

165 'Memorandum on the clauses of the Home Rule Bill', 29 January 1912 (NLI, Redmond Papers, MS 15266).

166 Memorandum, 4 March 1912 (NA, CAB 37/110/38).

167 Jalland, *Liberals and Ireland*, p. 41.

168 'Irish Finance, Suggested Modifications to Scheme', 25 March 1912 (NA, CAB 37/110/54).

169 Ibid. 'Government of Ireland Bill Outline of Financial Provisions', 1 April 1912 (NA, CAB 37/110/57). As Samuel feared might happen one day, Éamon de Valera's Irish Free State government elected to withhold land-annuity payments to the British Treasury in 1932.

170 Augustine Birrell to John Dillon, 2 April 1912 (NLI, Redmond Papers, MS 15182/19).

171 The prime minister had himself been unwell for a fortnight or so. The strain of the miners' strike had been so heavy that Margot Asquith feared that her husband had suffered a stroke. A doctor diagnosed mental fatigue and prescribed 'brain rest'; it was not until the day that the Home Rule Bill was introduced that Asquith felt fully himself again. Margot Asquith to John Burns, 3 April 1912 (BL, Burns Papers, Add. MS 46282); diary entry, 11 April 1912 (Bodl., Margot Asquith diaries, MS Eng. d. 3210).

172 Augustine Birrell to John Redmond, 10 April 1912 (NLI, Redmond Papers, MS 15169/3).
173 *Freeman's Journal*, 1 April 1912.
174 *Times*, 24 April 1912.
175 Ibid.
176 Senia Pašeta, *Irish Nationalist Women, 1900–1918* (Cambridge: Cambridge University Press, 2013), p. 79.
177 Ibid. p. 80.
178 *Times*, 22 April 1912.
179 'An Impression of the Convention', 24 April 1912 (NLI, Francis Sheehy-Skeffington Papers, MS 40475 (2)).
180 *Times*, 20 October 1912.
181 E.A. Aston to W.F. Trench, 5 March 1913 (TCD, Trench Papers, MS 9299).
182 Redmond to Lord Courtney of Penwith, 4 July 1912 (NLI, Redmond Papers, MS 15254).
183 John Redmond to Patrick O'Donnell, 12 December 1912 (TCD, Dillon Papers, MS 6748).
184 Warre B. Wells, *John Redmond: A biography* (London: Nisbet & Co., 1919), p. 129.
185 'Special Congress on the Political Situation', 22 March 1913 (UCDA, Sinn Féin Party Papers, P163).
186 Though James McConnel argued that place-hunting or political corruption may have inadvertently benefited the attainment of self-government in Ireland, by sustaining a strong nationalist political organisation and establishing a brokerage role that consolidated representative democracy. James McConnel, 'Jobbing with Tory and Liberal: Irish nationalists and the politics of patronage 1880–1914', *Past & Present*, no. 188 (August 2005), p. 131.
187 *Clarion*, 6 September 1912. 'Gombeen' is the Irish term for usury.
188 James McConnel, *The Irish Parliamentary Party and the Third Home Rule Crisis* (Dublin: Four Courts Press, 2013), pp. 57–8.
189 Joseph V. O'Brien, *Dear, Dirty Dublin: A city in distress, 1899–1916* (Berkeley CA: University of California Press, 1982), p. 99.
190 The Beresford Street buildings' lamentable state and the misery of their many inhabitants was simply an oversight, the journal sarcastically reassured readers, because 'statesmen have no time to bother about such microscopic matters as slum tenements'. *Lepracaun Cartoon Monthly*, November 1913.
191 McConnel, *Irish Parliamentary Party*, p. 136.
192 John O'Donovan, 'The All-for-Ireland League and the Home Rule Debate, 1910–14', in Gabriel Doherty (ed.), *The Third Home Rule Crisis, 1912–14* (Cork: Mercier Press, 2014), p. 150.
193 Anon., *If Ulster Revolts – Who Is Responsible? (An Indictment of Mr Joseph Devlin)* (Dublin, n.d.) (NLI, Francis Sheehy-Skeffington Papers, MS 40475 (2)).
194 R.F. Foster, *Vivid Faces: The revolutionary generation in Ireland, 1890–1923* (London: Allen Lane, 2014), p. 191. 'Advanced nationalist' is a term for those Irish nationalists who rejected the parliamentary route to national autonomy in favour of separatism. Advanced nationalists were often republicans, and sometimes advocates of physical force to expel British rule.
195 Stephen Gwynn to John Dillon, 14 January 1912 (TCD, Dillon Papers, MS 6754).
196 Francis Sheehy-Skeffington to unknown recipient, n.d. (NLI, Francis Sheehy-Skeffington Papers, MS 33612 (14)).

197 Jackson, *Home Rule*, p. 142.
198 Gwynn, *John Redmond*, p. 214.
199 David, *Hobhouse Diaries*, p. 124.
200 'The Fate of Ulster: How it would fare under the Provisional Government: Some unforeseen consequences', noted 'possibly Oct. 1912' (Bodl., MS Asquith 38). The reference to Covenanters dates this memorandum sometime after September 1912. On Ulster Day, 28 September 1912, after impressive public displays led by Sir Edward Carson, the Solemn League and Covenant, pledging loyalty to the Crown and resistance to Home Rule, was signed.
201 *Reynolds's Newspaper*, 21 July 1912; *Times*, 19 July 1912.
202 The celebratory mood was marred by a hatchet attack on the carriage by English suffragette Mary Leigh. The hatchet missed its intended prime-ministerial target and struck Redmond, injuring him slightly. *Times*, 19 July 1912.
203 Maurice Headlam, *Irish Reminiscences* (London: Robert Hale, 1947), pp. 124–5.
204 *Times*, 20 July 1912.
205 Francis Sheehy-Skeffington to Sylvia Pankhurst, 3 November 1912 (NLI, Francis Sheehy-Skeffington Papers, MS 33612 (12)); *Times*, 20 July 1912. Arthur Balfour was known in Ireland as 'Bloody Balfour' during his tenure as Unionist Irish chief secretary from 1887 to 1891.
206 Anon., *Mr Asquith's Visit to Dublin* (London: Home Rule Council, 1912), p. 1 (Bodl., MS Asquith 38).
207 *Times*, 20 July 1912.
208 *Daily News and Leader*, 1 April 1912; Anon., *Mr Asquith's Visit to Dublin*, p. 6 (Bodl., MS Asquith 38).
209 Charles Stewart Parnell's famously ambiguous motto, 'No man shall have the right to fix the boundary to the march of a nation', is inscribed on the monolith of Augustus Saint-Gaudens' Parnell Monument at the top of Dublin's O'Connell Street. Redmond unveiled the memorial in 1911.
210 *Times*, 19 July 1912.

Chapter 3: Answering the Challenge of Ulster, 1912–14

 1 1911 census figures (NLI, Redmond Papers, MS 15253).
 2 Memorandum, 19 May 1914 (BL, Bowood Papers, Add. MS 88906/27/10).
 3 Jonathan Bardon, '"Grotesque proceedings"? Localised responses to the Home Rule question in Ulster', in Doherty (ed.), *The Third Home Rule Crisis*, pp. 294–6.
 4 Jackson, *Home Rule*, pp. 137–9.
 5 *Lepracaun Cartoon Monthly*, January 1914, p. 253.
 6 *Catholic Times*, 24 January 1913; *Daily Citizen*, 18 December 1913.
 7 *Nation*, 7 February 1914.
 8 *Methodist Times*, 12 June 1913.
 9 *Reynolds's Newspaper*, 1 March 1914.
10 *Nation*, 30 May 1914.
11 *Reynolds's Newspaper*, 9 February 1913.
12 *Methodist Times*, 19 June 1913.
13 Ibid. 6 November 1913.
14 *Saturday Westminster Gazette*, 22 June 1912.
15 *Daily Citizen*, 3 July 1914.

16 *Nation*, 30 May 1914.

17 *Freeman's Journal*, 23 August 1912.

18 Lord Pirrie was the chairman of shipbuilders Harland & Wolff and a prominent Ulster supporter of Home Rule. *Nation*, 18 October 1913.

19 *Catholic Times*, 30 August 1912.

20 *Reynolds's Newspaper*, 13 July 1913.

21 *Daily Citizen*, 30 September 1913.

22 *Reynolds's Newspaper*, 26 May 1912.

23 Ibid. 7 December 1913.

24 Ibid. The reactionary Lord Willoughby de Broke was among the flintiest of diehards fighting against the Parliament Bill in 1911.

25 Anon., *Home Rule?s Answered*, p. 22.

26 Ibid. p. 38.

27 For example, *Baptist Times*, 19 April 1912; *Nation*, 5 May 1912.

28 *Saturday Westminster Gazette*, 13 April 1912.

29 MacVeigh, *Home Rule in a Nutshell*, pp. 77–83.

30 *Freeman's Journal*, 19 July 1912. Lord Carnarvon was a Tory Lord Lieutenant whom Parnell accused of promising and subsequently withdrawing a scheme for Home Rule in 1885. Richard Pigott was an Irish journalist who forged letters implicating Parnell in the 1882 Phoenix Park assassinations in Dublin. Pigott committed suicide when the forgery was exposed by Parnell's libel action against *The Times* in 1889.

31 *Baptist Times*, 19 April 1912.

32 Ibid. 5 December 1913.

33 *Catholic Times*, 30 August 1912.

34 *Reynolds's Newspaper*, 15 June 1913.

35 Ibid. 28 September 1913.

36 *Methodist Times*, 2 October 1913.

37 *Daily Citizen*, 27 June 1914.

38 Ibid. 2 December 1912.

39 Quoted in *Reynolds's Newspaper*, 30 November 1913.

40 *Nation*, 7 March 1914.

41 *Catholic Times*, 19 July 1912.

42 J.A. Hobson, *Traffic in Treason: A study of political parties* (London: T. Fisher Unwin, 1914), p. 39.

43 *Westminster Gazette*, 25 July 1914.

44 *Methodist Times*, 22 May 1913.

45 Ibid. 20 November 1913.

46 *Catholic Times*, 9 August 1912.

47 Quoted in *The Catholic Times*, 30 May 1913.

48 *Catholic Times*, 19 June 1914.

49 *Reynolds's Newspaper*, 15 March 1914.

50 *Catholic Times*, 3 July 1914.

51 *Methodist Times*, 15 August 1912.

52 *Nation*, 1 November 1913, 13 June 1914.

53 Ibid. 5 October 1912.

54 Rev. J.P. Mahaffy, Nicholas Gosselin and Rev. R.D.O. Martin, *Ulster and the Irish Minority* (London, 1912), p. 2.

55   *Times*, 18 November 1913.
56   *Nation*, 18 October 1913.
57   *Daily Citizen*, 3 December 1912. T.P. Gill wrote to Redmond and Birrell intimating the efficacy of just such blandishments. He suggested that it would be politic to give J.C. White of Belfast, president of the Northern Law Society, an honour to smooth the way for Home Rule among an influential set in Ulster. Gill's efforts were, in this instance, ineffective. Though White went on to be lord mayor of Belfast in 1919, he received no titular adornment in 1913–14. T.P. Gill to Augustine Birrell, 29 May 1913, T.P. Gill to John Redmond, 29 May 1913 (NLI, Gill Papers, MS 13485).
58   *Nation*, 2 November 1912, 20 June 1914.
59   *Times*, 9 January 1913.
60   *Nation*, 6 December 1913.
61   Anon., *The Way of Unity and Peace* (London: Smith, Elder & Co., 1914), pp. 14–16.
62   *Nation*, 20 December 1913.
63   Ibid. 13 December 1913, 11 April, 20 June 1914.
64   *Methodist Times*, 18 September 1913.
65   *Nation*, 6 December 1913.
66   *Reynolds's Newspaper*, 7 December 1913.
67   *Contemporary Review*, October 1913.
68   *Nation*, 18 July 1914.
69   Ibid. 26 June 1914.
70   *Saturday Westminster Gazette*, 21 February, 17 July 1914; *Westminster Gazette*, 21 March 1914.
71   *Westminster Gazette*, 27 July 1914.
72   *Daily News and Leader*, 24 April 1914.
73   *Catholic Times*, 18 May 1914.
74   *Nation*, 12 June 1914.
75   Ibid. 20 June 1914.
76   *Daily Citizen*, 23, 27 June 1914.
77   Ibid. 24 June 1914.
78   *Reynolds's Newspaper*, 14, 21 June 1914.
79   Ibid. 28 June 1914.
80   *Nation*, 21 March 1914.
81   *Catholic Times*, 10 July 1914.
82   *Nation*, 4, 11 July 1914.
83   Meleady, *John Redmond*, p. 297.
84   *Daily Chronicle*, 28, 29 July 1914. T.P. Gill wrote as an anonymous special correspondent for *The Daily Chronicle* in August 1914, and was in contact with its editor, Robert Donald, in July. These passages bear the tone of Gill's later contributions (NLI, Gill Papers, MS 13486 (8, 9, 10, 11)).
85   *Reynolds's Newspaper*, 2 August 1914.
86   *Daily Chronicle*, 30 July 1914.
87   *Nation*, 1 August 1914.
88   *Lepracaun Cartoon Monthly*, June 1914, p. 16.
89   Ibid. p. 25.
90   Ibid. p. 36.
91   *Reynolds's Newspaper*, 28 September 1913.
92   Clipping from unidentified newspaper, n.d. (UCDA, Kettle Papers, LA34/280).

93   *Daily Citizen*, 30 September 1913.
94   *Reynolds's Newspaper*, 30 November 1913.
95   Ibid. 23 November 1913.
96   *Nation*, 20 December 1913, 14 February, 11 April, 27 July 1914.
97   *Clarion*, 4 October 1912.
98   *Methodist Times*, 13 November 1913; *Catholic Times*, 22 May 1914.
99   *Daily Citizen*, 12, 13 November 1913.
100   *Methodist Times*, 25 September 1913.
101   *Nation*, 28 March 1914.
102   *Catholic Times*, 5 June 1914.
103   *Nation*, 21 March, 16 May 1914.
104   Retired General Sir George Richardson was the commander of the Ulster Volunteers. *Reynolds's Newspaper*, 21 September 1913; *Nation*, 21 March 1914.
105   *Reynolds's Newspaper*, 15 March 1914.
106   Ibid. 14 December 1913.
107   *Daily Citizen*, 13 November 1913.
108   *Nation*, 15 November 1913.
109   Ibid. 28 February 1914.
110   *Daily Citizen*, 22, 23 May 1914; *Catholic Times*, 24 July 1914.
111   Ibid. 25 May 1914.
112   *Nation*, 20 June 1914.
113   *Westminster Gazette*, 27 July 1914.
114   *Nation*, 20 June 1914.
115   *Baptist Times*, 8 August 1913.
116   *Reynolds's Newspaper*, 8 June 1913.
117   *Daily Citizen*, 16 November 1912.
118   *Catholic Times*, 2 August 1912.
119   *Daily News and Leader*, 17 June 1912.
120   *Daily Citizen*, 28 October 1912.
121   *Catholic Times*, 17 January 1913.
122   *Daily Citizen*, 28 October 1912.
123   *Nation*, 15 November 1913.
124   *Reynolds's Newspaper*, 15 March, 31 May 1914.
125   *Catholic Times*, 3 July 1914.
126   Henry de Rosenbach Walker, *The Need for the Parliament Act* (London: Liberal Publications Department, 1914), p. 16.
127   *Nation*, 17 August 1912.
128   Ibid. 14 March 1914.
129   *Reynolds's Newspaper*, 8 June 1913.
130   *Catholic Times*, 4 October 1912.
131   Ibid. 11 October 1912.
132   *Nation*, 7 June 1914.
133   *Catholic Times*, 22 May 1914.
134   *Nation*, 14 March 1914.
135   Ibid. 28 March 1914.
136   *Reynolds's Newspaper*, 26 April 1914.
137   Hobson, *Traffic in Treason*, p. 10.
138   Ibid. pp. 59–60.

139 Ibid. pp. 61–4.
140 *Westminster Gazette*, 25 July 1914.
141 *Nation*, 25 July 1914.
142 *Catholic Times*, 17 July 1914.
143 *Reynolds's Newspaper*, 2 August 1914.

Chapter 4: Tug of War

1 Jalland, *Liberals and Ireland*, pp. 116–17.
2 T.P. O'Connor to John Dillon, 2 June 1913 (TCD, Dillon Papers, MS 6740).
3 Koss, *Rise and Fall of the Political Press*, vol. ii, p. 675.
4 Gardiner, *Pillars of Society*, pp. 85–6.
5 Brooks, *Age of Upheaval*, pp. 154–5.
6 Fitzroy, *Memoirs*, vol. ii, pp. 492, 517–18.
7 Diary entry, 'The session of 1913, 10 March to 14 August' n.d. (Bodl., Margot Asquith diaries, MS Eng. d. 3210).
8 For example, 'Note of observations made to H.M. by Mr Bonar Law', 27 September 1912 (RA PS/PSO/GV/C/K/2553/1/2); Lord Stamfordham memoranda, 2 May, 12, 20 June, 1 July 1913 (RA PS/PSO/GV/C/K/2553/1/30, 31, 32, 36); memorandum, 11 July 1913 (RA PS/PSO/GV/C/K/2553/1/38); Walter Long memorandum, 22 July 1913 (RA PS/PSO/GV/C/K/2553/1/44).
9 *Times*, 25 January 1913; Maurice Brett (ed.), *Journals and Letters of Reginald, Viscount Esher*, vol. 3 (London: Nicholson & Watson, 1934), p. 117.
10 Copy of John St Loe Strachey memorandum, February 1913 (RA PS/PSO/GV/C/K/2553/1/19, 20).
11 Lord Stamfordham memorandum, 24 July 1913 (RA PS/PSO/GV/C/K/2553/1/45).
12 Augustine Birrell to H.H. Asquith, 24 July 1913 (Bodl., MS Asquith 38).
13 Lord Stamfordham memorandum, 24 July 1913 (RA PS/PSO/GV/C/K/2553/1/45).
14 Augustine Birrell to H.H. Asquith, 20 August 1913 (Bodl., MS Asquith 38).
15 Lord Stamfordham memorandum, 4 September 1913 (RA PS/PSO/GV/C/K/2553/1/78).
16 'Ld. L's conversation with the king', 6 September 1913 (BL, Bowood Papers, Add. MS 88906/27/7).
17 Jalland, *Liberals and Ireland*, p. 145; Andrew Bonar Law to Lord Lansdowne, 18 September 1913 (BL, Bowood Papers, Add. MS 88906/27/7).
18 Lord Loreburn to William O'Brien, 12 August 1913 (NLI, Michael MacDonagh Papers, MS 11439). Loreburn had been one of the most vocal opponents of extending the option of exclusion to Ulster counties when the proposal was mooted in Cabinet in February 1912.
19 Augustine Birrell to John Dillon, 14 September 1913 (TCD, Dillon Papers, MS 6799).
20 Augustine Birrell to H.H. Asquith, 8 September 1913 (Bodl., MS Asquith 38).
21 'Political Conditions in Ireland', 11 September 1913 (Bodl., MS Asquith 38).
22 H.H. Asquith to King George V, n.d., 1 October 1913 (Bodl., MS Asquith 38).
23 Winston Churchill to H.H. Asquith, 17 September 1913 (Bodl., MS Asquith 38).
24 Memorandum, 17 September 1913 (NLI, Redmond Papers, MS 15255/2); H.H. Asquith to Lord Loreburn, 20 September 1913 (PA, Lloyd George Papers, LG/C/19/3/7).
25 *Times*, 29 September 1913.

26   George Renwick to Robert Donald, 21 September 1913 (PA, Lloyd George Papers, LG/C/19/3/7).

27   Robert Donald to David Lloyd George, 5 October 1913 (PA, Lloyd George Papers, LG/C/4/8/5).

28   Augustine Birrell to H.H. Asquith, 26 September 1913 (Bodl., MS Asquith 38).

29   Brett (ed.), *Esher Journals*, vol. 3, p. 140. Haldane was ennobled upon his appointment as Lord Chancellor.

30   Augustine Birrell to H.H. Asquith, 26 September 1913 (Bodl., MS Asquith 38).

31   John Dillon to T.P. O'Connor, 1, 16 October 1913 (TCD, Dillon Papers, MS 6740).

32   McConnel, *Irish Parliamentary Party*, pp. 170–1.

33   Augustine Birrell to H.H. Asquith, 26 September 1913 (Bodl., MS Asquith 38).

34   Augustine Birrell to H.H. Asquith, 20 October 1913.

35   F.E. Smith to David Lloyd George, 26 September 1913 (PA, Lloyd George Papers, LG/C/7/1).

36   Jalland, *Liberals and Ireland*, p. 149. Sir Francis Hopwood, the king's confidant, dined with Lloyd George and Kitchin in Glasgow. Diary entry, 29 September 1913 (Bodl., Hopwood diaries, MS Eng. e. 3611/1).

37   David Lloyd George to F.E. Smith, 6 October 1913 (PA, Lloyd George Papers, LG/C/3/7/2).

38   T.P. O'Connor to Joseph Devlin, 7 October 1913 (misdated 1 October) (NLI, Redmond Papers, MS 15181/3).

39   Ibid.

40   John Dillon to T.P. O'Connor, 8 October 1913 (TCD, Dillon Papers, MS 6740).

41   John Dillon to T.P. O'Connor, 2 October 1913 (TCD, Dillon Papers, MS 6740).

42   John Dillon to T.P. O'Connor, 8 October 1913 (TCD, Dillon Papers, MS 6740).

43   Winston Churchill defected from the Unionist Party over the issue of free trade in 1904.

44   T.P. O'Connor to John Dillon, 13 October 1913 (TCD, Dillon Papers, MS 6740).

45   *Times*, 13 October 1913.

46   John Dillon to T.P. O'Connor, 15 October 1913 (TCD, Dillon Papers, MS 6740).

47   T.P. O'Connor to John Dillon, 15 October 1913 (TCD, Dillon Papers, MS 6740).

48   Augustine Birrell to H.H. Asquith, 16 October 1913; Leon Ó Broin, *The Chief Secretary: Augustine Birrell in Ireland* (London: Chatto & Windus, 1969), pp. 82–3.

49   Meeting notes, 15 October 1913 (Bodl., MS Asquith 38); Jalland, *Liberals and Ireland*, p. 154. Asquith's observation to his wife after this meeting is revealing of his estimation of Bonar Law, as well as of his own intellectual snobbery: 'He is very naïf, but a nice fellow: not at all clever, but clever enough to see his position is an impossible one.' Diary entry, 19 November 1913 (Bodl., Margot Asquith Papers, MS Eng. d. 3210).

50   David, *Hobhouse Diaries*, p. 146.

51   Jalland, *Liberals and Ireland*, p. 165.

52   T.P. O'Connor to John Dillon, 17 October 1913 (TCD, Dillon Papers, MS 6740).

53   Meeting notes, 17 October 1913 (Bodl., MS Asquith 38).

54   Augustine Birrell to H.H. Asquith, 3 October 1913 (Bodl., MS Asquith 38).

55   Augustine Birrell to H.H. Asquith, 28 October 1913 (Bodl., MS Asquith 38).

56   Meeting notes, 6 November 1913 (Bodl., MS Asquith 39).

57   H.H. Asquith memorandum for King George V, 7 November 1913 (RA PS/PSO/GV/C/K/2553/2/79).

58   Jalland, *Liberals and Ireland*, pp. 155–6.
59   Lord Stamfordham memorandum, 6 November 1913 (RA PS/PSO/GV/C/K/
      2553/2/76).
60   H.H. Asquith memorandum for King George V, 7 November 1913 (RA PS/PSO/
      GV/C/K/2553/2/79).
61   Lord Stamfordham memorandum, 8 November 1913 (RA PS/PSO/GV/C/K/
      2553/2/81). There was a strong case to be made that Irish over-representation in
      the Westminster parliament was a distorting anomaly.
62   David, *Hobhouse Diaries*, pp. 148–9.
63   Copy of a letter from H.H. Asquith to King George V, 14 November 1913 (RA
      PS/PSO/GV/C/K/2553/2/84). At Ladybank, Asquith noticed that his audience
      cheered when coercion of Ulster was mooted; their response was subdued when his
      tone became more conciliatory. Lord Stamfordham memorandum, 6 November
      1913 (RA PS/PSO/GV/C/K/2553/2/76).
64   Augustine Birrell to H.H. Asquith, 13 November 1913 (Bodl., MS Asquith 39).
65   Jalland, *Liberals and Ireland*, p. 167. Jalland cited this dinner as the debut of the
      Lloyd George plan of exclusion, a misattribution not supported by contemporary
      evidence. Lord Curzon had written to Lansdowne two months earlier, referring to
      'Asquith's idea … [of] a Home Rule parliament for the rest of Ireland and Ulster
      left out of it'. Lord Curzon to Lord Lansdowne, 14 September 1913 (BL, Bowood
      Papers, Add. MS 88906/27/7).
66   Copy of a letter from H.H. Asquith to King George V, 14 November 1913 (RA
      PS/PSO/GV/C/K/2553/2/84).
67   Augustine Birrell to H.H. Asquith, 13 November 1913 (Bodl., MS Asquith 39).
68   H.H. Asquith to John Redmond, 13 November 1913 (TCD, Dillon Papers, MS
      6740).
69   Meeting notes, 17 November 1913 (NLI, Redmond Papers, MS 15165/3).
70   Meeting notes, 17 November 1913 (Bodl., MS Asquith 39).
71   Meeting notes, 17 November 1913 (NLI, Redmond Papers, MS 15165/3).
72   'Interview with Mr John Dillon, at No. 11 Downing Street', 17 November 1913
      (PA, Lloyd George Papers, LG/C/20/2/4).
73   Memorandum, 18 November 1913 (Bodl., MS Asquith 39).
74   David, *Hobhouse Diaries*, p. 151.
75   John Redmond to H.H. Asquith, 24 November 1913 (Bodl., MS Asquith 39).
76   David, *Hobhouse Diaries*, pp. 151–2.
77   Ibid. p. 152.
78   T.P. O'Connor to John Dillon, 26 November 1913 (TCD, Dillon Papers, MS 6740).
79   Memorandum, 27 November 1913 (TCD, Dillon Papers, MS 6748).
80   T.P. O'Connor to John Dillon, 26 November 1913 (TCD, Dillon Papers, MS 6740).
      Conor Mulvagh cited this letter from O'Connor to Dillon as signifying the moment
      when Redmond acquiesced, in principle, to partition. This claim is not supported
      by Redmond's account of his meeting with Lloyd George that day, nor by the fact
      that Asquith was unable to announce an offer of temporary exclusion until the fol-
      lowing March. Redmond spent the next three months resisting exclusion proposals.
      To assert that he acceded to Ulster exclusion, much less partition, in the autumn of
      1913 is inaccurate. Mulvagh, *Irish Parliamentary Party at Westminster*, p. 107.
81   T.P. O'Connor to John Dillon, 27 November 1913 (TCD, Dillon Papers, MS
      6740); memorandum, 27 November 1913 (TCD, Dillon Papers, MS 6748).

82 Copy of a letter from H.H. Asquith to King George V, 26 November 1913 (RA PS/PSO/GV/C/K/2553/2/94).

83 'Further notes on the movement in Ulster', 10 November 1913 (PA, Lloyd George Papers, LGC/19/3/10).

84 David, *Hobhouse Diaries*, p. 152.

85 'Power to Prevent Importation of Arms &c. into Ulster' memorandum, 26 November 1913 (Bodl., Birrell Papers, MS Eng. 7035); 'Illegalities in Ulster' memorandum, 29 November 1913 (PA, Lloyd George Papers, LG/C/19/3/11).

86 'Extract from Prime Minister's Report of Cabinet Meeting of Decr 1st 1913', 2 December 1913 (RA PS/PSO/GV/C/K/2553/3/8).

87 Gwynn, *John Redmond*, p. 246.

88 Michael Tierney, *Eoin MacNeill: Scholar and man of action, 1867–1945*, ed. F.X. Martin (Oxford: Clarendon Press, 1980), p. 125.

89 Fanning, *Fatal Path*, p. 94.

90 For example, 'Further Notes on the Movement in Ulster', 10 November 1913 (PA, Lloyd George Papers, LG/C/19/3/10); 'Power to Prevent Importation of Arms &c. into Ulster' memorandum, 26 November 1913 (Bodl., Birrell Papers, MS Eng. 7035); 'Illegalities in Ulster' memorandum, 29 November 1913 (PA, Lloyd George Papers, LG/C/19/3/11).

91 Fanning, *Fatal Path*, p. 94.

92 If, as the evidence suggests, the proclamation was not issued in response to the formation of the nationalist Irish Volunteer force, there is no doubt that it was *enforced* with greater vigour in the south of Ireland, as Asquith later acknowledged in the House of Commons. *Times*, 17 June 1914.

93 John Dillon to T.P. O'Connor, 27 November 1913 (TCD, Dillon Papers, MS 6740).

94 T.P. O'Connor to John Dillon, 27 November 1913 (TCD, Dillon Papers, MS 6740). Though O'Connor suggested that awareness of the Irish Volunteers might have been one of the factors prompting the Cabinet to act, this does not mean that the emergence of a nationalist militia was perceived as a threat equal to that posed by the Ulster Volunteers. It must be remembered, too, that at the time O'Connor was writing, the only arms or ammunition to be seized were in the hands of, or bound for, the UVF.

95 Memorandum, 13 December 1913 (Bodl., MS Asquith 39).

96 'December 1913' memorandum, n.d. (Bodl., MS Asquith 39).

97 T.P. O'Connor to John Dillon, 17 December 1913 (TCD, Dillon Papers, MS 6740).

98 Jalland, *Liberals and Ireland*, pp. 180, 185.

99 Lord Stamfordham to King George V, 1 January 1914 (RA PS/PSO/GV/C/K/2553/3/46).

100 John Dillon to T.P. O'Connor, 20 December 1913 (TCD, Dillon Papers, MS 6740).

101 H.H. Asquith to Margot Asquith, 1 February 1914 (Bodl., Margot Asquith Papers, MS Eng. 6691).

102 Jalland, *Liberals and Ireland*, p. 159.

103 Meeting notes, 4 January 1914 (Bodl., MS Asquith 39).

104 Sir Edward Carson to H.H. Asquith, 7 January 1914 (Bodl., MS Asquith 39).

105 John Dillon to C.P. Scott, 5 January 1914 (TCD, Dillon Papers, MS 6843).

106 Extracts from a letter from Lord Morley to Lord Esher, 1 January 1914 (RA PS/PSO/GV/C/K/2553/3/56).

107 Fitzroy, *Memoirs*, vol. ii, p. 532.
108 Lord Morley to H.H. Asquith, 7 January 1914 (Bodl., MS Asquith 39).
109 Ibid.
110 Lord Esher to King George V, 6 January 1914, Brett (ed.), *Esher Journals*, vol. 3, p. 151.
111 Lord Stamfordham memorandum, 12 January 1914 (RA PS/PSO/GV/C/K/2553/3/62).
112 Brigadier General J.E. Gough claimed that the talk in the officers' mess was that sixty per cent of officers ordered to Ulster would refuse to go, and that thirty per cent of those not ordered into action would resign. Senior officers found the prospect of being the instrument of coercing Ulster intolerable, he reported, particularly at the behest of radicals and Irish nationalists who had been disloyal during the South African War. Lord Stamfordham memorandum, 7 November 1913 (RA PS/PSO/GV/C/K/2553/2/77).
113 Lord Stamfordham memorandum, 12 January 1914 (RA PS/PSO/GV/C/K/2553/3/62).
114 David, *Hobhouse Diaries*, p. 157. The king's peace continued to be disturbed by advice from Unionists to insist upon a general election over the Ulster question, to command Asquith to convene a cross-party conference, or to withhold the royal assent. George V had no wish, however, to be thrust to the centre of the controversy by appearing to act in a partisan manner. See, for example, Lord Esher to Lord Stamfordham, 28 December 1913, Brett (ed.), *Esher Journals*, vol. 3, p. 148; Lord Stamfordham memoranda, 8 November, 31 December 1913 (RA PS/PSO/GV/C/K/2553/2/81, PS/PSO/GV/C/K/2553/3/45); Lord Knollys to Lord Stamfordham, 3 December 1913 (RA PS/PSO/GV/C/K/2553/3/6).
115 David, *Hobhouse Diaries*, p. 157.
116 H.H. Asquith to Margot Asquith, 25 January 1914 (Bodl., Margot Asquith Papers, MS Eng. 6691).
117 Memorandum, 2 February 1914 (NLI, Redmond Papers, MS 15165/4). The Army Annual Bill authorised the maintenance of a standing army. It was widely reported that Unionists were considering using their majority in the House of Lords to amend the bill to forbid coercive operations in Ulster. Jeremy Smith argued that hints of this extreme tactic were intended to rattle the Liberals and hearten Unionist supporters, but that it was deemed potentially too toxic with the electorate to be seriously contemplated. However, Bonar Law wrote to a colleague in January 1914 that if Asquith refused to dissolve Parliament after the peers tampered with the Army Bill, 'from a party point of view that would be advantageous for us, I think, for it would mean bloodshed in Ulster'. Jeremy Smith, 'Bluff, Bluster and Brinkmanship: Andrew Bonar Law and the third Home Rule Bill', *Historical Journal*, vol. 36, no. 1 (March 1993), p. 177; idem, *The Tories and Ireland: Conservative Party politics and the Home Rule Crisis, 1910–1914* (Dublin: Irish Academic Press, 2000), p. 191; Andrew Bonar Law to Lord Lansdowne, 30 January 1914 (BL, Bowood Papers, Add. MS 88906/27/7).
118 Memorandum, 2 February 1914 (NLI, Redmond Papers, MS 15165/4).
119 Jalland, *Liberals and Ireland*, p. 191.
120 'The Leviathan' was Asquith's nickname for Redmond in his correspondence with Stanley. It is unclear whether this was intended to mock the Irish leader's short stature or his mental powers, which Asquith does not appear to have held in high regard.

121 H.H. Asquith to Venetia Stanley, 3 February 1914 (Bodl., Venetia Stanley Papers, MS Eng. 7091).

122 John Redmond to H.H. Asquith, 4 February 1914 (Bodl., MS Asquith 39).

123 Ibid.

124 Augustine Birrell to John Redmond, 4 February 1914 (NLI, Redmond Papers, MS 15169/4).

125 H.H. Asquith to Venetia Stanley, 5 February 1914 (Bodl., Venetia Stanley Papers, MS Eng. 7091); Augustine Birrell to John Redmond, 5 February 1914 (NLI, Redmond Papers, MS 15165/4).

126 Augustine Birrell to John Redmond, 9 February 1914 (NLI, Redmond Papers, MS 15169/4).

127 Bew, *Ideology and the Irish Question*, p. 103; Fitzroy, *Memoirs*, vol. ii, p. 536.

128 Memorandum, 16 February 1914 (Bodl., MS Asquith 39).

129 Memorandum, n.d. (NLI, Redmond Papers, MS 15266).

130 Memorandum, 23 February 1914 (TCD, Dillon Papers, MS 6754).

131 T.P. Gill to Robert Borden, 11 February 1914 (NLI, Gill Papers, MS 13486 (2)).

132 Robert Borden to T.P. Gill, n.d. (NLI, Gill Papers, MS 13486 (2)).

133 W.G.S. Adams to T.P. Gill, 27 February 1914 (NLI, Gill Papers, MS 13486 (3)).

134 T.P. Gill to John Redmond, 4 March 1914 (NLI, Gill Papers, MS 13486 (4)).

135 David, *Hobhouse Diaries*, pp. 161–2.

136 Memorandum, 27 February 1914 (NLI, Redmond Papers, MS 15257/2).

137 Diary entry, 9 March 1914 (Bodl., Margot Asquith Papers, MS Eng. 6691).

138 Note, n.d. (NLI, Redmond Papers, MS 15189).

139 Ó Broin, *Chief Secretary*, p. 85.

140 Memorandum, 2 March 1914 (Bodl., MS Asquith 39).

141 H.H. Asquith to John Redmond, 4 March 1914 (NLI, Redmond Papers, MS 15165/4).

142 Joseph Devlin to John Redmond, 4 March 1914 (NLI, Redmond Papers, MS 15181/3).

143 Joseph Devlin to John Redmond, 5 March 1914 (NLI, Redmond Papers, MS 15181/3).

144 Joseph Devlin to John Redmond, 6 March 1914 (NLI, Redmond Papers, MS 15181/3).

145 H.H. Asquith to John Redmond, 7 March 1914 (NLI, Redmond Papers, MS 15165/4).

146 Copy of a letter from H.H. Asquith to King George V, 14 November 1913 (RA PS/PSO/GV/C/K/2553/2/84); Lord Stamfordham memorandum, 13 December 1913 (RA PS/PSO/GV/C/K/2553/3/45).

147 Lord Stamfordham memorandum, 7 March 1914 (RA PS/PSO/GV/C/K/2553/4/11).

148 Gwynn, *John Redmond*, p. 394; Jackson, *Home Rule*, p. 172; diary entry, 10 July 1914 (Bodl., Margot Asquith diaries, MS Eng. d. 3210).

149 'Bonar Lisa' was Asquith's epithet for the Unionist leader, Redmond was 'The Leviathan', and Montagu was mocked as 'Cassandra-Tante' or 'The Assyrian'. Brock and Brock (eds), *Letters to Venetia Stanley*, p. 19.

150 Margot Asquith ranked the Irish third on her list of least favoured nationalities, after Americans and the Welsh. She recorded, however, that she 'always liked' Carson, whom she found 'much more truthful & genuine' than 'typical' Irishmen.

Redmond was pronounced 'a real bore', whose society, thankfully, only infrequently had to be endured. Diary entries, n.d.; 19 November 1913, 10 February 1914 (Bodl., Margot Asquith diaries, MS Eng. d. 3210); Jenkins, *Asquith*, p. 320.

151 See also Jackson, *Judging Redmond and Carson*, p. 115.

152 Maume, *Long Gestation*, p. 143.

153 Memorandum, 5 May 1914 (Bodl., MS Asquith 39).

154 There was also, of course, a strong financial incentive for the nationalists to seek to restrict the area of Ulster to be excluded, as the sum transferred to the Irish parliament would be reduced in proportion to the sources of revenue excluded from its jurisdiction. Unionists charged that nationalists wanted Ulster only for her tax revenues.

155 Lyons, *Culture and Anarchy in Ireland, 1890–1939* (Oxford: Clarendon Press, 1979), pp. 82–5, 143–5.

156 Bourke, *Peace in Ireland*, pp. 269–70.

157 Stephen Gwynn, *John Redmond's Last Years* (London: Arnold, 1926), p. 103, cited in Bew, *Ideology and the Irish Question*, pp. 105–7; Jackson, *Home Rule*, p. 162.

158 T.P. Gill to John Redmond, 8 March 1914 (NLI, Gill Papers, MS 13486 (4)).

159 David Marquand, *Ramsay MacDonald* (London: Cape, 1977), p. 159.

160 Ibid. pp. 159–60.

161 Clarke, *Lancashire and the New Liberalism*, p. 285.

162 Marquand, *Ramsay MacDonald*, p. 161.

163 Jalland, *Liberals and Ireland*, p. 196.

164 H.H. Asquith to Venetia Stanley, 16 March 1914 (Bodl., Venetia Stanley Papers, MS Eng. 7092).

165 Sir Horace Plunkett's proposed scheme, to exclude Ulster by plebiscite after a test period, was introduced in an article in *The Times*, 10 February 1914.

166 T.P. Gill to John Redmond, 18 March 1914 (NLI, Gill Papers, MS 13486 (4)).

167 Fitzroy, *Memoirs*, vol. ii, p. 541.

168 H.H. Asquith to Venetia Stanley, 16 March 1914 (Bodl., Venetia Stanley Papers, MS Eng. 7092).

169 Fitzroy, *Memoirs*, vol. ii, p. 541.

170 Diary entry, 19 March 1914 (Bodl., Margot Asquith diaries, MS Eng. d. 3210).

171 James Douglas to H.H. Asquith, 21 March 1914 (Bodl., MS Asquith 36). Douglas' alternative proposal of exclusion until the implementation of a federal scheme was similar to that advanced by Carson in his interview with the prime minister the previous December. Memorandum, 13 December 1913 (Bodl., MS Asquith 39).

172 *Times*, 25 March 1914.

173 Jalland, *Liberals and Ireland*, p. 205; memorandum, n.d. (Bodl., MS Asquith 39.

174 Randall Davidson to H.H. Asquith, 22 March 1914 (Bodl., MS Asquith 39).

175 Memorandum, n.d. (Bodl., MS Asquith 39).

176 David, *Hobhouse Diaries*, p. 163.

177 Memorandum, 6 March 1914 (Bodl., Birrell Papers, MS 7035).

178 Jalland, *Liberals and Ireland*, p. 222.

179 'Prime Minister to the King' Cabinet report, 18 March 1914 (Bodl., MS Asquith 4).

180 Jalland, *Liberals and Ireland*, pp. 223–9.

181 Ibid. p. 230.

182 Ibid. pp. 231–3.

183 Fitzroy, *Memoirs*, vol. ii, p. 543.

184 H.H. Asquith to Venetia Stanley, 22 March 1914 (Bodl., Venetia Stanley Papers, MS Eng. 7092).

185 Jenkins, *Asquith*, p. 310.

186 Diary entry, 23 March 1914 (Bodl., Margot Asquith diaries, MS Eng. 3210).

187 Historians to have asserted in recent years that the incident was an unambiguous mutiny include Keith Jeffery and Ronan Fanning. See Keith Jeffery, *Field Marshal Sir Henry Wilson: A political soldier* (Oxford: Oxford University Press, 2006), p. 124; Fanning, *Fatal Path*, p. 112.

188 The response of the Unionist press was instantaneous. Margot Asquith, returning to London the Monday after the resignations, observed large placards bearing the slogan 'The Plot that Failed' all over the city. Diary entry, 23 March 1914 (Bodl., Margot Asquith diaries, MS Eng. 3210).

189 'The State of Ireland' memorandum, 24 November 1914 (Bodl., Birrell Papers, MS 7035).

190 Jalland, *Liberals and Ireland*, p. 226.

191 Major General Charles Fergusson's confidential post-mortem on the Curragh Incident cited the widely held belief that officers holding high appointments in and out of the War Office were in communication with the Ulster Unionists, and were intent on obstructing the government and the army council. 'Report by Major General Sir Charles Fergusson', 19 April 1914, quoted in Ian W. Beckett (ed.), *The Army and the Curragh Incident, 1914* (London: Bodley Head, 1986), p. 368.

192 Wilson, having done everything in his power to ensure the downfall of Sir John French, cheerily related to Bonar Law his hopes of precipitating a Cabinet split by causing the resignations of Seely, Morley and Haldane. Fanning, *Fatal Path*, p. 115.

193 Diary entries 23, 24 March 1914 (Bodl., Margot Asquith diaries, MS Eng. d. 3210).

194 H.H. Asquith to Venetia Stanley, 25 March 1914 (Bodl., Venetia Stanley Papers, MS Eng. 7092). This revealing motto originated from the Disraeli novel *Henrietta Temple*: 'What we anticipate seldom occurs; but what we least expect generally happens.'

195 T.P. Gill to John Redmond, 30 March 1914 (NLI, Gill Papers, MS 13486 (4)).

196 T.P. Gill to W.G.S. Adams, n.d. (NLI, Gill Papers, MS 13486 (5)).

197 T.P. Gill to John Redmond, 30 March 1914 (NLI, Gill Papers, MS 13486 (4)).

198 Sir Francis Hopwood to Lord Stamfordham, 24 March 1914 (RA PS/PSO/GV/C/K/2553/4/46).

199 Lord Stamfordham memorandum, 19 March 1914 (RA PS/PSO/GV/C/K/2553/4/33). George V's position throughout was that it was for the politicians to decide whether Ireland should have Home Rule, but that the monarch should do everything in his power to avoid civil war. Lord Stamfordham memorandum, 5 February 1914 (RA PS/PSO/GV/C/K/2553/3/83).

200 Lord Stamfordham memorandum, 26 March 1914 (RA PS/PSO/GV/C/K/2553/4/51).

201 Fitzroy, *Memoirs*, vol. ii, p. 547.

202 A memorandum circulated to senior Unionists in April 1914 stressed the 'importance to us on party grounds to force an election before the Plural Voting Bill can become law'. Such an election, it submitted, could 'be forced by the setting up

of a Provisional Government' in Ulster. The potential for such a step being cast as a rebellion against the king and the imperial parliament militated in favour of delaying secession, its author counselled, perhaps until the first meeting of the Irish parliament. The Unionists detested the prospect of universal manhood suffrage no less than the abolition of plural voting, but this was politically awkward to oppose. It was privately predicted that the two electoral reforms could lose the Tories 105 seats in the House of Commons. 'Private and Confidential' memorandum, 4 April 1914 (Bodl., Milner Papers, MS dep. 96).

203   Grace A. Jones, 'Further Thoughts on the Franchise', *Past & Present*, no. 34 (July 1966), pp. 136–7.

204   Ian Packer, *Lloyd George, Liberalism and the Land: The land issue and party politics in England, 1906–1914* (Woodbridge: Boydell Press, 2001), p. 136.

205   Brooks, *Age of Upheaval*, p. 153.

206   'Report', 24 February 1914 (BL, Bowood Papers, Add. MS 88906/27/10). Jeremy Smith mentioned plural voting only in the context of the potential for its abolition to impair Unionist electoral prospects. Smith, *Tories and Ireland*, p. 40.

207   'Memorandum on the Present Political Situation' (attributed to F.S. Oliver), 3 March 1914 (RA PS/PSO/GV/C/K/2553/4/4).

208   Lord Stamfordham memorandum, 26 March 1914 (RA PS/PSO/GV/C/K/2553/4/51).

209   Winston Churchill to David Lloyd George, 3 April 1914 (PA, Lloyd George Papers, LG/C/3/16/11).

210   Petition, n.d. (Bodl., MS Asquith 39); Jalland, *Liberals and Ireland*, p. 250.

211   'Suggestions of a Settlement of the Irish Question' memorandum, n.d. (BL, Bowood Papers, Add. MS 88906/27/10).

212   'Suggestions for a Settlement of the Irish Question' memorandum, 6 April 1914 (NLI, Redmond Papers, MS 15266; Bodl., MS Asquith 39).

213   The Larne gunrunning coup was made possible by the support of a secretive group of wealthy Unionists, who financed the UVF. Among the largest amounts pledged to the Ulster cause were £30,000 from Waldorf Astor, and £10,000 each from Lord Rothschild, Lord Iveagh, the Duke of Bedford and a 'Mr Morrison'. Substantial donations were also promised by Australian graziers Sir Samuel McCaughey and J.S. Horsfall, stockbroker Sir Alexander Henderson, the Duke of Portland, and bankers Herbert Gosling and Sir Ernest Cassel. The British fund to support the UVF's activities stood, at one point, in excess of £30,000. 'Very Secret' memorandum, n.d. (Bodl., Milner Papers, MS dep. 156).

214   Gwynn, *John Redmond*, pp. 224–5.

215   David, *Hobhouse Diaries*, p. 169.

216   'Prime Minister to the King' Cabinet report, 27 April 1914 (Bodl., MS Asquith 4).

217   'Prime Minister to the King' Cabinet report, 2 May 1914 (Bodl., MS Asquith 4); (RA PS/PSO/GV/C/K/2553/5/13); Lord Stamfordham memorandum, 17 May 1914 (RA PS/PSO/GV/C/K/2553/5/28). Asquith told the king that the nationalist leaders strongly advised against taking action against the Larne gunrunners, fearing the creation of martyrs for the Ulster cause. The influence of Devlin was said to have been instrumental in halting prosecution. Lord Stamfordham memorandum, 15 May 1914 (RA PS/PSO/GV/C/K/2553/5/27); *Hibernian Journal*, January 1964, p. 53.

218   For example, *Times*, 30 April, 4 May 1914.

219 Edward Grigg to David Lloyd George, 24 April 1914 (PA, Lloyd George Papers, LG/C/4/15/1); *Times*, 2, 30 April, 2 May 1914.
220 Sir Francis Hopwood to Lord Stamfordham, 7 April 1914 (RA PS/PSO/ GV/C/K/2553/4/60).
221 Diary entry, 23 April 1914 (Bodl., Hopwood diaries, MS Eng. e. 3611/2).
222 Sir Francis Hopwood to Lord Stamfordham, 1 May 1914 (RA PS/PSO/ GV/C/K/2553/5/9).
223 John Redmond to H.H. Asquith, 28 April 1914 (Bodl., MS Asquith 39).
224 Memorandum, 5 May 1914 (Bodl., MS Asquith 39). The newspaper extract is not preserved in the Asquith Papers, but from the content and tone of Healy's speech at Castletownroche, County Cork on 2 May, it seems reasonable to speculate that this was what Redmond enclosed. It was the only public address by Healy reported by *The Times* or many of the Irish newspapers in over a fortnight.
225 *Irish Independent*, 4 May 1914.
226 H.H. Asquith to John Redmond, 6 May 1914 (Bodl., MS Asquith 39).
227 'Note of the Prime Minister's Meeting with B. Law and Sir E. Carson', 5 May 1914 (Bodl., MS Asquith 7).
228 'So the P.M. has learned something at the War Office', commented Lord Esher. Lord Esher to Lord Stamfordham, 10 May 1914, Brett (ed.), *Esher Journals*, vol. 3, p. 166.
229 H.H. Asquith to Venetia Stanley, 7 May 1914 (Bodl., Venetia Stanley Papers, MS Eng. 7092).
230 Fitzroy, *Memoirs*, vol. ii, p. 547.
231 *Times*, 13 May 1914; *Nation*, 16 May 1914.
232 The prime minister told the king that his announcement of the amending bill 'had not been at all popular with his Party'. His speech had been coldly received, a reception in contrast to loud Liberal and nationalist cheers for Redmond's 'decidedly antagonistic' response. Asquith also related the annoyance of Liberal members at the decision not to prosecute the Larne gunrunners. His position, he reportedly told the monarch, 'was not, for the moment, a strong one'. Lord Stamfordham memorandum, 17 May 1914 (RA PS/PSO/GV/C/K/2553/5/28).
233 John Redmond to Augustine Birrell, 15 May 1914 (NLI, Redmond Papers, MS 15520).
234 John Redmond to Percy Illingworth, 12 January 1914 (NLI, Redmond Papers, MS 15257/2).
235 John Redmond to Augustine Birrell, 15 May 1914 (NLI, Redmond Papers, MS 15520).
236 Ibid.
237 Hopwood recounted to Stamfordham the views of the 'old humbug' Lord Pirrie, a Home Ruler but eminently well connected in the Belfast business community: 'In spite of all that is going on, opinion among Ulster business men [Pirrie told him] is steadily growing in favour of trying to get on with a Dublin Parliament. – If we can tide over the crisis and there is good management, Ulster will soon come in.' This latter statement implies a presumption that the province or parts thereof would exclude themselves from Home Rule's initial operation. Sir Francis Hopwood to Lord Stamfordham, 19 May 1914 (RA PS/PSO/GV/C/K/2553/5/29).
238 'Synopsis of County Inspectors' Reports for the Month of March 1914' (NA, CO 904/93).

239   'Inspector-General's Confidential Report for the Month of May 1914' (NA, CO 904/93); 'Synopsis of County Inspectors' Reports for the Month of May 1914' (NA, CO 904/93).

240   'Synopsis of County Inspectors' Reports for the Month of May 1914' (NA, CO 904/93).

241   *Times*, 1 May, 2 June 1914.

242   'Inspector-General's Confidential Report for the Month of May 1914' (NA, CO 904/93).

243   'Synopsis of County Inspectors' Reports for the Month of June 1914' (NA, CO 904/93).

244   'Note of the Prime Minister's Meeting with B. Law and Sir E. Carson', 5 May 1914 (Bodl., MS Asquith 7); Lord Stamfordham memorandum, 15 May 1914 (RA PS/PSO/GV/C/K/2553/5/27).

245   H.H. Asquith to Venetia Stanley, 13 May 1914 (Bodl., Venetia Stanley Papers, MS Eng. 7092).

246   John Redmond to Augustine Birrell, 22 May 1914 (NLI, Redmond Papers, MS 15520).

247   Augustine Birrell to John Redmond, 23 May 1914 (NLI, Redmond Papers, MS 15520).

248   Wilfrid Scawen Blunt, *My Diaries: Being a personal narrative of events, 1888–1914*, vol. ii (London: Martin Secker, 1920), p. 444.

249   H.H. Asquith to Margot Asquith, 28 May, 30 May 1914 (Bodl., Margot Asquith Papers, MS Eng. 6691).

250   T.P. Gill to John Redmond, 3 June 1914 (NLI, Gill Papers, MS 13486 (7)).

251   T.P. Gill to John Redmond, 6 June 1914 (NLI, Gill Papers, MS 13486 (7)).

252   Alec Wilson to John Redmond, 20 June 1914 (NLI, Redmond Papers, MS 15257 (3)).

253   If the proposal was an authorised initiative, it also contradicts Paul Bew's judgement that the incidents at the Curragh and Larne had made any Unionist concession impossible. Bew, *John Redmond*, p. 36.

254   Redmond had a low opinion of Wilson, whom, Gill believed, was mistrusted in the north for his self-seeking ambition. John Redmond to Charles MacHugh, 14 November 1914 (TCD, Dillon Papers, MS 6748); T.P. Gill to John Redmond, 3 June 1914 (NLI, Gill Papers, MS 13486 (7)).

255   H.H. Asquith to Margot Asquith, 4 June 1914 (Bodl., Margot Asquith Papers, MS Eng. 6691).

256   Upon hearing this, Lord Morley exclaimed, 'We lawyers know! What a little Welsh attorney! He might as well have said we financiers!' Fitzroy, *Memoirs*, vol. ii, p. 551.

257   Fitzroy, *Memoirs*, vol. ii, p. 552. Both men found their interviews with the monarch distressing. The king appealed to Crewe, as a lifelong friend, not to place him in such a position; Crewe reportedly did not reply. Brett (ed.), *Esher Journals*, vol. 3, p. 171.

258   Fitzroy, *Memoirs*, vol. ii, p. 551.

259   Memorandum, 15 June 1914 (Bodl., Birrell Papers, MS Eng. 7035).

260   Sir Francis Hopwood to T.P. Gill, 23 May 1914 (NLI, Gill Papers, MS 13486 (5)).

Chapter 5: Home Rule in Liberal Britain

1 Diary entry, 16 August 1911 (Nuffield College Library, Oxford, J.A. Pease Papers, MS Gainford C85/33/3).
2 Peatling, *British Opinion*, pp. 72–4.
3 *Liberal Agent*, June 1913, p. 47.
4 *Freeman's Journal*, 23 February 1913.
5 *Liberal Agent*, January 1913, p. 139.
6 Ibid. January 1913, p. 145, July 1914, p. 46.
7 Ibid. July 1914, p. 185.
8 Ibid. June 1913, p. 25.
9 Ibid. July 1912, p. 28.
10 Ibid. April 1914, p. 212.
11 Ibid. April 1914, pp. 206, 212.
12 *Freeman's Journal*, 23 May 1914.
13 *Liberal Agent*, June 1913, p. 11.
14 *Times*, 23 October 1913.
15 Ibid. 16 September 1913.
16 *Reynolds's Newspaper*, 18 February 1912; *Irish Times*, 24 February 1912.
17 *Manchester Guardian*, 25 November 1912.
18 *Scotsman*, 16 September 1913; *Times*, 16 September 1913.
19 *Freeman's Journal*, 20 December 1913.
20 Ibid. 17 March 1914.
21 *Irish Times*, 19 September 1912.
22 *Observer*, 14 June 1914.
23 Anon., *Proceedings in Connection with the Thirty-second Annual Meeting of the National Liberal Federation, London, November 1910* (London: Liberal Publications Department, 1910), p. 68.
24 Anon., *Proceedings in Connection with the Thirty-fourth Annual Meeting of the National Liberal Federation, November 1912* (London: Liberal Publications Department, 1912), p. 69.
25 Anon., *Proceedings in Connection with the Thirty-fifth Annual Meeting of the National Liberal Federation, November 1913* (London: Liberal Publications Department, 1913), p. 80.
26 Diary entry, 20 January 1911 (Nuffield College Library, Oxford, J.A. Pease Papers, MS Gainford C85/33/3).
27 *Times*, 8, 21, 23 November 1912; *Daily Chronicle*, 9 November 1912; *Hansard*, 20 November 1912.
28 *Times*, 21 November 1912.
29 *Reynolds's Newspaper*, 21 April 1912.
30 *Hansard*, 20 November 1912.
31 *Nation*, 7 December 1912.
32 *Daily Chronicle*, 8 November 1912.
33 *Nation*, 22 November 1912.
34 *Hansard*, 19 November, 7 December 1912; *Daily Chronicle*, 22 November 1912.
35 Pašeta, *Irish Nationalist Women*, pp. 71–2.
36 Ibid. p. 77.
37 *Women's Liberal Federation News*, vol. iii, no. 8 (1 August 1912), p. 10.
38 'Redmond the Fox', 26 April 1912 (NLI, Francis Sheehy-Skeffington Papers, MS 40475 (2)).

39   *Women's Liberal Federation News*, vol. iii, no. 7 (1 July 1912), p. 12.
40   *Hansard*, 5 November 1912.
41   *Women's Liberal Federation News*, vol. iii, no. 12 (1 December 1912), p. 4.
42   Meleady, *John Redmond*, pp. 176–7.
43   'Notes for Interview with Mr John E. Redmond', April 1907 (NLI, Francis Sheehy-Skeffington Papers, MS 40474 (5)).
44   Trevor Wilson (ed.), *The Political Diaries of C.P. Scott, 1911–1928* (London: Collins, 1970), p. 66. Redmond's antipathy to votes for women was doubtless not diminished by physical attacks upon him by suffragettes in 1912 and 1913.
45   Wilson, *Scott Diaries*, pp. 65–6.
46   Pašeta, *Irish Nationalist Women*, pp. 64–8.
47   *Women's Liberal Federation News*, vol. iv, no. 2 (1 February 1913), p. 4.
48   *Women's Liberal Federation News*, vol. iv, no. 6 (1 June 1913), p. 18.
49   Ibid.
50   *Clarion*, 15 November 1912.
51   Pašeta, *Irish Nationalist Women*, pp. 84, 88.
52   Indeed, despite her humiliation before the WLF council meeting a year previously, Lady Carlisle sent a cheque for £300 to the Irish Volunteers' Defence of Ireland Fund in June 1914. *Times*, 2 July 1914.
53   *Irish Independent*, 7 February 1914; *Skibbereen Eagle*, 14 February 1914.
54   *Irish Independent*, 7 February 1914.
55   Ibid.
56   Quoted in the *Irish Independent*, 7 February 1914.
57   *Southern Star*, 28 February 1914.
58   *Hansard*, 24 February 1914.
59   *Freeman's Journal*, 17 March 1914.
60   Fitzroy, *Memoirs*, vol. ii, p. 529.
61   *Freeman's Journal*, 17 March 1914.
62   Diary entry, 22 April 1914 (Nuffield College Library, Oxford, J.A. Pease Papers, MS Gainford C85/33/3).
63   John Ward (1866–1934) was a trade unionist, politician and soldier who worked as a labourer from the age of seven and at the age of twenty-one became a labour agitator, alongside Tom Mann and John Burns. He represented Stoke-on-Trent as Lib-Lab MP from 1906 until his retirement in 1929. In the First World War, Ward raised the 'Navvies' Battalion', a unit in which he served as a colonel. A burly man over six feet tall, Ward was an instantly recognisable figure in his accustomed attire of a reefer jacket, large-brimmed hat and bell-bottomed trousers. His intervention at the time of the Curragh Incident marked the high point of his political career. *Scotsman*, 20 December 1934.
64   *Hansard*, 23 March 1914.
65   Ibid. 24 March 1914.
66   Ibid.; John Ward, *The Soldier and the Citizen* (London: T. Fisher Unwin, 1914), p. 30.
67   *Times*, 26 March 1914.
68   *Nation*, 28 March 1914.
69   *Saturday Westminster Gazette*, 28 March 1914.
70   *Freeman's Journal*, 17 March 1914.
71   *Times*, 23 April 1914.
72   *Daily News and Leader*, 14 May 1914.

73 *Reynolds's Newspaper*, 29 March 1914.
74 *Irish Independent*, 4 April 1914.
75 *Freeman's Journal*, 14 May 1914.
76 Ibid.
77 *Daily News and Leader*, 14 May 1914.
78 *Ulster Herald*, 16 May 1914.
79 'Annual Report, 21 May 1914' (U. Bris. Lib., Liberal Central Association minute book, DM 1913).
80 *Daily News and Leader, Manchester Guardian, Irish Times*, 19 May 1914.
81 *Times*, 3 June 1914.
82 *Manchester Guardian*, 3 June 1914.
83 Ward, *Soldier and Citizen*, pp. 46–50.
84 *Women's Liberal Federation News*, vol. v, no. 7 (1 July 1914), p. 10.
85 This elicited laughter but no response from Birrell. *Irish Independent*, 3 July 1914.
86 *Times*, 8 July 1914.
87 *Manchester Guardian*, 18 July 1914.
88 Ibid. 20 July 1914.
89 *Sunday Independent*, 26 July 1914.
90 *Manchester Guardian*, 29 July, 1 August 1914.
91 G.H. Mair to C.P. Scott, 22 July 1914 (BL, C.P. Scott Papers, Add. MS 50908).
92 Speakers at the meeting included the Nonconformist Sir Ryland Adkins, industrialists Sir Daniel Goddard and Sir Arthur Markham, radicals Neil Primrose and Thomas Lough, social reformer Jimmy Rowlands, and the rather Whiggish Robert Harcourt. *Daily News and Leader*, 22 July 1914.
93 *Irish Independent*, 22 July 1914.
94 *Daily News and Leader*, 22 July 1914.
95 *Freeman's Journal*, 22 July 1914.
96 *Donegal News*, 25 July 1914.
97 *Daily News and Leader*, 22 July 1914.
98 *Westminster Gazette*, 22 July 1914.
99 *Freeman's Journal*, 22 July 1914.
100 *Hansard*, 20 July 1914. Ginnell, a thorn in the side of the Irish Party, was reputedly used as a mouthpiece by advanced nationalists. He was one of only two men to have served both as an MP in the House of Commons and a TD in Dáil Éireann. Major Ivan Price to James O'Connor, 22 September 1917 (NLI, Redmond Papers, MS 15204).
101 *Daily News and Leader*, 23 July 1914.
102 *Times*, 21 July 1914. By the deferential standards of 1914, the alleged partiality of the monarch came in for severe criticism in the Liberal press.
103 *Daily News and Leader*, 23 July 1914.
104 Ibid.
105 *Daily News and Leader*, 25 July 1914. Sir John Brunner was an enormously wealthy industrialist and figure of great influence among back-bench Liberals.
106 *Freeman's Journal*, 21 July 1914.
107 *Donegal News*, 25 July 1914.
108 *Sunday Independent*, 26 July 1914.
109 *Westmeath Examiner*, 1 August 1914.
110 *Times*, 30 July 1914.

111 *Freeman's Journal*, 30 July 1914.
112 *Reynolds's Newspaper*, 2 August 1914.
113 *Freeman's Journal*, 30 July 1914.
114 *Reynolds's Newspaper*, 2 August 1914.
115 *Freeman's Journal*, 30 July 1914.
116 *Westminster Gazette*, 30 July 1914.
117 *Manchester Guardian*, 30 July 1914.
118 *Reynolds's Newspaper*, 2 August 1914.

Chapter 6: The Ferment of Nationalism
  1 Kelly, *Fenian Ideal*, pp. 207, 210–12.
  2 Ibid. p. 208.
  3 Caoimhe Nic Dháibhéid and Colin Reid (eds), *From Parnell to Paisley: Constitutional and revolutionary politics in modern Ireland* (Dublin: Irish Academic Press, 2010), pp. 36–7.
  4 Ronan Fanning's consideration of the question cited mid-twentieth-century Conservative historian Robert Blake's dramatic visions of bloody civil war, and argued that the success of the Larne gunrunning rendered a UVF revolt more likely. Alvin Jackson's research, however, cast doubt on the Larne incident's military value, the UVF level of preparedness, and Ulster Unionist resolve more generally. Fanning, *Fatal Path*, pp. 116, 119–20, 130; Jackson, 'Unionist Myths', pp. 180, 182–3. See also Jalland, *Liberals and Ireland*, p. 260.
  5 Eoin MacNeill to J.J. Horgan, 17 December 1913, in Tierney, *Eoin MacNeill*, p. 127.
  6 Eoin MacNeill to Stephen Gwynn, 20 May 1914 (NLI, Redmond Papers, MS 15204).
  7 Ibid.
  8 M.J. Kelly, 'The Irish Volunteers: A Machiavellian moment?', in D. George Boyce and Alan O'Day (eds), *The Ulster Crisis* (Basingstoke: Palgrave Macmillan, 2006), p. 68.
  9 Nic Dháibhéid and Reid (eds), *From Parnell to Paisley*, p. 36.
 10 Ibid. p. 219.
 11 Kelly, *Fenian Ideal*, p. 214.
 12 Tierney, *Eoin MacNeill*, pp. 118–19, 122–3.
 13 Witness statement of Patrick D. Little, BMH.WS1769, Military Archives, Ireland.
 14 Tierney, *Eoin MacNeill*, p. 125.
 15 Witness statement of Liam de Róiste, BMH.WS1698, Military Archives, Ireland.
 16 Blunt, *My Diaries*, Part II, p. 442; Kelly, *Fenian Ideal*, p. 226.
 17 Eoin MacNeill to J.J. Horgan, 17 December 1913, in Tierney, *Eoin MacNeill*, p. 127.
 18 Witness statement of Kevin O'Shiel, BMH.WS1770, Military Archives, Ireland.
 19 *Irish Independent*, 9 March 1914.
 20 Foster, *Vivid Faces*, p. 195; Witness statement of Archie Heron, BMH.WS577, Military Archives, Ireland; *Skibbereen Eagle*, 16 May 1914.
 21 Witness statements of William O'Brien and Sean O'Kelly, BMH.WS1766 and BMH.WS1765, Military Archives, Ireland.
 22 Witness statement of William O'Brien, BMH.WS1766, Military Archives, Ireland.
 23 Witness statement of Cahir Davitt, BMH.WS993, Military Archives, Ireland.
 24 *Irish Independent*, 23 March 1914; *Skibbereen Eagle*, 27 March 1914.

25 *Freeman's Journal*, 27 March 1914.
26 *Anglo-Celt*, 1 April 1914.
27 *Irish Independent*, 1 April 1914.
28 *Irish Times*, 6 April 1914.
29 Ibid.
30 *Freeman's Journal*, 11 April 1914; *Irish Independent*, 2 April 1914.
31 Ibid. 25 April 1914.
32 *Freeman's Journal*, 11 April, 22 April 1914.
33 *Irish Independent*, 16 April 1914.
34 Witness statement of Liam de Róiste, BMH.WS1698, Military Archives, Ireland.
35 Witness statement of Kevin O'Shiel, BMH.WS1770, Military Archives, Ireland.
36 Witness statement of Liam de Róiste, BMH.WS1698, Military Archives, Ireland.
37 Memorandum, 28 April 1914 (NAI, CSORP, 1914/17264).
38 Michael Wheatley, *Nationalism and the Irish Party: Provincial Ireland, 1910–1916* (Oxford: Oxford University Press, 2005), pp. 188–9.
39 Darrell Figgis, *Recollections of the Irish War* (New York: Ernest Benn, 1924), p. 12.
40 Tierney, *Eoin MacNeill*, pp. 129, 142.
41 T.P. Gill to John Redmond, 5 May 1914 (NLI, Gill Papers, MS 13486 (5)).
42 Tierney, *Eoin MacNeill*, p. 132.
43 Eoin MacNeill to Stephen Gwynn, 20 May 1914 (NLI, Redmond Papers, MS 15204).
44 Witness statement of Laurence Nugent, BMH.WS907, Military Archives, Ireland.
45 Kelly, *Fenian Ideal*, p. 228; witness statement of Diarmuid Coffey, BMH.WS1248, Military Archives, Ireland.
46 T.P. Gill to John Redmond, 6 June 1914 (NLI, Gill Papers, MS 13486 (7)).
47 Ibid.
48 T.P. Gill to John Redmond, 21 May 1914 (NLI, Gill Papers, MS 13486 (5)). The elderly and disabled General Kelly-Kenny was also, rather strangely, commended to Redmond by Sir Roger Casement. Tierney, *Eoin MacNeill*, p. 138.
49 For example, McConnel, 'John Redmond and Irish Catholic Loyalism', pp. 83–111; Jackson, *Judging Redmond and Carson*, pp. 136–44.
50 Witness statement of Laurence Nugent, BMH.WS907, Military Archives, Ireland; Gwynn, *John Redmond*, p. 245.
51 Thomas Plunkett to Provisional Committee, 14 June 1914 (NLI, Thomas MacDonagh Papers, MS 20643/9).
52 Tierney, *Eoin MacNeill*, pp. 139–40.
53 Headlam, *Irish Reminiscences*, pp. 140–1.
54 Captain Galligan to Thomas MacDonagh, n.d. (NLI, Thomas MacDonagh Papers, MS 20643/10).
55 Wheatley, *Nationalism*, pp. 190–5.
56 Witness statement of Liam de Róiste, BMH.WS1698, Military Archives, Ireland.
57 Memoranda 12, 27 June, 8 July 1914 (NAI, CSORP, 1914/17264).
58 *Hansard*, 9, 10 July 1914.
59 'Extract from the Inspector General's Monthly Report for May, 1914 – to the Under Secretary', n.d. (RA PS/PSO/GV/C/K/2553/5/15).
60 *Irish Times*, 13 June 1914.
61 Alec Wilson to John Redmond, 20 June 1914 (NLI, Redmond Papers, MS 15257 (3)).

62   Memorandum, 15 June 1914 (Bodl., Birrell Papers, MS 7035).
63   Pašeta, *Irish Nationalist Women*, pp. 135–7.
64   Ibid. p. 142.
65   *Sunday Independent*, 26 July 1914.
66   *Irish Independent*, 9 May, 22 August 1914.
67   *Westmeath Examiner*, 1 August 1914; *Irish Independent*, 24 August 1914; *Limerick Leader*, 31 August 1914.
68   *Daily Express*, 26 June 1914.
69   *Cork Free Press*, 2 June 1914; *Irish Independent*, 4 June 1914.
70   *Scotsman*, 4 June 1914.
71   J. Murphy to John Redmond, 21 June 1914, John McCafferty to John Redmond, 22 June 1914 (NLI, Redmond Papers, MS 15257 (3)).
72   This was probably a reference to The O'Rahilly. *Kildare Observer*, 20 June 1914.
73   *Meath Chronicle*, 27 June 1914; *Leitrim Observer*, 27 June 1914.
74   Witness statement of Kevin O'Shiel, BMH.WS1770, Military Archives, Ireland.
75   *Irish Independent*, 18 June 1914.
76   *Derry People*, 19 June 1914.
77   *Irish Times*, 27 June 1914.
78   *Irish Independent*, 29 June 1914.
79   *Irish Times*, 16 June 1914.
80   *Kildare Observer*, 13 June 1914.
81   *Irish Independent*, 8 July 1914.
82   Memorandum, n.d. (BL, Bowood Papers, Add. MS 88906/27/10).
83   *Anglo-Celt*, 2 May 1914.
84   *Daily News and Leader*, 2 June 1914.
85   *Irish Independent*, 15 June 1914.
86   Ibid.
87   *Irish Times*, 10 March, 25 May 1914.
88   Séamas Ó Buachalla (ed.), *The Letters of P.H. Pearse* (Gerrards Cross: Colin Smythe, 1980), p. 322.
89   Diary entry, 24 September 1914 (NLI, Diarmuid Coffey diaries, MS 46308/3).
90   Witness statement of Laurence Nugent, BMH.WS907, Military Archives, Ireland.
91   Witness statement of Liam de Róiste, BMH.WS1698, Military Archives, Ireland.
92   *Freeman's Journal*, 18 June 1914.
93   Walter D'Alton to T.P. Gill, 21 June 1914 (NLI, Gill Papers, MS 13486 (7)).
94   Ibid.
95   Circular to resident magistrates, 27 June 1914 (NAI, CSORP, 1914/14397).
96   Report of Belfast and Omagh resident magistrates, 27, 30 June 1914 (NAI, CSORP, 1914/14397).
97   Report of Omagh resident magistrate, 27 June 1914 (NAI, CSORP, 1914/14397).
98   Report of Bandon resident magistrate, 8 July 1914 (NAI, CSORP, 1914/14397).
99   Report of Sligo resident magistrate, 27 June 1914 (NAI, CSORP, 1914/14397).
100 Report of Ballinrobe resident magistrate, 29 June 1914 (NAI, CSORP, 1914/14397).
101 Reports of resident magistrates (NAI, CSORP, 1914/14397).
102 Dougherty's subordinates may also have been trying to cater to their chief's dismissive view of pessimistic provincial reports. Bew, *Ideology and the Irish Question*, p. 93.
103 Synopsis of reports of resident magistrates, 14 July 1914 (NAI, CSORP, 1914/14397).

104 Catriona Pennell, *A Kingdom United: Popular responses to the outbreak of the First World War in Britain and Ireland* (Oxford: Oxford University Press, 2012), pp. 196–7.

105 Beckett (ed.), *The Curragh Incident*, p. 320.

106 Diary entries, 8, 10, 27 August, 2 September 1914 (NLI, Diarmuid Coffey diaries, MS 46308/3).

107 Lord Stamfordham memorandum, 9 May 1914 (RA PS/PSO/GV/C/K/2553/5/21). MacCready was later to downplay the rebellious intentions and capabilities of the physical-force nationalists.

108 Witness statement of Liam de Róiste, BMH.WS1698, Military Archives, Ireland.

109 *Daily Chronicle*, 28 July 1914.

110 *Irish Independent*, 27 July 1914.

111 *Westminster Gazette*, 30 July 1914.

112 Ibid. 24 July 1914.

113 *Daily Chronicle*, 28 July 1914.

114 Similar language of a sanguinary baptism was used by *Irish Freedom*. Ó Buachalla (ed.), *Letters of Pearse*, p. 322.

115 Blunt, *My Diaries*, part ii, p. 446.

116 Kelly, *Fenian Ideal*, p. 188. Sales of *Sinn Féin* slumped to just half of their 1911 high of two thousand copies. Newspaper sales figures (Eason and Son Archive, EAS/A1/6/1/3/2).

117 Witness statement of Kevin O'Shiel, BMH.WS1770, Military Archives, Ireland.

118 Tierney, *Eoin MacNeill*, p. 144.

119 Blunt, *My Diaries*, part ii, p. 474.

120 Nic Dháibhéid and Reid (eds), *From Parnell to Paisley*, pp. 41–2.

121 Witness statement of Sean O'Kelly, BMH.WS1765, Military Archives, Ireland.

122 Francis Sheehy-Skeffington to George Lansbury, 3 August 1914 (NLI, Francis Sheehy-Skeffington Papers, MS 33612 (16)).

123 Witness statement of Liam de Róiste, BMH.WS1698, Military Archives, Ireland.

124 Witness statement of Kevin O'Shiel, BMH.WS1770, Military Archives, Ireland.

125 Ibid. The German army's destruction of the historic library at Louvain (Leuven) and the wanton killing of civilians in the city attracted worldwide condemnation.

126 Witness statement of Liam de Róiste, BMH.WS1698, Military Archives, Ireland.

127 Witness statement of Cahir Davitt, BMH.WS993, Military Archives, Ireland. Yet this viewpoint was far from universal. One observer, much later, recalled that opponents of the Irish Party could not believe their ears when Redmond pledged Irish soldiers to a 'holocaust – the most ghastly mistake any Irish leader has made'. Robert Brennan to W.G. Fallon, 27 April 1963 (NLI, W.G. Fallon Papers, MS 22589).

128 C. McSweeny to Sir James Dougherty, 8 August 1914, James Byrne to Augustine Birrell, 7 August 1914 (NAI, CSORP, 1914/13848); Patrick Mahon to Augustine Birrell, 2 August 1914 (NAI, CSORP, 1916/24668).

129 Charles O'Conor to Sir James Dougherty, 10 August 1914, W.D. Marsh to Lord Kitchener, 4 September 1914 (NAI, CSORP, 1916/24668).

130 Diary entry, 6 August 1914 (NLI, Diarmuid Coffey diaries, MS 46308/3); witness statement of Diarmuid Coffey, BMH.WS1248, Military Archives, Ireland.

131 Diary entry, 29 August 1914 (NLI, Diarmuid Coffey diaries, MS 46308/3); witness statement of Liam de Róiste, BMH.WS1698, Military Archives, Ireland.

132 *Limerick Leader*, 4 September 1914.

133 Draft letter for publication, n.d. (NLI, Francis Sheehy-Skeffington Papers, MS 33612 (16)).
134 Wheatley, *Nationalism*, pp. 204–5.
135 *Freeman's Journal*, n.d., enclosure, T.P. Gill to Robert Donald, 25 August 1914 (NLI, Gill Papers, MS 13486 (10)).
136 Diary entries, 28 August, 3, 7 September 1914 (NLI, Diarmuid Coffey diaries, MS 46308/3).
137 Diary entries, 1, 4 September 1914 (NLI, Diarmuid Coffey diaries, MS 46308/3). Coffey recorded a colleague's judgement of MacNeill, who said of him that 'he always conspires with each man he meets against the man he conspired with last'. Foster, *Vivid Faces*, p. 208.
138 Tierney, *Eoin MacNeill*, p. 148.
139 Diary entry, 10 September 1914 (NLI, Diarmuid Coffey diaries, MS 46308/3).
140 Diary entries, 6, 10, 15 September 1914 (NLI, Diarmuid Coffey diaries, MS 46308/3).
141 Tierney, *Eoin MacNeill*, p. 148.
142 T.P. Gill to Robert Donald, 25 August 1914 (NLI, Gill Papers, MS 13486 (10)).
143 Diary entry, 7 September 1914 (NLI, Diarmuid Coffey diaries, MS 46308/3).
144 'C.S.O. Notes 1914', p. 17 (N.A., CO 903/18); *Irish Independent*, 11 September 1914.
145 T.P. Gill to John Redmond, 12 September 1914 (NLI, Gill Papers, MS 13486 (11)).
146 *Irish Times*, 16 September 1914.
147 Diary entry, 15 September 1914 (NLI, Diarmuid Coffey diaries, MS 46308/3). Accusations of imperialism haunted the Young Ireland Branch in subsequent months, and eventually resulted in the branch's dissolution. Witness statement of Patrick J. Little, BMH.WS1769, Military Archives, Ireland.
148 Witness statement of Laurence Nugent, BMH.WS907, Military Archives, Ireland.
149 Diary entries, 21, 24 September 1914 (NLI, Diarmuid Coffey diaries, MS 46308/3).
150 Witness statement of Kevin O'Shiel, BMH.WS1770, Military Archives, Ireland.
151 Memorandum, 24 September 1914 (UCDA, Eoin MacNeill Papers, MS LA1/H).
152 *Times*, 26 September 1914.
153 Witness statement of Kevin O'Shiel, BMH.WS1770, Military Archives, Ireland.
154 Witness statement of William O'Brien, BMH.WS1766, Military Archives, Ireland.
155 *Irish Times*, 24 September 1914.
156 Pennell, *A Kingdom United*, p. 187.
157 Diary entries, 19, 24 September 1914 (NLI, Diarmuid Coffey diaries, MS 46308/3).
158 Witness statement of Cahir Davitt, BMH.WS993, Military Archives, Ireland.
159 Witness statement of Kevin O'Shiel, BMH.WS1770, Military Archives, Ireland.

Chapter 7: Impasse: Summer 1914

1 For example, Jalland, *Liberals and Ireland*, pp. 250–5; Patricia Jalland and John Stubbs, 'The Irish Question After the Outbreak of War in 1914: Some unfinished party business', *English Historical Review*, vol. 96, no. 381 (October, 1981), pp. 778–807; Chris Dooley, *Redmond: A life undone* (Dublin: Gill & Macmillan, 2015), pp. 213–25.
2 Meleady, *John Redmond*, p. 284.

3   Fanning, *Fatal Path*, p. 134.

4   'Draft of a Bill to Amend the Government of Ireland Act, 1914', 19 June 1914 (PA, Lloyd George Papers, LG/C/19/2/8).

5   Memorandum, 27 June 1914 (BL, Bowood Papers, Add. MS 88906/27/10).

6   Memoranda, 16, 27 June 1914 (BL, Bowood Papers, Add. MS 88906/27/10).

7   Diary entry, 22 June 1914 (Bodl., Margot Asquith diaries, MS Eng. d. 3210).

8   Wilson, *Scott Diaries*, p. 88.

9   Sir Francis Hopwood to Lord Stamfordham, 17 June 1914 (RA PS/PSO/GV/C/K/2553/5/52).

10 Sir Francis Hopwood to Lord Stamfordham, 20 June 1914 (RA PS/PSO/GV/C/K/2553/5/59).

11 H.H. Asquith to Venetia Stanley, 24 June 1914 (Bodl., Venetia Stanley Papers, MS Eng. 7092).

12 S.D. Waley, *Edwin Montagu: A memoir and an account of his visits to India* (London: Asia Publishing House, 1964), p. 61.

13 Lord Murray to H.H. Asquith, 30 June 1914 (Bodl., Venetia Stanley Papers, MS Eng. 7092); Gwynn, *John Redmond*, pp. 327–30.

14 Dooley, *Redmond: A life undone*, p. 190.

15 Lord Stamfordham memorandum, 2 July 1914 (RA PS/PSO/GV/C/K/2553/5/76).

16 1911 census figures (NLI, Redmond Papers, MS 15253).

17 Tom Garvin, *The Evolution of Irish Nationalist Politics* (Dublin: Gill & Macmillan, 1981), p. 112; *C.S.O. Judicial Division Intelligence Notes 1914*, p. 10 (N.A., CO 903/18); *Irish Independent*, 8 July 1914.

18 *Freeman's Journal*, 7 July 1914.

19 *Southern Star*, 4 July 1914.

20 Resident magistrate's report, 28 July 1914 (NAI, CSORP, 1914/14397).

21 Ibid.; *C.S.O. Judicial Division Intelligence Notes 1914*, p. 10 (NA, CO 903/18).

22 H.H. Asquith to Venetia Stanley, 4 July 1914 (Bodl., Venetia Stanley Papers, MS Eng. 7092); Lord Murray to H.H. Asquith, 30 June 1914 (Bodl., Venetia Stanley Papers, MS Eng. 7092).

23 H.H. Asquith to Venetia Stanley, 4 July 1914 (Bodl., Venetia Stanley Papers, MS Eng. 7092).

24 H.H. Asquith to Venetia Stanley, 6 July 1914 (Bodl., Venetia Stanley Papers, MS Eng. 7092).

25 Though the generals could not, of course, have known it, they wrote the day after Germany gave its 'blank cheque' to Austria-Hungary, emboldening the Austrians towards war with Serbia.

26 Beckett (ed.), *The Curragh Incident*, pp. 379–80. In the light of the Cabinet's agonised decision to enter the European conflict that erupted three weeks later, the contrast between the generals' sense of a lack of direction in Ireland and their apparent clarity as to Britain's Continental obligations is interesting. There appears to have been little doubt among the general staff about the extent of Britain's commitment to France. The absence of any mention of Ulster may be indicative of the generals' presumption that the south of Ireland was to be the theatre of operations there.

27 Lord Stamfordham memorandum, 5 July 1914 (RA PS/PSO/GV/C/K/2553/5/104).

28 Sir Francis Hopwood to Lord Stamfordham, 8 July 1914 (RA PS/PSO/GV/C/K/2553/5/110).

29　Sir Francis Hopwood to Lord Stamfordham, 30 June 1914 (RA PS/PSO/GV/
　　C/K/2553/5/74). Macnamara told Hopwood that Liberal disaffection arose from
　　a number of grievances, but at bottom, 'it is simply that the men are tired & sore
　　& nervous & disappointed about Ireland'.
30　Ibid. Lord Devonport was the chair of the Port of London Authority.
31　Diary entry, 10 July 1914 (Bodl., Margot Asquith diaries, MS Eng. d. 3210).
32　H.H. Asquith to Venetia Stanley, 8 July 1914 (Bodl., Venetia Stanley Papers, MS
　　Eng. 7092).
33　Lord Stamfordham memorandum, 9 July 1914 (RA PS/PSO/GV/C/K/2553/5/111).
34　Lord Stamfordham memorandum, 8 July 1914 (RA PS/PSO/GV/C/K/2553/5/108).
　　Carson claimed that he told the prime minister (the day after Mrs Asquith's clan-
　　destine meeting with Redmond) that 'the people would murder him' if he accepted
　　less than six-county exclusion.
35　Lord Stamfordham memorandum, 8 July 1914 (RA PS/PSO/GV/C/K/2553/5/108).
36　Memorandum, 21 June 1914 (BL, Bowood Papers, Add. MS 88906/27/10).
37　Waley, *Edwin Montagu*, p. 61. In lawyerly fashion, Carson continued to set his claims
　　high. He reportedly told Murray's emissary, Rothermere, that a panic in the City
　　of London occasioned by a repudiation of loan agreements by Belfast firms would
　　bring the government to its senses, forcing it to concede to Unionist demands.
38　John Redmond to H.H. Asquith, 9 July 1914 (NLI, Redmond Papers, MS 15165 (4)).
39　Lord Stamfordham memorandum, 9 July 1914 (RA PS/PSO/GV/C/K/2553/5/111).
40　Lord Stamfordham memoranda, 11 June, 9 July 1914 (RA PS/PSO/GV/C/K/
　　2553/5/48, 111).
41　Fitzroy, *Memoirs*, vol. ii, p. 556.
42　T.P. O'Connor to John Redmond, 10 July 1914 (NLI, Redmond Papers, MS 15215/
　　2/A).
43　H.H. Asquith to Venetia Stanley, 13 July 1914 (Bodl., Venetia Stanley Papers, MS
　　Eng. 7092).
44　Redmond memoranda, 13 July, 16 July 1914, in Gwynn, *John Redmond*, pp. 334–5.
45　J.A. Spender to H.H. Asquith, 14 July 1914 (Bodl., Venetia Stanley Papers, MS
　　Eng. 7092).
46　Sir Francis Hopwood to Lord Stamfordham, 14, 15 July 1914 (RA PS/PSO/GV/C/K/
　　2553/5/113, PS/PSO/GV/C/K/2553/6/1). Lord Granard was an Irish peer and
　　intimate of the king; Theobald Mathew was the brother of Dillon's wife, Elizabeth.
47　Jalland, *Liberals and Ireland*, pp. 251–2.
48　H.H. Asquith to Venetia Stanley, 15 July 1914 (Bodl., Venetia Stanley Papers, MS
　　Eng. 7092).
49　Sir Francis Hopwood to Lord Stamfordham, 15 July 1914 (RA PS/PSO/GV/C/K/
　　2553/6/2).
50　H.H. Asquith memorandum, 16 July 1914 (RA PS/PSO/GV/C/K/2553/6/5).
　　The Liberal whips had that day reported to Asquith the strength of feeling against
　　concession among the rank and file.
51　Lord Stamfordham memorandum, 16 July 1914 (RA PS/PSO/GV/C/K/2553/6/6).
52　H.H. Asquith to King George V, 17 July 1914 (RA PS/PSO/GV/C/K/2553/6/13).
53　H.H. Asquith to Lord Stamfordham, 18 July 1914 (RA PS/PSO/GV/C/K/
　　2553/6/14).
54　'Memoranda and Extracts on the Constitutional Position', n.d. (PA, Lloyd George
　　Papers, LG/C/20/2/12). Lloyd George's authorship of the undated memorandum

on the constitutional position is not certain, but since the document is collected in his papers, printed on Treasury notepaper, and its content is characteristic of his keen political instincts, it seems reasonable to assume that the arguments are his.

55   Ibid.
56   Ibid.
57   Northcliffe authorised Rothermere to disclose the source of the leak to Asquith: 'The object was to save a day in Ireland, that is to let everybody there in Ulster know about the conference before it was held.' Sir Francis Hopwood to Lord Stamfordham, 21 July 1914 (RA PS/PSO/GV/C/K/2553/6/37).
58   H.H. Asquith to Venetia Stanley, 20 July 1914 (Bodl., Venetia Stanley Papers, MS Eng. 7092).
59   For example, Gwynn, *John Redmond*, pp. 336–42; Jenkins, *Asquith*, pp. 319–22; Jalland, *Liberals and Ireland*, pp. 254–5.
60   Memorandum, 21 July 1914 (NLI, Redmond Papers, MS 15257/3).
61   'Redmond's Address', 21 July 1914 (PA, Lloyd George Papers, LG/C/20/2/9).
62   Memorandum, 21 July 1914 (NLI, Redmond Papers, MS 15257/3).
63   H.H. Asquith to Venetia Stanley, 22 July 1914 (Bodl., Venetia Stanley Papers, MS Eng. 7092).
64   Note, 23 July 1914 (NLI, Redmond Papers, MS 15169/4).
65   Mcmorandum, n.d. (PA, Lloyd George Papers, LG/C/20/2/10).
66   Memorandum, 21 July 1914 (NLI, Redmond Papers, MS 15257/3).
67   Asquith used the phrase to describe the Dublin shootings to Stanley. H.H. Asquith to Venetia Stanley, 27 July 1914 (Bodl., Venetia Stanley Papers, MS Eng. 7092).
68   Translation: 'Ireland is an incurable malady, but never a fatal one.' Diary entry, 24 July 1914 (Bodl., Margot Asquith diaries, MS Eng. d. 3210). Stamfordham recorded that Redmond, in his interview with the king at the break-up of the conference, admitted that exclusion of the whole of Ulster would be the best solution, but that his people would never agree to it. Lord Stamfordham memorandum, 24 July 1914 (RA PS/PSO/GV/C/K/2553/6/49).
69   H.H. Asquith to Venetia Stanley, 24 July 1914 (Bodl., Venetia Stanley Papers, MS Eng. 7092).
70   Ibid.
71   'Extract from Cabinet Letter' from H.H. Asquith to King George V, 25 July 1914 (RA PS/PSO/GV/C/K/2553/6/50).
72   H.H. Asquith to Venetia Stanley, 26 July 1914 (Bodl., Venetia Stanley Papers, MS Eng. 7092).
73   H.H. Asquith to Venetia Stanley, 27 July 1914 (Bodl., Venetia Stanley Papers, MS Eng. 7092).
74   Wilson, *Scott Diaries*, p. 90.
75   John Redmond to H.H. Asquith, 27 July 1914 (NLI, Redmond Papers, MS 15520).
76   John Dillon to C.P. Scott, 25 July 1914 (BL, C.P. Scott Papers, Add. MS 50908).
77   Diary entry, 29 July 1914 (Bodl., Margot Asquith diaries, MS Eng. 3210).
78   In fact, the king's advisers had resolved that the monarch's duty was to give his assent to the bill, with the reservation that, because no specific mandate had been obtained from the electorate, ministers should supply a statement of reasons why the king's assent was in the best interest of the people. Events rendered issuance of such a command unnecessary. Draft letter, possibly to be sent by Lord Stamfordham to the prime minister, 31 July 1914 (RA PS/PSO/GV/C/K/2553/6/56).

79   Blunt, *My Diaries*, part ii, p. 446.
80   H.H. Asquith to Venetia Stanley, 29 July 1914 (Bodl., Venetia Stanley Papers, MS Eng. 7092).
81   Ibid.
82   Jenkins, *Asquith*, p. 325.
83   H.H. Asquith to Venetia Stanley, 30 July 1914 (Bodl., Venetia Stanley Papers, MS Eng. 7092).
84   H.H. Asquith to Lord Stamfordham, 30 July 1914 (RA PS/PSO/GV/C/K/ 2553/6/55).
85   Meleady, *John Redmond*, p. 284.
86   H.H. Asquith to Venetia Stanley, 30 July 1914 (Bodl., Venetia Stanley Papers, MS Eng. 7092).
87   H.H. Asquith to Lord Stamfordham, 30 July 1914 (RA PS/PSO/GV/C/K/ 2553/6/55).
88   George Dangerfield asserted that not only was the suspensory bill imposed upon Redmond, it was sprung on him by surprise; Paul Bew also wrote that suspension was forced upon him. The accounts of Patricia Jalland and Dermot Meleady did not attribute the proposal to Redmond. George Dangerfield, *The Damnable Question: A study in Anglo-Irish relations* (London: Little, Brown, 1976), p. 129; Bew, *John Redmond*, p. 37; Jalland, *Liberals and Ireland*, p. 259; Meleady, *John Redmond*, p. 302.
89   Fanning, *Fatal Path*, p. 134.
90   Jalland and Stubbs, 'The Irish Question After the Outbreak of War in 1914', p. 804.
91   *Irish Independent*, 5 June 1914.
92   Ibid. 30 July 1914 (newspaper clipping, NLI, Redmond Papers, MS 15266).
93   Lord Milner to Andrew Bonar Law, 15 July 1914 (PA, Bonar Law Papers, MS BL/33/1/28).
94   G.W. de Tunzelmann to Lord Milner, 7 July 1914 (Bodl., Milner Papers, MS dep. 71); *Chief Secretary's Office Judicial Division Intelligence Notes 1914*, pp. 1–2, 6 (NA, CO 903/18).
95   H.A. Gwynne to Sir Edward Carson, 17 July 1914 (PA, Bonar Law Papers, MS BL/33/1/32).
96   Ibid.
97   John Vincent (ed.), *The Crawford Papers: The journals of David Lindsay, twenty-seventh Earl of Crawford and tenth Earl of Balcarres, 1871–1940: during the years 1892–1940* (Manchester: Manchester University Press, 1984), p. 344.
98   H.H. Asquith to Venetia Stanley, 31 July 1914 (Bodl., Venetia Stanley Papers, MS Eng. 7092).
99   The consensus at a political dinner party on 30 July was that it would last three weeks to three months. Kitchener, however, believed it would last for over a year. Diary entry, 30 July 1914 (Bodl., Margot Asquith diaries, MS Eng. d. 3210).
100   Diary entry, 1 August 1914 (Bodl., Margot Asquith diaries, MS Eng. d. 3210). As has been seen, Redmond intimated to the prime minister that he might make such an offer two days before Margot Asquith's letter. It cannot so readily be taken, as Conor Mulvagh speculated, that Redmond acted on Mrs Asquith's advice. Mulvagh, *Irish Parliamentary Party at Westminster*, p. 120.
101   Dangerfield, *Damnable Question*, p. 122.

102 John Redmond to John Dillon, 4 August 1914 (TCD, Dillon Papers, MS 6748).
103 Diary entry, 1 August 1914 [evidently recorded at a later date] (Bodl., Margot Asquith diaries, MS Eng. 3210).
104 Christopher Addison, *Four and a Half Years: A personal diary from June 1914 to January 1919* (London: Hutchinson, 1934), p. 32, quoted in Jalland and Stubbs, 'The Irish Question After the Outbreak of War in 1914', p. 782.
105 T.P. O'Connor to John Dillon, 4 August 1914 (TCD, Dillon Papers, MS 6740).
106 John Redmond to John Dillon, 4 August 1914 (TCD, Dillon Papers, MS 6748).
107 Bew, in his volume of biography, suggested that it was likely that this was a quid pro quo; however, his entry for Redmond in the *Oxford Dictionary of National Biography* states that it was a calculated exchange. Bew, *John Redmond*, p. 37; idem, 'Redmond, John Edward (1856–1918)', *Oxford Dictionary of National Biography* (Oxford: Oxford University Press, 2004), p. 4.
108 *Times*, 3 August 1914.
109 John Redmond to H.H. Asquith, 4 August 1914 (Bodl., MS Asquith 36).
110 John Redmond to David Lloyd George, 4 August 1914 (PA, Lloyd George Papers, LG/C/7/3/11).
111 H.H. Asquith to Venetia Stanley, 4 August 1914 (Bodl., Venetia Stanley Papers, MS Eng. 7093); Sir Edward Carson to H.H. Asquith, 5 August 1914 (Bodl., MS Asquith 36).
112 H.H. Asquith to Venetia Stanley, 4 August 1914 (Bodl., Venetia Stanley Papers, MS Eng. 7093); Dangerfield, *Damnable Question*, p. 125.
113 John Redmond to H.H. Asquith, 5 August 1914 (NLI, Redmond Papers, MS 15520).
114 H.H. Asquith to John Redmond, 6 August 1914 (NLI, Redmond Papers, MS 15520); H.H. Asquith to Venetia Stanley, 6 August 1914 (Bodl., Venetia Stanley Papers, MS Eng. 7093).
115 Diary entry, 7 August 1914 (Bodl., Margot Asquith diaries, MS Eng. d. 3210).
116 Jalland and Stubbs, 'The Irish Question After the Outbreak of War in 1914', p. 788.
117 H.H. Asquith to Venetia Stanley, 7 August 1914 (Bodl., Venetia Stanley Papers, MS Eng. 7093).
118 Lyons, *John Dillon*, p. 359. Within a fortnight of the war's commencement, Dillon presciently wrote to C.P. Scott, 'I take it for granted Germany will be beaten – but after a titanic struggle … What a prospect for Europe – if Germany is beaten Germany and Austria will be dissected – and goodbye to peace in Europe for some generations.' John Dillon to C.P. Scott, 12 August 1914 (TCD, Dillon Papers, MS 6843).
119 John Redmond to John Dillon, 13 August 1914 (TCD, Dillon Papers, MS 6748).
120 Lyons, *John Dillon*, p. 359. Mahon's prominent support for the Orange cause may have made Redmond's relations with him difficult. The Irish Party chairman's views about Volunteer recruitment for the Western Front, or at least about the public stance on the issue that he should adopt, seem to have evolved in the first weeks of war. The firm conditions attached to use of the Volunteers in August were jettisoned by mid-September.
121 Andrew Bonar Law to Sir Edward Grey, 6 August 1914 (Bodl., MS Asquith 36).
122 H.H. Asquith to Venetia Stanley, 10 August 1914 (Bodl., Venetia Stanley Papers, MS Eng. 7093).

123   Augustine Birrell to John Redmond, 12 August 1914 (NLI, Redmond Papers, MS 15520).
124   Jalland and Stubbs, 'The Irish Question After the Outbreak of War in 1914', p. 791.
125   H.H. Asquith to Venetia Stanley, 12, 18 August 1914 (Bodl., Venetia Stanley Papers, MS Eng. 7093).
126   H.H. Asquith to Venetia Stanley, 19 August 1914 (Bodl., Venetia Stanley Papers, MS Eng. 7093).
127   Ibid.
128   Augustine Birrell to John Redmond, 19 August 1914 (NLI, Redmond Papers, MS 15520).
129   John Redmond to T.P. Gill, 19 August 1914 (NLI, Gill Papers, MS 13486 (10)).
130   T.P. Gill to Robert Donald, 19 August 1914 (NLI, Gill Papers, MS 13486 (10)),
131   Fyfe, *T.P. O'Connor*, p. 235.
132   John Redmond to John Dillon, 19 August 1914 (TCD, Dillon Papers, MS 6748).
133   H.H. Asquith to Venetia Stanley, 20 August 1914 (Bodl., Venetia Stanley Papers, MS Eng. 7093).
134   H.H. Asquith to Venetia Stanley, 21 August 1914 (Bodl., Venetia Stanley Papers, MS Eng. 7093).
135   H.H. Asquith to Venetia Stanley, 22 August 1914 (Bodl., Venetia Stanley Papers, MS Eng. 7093).
136   Gwynn, *John Redmond*, p. 376.
137   John Redmond to H.H. Asquith, 22 August 1914 (Bodl., MS Asquith 36).
138   Note, 22 August 1914 (Bodl., MS Asquith 39). Despite the definitive tone of Asquith's preface to the note, and perhaps mindful of the fruitlessness of the negotiations of the preceding months, he appended the alternative of a one-clause bill suspending the operation of the Government of Ireland Act for twelve months.
139   H.H. Asquith to Venetia Stanley, 24 August 1914 (Bodl., Venetia Stanley Papers, MS Eng. 7093).
140   H.H. Asquith to Venetia Stanley, 26 August 1914 (Bodl., Venetia Stanley Papers, MS Eng. 7093).
141   H.H. Asquith to Venetia Stanley, 24 August 1914 (Bodl., Venetia Stanley Papers, MS Eng. 7093).
142   Robert Donald to T.P. Gill, 18 August 1914, T.P. Gill to Robert Donald, 25 August 1914 (NLI, Gill Papers, MS 13486 (10)).
143   T.P. Gill to Robert Donald, 25, 29 August 1914 (NLI, Gill Papers, MS 13486 (10)).
144   Augustine Birrell to John Redmond, 28 August 1914 (NLI, Redmond Papers, MS 15520).
145   Gwynn, *John Redmond*, p. 358.
146   Clan-na-Gael was the physical-force republican counterpart to the IRB in the United States.
147   Robert Donald to David Lloyd George, 30 August 1914 (PA, Lloyd George Papers, LG/C/4/8/8).
148   'Extract from Cabinet Letter' from H.H. Asquith to King George V, 12 September 1914 (RA PS/PSO/GV/C/K/2553/6/85). Alvin Jackson singles out Redmond's avoidance of this international argument for Home Rule in time of war as a characteristic excess of caution. At a moment when it was critical to stress Irish loyalty, it may not have been altogether wise to emphasise Clan-na-Gael's subversive

intent and Irish-American hostility. The message, however, was being disseminated privately in Cabinet circles by proxies (Gill and Donald), as the Irish Party chairman was doubtless aware. Jackson, *Judging Redmond and Carson*, p. 184.

149   Robert Donald to David Lloyd George, 30 August 1914 (PA, Lloyd George Papers, LG/C/4/8/8); T.P. Gill to Robert Donald, 29 August 1914 (NLI, Gill Papers, MS 13486 (10)).

150   T.P. Gill to Robert Donald, 2 September 1914 (NLI, Gill Papers, MS 13486 (11)).

151   Ibid.

152   *Times*, 4 September 1914.

153   John Dillon to T.P. O'Connor, 5 September 1914 (TCD, Dillon Papers, MS 6740).

154   This was a reference to *The Resurrection of Hungary*, Sinn Féin founder Arthur Griffith's 1904 book advocating a policy of parliamentary abstentionism in emulation of nineteenth-century Hungarian nationalists.

155   T.P. Gill to Walter D'Alton, 6 September 1914 (NLI, Gill Papers, MS 13486 (11)).

156   Ibid.; Denis Kelly to T.P. Gill, Maurice Moore to T.P. Gill, 3 September 1914, T.P. Gill to John Redmond, 8 September 1914 (NLI, Gill Papers, MS 13486 (11)).

157   T.P. Gill to John Redmond, 8 September 1914 (NLI, Gill Papers, MS 13486 (11)). Colonel Moore must be assumed to have dissented to this consensus, though his views with regard to service in the British army were inconsistent. In May 1914 he appears to have considered offering the Volunteers to the army as a territorial force. On the eve of the outbreak of war, however, Moore urged Redmond to use the Volunteers as a bargaining chip, and he deplored the nationalist leader's Woodenbridge declaration. By November 1914, however, Moore was durifully recruiting for the Expeditionary Force. Wells, *John Redmond*, p. 168; Dangerfield, *Damnable Question*, p. 122; Pennell, *A Kingdom United*, p. 187.

158   For example, Pennell, *A Kingdom United*, p. 183; Lyons, *John Dillon*, p. 359.

159   Bew, 'John Redmond', p. 4.

160   Roy Foster and Catriona Pennell have speculated that Redmond's call for Irish Volunteer enlistment in the British army was a tactic designed to provoke a split in the Irish Volunteers, a course being urged upon him by some moderates in the corps' command. In view of the larger objective that Gill seems to have had in mind, however, isolation of the extremists of the provisional committee was probably seen as an incidental benefit. Foster, *Vivid Faces*, p. 210; Pennell, *A Kingdom United*, p. 182.

161   T.P. Gill to Sir Francis Hopwood, 9 September 1914 (NLI, Gill Papers, MS 13486 (12)).

162   Ibid. Hopwood appears to have been unmoved by Gill's appeal. His advice to the king, in the final days of the controversy, placed greater emphasis on forestalling the enactment of Home Rule in order to preserve the spirit of national unity in wartime that George V desired above all else.

163   Augustine Birrell to John Redmond, 8 September 1914 (NLI, Redmond Papers, MS 15520).

164   'Headings for a Settlement as to the Government of Ireland', n.d. (NLI, Redmond Papers, MS 15266).

165   Lord Stamfordham memorandum, 8 September 1914 (RA PS/PSO/GV/C/K/2553/6/76); H.H. Asquith to Lord Stamfordham, 8 September 1914 (RA PS/PSO/GV/C/K/2553/6/77).

166   Lord Stamfordham to H.H. Asquith, 8 September 1914 (Bodl., MS Asquith 4).

167 H.H. Asquith to Venetia Stanley, 9 September 1914 (Bodl., Venetia Stanley Papers, MS Eng. 7093).

168 In Cabinet Sir Edward Grey emphasised the important effect that putting Home Rule on the statute book would have on American opinion. 'Prime Minister to the King' Cabinet report, 12 September 1914 (Bodl., MS Asquith 7); Lord Stamfordham to H.H. Asquith, 10, 11 September 1914 (Bodl., MS Asquith 4).

169 H.H. Asquith to Margot Asquith, 12 September 1914 (Bodl., Margot Asquith diaries, MS Eng. d. 6691).

170 H.H. Asquith to Venetia Stanley, 13 September 1914 (Bodl., Venetia Stanley Papers, MS Eng. 7093).

171 King George V to H.H. Asquith, 13 September 1914 (Bodl., MS Asquith 4).

172 H.H. Asquith to King George V, 14 September 1914 (RA PS/PSO/GV/C/K/ 2553/6/89).

173 Augustine Birrell to John Redmond, 15 September 1914 (NLI, Redmond Papers, MS 15520).

174 *Hansard*, 15 September 1914.

175 Ibid.

176 H.H. Asquith to Venetia Stanley, 15 September 1914 (Bodl., Venetia Stanley Papers, MS Eng. 7093).

177 Asquith wrote to Stanley that he anticipated a summons from the king, to allow the monarch 'to blow off a little regal steam; but he is well advised to acquiesce without further protest or demur'. H.H. Asquith to Venetia Stanley, 17 September 1914 (Bodl., Venetia Stanley Papers, MS Eng. 7093).

178 Augustine Birrell to John Redmond, 15 September 1914 (NLI, Redmond Papers, MS 15520). The king's only comment to Asquith upon granting assent to the Act was to express the hope that the attitudes of the parties in respect of Ireland would improve by the war's end. King George V to H.H. Asquith, 17 September 1914 (Bodl., MS Asquith 4).

179 T.P. Gill to John Redmond, 12 September 1914 (NLI, Gill Papers, MS 13486 (11)).

180 Memorandum, n.d. (NLI, Gill Papers, MS 13486 (11)).

181 Ibid.

182 *Freeman's Journal*, 21 September 1914.

183 'Irish Volunteer Force (Territorial)' memorandum, n.d. (NLI, Gill Papers, MS 13486 (9)).

184 T.P. Gill to Sir Francis Hopwood, 8 October 1914 (NLI, Gill Papers, MS 13486 (14)).

185 Bew, *Ideology and the Irish Question*, pp. 122–3.

186 John Redmond to T.P. O'Connor, 6 October 1914 (TCD, Dillon Papers, MS 6740).

187 Augustine Birrell to John Dillon, 24 September 1914 (TCD, Dillon Papers, MS 6799).

188 'C.S.O. Judicial Division Intelligence Notes 1914', p. 64 (NA, CO 903/18).

189 P.T. Barry to John Redmond, 31 October 1914 (NLI, Redmond Papers, MS 15236/1).

190 Thomas B. Fitzpatrick to John Redmond, 16 December 1914 (NLI, Redmond Papers, MS 15236/5).

191 Bew, *John Redmond*, pp. 38–9.

Chapter 8: Auguries
1 DMP Report, 15 November 1914 (NAI, CSORP 1914/23136).
2 Ibid.
3 Ibid.
4 Ibid.
5 Ibid.
6 Sir Matthew Nathan to Sir John Simon, 16 November 1914 (NAI, CSORP, 1914/23136).
7 Sir John Simon to Sir Matthew Nathan, 16 February 1915 (NAI, CSORP, 1914/23136).

Conclusion: An 'endless legacy of trouble'
1 A.J.P. Taylor, *Essays in English History* (Harmondsworth: Penguin, 1976), p. 227.
2 H.C.G. Matthew, *The Liberal Imperialists: The ideas and politics of a post-Gladstonian elite* (London: Oxford University Press, 1973), p. 128.
3 An attraction to coalition lingered in certain quarters of both parties. J.L. Garvin reported that Lloyd George spoke privately in May 1911 'with but little admiration of his own side: he sees danger for the State which he says can only be met by the cooperation of the best men of both parties'. A gloomy J.A. Spender believed in April 1913 that Lloyd George and Churchill were once again angling for a 'National Party' that would spell the end of Liberalism. Churchill, whom Bonar Law had baited with prospective collaboration, lamented the 'lost opportunity' of the 1910 coalition scheme to Austen Chamberlain in September 1913. Early in 1914 Garvin wrote flatteringly to Lloyd George as a 'Merlin' who had 'attempted that larger settlement with the nerve and insight of genius'. J.S. Sandars to Arthur Balfour, 6 May 1911 (BL, Balfour Papers, Add. MS 49736); Winston Churchill to H.H. Asquith, 17 September 1913 (Bodl., MS Asquith 38); Lord Esher to 'L.B.', 25 April 1913, Brett (ed.), *Esher Journals*, vol. 3, p. 123; G.R. Searle, *A New England? Peace and war, 1886–1914* (Oxford: Oxford University Press, 2004), p. 430; J.L. Garvin to David Lloyd George, 1 January 1914 (PA, Lloyd George Papers, LG/C/4/13/2).
4 For example, Lord Crewe to David Lloyd George, 21 October 1910 (PA, Lloyd George Papers, LG/C/4/1/2); Edward Grey to H.H. Asquith, 26 October 1910, in Scally, *The Origins of the Lloyd George Coalition*, p. 128.
5 *Catholic Times*, 22 May 1914.
6 Clarke, *Lancashire and the New Liberalism*, p. 6.
7 Ibid. p. 399.
8 J.A. Pease to D.L. Winter, 29 April 1914 (Nuffield College Library, Oxford, J.A. Pease Papers, MS Gainford C33/3).
9 Liberal theorist and *Traffic in Treason* author J.A. Hobson was also among the leaders of a movement that was to remain influential in the Labour Party for two decades. Keith Robbins, *The Abolition of War: The 'peace movement' in Britain, 1914–1919* (Cardiff: University of Wales Press, 1976), pp. 38–46.
10 *Manchester Guardian*, 24 July 1914.
11 Margaret O'Callaghan, *British High Politics and a Nationalist Ireland: Criminality, land and the law under Forster and Balfour* (Cork: Cork University Press, 1994), p. 120.
12 Lyons, *Culture and Anarchy in Ireland*, pp. 57–61.

13   Ibid. pp. 87–93.

14   Bull, *Land, Politics and Nationalism*, pp. 169–70.

15   McConnel, *Irish Parliamentary Party*, p. 189.

16   When asked in an interview in 1907 whether he believed that Ireland's future lay inside or outside the British Empire, Redmond refused to express an opinion, but implied that his view inclined to separation by gradual means. 'Parnell's words, were the wisest', he said. 'No man can set the bounds to the onward march of a nation.' 'Interview with Mr John E. Redmond', April 1907 (NLI, Francis Sheehy-Skeffington Papers, MS 40474 (5)).

17   Foster, *Modern Ireland*, pp. 402, 428.

18   The constituent area of 'Ulster' was not defined in this conversation. 'A.P.G. meeting with Sir Edward Carson' memorandum, 13 March 1915 (BL, C.P. Scott Papers, Add. MS 50908).

19   Conor Cruise O'Brien, *Ancestral Voices: Religion and nationalism in Ireland* (Dublin: Poolbeg, 1994), p. 100.

20   Jackson, 'Unionist Myths', pp. 173–4. Paul Bew also cited evidence of social and commercial pressures being brought to bear upon northern businessmen to hold the Carsonite line. Bew, *Ideology and the Irish Question*, p. 93.

21   Jackson, 'Unionist Myths', p. 183.

22   Timothy Bowman, *Carson's Army: The Ulster Volunteer Force, 1910–22* (Manchester: Manchester University Press, 2007), p. 106.

23   Ibid. pp. 105–6.

24   One biographer of Carson asserted that, in the final days of July 1914, James Craig was preparing for a UVF rising in Belfast. Yet the same author records that, at the end of the Buckingham Palace conference, Craig told the king that he disagreed with Carson's fear that Ulster might rebel if the Home Rule Bill became law. Craig favoured casting Ulster's lot on the result of a general election, claiming to be so confident of Unionist strength that she would be excluded from Home Rule whichever party was returned to office. On 30 July Craig urged Carson to take advantage of the international crisis to propose a truce on the Home Rule question. Geoffrey Lewis, *Carson: The man who divided Ireland* (London: Hambledon & London, 2005), pp. 164–6.

25   Bowman, *Carson's Army*, p. 138.

26   'Continuation of Diary of Colonel Crawford', 20 July 1914 (PRONI, D1700/5/17/2/3).

27   Ibid.; 'Notes from Diary Kept by Major Crawford' n.d. (PRONI, D1700/5/17/1/127).

28   'Notes from Diary Kept by Major Crawford' n.d. (PRONI, D1700/5/17/1/127).

29   Jackson, *Redmond and Carson*, p. 93.

30   Bowman, *Carson's Army*, p. 106.

31   Foster, *Modern Ireland*, p. 456.

32   Witness statement of Kevin O'Shiel, BMH.WS1770, Military Archives, Ireland.

33   'Memorandum of a Conversation with Sir Edward Carson Which Took Place on March 13th, 1915' (BL, C.P. Scott Papers, Add. MS 50908).

34   Ibid.

35   Kelly, *Fenian Ideal*, pp. 238–46.

36   *Times*, 9 March 1918.

37   Foster, *Modern Ireland*, p. 472.

38   J.J. Lee, *Ireland, 1912–1985: Politics and society* (Cambridge: Cambridge University Press, 1989), p. 21.

39   Lest it be thought that Healy had gone soft on his dead rival, the speech continued, 'They [the Sinn Féin leaders] might, perhaps, be asked to fold aside the banner of the republic in reverent repose, but how could any leaders trail the flag of Ireland below the Redmond level?' *Irish Independent*, 19 October 1921.

40   Bew, *John Redmond*, p. 51.

41   Mary E. Daly, 'Recent Writings on Modern Irish History: The interaction between past and present', *Journal of Modern History*, vol. 69, no. 3 (September 1997), pp. 516, 533.

42   Foster, *Modern Ireland*, p. 506.

43   In the last year of John Dillon's life, C.P. Scott wrote a letter of consolation to the seventy-five-year-old former nationalist leader. Tory recklessness, he wrote, had broken Ireland in two. 'What sane man', he wrote, 'will not now recognise that a smaller measure (with the element of growth) would have been infinitely better for Ireland and for us than Dominion Home Rule with Ulster left out. But that is all over. You fought the good fight and only the extremity of folly and the cruelty of fate defeated you.' Interestingly, Dillon himself blamed the Liberal government of 1910–15 and the wartime coalition of May 1915, even more than Carson, for Ireland's divided state. C.P. Scott to John Dillon, 26 October 1926 (TCD, Dillon Papers, MS 6843); diary entry, 13 March 1921 (TCD, Dillon Papers, MS 6582).

Bibliography

MANUSCRIPT SOURCES
BODLEIAN LIBRARIES
Asquith Papers
Margot Asquith Diaries
Augustine Birrell Papers
Maurice Bonham Carter Papers
Francis Hopwood Papers
Alfred Milner Papers
Venetia Stanley Papers

BRITISH LIBRARY
Balfour Papers
Bowood Papers
John Burns Papers
C.P. Scott Papers

BUREAU OF MILITARY HISTORY
Witness Statement of Diarmuid Coffey, BMH.WS1248
Witness Statement of Cahir Davitt, BMH.WS993
Witness Statement of Liam de Róiste, BMH.WS1698
Witness Statement of Archie Heron, BMH.WS577
Witness Statement of Patrick D. Little, BMH.WS1769
Witness Statement of Laurence Nugent, BMH.WS907
Witness Statement of William O'Brien, BMH.WS1766
Witness Statement of Sean O'Kelly, BMH.WS1766
Witness Statement of Kevin O'Shiel, BMH.WS1770

EASON AND SON COMPANY ARCHIVE
Newspaper and periodical sales records

NATIONAL ARCHIVES (IRELAND)
Chief Secretary's Office Registered Papers

(1914) 13512	(1914) 17264
(1914) 13848	(1914) 23136
(1914) 14397	(1916) 24668

NATIONAL ARCHIVES (UK)
Cabinet Office Papers

NATIONAL LIBRARY OF IRELAND
Diarmuid Coffey Papers
Francis Sheehy-Skeffington Papers
John Redmond Papers
Michael MacDonagh Papers
Thomas MacDonagh Papers
T.P. Gill Papers
W.G. Fallon Papers

NUFFIELD COLLEGE LIBRARY, OXFORD
Gainford Papers

PARLIAMENTARY ARCHIVES
Bonar Law Papers
Lloyd George Papers

PUBLIC RECORD OFFICE OF NORTHERN IRELAND
Crawford Papers

TRINITY COLLEGE, DUBLIN
Papers of John Dillon
Papers of W.F. Trench

UNIVERSITY COLLEGE, DUBLIN ARCHIVES
Eoin MacNeill Papers
Sinn Féin Party Papers
T.M. Kettle Papers

UNIVERSITY OF BIRMINGHAM SPECIAL COLLECTIONS
Austen Chamberlain Papers

UNIVERSITY OF BRISTOL SPECIAL COLLECTIONS
Liberal Central Association Annual Reports

OFFICIAL PRINTED SOURCE
Hansard's Parliamentary Debates, series 5

NEWSPAPERS
Anglo-Celt
Baptist Times and Freeman
Catholic Times and Catholic Opinion
Clarion
Cork Free Press
Daily Chronicle
Daily Citizen
Daily Express

Daily News and Leader
Derry People
Donegal News
Freeman's Journal
Irish Independent
Irish Times
Kildare Observer
Leader
Leitrim Observer
Limerick Leader
Manchester Guardian
Meath Chronicle
Methodist Times
Morning Post
Nation
Reynolds's Newspaper
Saturday Westminster Gazette
Scotsman
Sinn Féin
Skibbereen Eagle
Southern Star
Sunday Independent
Times
Ulster Herald
Westmeath Examiner
Westminster Gazette

PERIODICALS

Academy and Literature
Contemporary Review
East Hants Liberal Monthly Magazine
English Review
Fortnightly Review
Gleanings and Memoranda [published by National Unionist Association and Conservative and Liberal Unionist organisations]
Hibernian Journal
Lepracaun Cartoon Monthly
Liberal Agent
Quarterly Review
Review of Reviews
Women's Liberal Federation News

PAMPHLETS

Anon., *Home Rule ?s Answered* (London: Home Rule Council, 1912)

_____, *If Ulster Revolts – Who Is Responsible? (An Indictment of Mr Joseph Devlin)* (Dublin, n.d.)

_____, *Mr Asquith's Visit to Dublin* (London: Home Rule Council, 1912)

_____, *Proceedings in Connection with the Thirty-fifth Annual Meeting of the National Liberal Federation, London, November 1913* (London: Liberal Publications Department, 1913)

_____, *Proceedings in Connection with the Thirty-fourth Annual Meeting of the National Liberal Federation, London, November 1912* (London: Liberal Publications Department, 1912)

_____, *Proceedings in Connection with the Thirty-second Annual Meeting of the National Liberal Federation, London, November 1910* (London: Liberal Publications Department, 1910)

_____, *Proceedings in Connection with the Thirty-third Annual Meeting of the National Liberal Federation, London, November 1911* (London: Liberal Publications Department, 1911)

_____, *The Home Rule Library (No. 1)* (London: Home Rule Council, 1912)

_____, *The Way of Unity and Peace* (London: Smith, Elder & Co., 1914)

_____, *What the Home Rule Bill Will Do* (London: Home Rule Council, 1912)

Evans, Fred W., *A Workman's Views of the Irish Question* (London: National Press Agency, 1887)

Mahaffy, J.P., Nicholas Gosselin and R.D.O. Martin, *Ulster and the Irish Minority* (London, 1912)

Redmond, John E., *Some Arguments for Home Rule: Being a series of speeches delivered in the autumn of 1907 by J.E. Redmond, M.P.* (Dublin: Sealy, Bryers & Co., 1908)

Walker, Henry de Rosenbach, *The Need for the Parliament Act* (London: Liberal Publications Department, 1914)

Ward, John, *The Soldier and the Citizen* (London: T. Fisher Unwin, 1914)

CONTEMPORARY BOOKS

Beerbohm, Max, *Fifty Caricatures* (London: William Heinemann, 1914)

Begbie, Harold, *The Lady Next Door* (London: Hodder & Stoughton, 1912)

Buxton, C.R. (ed.), *The ABC Home Rule Handbook* (London: Home Rule Council, 1912)

Childers, Erskine, *The Framework of Home Rule* (London: Edward Arnold, 1911)

Gardiner, A.G., *Pillars of Society* (London: James Nisbet & Co., 1913)

Hobson, J.A., *Traffic in Treason: A study of political parties* (London: T. Fisher Unwin, 1914)

Hocking, Joseph, *Is Home Rule Rome Rule?* (London: Ward, Lock & Co., 1912)

Kettle T.M., *Home Rule Finance: An experiment in justice* (Dublin: Maunsel & Co., 1911)

_____, *The Open Secret of Ireland* [1912], ed. Senia Pašeta (University College Dublin Press, 2007)

MacVeagh, Jeremiah, *Home Rule in a Nutshell* (London: Home Rule Council, 1911)

Morgan, J.H. (ed.), *The New Irish Constitution* (London: Hodder & Stoughton, 1912)

Palmer, William, *Under Home Rule: A novel* (London: Baines & Scarsbrook, 1912)

Williams, Basil (ed.), *Home Rule Problems* (London: P.S. King, 1911)

SECONDARY SOURCES

Addison, Christopher, *Four and a Half Years: A personal diary from June 1914 to January 1919* (London: Hutchinson, 1934)

Baylen, J.O., '"What Mr Redmond Thought": An unpublished interview with John Redmond, December 1906', *Irish Historical Studies*, vol. 19, no. 74 (September 1974)

Beckett, Ian W. (ed.), *The Army and the Curragh Incident, 1914* (London: Bodley Head, 1986)

Bentley, Michael, *The Climax of Liberal Politics: British Liberalism in theory and practice, 1868–1918* (London: Edward Arnold, 1987)

Bew, Paul, *Ideology and the Irish Question: Ulster Unionism and Irish nationalism, 1912–1916* (Oxford: Clarendon Press, 1994)

_____, *John Redmond* (Dundalk: Dundalgan Press, 1996)

_____, 'Redmond, John Edward (1856–1918)', *Oxford Dictionary of National Biography* (Oxford: Oxford University Press, 2004)

Biagini, Eugenio F., *British Democracy and Irish Nationalism, 1876–1906* (Cambridge: Cambridge University Press, 2007)

Blewett, Neal, *The Peers, the Parties and the People: The general elections of 1910* (London: Macmillan, 1972)

Blunt, Wilfrid Scawen, *My Diaries: Being a personal narrative of events, 1888–1914*, vol. ii (London: Martin Secker, 1920)

Bowman, Timothy, *Carson's Army: The Ulster Volunteer Force, 1910–22* (Manchester: Manchester University Press, 2007)

Bourke, Richard, *Peace in Ireland: The war of ideas* (London: Pimlico, 2003)

Boyce, D. George and Alan O'Day (eds), *The Ulster Crisis* (Basingstoke: Palgrave Macmillan, 2006)

Brady, Ciaran (ed.), *Worsted in the Game: Losers in Irish history* (Dublin: Lilliput Press, 1989)

Brett, Maurice (ed.), *Journals and Letters of Reginald, Viscount Esher*, vol. 3 (London: Nicholson & Watson, 1934)

Brock, Michael and Eleanor Brock (eds), *H.H. Asquith Letters to Venetia Stanley* (Oxford: Oxford University Press, 2014)

Brooks, David, *The Age of Upheaval: Edwardian politics, 1899–1914* (Manchester: Manchester University Press, 1995)

Bull, Philip, *Land, Politics and Nationalism: A study of the Irish land question* (Dublin: Gill & Macmillan, 1996)

Chamberlain, Austen, *Politics from Inside: An epistolary chronicle, 1906–1914* (London: Cassell & Co., 1936)

Clarke, P.F., *Lancashire and the New Liberalism* (Cambridge: Cambridge University Press, 1971)

_____, *Liberals and Social Democrats* (Cambridge: Cambridge University Press, 1978)

Close, David H., 'The Collapse of Resistance to Democracy: Conservatives, adult suffrage, and Second Chamber reform, 1911–1928', *Historical Journal*, vol. 20, no. 4 (1977), pp. 893–918

Cooke, A.B. and John Vincent, *The Governing Passion: Cabinet government and party politics in Britain, 1885–86* (Brighton: Harvester Press, 1974)

Cruise O'Brien, Conor, *Ancestral Voices: Religion and nationalism in Ireland* (Dublin: Poolbeg, 1994)

Daly, Mary E., 'Recent Writings on Modern Irish History: The interaction between past and present', *Journal of Modern History*, vol. 69, no. 3 (September 1997)

Dangerfield, George, *The Damnable Question: A study in Anglo-Irish relations* (London: Little, Brown, 1976)

_____, *The Strange Death of Liberal England* (London: Constable & Co., 1936)

David, Edward (ed.), *Inside Asquith's Cabinet: From the diaries of Charles Hobhouse* (London: J. Murray, 1977)

Doherty, Gabriel (ed.), *The Third Home Rule Crisis, 1912–14* (Cork: Mercier Press, 2014)

Dooley, Chris, *Redmond: A life undone* (Dublin: Gill & Macmillan, 2015)

Fair, John D., *British Inter-party Conferences: A study of procedure of conciliation in British politics, 1867–1921* (Oxford: Clarendon Press, 1980)

Fanning, Ronan, *Fatal Path: British government and Irish revolution, 1910–1922* (London: Faber & Faber, 2013)

_____, 'The Irish Policy of Asquith's Government and the Cabinet Crisis of 1910', in A. Cosgrove and D. MacCartney (eds), *Studies in Irish History Presented to R. Dudley Edwards* (Dublin: University College Dublin Press, 1979)

Fergusson, James, *The Curragh Incident* (London: Faber & Faber, 1964)

Fergusson, Rosalind (ed.), *Shorter Dictionary of Catch Phrases* (London: Routledge, 1994)

Figgis, Darrell, *Recollections of the Irish War* (New York: Ernest Benn, 1924)

Fitzroy, Almeric, *The Memoirs of Sir Almeric Fitzroy*, vol. ii (London: Hutchinson, 1925)

Foster, R.F., *Modern Ireland, 1600–1972* (London: Allen Lane, 1988)

_____, *Vivid Faces: The revolutionary generation in Ireland, 1890–1923* (London: Allen Lane, 2014)

Fyfe, Hamilton, *T.P. O'Connor* (London: Allen & Unwin, 1934)

Garvin, Tom, *The Evolution of Irish Nationalist Politics* (Dublin: Gill & Macmillan, 1981)

Gollin, A.M., *The Observer and J.L. Garvin* (London: Oxford University Press, 1960)

Grigg, John, *Lloyd George: The people's champion, 1902–1911* (London: HarperCollins, 1978)

Gwynn, Denis, *The Life of John Redmond* (London: George G. Harrap, 1932)

Gwynn, Stephen, *John Redmond's Last Years* (London: Arnold, 1926)

Hazlehurst, Cameron and Christine Woodland, *A Liberal Chronicle: Journals and papers of J.A. Pease, first Lord Gainford, 1908–1910* (London: Historian's Press, 1994)

Headlam, Maurice, *Irish Reminiscences* (London: Robert Hale, 1947)

Hobhouse, L.T., *Democracy and Reaction*, ed. P.F. Clarke (New York: Barnes & Noble Books, 1973)

Horgan, J.J., *From Parnell to Pearse: Some recollections and reflections* (Dublin: Browne & Nolan, 1948)

Jackson, Alvin, *Home Rule: An Irish history, 1800–2000* (London: Weidenfeld & Nicolson, 2004)

_____, *Judging Redmond and Carson: Comparative Irish lives* (Dublin: Prism, 2018)

_____, 'Unionist Myths, 1914–1985', *Past & Present*, no. 136 (August 1992)

Jalland, Patricia, *The Liberals and Ireland: The Ulster question in British politics to 1914* (Brighton: Harvester Press, 1980)

_____ and John Stubbs, 'The Irish Question After the Outbreak of War in 1914: Some unfinished party business', *English Historical Review*, vol. 96, no. 381 (October 1981)

Jeffery, Keith, *Field Marshal Sir Henry Wilson: A political soldier* (Oxford: Oxford University Press, 2006)

Jenkins, Roy, *Asquith* (London: Collins, 1964)

Jones, Grace A., 'Further Thoughts on the Franchise', *Past & Present*, no. 34 (July 1966)

Kelly, M.J., *The Fenian Ideal and Irish Nationalism, 1882–1916* (Woodbridge: Boydell, 2006)

Koss, Stephen, 'The Destruction of the Last Liberal Government', *Journal of Modern History*, vol. 40, no. 2 (June 1968)

_____, *The Rise and Fall of the Political Press in Britain*, vol. ii (London: Hamish Hamilton, 1984)

Lee, J.J., *Ireland, 1912–1985: Politics and society* (Cambridge: Cambridge University Press, 1989)

Lewis, Geoffrey, *Carson: The man who divided Ireland* (London: Hambledon & London, 2005)

Lyons, F.S.L., *Culture and Anarchy in Ireland, 1890–1939* (Oxford: Clarendon Press, 1979)

_____, *The Irish Parliamentary Party, 1890–1910* (London: Faber & Faber, 1951)

_____, *John Dillon: A biography* (London: Routledge & Kegan Paul, 1968)

Mansergh, Nicholas, *The Irish Question, 1840–1921* (London: Allen & Unwin, 1965)

Marquand, David, *Ramsay MacDonald* (London: Cape, 1977)

Martin, F.X. (ed.), *The Howth Gun-running and the Kilcoole Gun-running, 1914* (Dublin: Browne & Nolan, 1964)

Masterman, Lucy, *C.F.G. Masterman: A biography* (London: Nicholson & Watson, 1939)

Matthew, H.C.G., *The Liberal Imperialists: The ideas and politics of a post-Gladstonian elite* (London: Oxford University Press, 1973)

Maume, Patrick, *The Long Gestation: Irish nationalist life, 1891–1918* (Dublin: Gill & Macmillan, 1999)

McConnel, James, 'The Franchise Factor in the Defeat of the Irish Parliamentary Party, 1885–1918', *Historical Journal*, vol. 47, no. 2 (June 2004)

_____, *The Irish Parliamentary Party and the Third Home Rule Crisis* (Dublin: Four Courts Press, 2013)

_____, 'Jobbing with Tory and Liberal: Irish nationalists and the politics of patronage 1880–1914', *Past & Present*, no. 188 (August 2005)

_____, 'John Redmond and Irish Catholic Loyalism', *English Historical Review*, vol. cxxv, no. 512 (2010)

_____, '"Après la guerre": John Redmond, the Irish Volunteers, and armed constitutionalism, 1913–1915', *English Historical Review*, vol. 131, no. 553 (December 2016)

Meleady, Dermot, *John Redmond: The national leader* (Dublin: Merrion Press, 2013)

Mulvagh, Conor, *The Irish Parliamentary Party at Westminster, 1900–18* (Manchester: Manchester University Press, 2016)

Nic Dháibhéid, Caoimhe and Colin Reid (eds), *From Parnell to Paisley: Constitutional and revolutionary politics in modern Ireland* (Dublin: Irish Academic Press, 2010)

Nowlan, Kevin B. (ed.), *The Making of 1916: Studies in the history of the Rising* (Dublin: Stationery Office, 1969)

O'Brien, Joseph V., *Dear, Dirty Dublin: A city in distress, 1899–1916* (Berkeley, CA: University of California Press, 1982)

_____, *William O'Brien and the Course of Irish Politics, 1881–1918* (Berkeley, CA: University of California Press, 1976)

Ó Broin, Leon, *The Chief Secretary: Augustine Birrell in Ireland* (London: Chatto & Windus, 1969)

Ó Buachalla, Séamas (ed.), *The Letters of P.H. Pearse* (Gerrards Cross: Colin Smythe, 1980)

O'Callaghan, Margaret, *British High Politics and a Nationalist Ireland: Criminality, land and the law under Forster and Balfour* (Cork: Cork University Press, 1994)

Ó Gráda, Cormac, '"The Greatest Blessing of All": The old age pension in Ireland', *Past & Present*, no. 175 (May 2002)

Packer, Ian, *Lloyd George, Liberalism and the Land: The land issue and party politics in England, 1906–1914* (London: Boydell Press, 2001)

Pašeta, Senia, *Irish Nationalist Women, 1900–1918* (Cambridge: Cambridge University Press, 2013)

Peatling, G.K., *British Opinion and Irish Self-government, 1865–1925: From Unionism to Liberal Commonwealth* (Dublin: Irish Academic Press, 2001)

Pennell, Catriona, *A Kingdom United: Popular responses to the outbreak of the First World War in Britain and Ireland* (Oxford: Oxford University Press, 2012)

Robbins, Keith, *The Abolition of War: The 'peace movement' in Britain, 1914–1919* (Cardiff: University of Wales Press, 1976)

Scally, R.J., *The Origins of the Lloyd George Coalition* (London: Princeton University Press, 1975)

Searle, G.R., 'A.J. Balfour's Secret Coalition Talks Memorandum, 1910', *Historical Research*, vol. 66, no. 160 (1993)

_____, *A New England? Peace and War, 1886–1914* (Oxford: Oxford University Press, 2004)

_____, *The Quest for National Efficiency: A study in British politics and British political thought, 1899–1914* (Oxford: Blackwell, 1971)

Shannon, Catherine B., *Arthur J. Balfour and Ireland* (Washington DC: Catholic University of America Press, 1998)

Smith, Jeremy, 'Bluff, Bluster and Brinkmanship: Andrew Bonar Law and the third Home Rule Bill', *Historical Journal*, vol. 36, no. 1 (March 1993)

_____, *The Tories and Ireland: Conservative Party politics and the Home Rule Crisis, 1910–1914* (Dublin: Irish Academic Press, 2000)

Spender, J.A. and Cyril Asquith, *Life of Herbert Henry Asquith, Earl of Oxford and Asquith* (London: Hutchinson & Co., 1932)

Taylor, A.J.P., *Essays in English History* (Harmondsworth: Penguin, 1976)

Taylor, H.A., *Robert Donald: Being the authorised biography of Robert Donald, G.B.E., Ll.B., journalist, editor and friend of statesmen, etc.* (London: Stanley Paul & Co., 1934)

Thompson, J.A., 'Historians and the Decline of the Liberal Party', *Albion: A Quarterly Journal Concerned with British Studies*, vol. 22, no. 1 (spring 1990)

Tierney, Michael, *Eoin MacNeill: Scholar and man of action, 1867–1945*, ed. F.X. Martin (Oxford: Clarendon Press, 1980)

Vincent, John (ed.), *The Crawford Papers: The journals of David Lindsay, twenty-seventh Earl of Crawford and tenth Earl of Balcarres, 1871–1940: during the years 1892–1940* (Manchester: Manchester University Press, 1984)

Waley, S.D., *Edwin Montagu: A memoir and an account of his visits to India* (London: Asia Publishing House, 1964)

Wells, Warre B., *John Redmond: A biography* (London: Nisbet & Co., 1919)

Weston, C.C., 'The Liberal Leadership and the Lords Veto, 1907–1910', *Historical Journal*, vol. 11, no. 3 (1968)

Wheatley, Michael, 'John Redmond and Federalism in 1910', *Irish Historical Studies*, vol. 32, no. 127 (May 2001)

_____, *Nationalism and the Irish Party: Provincial Ireland, 1910–1916* (Oxford: Oxford University Press, 2005)

Wilson, Trevor, *The Downfall of the Liberal Party, 1914–1935* (London: Faber & Faber, 1966)

_____ (ed.), *The Political Diaries of C.P. Scott, 1911–1928* (London: Collins, 1970)

Index